# The Truth of Christianity

Being an Examination of the More Important Arguments For and Against Believing in T' Religion

W. H. Turton

**Alpha Editions**

This edition published in 2024

ISBN : 9789362511850

Design and Setting By
**Alpha Editions**
www.alphaedis.com
Email - info@alphaedis.com

As per information held with us this book is in Public Domain. This book is a reproduction of an important historical work. Alpha Editions uses the best technology to reproduce historical work in the same manner it was first published to preserve its original nature. Any marks or number seen are left intentionally to preserve its true form.

# PREFACE TO NINTH EDITION.

I have again carefully revised the whole book. Some additions have been made here and there, especially in Chapter XIX.; but as a rule the alterations have been merely to shorten and condense the arguments where this could be done without spoiling them, and to simplify the language as much as possible. The book is thus shorter, and I hope simpler than any previous edition. Another slight improvement, which will commend itself to most purchasers, is reducing the price to 2s. net. The work, as before stated, lays no claim to originality, and I have not hesitated to borrow arguments and illustrations from any source. The references to the Bible are all to the Revised Version.

W. H. T.

29, CALEDONIA PLACE,
CLIFTON, BRISTOL,
*October 1, 1919.*

# PART I.
## NATURAL RELIGION.

| CHAP. | I. | THAT THE UNIVERSE HAD A CREATOR. |
|---|---|---|
| " | II. | THAT THE CREATOR DESIGNED THE UNIVERSE. |
| " | III. | THAT THE EXISTENCE OF GOD IS EXTREMELY PROBABLE. |
| " | IV. | THAT MAN IS A FREE AND RESPONSIBLE BEING. |
| " | V. | THAT GOD TAKES AN INTEREST IN MAN'S WELFARE. |
| " | VI. | THAT GOD MIGHT MAKE SOME REVELATION TO MAN. |
| " | VII. | THAT A MIRACULOUS REVELATION IS CREDIBLE. |

# CHAPTER I.
## THAT THE UNIVERSE HAD A CREATOR

(*A.*) THE ORIGIN OF THE UNIVERSE.

Explanation of the universe, its origin, a Free Force.

(1.) The Philosophical Argument. If the universe had not an origin, all events must have occurred before, and this seems incredible.

(2.) The Scientific Argument. From the process of evolution and the degradation of energy.

(*B.*) THE CREATOR OF THE UNIVERSE.

The Single Supernatural Cause, which originated it.

It is proposed in this Essay to consider the reasons for and against believing in the truth of Christianity, meaning by that term, as will be explained later on (Chapter XIII.), the doctrines contained in the Three Creeds. For convenience the subject has been divided into three Parts, Natural Religion, the Jewish Religion, and the Christian Religion; but the second of these may be omitted by anyone not specially interested in that subject. At present we are considering *Natural Religion* only, which deals with the great questions of the Existence of God, and the probability, or otherwise, of His making some Revelation to man. And we will commence at the very beginning, though the first chapter will unfortunately have to be rather technical.

### (*A.*) THE ORIGIN OF THE UNIVERSE.

Now by the universe is meant the *material* universe, which includes everything that exists (earth, sun, stars, and all they contain), with the exception of immaterial or spiritual beings, if there are any such. And by this universe having had an *origin* is meant that it was at some time acted on by a *Free* Force, that is to say, by a force which does not always act the same under the same circumstances, but which can act or not as it pleases. No doubt such a force would be totally different from all the known forces of nature; but there is no difficulty in understanding what is meant by the term, since man himself *seems* to possess such a force in his own free will. He *seems* for instance to be able to raise his hand, or not, as he likes. We are not, of course, assuming that man's will is really free, but merely that the idea of a free force, able to act or not as it pleases, is well known and generally understood.

Hence the statement that the universe had an origin means that at some time or other it was acted on by such a Free Force; in other words, it has not existed for ever under the fixed and invariable forces of nature, and without any external interference. We have now to consider the two arguments in favour of this, which may be called the Philosophical and the Scientific argument.

### (1.) The Philosophical Argument.

By this is meant that, when we reflect on the subject, it seems inevitable that if the universe had not an origin, all present events must have occurred before. The reason for thinking this is, that if all free force is excluded, it is plain that matter must be eternal, since its coming into existence at any time could not have been a necessity, and must therefore have been due to some free force. It is equally plain that what we call the forces of nature and the properties of matter must also be eternal, since any alteration in them at any time would also have required a free force. And from this it follows that no *new* event can happen *now*. For every event which the forces of nature could possibly bring about of themselves would, since they have been acting from eternity, have been brought about long ago. Therefore present events are not new, but must have occurred before.

This is no doubt a possible theory. For example, if we assume that the universe will in process of time work itself back into precisely the same condition in which it was long ago as a *nebula* or anything else, when it will begin again precisely the same changes as before; then, and only then, is it possible that it has been going on doing so from all eternity. But this theory, though possible, is certainly not credible. For it requires that all events, past, present, and future, down to the minutest detail, have occurred, and will occur, over and over again. They must, in fact, form a *recurring series*. And when applied to a single example, say the history of the human race, this is seen to be quite incredible.

We must hence conclude that the universe has not existed for ever under the fixed forces of nature, and without any external interference; in other words, that it had an origin. No doubt there are difficulties in regard to this theory also, but they are mostly due to our ignorance. We may not know, for instance, whether matter itself is eternal. Nor may we know why, if a free force once acted on the universe, it never apparently does so at present, and still less can we picture to ourselves what such a force would be like; though the difficulty here is no greater than that of picturing a force which is not free, say gravity.

But our ignorance about all this is no reason for doubting what we do know. And it appears to the writer that we do know that, unless present events have occurred before, which seems incredible, the universe cannot have existed for ever without some *Free Force* having acted on it at some time. In short, it seems less difficult to believe that the universe had an origin than to believe that it had not.

## (2.) The Scientific Argument.

And this conclusion is greatly strengthened by two scientific theories now generally accepted—that of the process of evolution and the degradation of energy; both of which seem to show that the universe had a beginning.

The first subject, that of *Evolution*, will be discussed more fully in the next chapter. All that need be said here is, that the atoms of the universe, with their evolving properties, cannot have existed eternally; for then the course of evolution would have commenced in the eternal past, and would therefore have been finished now. But this is certainly not the case, and evolution is still in progress, or at all events was so a few thousand years ago; and a state of progress cannot be *eternal*. It thus differs from a mere state of *change* which as we have seen, might be eternal, if the changes were recurring. But a state of *progress*, in which the changes are not recurring, but all tend in one direction, can never be eternal. It must have had a commencement. And this commencement cannot have been a necessity, so it must have been due to some Free Force. In short, evolution requires a previous *Evolver*; since it cannot have been going on for ever, and it cannot have started itself.

The other theory, that of the *Degradation of Energy*, is that all energy (motion, etc.) tends to *heat*; the simplest instance being that of two bodies hitting each other when a certain amount of motion is lost, and a corresponding amount of heat is produced. And heat tends to be equally distributed. The heat, for instance, which is now stored up in the sun will in process of time be distributed throughout space, and the same applies to the whole universe; so that everything will eventually have the same temperature. And though this may take millions of years, they are yet nothing to eternity. Therefore, if the universe with all its present forces has existed from eternity, and without any external interference, it must have been reduced to this state long ago. So if this theory is correct (and the only reason for doubting it, is the curious behaviour of *radium*), it seems not only probable, but certain, that the universe had an origin.

But an objection has now to be considered. It may be said that the above reasoning is merely another form of the old argument, 'Everything must have a cause, and therefore there must have been a First Cause;' the obvious answer to which is, that then this First Cause must also have had a cause, and so on indefinitely. But this is not the case; for the alleged First Cause is of a different *kind* from all the others. It is a *Free* Cause, whereas natural causes are not free, but are themselves effects of other natural causes; and these, again, of previous ones. What we want is a cause which is *not* also an effect, in other words, a cause which is not moved by anything else, but is moved by itself, or *Free*. When once we get to such a cause as this, there is no need for a previous one.

This objection, then, cannot be maintained, and we therefore decide that the universe had an origin. And all we know at present about the Force which originated it, is that it was a Free Force. And the conclusion at which we have arrived may be concisely expressed by saying, that before all natural causes which acted necessarily, there was a *First Cause* which acted voluntarily.

## (*B.*) THE CREATOR OF THE UNIVERSE.

We have next to consider what else we can ascertain in regard to this First Cause. To begin with it can scarcely be disputed at the present day that it was a *Single* Cause, as modern science has completely established the unity which pervades the universe. We know for instance that the same materials are used everywhere, many of the elements which exist on this earth being also found in the sun and stars. Then there is the force of gravity, which is all-embracing, and applies equally to the most distant stars, and to the most minute objects on this earth; and many other examples might be given. But it is scarcely necessary, as everyone now admits that the universe (as the word implies) is one whole, and this plainly points to a *Single* First Cause.

Nor can it be disputed that this First Cause was *Supernatural*, which merely means that it differs from natural forces in being *free*; for this is exactly what we have shown. It was thus no kind of gravitation, or electricity, or anything of that sort. All these and all similar forces would always act the same under the same conditions; while the Force we are considering was of a different kind. It was a *Free* Force, a Force which voluntarily chose to originate the universe at a certain time. And such a Force must clearly have been Supernatural.

In conclusion we will call this *Single Supernatural Cause*, which originated the universe, its *Creator*. And if it be objected that the universe may have had no *origin*, owing to some Free Force having been always acting on it, such a Force must also be Single and Supernatural, and may equally well be called its Creator.

# CHAPTER II.
## THAT THE CREATOR DESIGNED THE UNIVERSE.

Design means voluntary action, combined with foreknowledge.

(*A.*) EVIDENCE OF DESIGN.

Seems overwhelming throughout organic nature; and we are not appealing to it to show the Creator's existence, but merely His foreknowledge.

(1.) The example of a watch: its marks of design show that it had a maker who foresaw its use.

(2.) The example of an eye: this also has marks of design, and must also have had a Designer.

(3.) The evidence cumulative.

(*B.*) THE EVOLUTION OBJECTION.

(1.) The meaning of Evolution: it is a process, not a cause.

(2.) The effect of Evolution on the present argument: it increases the evidence for design.

(*C.*) THE FREE WILL OBJECTION.

(1.) Its great improbability: for several reasons.

(2.) Free Will and Foreknowledge not inconsistent; so the chief argument in its favour cannot be maintained. Conclusion.

Having decided that the universe had a Creator, we have next to examine whether the Creator designed the universe. Now by *Design* is meant any voluntary action, combined with foreknowledge of the results that will follow from such action. So when the Creator originated the universe, if He foreknew the results of His action, it would be to *design* those results, as the word is here used. And these include, either directly or indirectly, the whole course of the universe, everything that exists, or that ever has existed in the world.

By the word *foreknew* it is not meant that the Creator necessarily *thought* of all future events, however insignificant, such as the position of the leaves on each tree; but merely that He was able to foresee any of them He wished, and in this sense foreknew them. Compare the case of memory; a man may be able to remember a thousand events in his life; but they are not all before his mind's eye at the same time, and the insignificant ones may never be. In the same way the Creator may have been able to foresee all future events in the world's history without actually thinking about them. At all events, this is the kind of foresight, or rather foreknowledge, which is meant to be included in the term *design*.

## (*A*.) EVIDENCE OF DESIGN.

Passing on now to the evidence of design, this is of the most varied kind, especially throughout organic nature, where we find countless objects, which seem to point to the foresight of the Cause which produced them. The evidence is indeed so vast that it is difficult to deal with it satisfactorily. Perhaps the best way will be to follow the well-known *watch* argument of Paley, first showing by the example of a watch what it is that constitutes marks of design; next, how a single organ, say the human eye, possesses these marks; and then, the cumulative nature of the evidence.

### (1.) The example of a watch.

Now, when we examine a watch, we see that it has marks of design, because the several parts are put together for a *purpose*. They are so shaped and arranged as to produce motion, and this motion is so regulated as to point out the hour of the day. While, if they had been differently shaped or differently arranged, either no motion at all would have been produced, or none which would have answered the same purpose. And from this, we may infer two things. The first is that the watch had a *maker* somewhere and at some time; and the second is that this maker understood its construction, and *designed* it for the purpose which it actually serves.

These conclusions, it will be noticed, would not be altered by the fact that we had never seen a watch made; never knew a man capable of making one; and had no idea how the work could be done. All this would only exalt our opinion of the unknown watchmaker's skill, but would raise no doubt in our minds either as to his existence, or as to his having made the watch for the purpose of telling the time.

Nor should we feel that the watch was explained by being told that every part of it worked in strict accordance with natural laws, and could not possibly move otherwise than it did; in fact, that there was no design to account for. We should feel that, though the action of every part might be in strict accordance with law, yet the fact that all these parts agreed in this one particular, that they all helped to enable the watch to tell the time, did show design somewhere. In other words, we should feel that the properties of matter could only partly account for the watch, and that it required a skilful watchmaker as well, who made use of these properties so as to enable the watch to tell the time.

Now suppose on further investigation we found that the watch also possessed the unexpected property of producing in the course of its movements another watch very like itself. It might, for instance, contain a mould in which the new works were cast, and some machinery which fitted them together. What effect would this have on our former conclusions? It would plainly increase our admiration for the watch, and for the skill of its unknown maker. If without this extra property, the watch required a skilful maker, still more would it do so with it. And this conclusion would not be altered by the fact that very possibly the watch we were examining was itself produced in this way from some previous one, and perhaps that from another. We should feel that, though each watch might be thus produced from a previous one, it was in no sense *designed* by it. And hence this would not in any way weaken our conviction as to the existence of a watchmaker somewhere and at some time who designed the whole series.

This, then, is the watch argument. Wherever we find marks of design, there must be a designer somewhere; and this conclusion cannot be altered by any other considerations whatever. If, then, we find in nature any objects showing marks of design, the obvious inference is that they also had a designer. And this inference, it should be noticed, does not depend on any supposed *analogy* between the works of man and the works of nature. The example of the watch is merely given *as an example*, to show clearly what the design argument is; but the argument itself would be just as sound if man never had made, and never could make, any object showing marks of design.

Moreover, to complete the example, we must assume that the *existence* of the watchmaker, and the fact of his having made the watch, are already admitted for other reasons. And we are only appealing to these marks of design to show that *when* he made the watch, he must have known that it would be able to tell the time, and presumably made it for that purpose. And in this case the inference seems, if possible, to be still stronger.

**(2.) The example of an eye.**

We will next consider the *human eye* as an example of natural organs showing marks of design. It is a well-known instance, but none the worse on that account. Now, in order to see anything clearly, it is necessary that an image or picture of it should be formed at the back of the eye, that is, on the *retina* from whence the impression is communicated to the brain. And the eye is an instrument used for producing this picture, and in some respects very similar to a telescope. And its marks of design are abundant and overwhelming.

To begin with, in both the eye and the telescope the rays of light have to be *refracted*, so as to produce a distinct image; and the lens, and humours in the eye, which effect this, somewhat resemble the lenses of a telescope. While the *different* humours through which the rays pass, prevent them from being partly split up into different colours. The same difficulty had of course to be overcome in telescopes, and this does not seem to have been effected till it occurred to some one to imitate in glasses made from different materials the effect of the different humours in the eye.[1]

[1] Encyc. Brit., 9th edit., vol. xxiii., p. 137.

In the next place, the eye has to be suited to perceive objects at different *distances*, varying from inches to miles. In telescopes this would be done either by putting in another lens, or by some focussing arrangement. In the eye it is effected by slightly altering the *shape* of the lens, making it more or less convex. A landscape of several miles is thus brought within a space of half an inch in diameter, though the objects it contains, at least the larger ones, are all preserved, and can each be distinguished in its size, shape, colour, and position. Yet the same eye that can do this can read a book at the distance of a few inches.

Again, the eye has to be adapted to different *degrees of light*. This is effected by the *iris*, which is a kind of screen in the shape of a ring, capable of expanding or contracting so as to alter the size of the central hole or pupil, yet always retaining its circular form. Moreover, it is somehow or other self-adjusting; for if the light is too strong, the pupil at once contracts. It is needless to point out how useful such a contrivance would be in photography, and how much we should admire the skill of its inventor.

Again, the eye can perceive objects in different *directions*; for it is so constructed that it can turn with the greatest rapidity right or left, up or down, without moving the head. It is also provided *in duplicate*, the two eyes being so arranged that though each can see separately should the other get injured, they can, as a rule, see together with perfect harmony. Lastly, our admiration for the eye is still further increased when we remember that it was formed *before birth*. It was what is called a *prospective* organ, of no use at the time when it was made; and this, when carefully considered, shows design more plainly than anything else.

On the whole, then, the eye appears to be an optical instrument of great ingenuity; and the conclusion that it must have been made by someone, and that whoever made it must have known and designed its use, seems inevitable.

These conclusions, it will be noticed, like the similar ones in regard to the watch, are not affected by our ignorance on many points. We may have no idea as to how an eye can be made, and yet feel certain that, as it exists, it must have been made by someone, and that its maker designed it for the purpose it serves.

Nor should we feel that the eye is explained by being told that every part of it has been produced in strict accordance with natural laws, and could not have been otherwise; in fact, that there is no design to account for. No doubt every single part has been thus produced, and if it stood alone there might be little to account for. But it does not stand alone. All the various and complicated parts of the eye agree in this one remarkable point, and in this one only, that they all help to enable man to see; and it is this that requires explanation. We feel that there must be some connection between the cause which brought all these parts together and the fact of man's seeing. In other words, the result must have been designed.

Nor does the fact that every organism in nature is produced from a previous one of the same kind alter this conclusion. Indeed, as was shown with reference to the watch, it can only increase our admiration for the skill which must have been spent on the first organism of each kind. Moreover, no part of the design can be attributed to the *parents*. If, for instance, the eyes of a child show design, it is not due to the intelligence or designing power of its father and mother. *They* have not calculated the proper shape for the lens, or the mechanism of the iris, and as a rule know nothing whatever about it. And the same applies to *their* parents, so that our going back ever so far in this way brings us no nearer to what we are in search of. The design is still unaccounted for, we still want a designer.

We hence conclude that the marks of design in the eye afford, at all events, what seems to be a very strong argument in favour of a *Designer*. And if only one eye existed in the universe, and there were no other mark of design in nature, this conclusion would be none the less clear.

**(3.) The evidence cumulative.**

But the argument is far stronger than this. It is cumulative in a *triple* sense. To begin with, an eye is found not in one man only, but in millions of men, each separately showing marks of design, and each separately requiring a designer. Secondly, the human eye is only one example out of hundreds in the human body. The ear or the mouth would lead to the same conclusion, and so would the lungs or the heart. While, thirdly, human beings are but one out of many thousands of organisms in nature, all bearing marks of design, and showing in some cases an even greater ingenuity than in the human eye. Of course, as a rule, the lower organisms, being less complicated than the higher ones, have less striking marks of design, but their existence is equally clear; the flowers of plants affording some well-known examples.

Nor is this all, for even the world itself bears traces of having been designed. Had it been a mere chaos, we might have thought that the Creator was unaware of what would be the result of His action. But a planet like our earth, so admirably adapted for the support of life, can scarcely have been brought about by accident.

We conclude then, on reviewing the whole subject, that there are countless objects in nature, more especially organs like the eye, which bear strong marks of having been *designed*. And then the Unity of Nature, and the fact that all its parts act on one another in so many ways (the eye for instance being useless without light), shows that if anything has been designed, everything has been designed. Now there are two, and only two, important objections to this argument, which may be called the *Evolution* and the *Free Will* objection.

## (*B.*) THE EVOLUTION OBJECTION.

The first objection is that the whole of nature has been brought about in accordance with fixed laws by the process of *Evolution*. Therefore, though it is possible the Creator may have foreseen everything that exists; yet the apparent marks of design in nature, being all the necessary results of these laws, do not afford any evidence that He actually did so. And before discussing this objection we must first consider what we mean by laws of nature and natural forces.

Now by a *law of nature* is meant any regular, or uniform action which we observe in nature. For example, it is called a law, or rule of nature that (with certain exceptions) heat should expand bodies, which merely means that we see that it does so. In other words, we observe that heat is followed by expansion, and we therefore assume that the one is the cause of the other. But calling it a law of nature for heat to expand bodies, does not in any way account for its doing so. And the same is true in other cases, so that a law of nature *explains* nothing, it is merely a summary of the facts to be explained.

It should also be noticed that a law of nature *effects* nothing. It has no coercive, or compelling power whatever. The law of gravitation, for instance, has never moved a planet, any more than the rules of navigation have steered a ship. In each case it is some power or force acting according to law which does it. And *natural forces* are those which, as far as we know, *always* act according to some fixed law. They have no freedom of choice, they cannot act or not as they like; they must always and everywhere act the same under the same circumstances. We pass on now to the subject of Evolution, first considering its meaning, and then its effect on the present argument.

**(1.) The meaning of Evolution.**

Now by the term Evolution is meant to be included the processes of Organic Evolution, Natural Selection, and the Survival of the Fittest. The former may be described as meaning that all the different forms of life now existing, or that ever have existed on this earth, are the descendants of earlier and less developed forms, and those again of simpler ones; and so on, till we get back to the earliest form of life, whatever that may have been.

And the theories of *Natural Selection* and *the Survival of the Fittest* explain how this may have taken place. For among the slight modifications that would most likely occur in every organism, those, and only those, would be perpetuated which were of advantage to it in the struggle for existence. And they would in time, it is assumed, become hereditary in its descendants, and thus higher forms of life would be gradually produced. And the value of these theories is that they show how Organic Evolution may have taken place without involving any sudden change, such as a monkey giving birth to a man. We must remember, however, that the subject is far from settled; and even now naturalists are beginning to doubt whether all the modifications were in reality very slight. But still, speaking broadly, this is the theory we have to discuss.

It will, of course, be noticed that Evolution is thus a *process*, and not a *cause*. It is the method in which certain changes have been brought about, and not the cause which brings them about. Every slight modification must have been caused somehow. When such modifications were caused, then Natural Selection can explain how the useful ones alone were perpetuated, but it cannot explain how the modifications themselves arose. On the contrary, it supposes them as already existing, otherwise there would be nothing to select from. Natural Selection, then, rather weeds than plants, and would be better described as Natural *Rejection*. It merely shows how, as a rule, among the various modifications in an organism, some good and some bad, the useless ones would disappear, and the useful ones would remain; in other words, how the fittest would survive. But this survival of the fittest does not explain in the slightest degree how the fitness arose. If, as an extreme example, out of a hundred animals, fifty had eyes and fifty had not, it is easy to understand how those that had eyes would be more likely to have descendants; but this does not explain how they first got eyes. And the same applies in other cases.

How, then, did the variations in each organism first arise? In common language they may be ascribed to chance; but, strictly speaking, such a thing is impossible. The word *chance* is merely a convenient term for the results of certain forces of nature when we are unable to calculate them. Chance, then, must be excluded; and there seem to be only two alternatives. Either the organisms in nature possessed free will, and acted as they did *voluntarily*; or else they did not possess free will, and acted as they did *necessarily*. The former theory will be examined later on; the latter is the one we are now considering.

## (2.) The effect of Evolution.

How then would this theory affect our previous conclusion that the Creator designed all the organs of nature, such as the eye, and hence presumably the whole of the universe? As we shall see, it only confirms it. For to put it plainly, if all free will on the part of the organisms is excluded, so that they were all bound to act exactly as they did, it is clear that the earth and all it contains is like a vast mass of machinery. And however complicated its parts, and however much they may act on one another, and however long they may take in doing so, yet if in the end they produce an organ showing design, this must have been foreseen and intended by the Maker of the machinery. In the same way if a mass of machinery after working for a long time eventually turned out a watch, we should have no hesitation in saying that whoever made the machinery, and set it going, intended it to do so. And is the inference less clear, if it not only turned out a watch, but a watchmaker as well, and everything else that exists on this planet?

All then that evolution does is this. It shows that the whole of nature forms such a long and continuous process; that if the end has been foreseen at all, it must have been foreseen from the beginning. In other words, just as the Unity of Nature shows that if anything has been designed, everything has been designed; so Evolution shows that if it has been designed at all, it has been designed *from the beginning*. We must hence conclude that the organs in nature, such as the eye, which undoubtedly show design, were not designed separately or as *after-thoughts*, but were all included in one grand design from the beginning. And this can only increase our admiration for the Designer. Thus evolution, even in its most extreme and automatic form, cannot get rid of a Designer. Still less can it do so, if (as is probable) it is not automatic at all; but is due to the *continuous* action of the Creator, who is what is called *immanent* in nature, and directs every step.

It should be noticed, moreover, that in one respect evolution rather *increases* the evidence of design. For if, to take a single example, a human hand has been evolved from a monkey's foot merely by the monkey using it as a hand, and taking hold of things; it increases the amount of design which must have been spent on the foot to enable it to do so. And if *all* the organs in nature have been evolved in this way from simpler ones, it increases the amount of design which must have been spent on those simpler ones to an extent which is practically infinite.

Thus Evolution implies a previous *Involution*; since all forms of life must have been involved in the first form before they could be evolved from it; so that creation by evolution is more wonderful than creation by direct manufacture. And it seems to many to be a far nobler conception of the Creator that He should obtain all the results He desired, by one grand system of evolution, rather than by a large number of separate creations. For then the *method* in which the results were obtained would be as marvellous, and show as much wisdom and foresight as the results themselves; and each would be worthy of the other. Evolution, then, seems to be the highest form of creation; and so far from destroying the present argument, it only destroys its difficulties, by showing that every single part of every single organism may have been *designed*, and yet in a manner worthy of the great Creator.

Nor is the conclusion altered if we carry back the process of evolution, and assume that the earliest form of life was itself evolved from some previous form of inanimate matter; and this again from a simpler one, and so on till we get back to the original form of matter, whatever that may have been. For if the results as we now see them show design, then the argument for a Designer is not weakened, but our ideas of His skill are still further increased, if we believe that they were already secured when our earth was merely a nebula.

### (*C.*) THE FREE WILL OBJECTION.

We have, lastly, to consider the other, and more important objection, that arising from *Free Will*. Why, it is urged, may not all organisms in nature have possessed free will within certain limits, and have selected those forms which suited them best? For example, referring to the case of a watch, if telling the time were of any advantage to the watch itself, and if the spring, wheels, and hands possessed free will; then it might be thought that they had formed themselves into that arrangement which suited them best. And if so, the idea that the watchmaker foresaw and intended them to adopt this arrangement seems unnecessary.

Now, in the case before us, as the organs showing design in nature, such as the eye, always conduce to the welfare of their possessor, the objection is certainly worth considering. But as we shall see, it is most improbable, while the chief argument in its favour cannot be maintained. It need scarcely be pointed out that we are not assuming that the organisms have free will, but merely admitting that they may have it; and if anyone denies this, the objection, as far as he is concerned, falls to the ground at once.

### (1.) Its great improbability.

This is apparent because low down in the scale of nature (plants, trees, etc.), the free will of the organisms, if they have any, must be extremely limited; yet they bear unmistakable marks of design. While, in higher beings which have (or may have) an undoubted free will, it is hard to believe that it can effect anything like what is required. Would, for instance, wishing to see or trying to see, even if blind animals were capable of either, have ever given them eyes? And the same applies in other cases. It is hence most improbable that the marks of design in nature are due to the organisms themselves, rather than to their Creator.

But there is one important argument on the other side, which, if it could be maintained, would be sufficient to outweigh all this improbability. It is, that some beings, such as man, do, as a matter of fact, possess a free will, and that man can and does alter his condition, to a slight extent, by using that free will. Therefore, it is said, it is impossible for the Creator to have foreknown what man's condition would be, because free will and foreknowledge are *necessarily* inconsistent. But this latter point is disputed.

### (2.) Free Will and Foreknowledge not inconsistent.

Now, although at first sight freedom of action seems inconsistent with any foreknowledge of what that action will be, yet on closer examination this will be found to be at least doubtful. For our own experience seems to show that in some cases, at all events, it is not in the nature of things impossible to know how a free being will act.

For example, I myself may know how, under given external conditions, I will act to-morrow. Never being sure of these, I cannot be said to actually foreknow the event; so that foreknowing with man is never more than foreguessing. But I may be quite sure how, *under given conditions*, I will act. For instance, I may know that, provided I keep in good health, provided I receive no news from anyone, provided, etc, I will go to my office some time to-morrow morning.

Yet I feel equally sure that this foreknowledge of mine does not prevent the act when it comes from being quite free on my part. My knowing this evening what I will do to-morrow does not oblige me to do it. My foreknowledge of the event does not bring the event about. It is in no sense its *cause*. The act when it comes is due to my own free will, I merely foreknow *what use I will make of my freedom*. And these are probably the common feelings of mankind on the subject.

It seems, then, that my foreknowledge need not be inconsistent with my free will. And hence, if I tell someone else how I will act, *his* foreknowledge would not be inconsistent with my free will. So that in some cases, and under given conditions, it does not seem impossible for a man to foreknow how another man will act, yet without interfering with his freedom. In short, free will does not seem to be *necessarily* inconsistent with the foreknowledge even of man, though it is always practically so, owing to man's imperfect knowledge of the surrounding circumstances. But the Creator knows, or may know, these circumstances fully, therefore it must be still less inconsistent with *His* foreknowledge.

Of course it may be said that if the Creator foreknows how I will act tomorrow, I am *certain* to act in that way; and this is doubtless true. But it does not follow that I *need* act in that way; for *certainty* is not the same as *necessity*. This is obvious enough in regard to a past event. I certainly did it, but I need not have done it; and it may be equally true in regard to a future event. I will certainly do it, but I need not do it. Therefore the Creator may know that I will do it, though it will still be *free* on my part.

And this is strongly confirmed when we reflect that the difficulty of knowing how a free being will act, however great in itself, seems as nothing compared with the difficulty of *creating* a free being. Apart from experience, we should probably have thought this to be impossible. Yet man has been created somehow. Is it then unlikely that the Being who was able to overcome the greater difficulty, and create a free man, should also be able to overcome the lesser difficulty, and foreknow how he would act?

Moreover, if free will and foreknowledge are *always* and *necessarily* inconsistent, then the Creator cannot have any foreknowledge of *His Own* acts, or else they are not free on His part; neither of which seems at all probable. We are not, of course, arguing from this that He actually does foreknow how He will act Himself, or how a free man will act, but only that it is not in the nature of things impossible that He should do so; in other words, that free will and foreknowledge are not *necessarily* inconsistent.

And this is precisely what we had to show. The marks of design in nature afford what seems to be overwhelming evidence in favour of the foreknowledge of the Creator. The objection we are considering is that, in spite of all this evidence, we must still deny it, because some of the organisms in nature, such as man, possess a free will; and therefore any foreknowledge is in the nature of things impossible. And the instant it is shown that such foreknowledge is not impossible, the objection falls to the ground.

We may now sum up the argument in this chapter. We first explained that by *Design* was meant any voluntary action combined with foreknowledge of the results of that action. We next considered the evidence for design in nature, taking, as a single example, the human eye. And this evidence appeared complete and overwhelming; more especially as we were not appealing to it to show the existence of a Creator, which is already admitted, but merely His foreknowledge. And we have since considered the two apparent objections to this argument arising from Evolution and Free Will.

But when carefully examined, the former only strengthens the argument, while the latter does not weaken it. We therefore conclude, on reviewing the whole subject, that the Creator *designed the universe.*

# CHAPTER III.
## THAT THE EXISTENCE OF GOD IS EXTREMELY PROBABLE.

(*A.*) MEANING OF THE TERM GOD.

The Personal Being who designed and created the universe.

(*B.*) TWO OF GOD'S ATTRIBUTES.

Wisdom and Power. He is also Omnipresent.

(*C.*) THE OBJECTION THAT GOD IS UNKNOWABLE.

This is partly true; but everything is unknowable in its real nature, though in each case the partial knowledge we can obtain is all we require.

(*D.*) SUMMARY OF ARGUMENT.

The position in the argument at which we have now arrived is this. We showed in the last chapter that the Creator designed the universe; in other words, that when he created it, He foreknew its future history. And from this the next step, as to the existence of God, is quite plain; in fact, it is merely a question of words.

**(A.) MEANING OF THE TERM GOD.**

Now any being who is able to design we will call a *personal being*. And GOD is the name given to the Personal Being who designed and created the universe.

But it ought to be noticed, before we pass on, that the term *personal being* is also applied to *man*, and is said by many writers to involve the three ideas of *thought*, *desire*, and *will*. But these seem to be all included in design; for if I design anything, I must first of all *think* of it, then *wish* it, and then *accomplish* it.

We will examine in the next chapter whether man is a personal being as we have used the term; but if we admit that he is, we have another and independent argument in favour of the Creator being so too. For the Creator has somehow or other produced man, with all his attributes; so He cannot be a mere impersonal Being or Force, since a cause must be able to account for its effect. And a free and intelligent man cannot be due to a Force, which is neither free nor intelligent. Therefore, if man is a personal being, it follows that man's *Maker* must be so too.

It should also be noticed that man's mind and spirit, which make him a personal being, cannot be discovered by any physical means. And this meets the objection that we cannot discover God by any physical means. It would be much more surprising if we could. But though the telescope can find no

God in the heavens, just as the microscope can find no mind in man, the existence of each may be quite certain for other reasons. In popular language, all we can see is the *house*, not the *tenant*, in either case.

## (*B.*) TWO OF GOD'S ATTRIBUTES.

We must next notice somewhat carefully two of God's attributes, *Wisdom* and *Power*. Both of these are involved in the idea of a Personal Being able to design. For *design*, as used in this Essay, means originating or freely doing anything, as well as previously planning it. Therefore, if we use the word, as is often done, for planning alone, we must remember that a personal being is one who can both design and accomplish. The former implies a mind able to form some plan, and the latter a free force, or will, able to carry it out. So a personal being must of necessity have *wisdom* to design and *power* to accomplish. And considering the vastness of the universe and the variety of its organisms, it seems only reasonable to conclude that the Creator possesses these attributes to the greatest possible extent, so that He is both Omniscient and Omnipotent.

It is important, however, to notice the meaning given to these words. By *Omniscient*, then, we mean possessing all possible knowledge. Now the only knowledge which might be thought impossible is how a free being would act in the future, and we have already shown that such knowledge is not in the nature of things impossible; so there does not seem to be any necessary restriction here.

But with *Omnipotent* the case is different. This means, as just said, possessing all possible power; that is to say, being able to do anything which is not impossible. Of course some Christians may be inclined to answer, that *with God all things are possible*; but as He who said so began one of His own prayers with the words *if it be possible*, this cannot be taken in its widest sense.[2] And provided the word *impossible* is used in its strict meaning, we have no reason for thinking that God could do impossible things; such as make a triangle with the properties of a circle, or allow a man a free choice between two alternatives, and yet force him to choose one of them. These, then, are two of the great attributes of God, Wisdom and Power. There is a third, which will be considered in Chapter V.

[2] Matt. 19. 26; 26. 39.

It should also be noticed that besides being the Designer and Creator of the universe in the past, God seems to be also its *Preserver* at the present, being, in fact, the *Omnipresent* Power which is still working throughout nature. That there is such a Power can scarcely be denied (however hard it may be to realise), and that it is the same as the Creating Power is plainly the most probable view. God is thus the Cause of all natural forces now, just as He was their Creator in times past; and what are called secondary or natural causes, have probably no existence. They may, indeed, be called secondary *forces*, but they are not *causes* at all in the strict sense; for a cause must be *free*, it must have the power of initiative. Thus man's free will, if it is free, would be a real secondary cause, but the forces of nature are mere links in a chain of events, each of which is bound to follow the previous one. This is often spoken of as the Divine *Immanence* in nature, and means little else than the Omnipresence of a Personal God—the all-pervading influence of One 'who is never so far off as even to be called near.'

### (*C.*) THE OBJECTION THAT GOD IS UNKNOWABLE.

We must lastly consider an important objection which may be made to the whole of these chapters. It may be said that the human mind is unable to argue about the *First Cause*, because we have no faculties for comprehending the Infinite; or, as it is commonly expressed, because God is *Unknowable*.

Now this objection is partly true. There is a sense in which all will admit that God is Unknowable. His existence and attributes are too great for any human mind to comprehend entirely, or for any human language to express completely and accurately. Therefore our statements on the subject are at best only approximations to the truth. We can apprehend His existence, but we cannot comprehend it, and God in His true nature is certainly *Unknowable*.

But, strictly speaking, it is the same with everything. Man in his true nature is also unknowable, yet we know something about man. So, again, the forces of nature are all unseen and unknowable in themselves, yet from their effects we know something about them. And even matter when reduced to atoms, or electrons, or anything else, is still a mystery, yet we know a good deal about matter. And in each case this knowledge is not incorrect because it is incomplete. Why, then, should the fact of God being in His true nature unknowable prevent our having some real, though partial, knowledge of Him? In short, we may know something about God, though we cannot know everything about Him.

And it should be noticed that Natural Religion and Natural Science are alike in this respect—they are both founded on inferences drawn from the observed facts of nature. For example, we observe the motion of falling bodies, and infer the existence of some force, gravity, to account for this. Similarly, we observe the marks of design in nature, and infer the existence, or at least foresight, of some Being who designed them. In neither case have we any direct knowledge as to the cause of what we see. And in some respects Religion is not so unknowable as Science. For our own, real or apparent, mind and free will do give us some kind of idea as to the existence of a personal being, apart from what he does; while of a natural force, such as gravity, apart from its effects, we can form no idea whatever. Thus our knowledge of every subject is but partial, and it finally leads us into the Unknowable.

But now comes the important point. This partial knowledge, which is all we can obtain in either Science or Religion, is all we require. It is not a perfect knowledge, but it is sufficient for all practical purposes. Whatever the force of gravity may be in itself, we know what it is *to us*. We know that if we jump off a cliff we shall fall to the ground. And so in regard to Religion. Whatever God may be in Himself, we know what He is *to us*. We know that He is our Maker, and therefore, as will be shown in the next chapter, He is the Being to whom we are responsible. This is the practical knowledge which we require, and this is the knowledge which we can obtain.

Moreover, though our reason may be to some extent unfit to judge of such matters, the vast importance of the subject seems to demand our coming to some conclusion one way or the other. This is especially the case because important results affecting a man's daily life follow from his deciding that there is a God, and to leave the question undecided is practically the same as deciding that there is not a God. In the same way, if a ship were in danger of sinking, and a steamer also in distress offered to take off the passengers, for one of them to say that he did not know whether it was safer to go in the steamer or not, and would therefore do nothing and stay where he was, would be practically the same as deciding not to go in the steamer. So in the case before us. To refuse to decide the question because of the supposed inadequacy of human reason is practically the same as to deny the existence of God.

Still, it may be urged, granting that our reason must decide the question one way or the other, and granting that our reason seems to force us to conclude in the existence of God, are there not great difficulties in honestly believing this conclusion? No doubt there are, and no thoughtful man would think of ignoring them. But after all it is only a choice of difficulties; and, as we have shown, there is *less* difficulty in believing what we have here maintained than the contrary. It is less difficult, for instance, to believe that the universe had an origin, than to believe that it had not. Similarly as to the existence of God; the theory is not free from difficulties, but, with all its difficulties, it is still by far the most probable theory to explain the origin and present state of the universe. We therefore decide, judging by reason alone (which is the line adopted in this Essay), that the existence of God is *extremely probable*.

### (*D*.) SUMMARY OF ARGUMENT.

In conclusion, we will repeat very briefly, the main line of argument thus far. To begin with, in the present universe we observe a succession of changes. If these changes are not recurring, which seems incredible, they must have had a commencement; and this is supported by the theories of Evolution and the Degradation of Energy. Therefore, as this commencement cannot have been a necessity, it must have been due to some *Free Force*. And a Free Force must be a *Supernatural* Force, since natural forces are not free, but always act according to some fixed law, while the unity of nature points to its being a *Single* Supernatural Force, which we called the Creator.

Next, it follows that the Creator must have foreknown the consequences of His acts, judging by the marks of design which they present. And this conclusion was shown to be not inconsistent with either the process of evolution, or the existence of free will in man or other beings. Hence He must have been a *Personal Being*, possessing both Wisdom to design, and Power to accomplish.

Or the whole argument may be repeated in an even shorter form. The universe (in its present condition) has not existed always, it is therefore an *effect*,—something that has been effected, or brought about somehow; and therefore like every effect, it must have had a *Cause*. Then since the effect shows a certain unity throughout, the Cause must have been One. Since the effect shows in some parts evidence of having been planned and arranged, the capacity for planning and arranging must have existed in the Cause. In other words, a universe showing marks of design is the effect, and nothing less than a Personal Being who designed it can be the Cause. And GOD is the name given to this Personal Being.

# CHAPTER IV.
## THAT MAN IS A FREE AND RESPONSIBLE BEING.

(*A.*) MAN'S MENTAL ATTRIBUTES.

Man possesses a mind as well as a body; the opposite theory, materialism, has great difficulties.

(*B.*) MAN'S MORAL ATTRIBUTES.

(1.) Man possesses a will.

(2.) Man's acts are partly determined by his will.

(3.) Man's will is *free*.

(4.) Man knows that his will is free; and this enables him to design, and makes him a personal being.

(5.) Man's *responsibility* for his acts.

(6.) Man's moral sense of right and wrong; which enables him to distinguish the quality of acts, and makes him a moral being.

(7.) Man's conscience, by which he can judge of this quality in some cases.

(*C.*) DIFFERENCE BETWEEN ANIMALS AND MEN.

There is a great mental difference, though probably only of degree; and entire moral difference, since animals, even if free, do not possess a *known* freedom, and are hence not personal beings.

(*D.*) CONCLUSION.

Man consists of three parts, body, mind, and spirit: his unique position.

Having decided on the Existence of God, which is the great truth of *Natural* Religion, the question now arises whether, if nature can lead us so far, there is no means of getting further. No one will deny that further knowledge is desirable, both as to God, ourselves, and our future destiny, and is there no means of obtaining it? And this brings us to the subject of *Revealed* Religion, that is to say, of God's making some Revelation to man. And the probability of this will depend partly on the *character of man*—is he a being at all worthy of a revelation; and partly on the *Character of God*—is He a Being at all likely to make one? The former question alone will be discussed in this chapter, and we will consider man's *mental* and *moral* attributes separately. Nothing need be said about his bodily or *physical* characteristics, as they have no bearing on the present argument.

## (A.) MAN'S MENTAL ATTRIBUTES.

By these are meant man's thoughts and feelings, and that they are different from the matter composing his body seems self-evident. Matter possesses size, weight, colour, shape, and hardness. Mind does not possess any of these. They have no conceivable meaning when applied to thoughts and feelings. Yet both mind and matter exist in man. We each feel conscious that we have something which *thinks*, and which we call mind; as well as something which *moves*, and which we call matter (*i.e.*, our bodies); and that these are absolutely distinct from one another. And from the nature of the case this *inherent conviction* is all we can appeal to. For mind, if it exists at all, being different from matter, is beyond the reach of ordinary scientific discovery. We cannot however be more certain of anything than of these inherent convictions, which form the basis of all our knowledge. Even the propositions of Euclid are only deductions from some other of our convictions, such as that the whole is greater than its part.

Still the difficulty of understanding this compound nature in man, part mind and part body, has led some persons to adopt the theory of *materialism*. According to this there is no such thing as *mind*; what we call thoughts and feelings being merely complicated motions of the molecules of the brain. Now, that the mind and brain are closely associated together none will deny, but it does not follow that they are identical. The brain may be merely the instrument of the mind through which it acts. And though, as far as we know, the mind can never act without the brain, it may certainly have a separate existence, and possibly, under different conditions, may be able to act separately. It is in fact no more difficult to conceive of thought without a brain, than to conceive of thought with a brain. All we can say is, that within the range of our experience the two seem to be somehow connected together.

Recent investigations, however, in what is called *telepathy* (or thought-transference) seem to show that in some cases one mind can influence another *at a distance*, and without any material connection. And this (if admitted) proves that the mind is something more than a mere collection of particles of matter.

Moreover materialism, to be consistent, must deny not only that man has a mind, but that he has anything immaterial at all; he must be matter in motion, and nothing else. But this is disproved by our *memory*, which convinces us that we are the *same* persons now as we were ten years ago; yet we know that every particle of our bodies, including our brains, has changed in the interval. We must then have something immaterial which survives, in spite of everything material changing.

The case, it should be noticed, is not like that of a tree, which may be popularly said to be the same now as it was ten years ago, though every particle of it has changed in the interval. For as far as we know, the tree has nothing which connects its present state with its former state, it has no memory of what happened to it then. We *have*, that is just the difference. We can remember now what happened to us ten years ago, though our bodies now do not contain a single atom or molecule which they did then. We must, therefore, have something else besides atoms and molecules, in other words, something *immaterial*; and if so, there is an end of materialism in its only logical form.

This theory then cannot possibly be accepted, and we must abide by our inherent conviction that we have a mind as well as a body. This is an ultimate fact in human nature; and we are as certain of it as we are of anything, though like some other ultimate facts it has to be assumed, because it can be neither proved nor doubted.

### (*B*.) MAN'S MORAL ATTRIBUTES.

We pass on now to man's moral attributes, which we will consider in detail.

### (1.) Man possesses a will.

In the first place man possesses what, in common language, is called a *will*. Strictly speaking, of course, the will is not anything independent of the man, which he *possesses*, as he might possess a dog; it is the man himself *who wills*, or who possesses the power of willing. But the common language is so generally understood, that it will be used here. Now the chief reason for believing that man has a will is his own inherent conviction. He feels certain that he does possess a will which is distinct from his body and his mind, though closely associated with both, and apparently to some extent controlling both. For example, I may resolve to raise my hand, and then do it; or I may resolve to think out a problem, and then do it. In each case the will is felt to be something distinct from the subsequent bodily or mental action.

### (2.) Man's acts are partly determined by his will.

In the next place, a man's acts (and also his thoughts) are partly determined by his will. By this is meant that a man's will is able to move his limbs, so that, for instance, he can raise his hand when he wishes, and this gives him the power of determining his acts. It is not meant that a man's will can move his limbs directly; his limbs are moved by his muscles, which are directed by his nerves, and these by certain motions in the brain. All that the will can do is to give a particular direction to these motions, which, combined with various other forces, brings about the observed result.

Now we have in favour of this action of the human will on the human body the universal experience of mankind, which is that a man can somehow or other move his limbs at pleasure. Indeed, the question whether a man can walk across the room when he wishes, seems to most people to admit of a convincing answer: *solvitur ambulando*. But still, the action of will on matter seems so improbable, and so difficult to understand, that attempts have naturally been made to find some other explanation.

But no satisfactory one can be suggested. For my wishing to move my body, is followed by my moving it so frequently and so universally, that there must be some connection between them. And though we cannot imagine how a mere wish can move particles of matter (in the brain or anywhere else), it is just as hard to imagine how the movement of particles of matter can produce a wish. The latter theory is no easier to understand than the other; and, as just said, it is opposed to *the daily experience of mankind*, which is that a man's will can, somehow or other, move his limbs, and hence determine his acts.

### (3.) Man's will is free.

It must next be noticed that man's will is a *free* will, and this is a most important point. It is quite distinct from the previous question. Then we decided that a man's raising his hand, for instance, was the result of his wishing to do so. We have now to consider whether this wish was free on the man's part, or whether he could not help it; the latter view being called that of *Necessity*, or *Determinism*, and meaning that a man's acts are necessarily determined, and not free. Of course everyone admits that there are *limits* to human freedom. A man cannot always raise his hand when he likes, it may be paralyzed. The important point is whether he is *ever* free; and there are two main arguments on each side.

Now the great argument in favour of free will is, again, our own inherent conviction. It is one of the most universal, and one of the most certain, beliefs of mankind that he has free will. This belief is forced upon him by his own daily experience. He feels, for instance, that he is free to raise his hand or not. And what is more, he can verify the fact by actually raising it, whenever he likes; so it is literally true to say that the conviction rests on the daily experience of the human race. And to many, this argument alone seems conclusive.

But, as a matter of fact, it is fully confirmed by *human conduct*. For a man's conduct is *variable* and quite unlike the uniformity which we find in chemistry and physics, where there is no free force, and everything is brought about in accordance with fixed laws. So we seem to require some free force in man to account for his variable conduct. These, then, are the two arguments in favour of free will—man's *inherent conviction*, confirmed by his *variable conduct*; and no more powerful arguments can be imagined.

On the other hand, the chief argument against human freedom is that it would be an *anomaly* in nature; since natural forces always act in the same way, and any free force, able to act or not as it likes, is quite unknown. If, then, man possesses such a force, no matter how limited it may be, he is partly, at least, a *supernatural* being, not bound by fixed laws.

Now all this may be admitted, but what then? Why should not man be a partly supernatural being? God, Who has made man, is Supernatural; He possesses free will, and He might, if He thought fit, bestow some of this attribute on man, allowing him, that is to say, within certain limits, to act in one way or another. No doubt, to persons who study physical science alone, the existence of any free force in man seems most improbable. But, on the other hand, to those who study the actions of men, such as barristers, soldiers, or politicians, the idea that man is a mere machine seems equally improbable.

And does not the same principle apply in other cases? Suppose, for instance, that a man were to study inorganic chemistry alone, living on an island where vegetation was unknown, would not a tree be a complete anomaly to him? Yet trees exist and have to be allowed for. In the same way man's free will may be an anomaly, but the evidence for it is overwhelming.

Moreover, the anomaly is greatly lessened by the fact that man already occupies a very anomalous position. For as we have seen, his acts are often determined by his *will*, and this is utterly unlike anything that we find elsewhere in nature. Indeed the *action* of a will is as great an anomaly as its *freedom*; and with the possible exception of animals (see further on) we have no experience whatever of a will that can act and is *not* free. Therefore claiming freedom for a man, is not like claiming freedom for a mineral, or a plant. He is anyhow a unique being, by far the highest and most important on this planet; and that he should be partly supernatural as well does not seem so very unlikely after all.

We must also remember that we know more about ourselves where we are conscious of freedom, than we do about the surrounding universe, where we infer a rigid uniformity. Indeed, our own free will is the only force of which we have any *direct* knowledge, and the so-called forces of nature, such as gravity, are, strictly speaking, only assumptions which we make to account for observed facts. And, as we have shown, even these forces seem to have originated in the Free Will of the Creator; so as far as we can judge, *free will*, of some kind is the ultimate cause of all force.

The other important argument against free will is that it would be inconsistent with what is called the *Conservation of Energy*, since it is said any voluntary act would involve the creation of energy. But this is at least doubtful; for the will might be free as to its acts, were it only able to control energy without producing it. And it could do this if it possessed the power of altering either the time, or the direction of force; deciding, for instance, whether to raise my hand now, or a minute hence, or whether to raise my right hand or my left. And if it possessed either of these powers, it could turn the latent force, which a man possesses, into actual motion when and how it pleased. And it would thus be free as to its acts, without creating any energy at all.

We therefore decide on reviewing the whole subject, that man's will is free; since this alone agrees with his own inherent *conviction*, and fully accounts for his variable *conduct*. While, on the other hand, though an *anomaly* in nature, it is not on that account incredible; nor is it inconsistent with the *conservation of energy*.

**(4.) Man knows that his will is free.**

Having now decided that man's will is free, little need be said about the next point, which is that man *knows* that his will is free, since, as we have shown, this is the chief argument for admitting its freedom. There are, however, many other arguments for proving that man believes that he has a free will, for it is shown by his acts. It is this known freedom which enables a man to set before him an end, and deliberately work towards it; in other words, it enables him to *design*, and makes him a *personal being*, as we have used the term. And it is needless to point out that the evidence of human design is universal. Again, human language affords a conclusive proof that man has always and everywhere believed himself to be free; for such terms as *I will*, *I choose*, *I decide*, exist in all languages. However, we need not pursue this subject, since it is undisputed that man *believes* that he has a free will; and it is taken for granted in all human affairs.

**(5.) Man's responsibility for his acts.**

By this is meant that a man is responsible for the way in which he uses his freedom; and this seems to follow at once from his knowing that he is free. Moreover, a sense of responsibility is among the inherent convictions of mankind. Of course, there may be exceptions to this as to most other rules; but taking mankind as a whole, he certainly believes in his own responsibility.

He also believes that this responsibility is in the first place to God, or some other supernatural Being. No doubt he is also responsible to his fellow-men, more especially to those among whom he is living; but a moment's reflection will show that this is not the leading idea. For a man must in the first place be responsible to his Maker rather than to his fellow-men. In the same way a child is first of all responsible to his parents, and then, secondly and consequently, to his brothers and sisters. Therefore, because God has made us, we are responsible to Him; and because He has placed us among other men, and presumably wishes us to take some part in human society, we are in a lesser degree responsible to them also. So the *brotherhood of man*, as it is called, naturally follows from the Fatherhood of God.

### (6.) Man's moral sense of right and wrong.

In the next place, man has the remarkable faculty of distinguishing the *quality* of acts which are free, regarding some as right and others as wrong, the latter being called *sins*. And it may be noticed in passing, that the existence of moral evil or sin seems to many to be an additional argument in favour of man's freedom; otherwise God would be the sole author of man's misdeeds. Of course, in this case, they would not be really *sins*, for if man has no free will, he is a mere machine, and can no more sin against God (or man either) than a watch can sin against its maker. Such a man might be imperfect, and so might a watch, but he could not be *wicked*; yet few will say that there are no wicked men in the world. Now we will call a being who is thus able to distinguish the quality of acts a *moral being*. Man is therefore a moral being, having this *moral sense*, as it is called, of distinguishing right from wrong.

It will perhaps make the meaning of this moral sense plainer if we compare it with one of man's other senses, say that of sight. The one, then, distinguishes right from wrong, just as the other distinguishes red from yellow, or blue from green. And as man's sense of colours is not disproved by one man thinking a colour blue which another thinks green—or his sense of taste, by one man thinking a taste nice, which another thinks nasty—so his moral sense is not disproved by one man thinking an act right which another thinks wrong.

Moreover this sense of right and wrong is quite distinct from the pleasant or unpleasant consequences which are associated with certain acts. For instance, I may avoid putting my hand into hot water, because I remember having done so before, and it was painful; but this is quite different from avoiding an act because it is *wrong*. It is also quite distinct from expediency, or the idea of benefiting by an act. For an act may not benefit us at all, or may even injure us, and yet it may be right. In short, 'fifty experiences of what is pleasant or what is profitable do not, and cannot, make one conviction of what is right'; the ideas differ in kind; and not merely in degree.

## (7.) Man's conscience.

Lastly, as to man's conscience. This is often confused with his moral sense, but a little reflection will show that the two are distinct. For a man might possess a moral sense, and be able to classify acts as right or wrong, yet have no direct means of knowing to which class any particular act belonged. He might have to work this out by reasoning; and in difficult cases we sometimes do so. But as a rule this is unnecessary. For mankind possesses a very remarkable *something*, called a conscience, which tells him at once, and without either argument or reasoning, that certain acts are right and others wrong. Conscience is thus like an organ of the moral sense, and may be compared to the eye or organ of sight; for just as the eye perceives that certain colours are red and others blue, so conscience perceives that certain acts are right and others wrong. In each case the perception is almost instantaneous, and quite distinct from any kind of reasoning.

Conscience, it will be noticed, does not *make* the act right or wrong, any more than the eye makes the colour red or blue; it merely tells us what acts are right and what wrong. It is thus an *intermediary* between Someone else and ourselves; and this Someone else can only be God, Who gave us our conscience, so that in popular language it may be called *the Voice of God*. And it tells us we ought to act right, because this is the way in which God wishes us to act.

Now that mankind possesses a conscience is indisputable. It is shared alike by young and old, rich and poor, educated and uneducated. It has existed in all ages, countries and races. We all have it, and what is very remarkable it seems to be independent of our will, and not at our disposal. We do not correct it, but it corrects us; for it not only tells us what acts are right and what wrong, but it approves definitely of our doing the former, and disapproves just as definitely of our doing the latter. Indeed, one of the most striking effects of conscience is this feeling of *remorse* or self-condemnation after wrong-doing; and such a feeling is practically universal.

And if it be objected that one man's conscience may say that an act is right, which another man's conscience says is wrong, we must remember that the decision of a man's conscience, only refers to the man himself. It tells a man what is right *for him*, with his knowledge and surroundings, and it is quite possible that this may be wrong for another man.

These, then, are the moral attributes of the human race, and it follows at once that man is a *free and responsible being*. But as this conclusion is often disputed, because of the similarity between animals and men, and the difficulty of admitting that they also are free and responsible beings, or else of showing where the distinction lies, we must examine this subject.

## (*C.*) DIFFERENCE BETWEEN ANIMALS AND MEN.

Now the *bodily* difference between certain animals and men is admittedly small; and though the accompanying *mental* difference is enormous, it is probably only one of degree; for all animals seem, to some slight extent, to possess a mind, which enables them at least to feel conscious of pleasure and pain. We must therefore pass on to the *moral* attributes of animals; and as we know nothing as to their feelings on the subject, it is difficult to say (referring to the first three points) whether they have a *free will* or not. Of course, if they have *not*, that would be a clear distinction between animals and men. But we have no right to assume this, and there is a good deal to be said on the other side, at least in regard to the higher animals, so the question had better be left open.

But with regard to the next point, that of *known* freedom, we are on surer ground; for the proof of man's *believing* himself to be free does not depend solely on his own feelings. It is shown by his acts, as it enables him to *design*, and it is doubtful if there is anything corresponding to this in animals. For though many of their works show design somewhere, it does not seem to be due to *them*. This kind of unconscious designing (which strange to say is most apparent in the *lower* forms of animal life) is called *instinct*, and there are at least three reasons for thinking that it differs from real design implying forethought.

The first is, that, if these works were due to the design of the animals themselves, they must possess intellectual powers of a very high order. Take, for instance, the well known example of the *cells of bees*. These are built on the most perfect mathematical principles, the three rhombs which close the hexagonal columns having the exact angles so as to contain the greatest amount of honey, with the least expenditure of wax. And as we require advanced mathematics and a book of logarithms to work out such problems, it is hard to see how the bees can do it. Nor is heredity of any use, for the bees which build cells are all *workers* (as they are called) and have no descendants; while those which have descendants are either *drones* or *queens*, and these do no building. Thus the cells are built by bees, none of whose ancestors have ever built cells; so the design cannot be ascribed to anything they have inherited from their parents.[3] Secondly, animals are only able to design in a few special cases, and in other respects they often act with the greatest stupidity. A bee, for example, with all its mathematics, cannot very often, if it has flown in through an open window, retrace its way, but will buzz helplessly against another which is shut.

[3] Encyc. Brit., 9th edit., vol. iii., pp. 490, 484. The angles are 109° 28' and 70° 32'.

Thirdly, the instincts of animals are practically the same, always and everywhere. They are not more advanced in some countries, than in others; or in some individuals, than in others. They are not even more advanced as time goes on. The last cell built by a bee is no better than the first, and no better, as far as we know, than cells built by bees thousands of years ago; while the young of animals, without any experience to guide them, have the same instincts as the old. Clearly, then, an animal's instinct is born with it, and not acquired; and therefore, any apparent design there may be in what is done by instinct cannot be attributed to the animal itself, any more than the design shown in its eyes, but to its Maker.

So far all is plain. It may, however, be urged that in some of the higher animals, especially those in contact with man, we do find certain acts which seem to imply forethought and design. A dog, for example, will bury a bone one day, and go and look for it the next. But when once it is admitted that what are apparently far more striking instances of design are to be explained by instinct, it seems better to explain them all in the same way.

And this is confirmed by the fact that even the higher animals do not appear to have any idea of *responsibility*, or any sense of *right* and *wrong*, which in man are the result of his known freedom. Of course, this also may be disputed, since as we punish a dog for doing what we dislike, it looks as if we held it responsible for the act. But this does not follow. We punish the dog to prevent its repeating the act. And it may avoid doing so, because its memory associates the act with *pain*, and not because it feels responsible for it, or considers it to be *wrong*. While in the vast majority of cases we never think of holding an animal responsible for its acts, or look upon its injuring anyone as a sin. We conclude, then, that *moral* attributes form the great distinction between animals and men; because though animals have, or may have, a free will, it is not a *known* freedom, so they are not able, like men, to *design*, and are hence not *personal beings*.

Two further remarks may be made before leaving this subject. The first is, that though there are difficulties in placing this known freedom as the difference between animals and men, there are as great, if not greater, difficulties in placing it anywhere else. If we say that an ape or a dog can design, the difficulty is not lessened; it is merely transferred lower down the scale. Can a jellyfish design? The momentous attribute of known freedom must begin *somewhere*; and it seems less difficult to place it between animals and men than anywhere else.

The second and more important point is, that our ignorance about animals is no reason for doubting what we do know about man. To do this would be most illogical. Indeed, we might as well deny that a man could see, or hear, because there are difficulties in deciding where sight and hearing commence in the scale of animal life.

## (*D.*) CONCLUSION.

We may now conclude this chapter. With regard to man, it is clear that his bodily, mental, and moral attributes are quite distinct. A man may be strong in body, yet of weak intellectual power; or he may have a great intellect, yet be of weak moral character. This makes it probable that human nature consists of three parts—*body*, *mind*, and *spirit*; the mind corresponding to the mental reasoning part of man, and the spirit to the free moral part, the word *soul* being often used for either of these latter.

And the difference between animals and men is probably that the former have no *spirits*, but only bodies and (undeveloped) minds. All life on this planet would then form three great groups—*vegetation*, consisting of matter alone; *animals*, of matter and mind; *man*, of matter, mind, and spirit. And from this it seems to follow that while a man's *body* may (conceivably) have been evolved from any other form of matter, and his *mind* from any other form of mind, yet his *spirit* is essentially distinct, and cannot have been evolved from anything else.

Moreover, as a man's body and mind are both (to some extent) under the known control of his free will, or spirit, this latter must be looked upon as his real *self*. Thus he is not, strictly speaking, an organism at all, but a free being served by organs both of body and mind. They are *his*; they do not constitute *him*. He is the personal being, who controls both. In other words man *is* a spirit, and *has* a body and mind.

And our present conclusion is quite plain. We have shown that man is a *free* being, his freedom distinguishing him from natural forces, and making him in part supernatural. And he is a *responsible* being, his responsibility being due to his known freedom, and distinguishing him from animals. He has thus a unique position. Nothing else on this planet resembles him, and in his attribute of known freedom which enables him to design, and makes him a *personal being*, he resembles God alone.

# CHAPTER V.
## THAT GOD TAKES AN INTEREST IN MAN'S WELFARE.

(*A.*) THE EVIDENCE IN ITS FAVOUR.

Since God is a *Moral* as well as a Personal Being, He must be capable of caring for all His creatures; and we have abundant evidence that He does so, especially for man. But there are two great difficulties.

(*B.*) THE INSIGNIFICANCE OF MAN.

(1.) Some counter-arguments, showing that even if insignificant, God might still care for him.

(2.) Man's real importance, due to his mind and spirit.

(3.) The supposed inhabitants of other planets.

(*C.*) THE EXISTENCE OF EVIL.

(1.) Physical evil in animals. The objection that it is vast in amount, wholly unmerited, and perfectly useless, cannot be maintained.

(2.) Physical evil in man. Several ways of lessening the difficulty. Its explanation seems to be that God's designing evil does not mean His desiring it, as it is essential for forming a man's character.

(3.) Moral evil in man. The possibility of this is essential to free will; and wicked men are as necessary as any other form of evil.

(*D.*) CONCLUSION.

God's *Goodness* includes Beneficence and Righteousness.

Having discussed in the last chapter the character of man, we have next to consider, as far as we have any means of doing so, *the Character of God*; more especially whether He seems to take any interest in man's welfare. And we will first examine the evidence in favour of this; then the two arguments on the other side from the insignificance of man, and the existence of evil; and will conclude by considering in what sense the term *Goodness* can be ascribed to God.

**(*A.*) THE EVIDENCE IN ITS FAVOUR.**

To begin with, God is certainly capable of taking an interest in man's welfare, for He is not only a Personal Being, but also a Moral Being. This follows at once from what may be called the *moral argument* for the Existence of God, or that depending on man's free will. It is briefly this, that no combination of natural forces, which are uniform and always act the same under the same circumstances, can ever produce a *free* force, able to act or not as it likes. The idea seems inconceivable. If, then, man possesses such a force, which we have already admitted, it cannot have come from any natural forces, nor can it have made itself, so it must have been derived from some *previous* free force, and this, again, from a previous one, and so on till we finally arrive at a *Free Force*, which was *not* derived from any other, but which existed eternally. And this, it will be remembered, was precisely the conclusion we reached in Chapter I., though from quite a different argument. And then it follows that this Free Force, or Free Being, must know that He is free; and must therefore be a *moral* Being, able to distinguish the quality of acts as right or wrong. Indeed, the mere fact that man possesses this remarkable faculty makes it certain that man's Maker must possess it too.

Now a personal and moral God must clearly be able to take an interest in the welfare of His creatures; and there is abundant evidence that He actually does so. For everywhere in nature, and especially in man, we meet with marks, not only of design, but of *beneficent* design—that is to say of design tending to the welfare and happiness of the beings in question. Take, for instance, the human eye, which we considered in Chapter II. Everyone will admit that this conduces very greatly to man's happiness; and therefore the conclusion that God, when He designed the eye, did so with the object of benefiting man seems irresistible. Nor is this altered by the fact that the eye has a few defects, in being liable to various kinds of disease. For no one can think that it was made for the sake of these defects. It was evidently made to see, and not to ache. That it does ache now and then is in all probability due to its being such a complicated instrument; and perhaps also to its being often used too much.

But it may be said, beneficial organs like the eye, though they abound throughout nature, are not the only ones we meet with. There are others, like the claws and teeth of wild animals, which are just the opposite, and seem designed to give pain to other creatures. But this is quite untenable. They were plainly designed to enable the animal to secure its food, and are perhaps necessary for that purpose, and they all tend to the welfare of their possessor, and sometimes also to that of their victim, as it hastens death. There is not, in fact, a single organ in nature the *object* of which is to produce pain. Where pain is produced it is merely a sort of *by-product*. Thus far then, we are quite justified in concluding that God takes an interest in man's welfare. But there are two great difficulties.

### (*B.*) THE INSIGNIFICANCE OF MAN.

The first is from the apparent *insignificance* of man. For though he is doubtless by far the most important being on this planet, and endowed with some of the Divine attributes, yet, after all how utterly insignificant he is in comparison with his Maker. This is no new difficulty,[4] but modern science has increased its force by showing that our earth is only one among the planets which go round the sun, while the sun itself is only one among many millions of stars. And, we may ask, is it likely that the God Who rules these millions of stars should take any interest in the beings on a small planet like our earth?

[4] Ps. 8. 3, 4.

This is the difficulty we have to face; but a good deal depends on the way in which it is stated. Would it not be better to argue from the known to the unknown, and ask—Is it likely that the God Who has made this earth, and Who we know (from the marks of design) takes an interest in its inhabitants, should be *also* the Ruler of the distant stars? And when so stated, the unity of nature compels us to say that it is not only likely, but practically certain. However, we will discuss the subject more in detail, first considering some counter-arguments, which show that even if man were insignificant God might still care for him; then man's real importance; and lastly, the question of other planets being inhabited.

**(1.) Some Counter-arguments.**

To begin with, though it seems unlikely that God should take any interest in such insignificant beings as us men, it also seems unlikely that He should ever have designed and created such beings. Yet He has done so. And having created them, there is at most only a slight *additional* improbability, if any at all, that He should take an interest in their welfare. And this is especially the case when we remember that man is not only the highest and noblest being on this planet, but as far as we know on any planet. Therefore though we may be quite unworthy of God's care, we do not know of any other being who is more worthy of it. And it is most unlikely that a Creator would not take an interest in *any* of His works.

Next, as to the analogy of nature. Here we find nothing resembling a neglect of small things. On the contrary, everything, down to the minutest insect, seems finished with as much perfection as if it alone existed in the universe. And this is surely what we should expect. For true greatness does not exist in despising that which is small; and it may be a very part of God's infinite greatness that nothing should be too small for Him to care about, just as nothing is too large. And while a Being, Who can govern the universe, and attend to its millions of stars, is no doubt great—inconceivably great; yet He is surely greater still—*inconceivably greater*—if He can *also* attend to our little planet, and its inhabitants; and can do this so thoroughly, as not only to take an interest in the human race, but in the welfare of each one of its members.

And the whole analogy of nature is in favour of His doing so; for the forces of nature never deal with matter in bulk, but with each particle separately. A stone, for instance, is attracted to the ground, because, and only because, each particle of it is so attracted. In the same way if God takes an interest in the human race (and, as just said, it is hard to imagine His not doing so, since it is His noblest work) it may be because, and only because, He takes an interest in each individual member of it.

Thirdly, the difficulty of thus believing that God takes an interest in the daily life of an individual man, though undoubtedly great, is really no more than that of believing that He knows about it. For if He knows about it, why should He not care about it? Yet, as said in Chapter II., a world like ours cannot have been made without both knowledge, and foreknowledge, on the part of its Maker. And though we might at first be inclined to limit this to important matters, a little consideration will show that such a distinction is untenable; and that if God knows anything, He knows everything. And if He knows everything, why should He not care about everything?

Fourthly, and this is very important, whether we are insignificant or not, we are each of us *unique*. We are not like particles of matter. Millions of these are (or may be) exactly alike, but no two *men* are exactly alike; not even to the same extent as plants and animals. For each man is a separate spirit, a *personal being* distinct from all else in the world. And since he possesses a free will, his character is also distinct; for this depends to a large extent on how he uses his free will, what he says, and what he does, day by day. So it is out of the question to think that any two men are exactly alike. And this is the common belief of mankind, for however much we may think other people alike, we each feel sure that there is no one else in the world exactly like *ourselves*.

Nor can there be. For though God might, if He chose, make two trees exactly alike, or two men exactly alike in their external features, He could not make them alike *in their character*. For this, as just said, depends on their own free use of their own free will; and if God were to force them to decide in the same way, they would cease to be free. And from this it follows that each man is not only unique, but *irreplaceable*. No other can be made like him. Therefore, as we each have something special about us, God may take a *special* interest in each of us. Doubtless such an idea seems very wonderful; but no one who has any knowledge of the marvels of nature will think it, on that account, incredible. Indeed, from one point of view, it is only what we should expect. For we all know how a naturalist will value a unique specimen, which cannot be replaced, in spite of its having some defects. And if each man is really *unique*, and *irreplaceable*, why may not the God of Nature value him too (in spite of his faults), and take an interest in his welfare?

Then, fifthly, as to the discoveries of science, there is here also a good deal to be said on the other side. For though the telescope has shown us that our world is like a mere drop in the ocean, the microscope has shown us a new world in each drop; and the *infinitely little*, as it is called, is as wonderful as the infinitely great, and man still occupies a sort of central position.

When, for instance, we examine a single organ, say the human eye, we find that it consists of an immense number of parts, each of which is seen to be more and more complicated the more we are able to magnify it, and so on without apparently any limit. And this makes it more than ever likely that the God, Who has shown such marvellous skill in the various organs of a man's body, should care for the man himself, the personal and moral being, who possesses these organs. Nor is the argument weakened by the fact that the organs of animals also show a wonderful amount of design, for as far as we know, in their case, there is no personal and moral being to care about.

Again, science has not only shown us the *magnitude* of the universe, and that there are millions of stars, millions of miles apart, but it has also shown us its *unity*, and that all its parts are closely connected together. And certainly the idea that the God, Who rules these stars, should take an interest in us men, is no harder to believe than that the gases, which are burning in these stars, should influence our spectroscopes. Yet they do; so if this were all, it would still lessen the difficulty a good deal.

## (2.) Man's real importance.

But this is not all, for science has also taught us a great deal about man himself, and his long development; which has a most important bearing on the argument. For we now know that our earth has existed for thousands of centuries, gradually evolving higher and higher forms of life, all leading up to *man*, who is the heir of all the ages, the inheritor of all that is useful and best in his long line of ancestors.

And (what is very important) organic evolution seems obliged to stop here. Man is not merely a link in a series leading on to still more perfect beings, but he is the *end* of the series. In all probability there will never be a higher being on the earth, for the causes which have produced his evolution thus far, can carry it no further. When, for instance, man acquired an erect position, there was an end to any further improvement in that respect. When he took to wearing clothes, there was an end to the body becoming hardier and stronger through exposure. When he took to using weapons and inventing machinery, mere physical strength was no longer essential, and could no longer be increased.

In short, when Evolution began to take a *mental* turn, there was an end to bodily development. Henceforth there was to be no evolution of any higher being, but rather the gradual perfecting of this one being, by mental and moral, and not physical improvements. Man is thus not only the highest being that ever has been evolved, but, as far as we can judge, the highest being that ever will be evolved on this earth. So the vast scheme of evolution, inconceivable alike in magnitude, in duration, and in complexity, is all seen to be one plan, with *man* apparently at the end of it. And consequently, as everything was designed by God, he must have been the foreknown and intended end, from the very beginning; the first thought in creation, as well as the last.

And when we thus regard man as the goal towards which nature has all along tended, and therefore as the *chief* object which God—the Author of Nature—had in view all the time, it seems to increase his importance tenfold; and shows conclusively that in God's sight he must be anything but insignificant.

Nor is it difficult to suggest a reason for this. For man, as we know, has a *mind*, as well as a body; and though the discoveries of science have in some respects lessened the importance of his *body*, by showing its evolution from other animals; they have at the same time increased that of his *mind*, for it is his mind that has discovered them. And every fresh discovery man makes can only exalt him still higher for making it; so that the mind of man now shows him to be a far nobler being than could possibly have been imagined some centuries ago. And certainly, a mind that can discover the motions of distant stars, and the elements of which they are composed, cannot be thought insignificant. In fact, in one respect man is greater than any of the stars; for he can think about them, but they cannot think about him.

Moreover, man has not only a mind, but also a *spirit*, or free will, able to act right or wrong. And even his acting *wrong*, however sad it may be in other respects, is a powerful witness to his greatness; for who but a great being could act in opposition to the will of the Almighty? But then; if his acting *wrong* proves his greatness, still more does his acting *right*. Indeed (if we were not so far from it ourselves) we should probably see that moral perfection, or *always* acting right, though one might act wrong, is the noblest thing in the whole universe; and as far above mental greatness, as this latter is above mere physical strength.

But though *we* cannot properly appreciate it, God can. He is Himself a Spirit, and therefore, in His sight, a man possessing a mind and spirit, and thus made to some extent in His own image, and capable of developing moral perfection, may be of more value (because more like Himself) than a universe of dead matter. In the same way (to quote a well-known analogy) a king will value his child more than his palace: for the simple reason that the child is more like himself. Thus *persons* are always more valuable than *things*. And they are *incomparably* more valuable, for they have nothing in common by which they can be compared. We cannot class an astronomer with his telescopes, or say that one geologist is worth so many fossils, or one bricklayer so many bricks. And this being so, what shall we say of the millions of men who have lived, and are now living, on this earth? Surely *their* welfare cannot be thought insignificant by anyone, least of all by their Creator.

### (3.) The supposed inhabitants of other planets.

But it may be said, what about other planets? Are not some of these inhabited, and does not this weaken the argument a good deal, and show that God cannot take any special interest in man, or other beings on this earth?

Now there is, of course, no reason why God should take any *special* interest in the beings on this planet, more than in similar beings on other planets, if such exist; but this is very doubtful. For modern science has shown that not only are the same *materials* found in the other planets (and also in the fixed stars) as are found here; but that *natural laws*, such as those of gravity, light, and heat, are the same throughout the entire universe. And this makes it probable that the laws of life are also the same; so that if living beings exist on other planets, we should expect them to be somewhat similar to the living beings here; and to have been evolved in a somewhat similar manner. And this requires that a large number of favourable circumstances, such as a moderate temperature, a suitable atmosphere, sufficient water, etc., should all be found on some other planet, not only now, but during the long ages which (judging by this earth) appear necessary for the development of the higher forms of life; and this certainly seems unlikely.

On the other hand, it is difficult to believe that God would create an immense number of suns or stars, many of which have probably planets round them, if only one out of the whole series was to be inhabited by personal beings. But however strange this may seem to us, it entirely agrees with God's methods in nature, where what seems to be needless waste is the universal rule. So this is not an insuperable difficulty. The question, however, may well be left open, for even if other planets are inhabited, there is no reason why God should not take an interest—and perhaps a great interest—in their inhabitants, as well as in ourselves; since all His capacities are boundless, and even the smallest part of *infinity* may be very large.

### (*C.*) THE EXISTENCE OF EVIL.

We now come to the other, and perhaps more important, difficulty—that arising from the *existence of evil*. This term in its widest sense includes both *pain*, which affects a man's body; *sorrow*, which affects his mind; and *sin*, which affects his spirit. The two former may be called *physical evil*, and apply also to animals; while the latter is *moral evil*, and applies only to man. And as the world is full of pain, sorrow, and sin, one may naturally ask how could it have been designed and created by a God Who cares for the welfare of His creatures? Or, to put the objection in other words, does not the existence of this evil show that God either could not or would not prevent it? If He *could* not, he is not All-Powerful; if He *would* not, He is not All-Good. This is an undoubted difficulty; and we will examine it in detail, both as it affects animals and men.

**(1.) Physical evil in animals.**

The objection here is that animals of all kinds suffer a vast *amount* of pain and misery, which is wholly *unmerited* and perfectly *useless*; since, having no moral nature, they can neither deserve pain nor profit by it. We will consider these points in turn.

And first, as to the *amount* which animals suffer. One animal does not suffer more because a million suffer likewise, so we must consider the suffering as it affects the individual, and not the *total* amount. And as to its extent we know but little. That animals appear to suffer greatly, *e.g.*, a mouse being caught by a cat, is obvious; but how far they really suffer is doubtful, as their feelings are probably far less sensitive than those of man; so it is quite misleading to think what we should feel like in similar circumstances. This is indeed evident when we reflect that suffering is connected with the brain, as is shown by the fact that savages suffer much less than civilised nations. And therefore we should expect animals, whose mental development is far less advanced, to suffer still less; while the lower forms of life we should not expect to suffer at all.

And this is confirmed by observation, as several facts have been noticed which almost force us to this conclusion. A crab, for instance, will continue to eat, and apparently relish, a smaller crab, while being itself slowly devoured by a larger one; and this shows that the crab can feel scarcely any pain, since the almost universal effect of pain is to destroy the pleasure of eating. And many other instances are known.[5]

[5] Transactions of Victoria Institute, vol. xxv., 1891, p. 257.

Moreover, animals, except domestic ones which are partly trained and civilised, appear to have no anticipation of suffering, and no power of concentrating their thoughts upon it, which increases it so greatly in man. And assuming, with reference to the above example, that the mouse is not to live for ever, its being destroyed by a cat is at most a very short misery, and perhaps involving altogether less pain than if it died from disease or old age. Indeed few things could be worse than for old and weak animals to be left to themselves, and gradually die of starvation. And we must remember, in a state of nature, with uncertain meals the cat would never *play* at capturing the mouse, thus giving it needless and repeated sufferings, but it would kill it at once.

Then as to the so-called *struggle for existence*. It is nothing like what is commonly supposed, as has been recognised by leading naturalists. Thus *Darwin* says:—'When we reflect on this struggle we may console ourselves with the full belief that the war of nature is not incessant, that no fear is felt, that death is generally prompt, and that the vigorous, the healthy, and the happy survive and multiply.' And *Wallace* says:—'The popular idea of the struggle for existence entailing misery and pain on the animal world is the very reverse of the truth. What it really brings about is the maximum of life, and of the enjoyment of life, with the minimum of suffering and pain.'[6] On the whole, then, it seems probable that pain among animals is far less than is commonly assumed, and in the lower forms of life almost entirely absent.

[6] C. Darwin. Origin of Species. 6th edit., 1888, p. 96. A. R. Wallace. Darwinism, 1889, p. 40.

Still it may be said, this only lessens the difficulty; for why should animals suffer pain at all? As far as we can judge, it is wholly *unmerited*, since, having no moral nature, and therefore no responsibility, they cannot have done anything wrong to deserve it. But then, the pleasure which they enjoy is also unmerited. The two must in all fairness be taken together, and as a matter of fact, animals seem to have a much greater amount of pleasure than of pain. Their life (except when ill-treated by man) is, as a rule, one of continual enjoyment, and probably, at any given moment, the number of animals of any particular kind that are happy is incomparably greater than those that are miserable. In short, health and happiness is the rule, sickness and pain the exception.

Nor can it be said that pain is *useless* to animals; for though they have no moral nature to be improved, they have a physical nature to be preserved and transmitted, and the sense of pain may be essential for this. It is indeed a kind of sentry, warning them of dangers, which might otherwise lead to their destruction. If for example, animals felt no pain from excessive heat, they might not escape when a forest was burning; or, if they felt no pain from hunger, they might die of starvation. Thus pain is, in reality, a *preservative of life*; and it is often not an evil at all; so no part of this objection can be maintained.

**(2.) Physical evil in man.**

We now pass on to the case of man. There is unfortunately no doubt about the suffering which he endures. The struggling lives, the painful diseases, the lingering deaths, not to mention accidents of all kinds, are but too evident. And we may ask, would an Omnipotent God, Who cared for man's welfare, have ever designed all this?

Now it is important to remember that a great deal of physical evil originates in *moral* evil, which will be considered later on. By far the greater part of the pain and misery which men endure is brought about by their own wickedness and folly, or by that of their fellow-men. The recent war—worse in *extent*, though not worse in kind, than all previous wars—has been a terrible example of this. But it was man's doing, not God's; and man alone must be blamed for it.

In the next place, many of the so-called evils of life do not involve any actual suffering. If for instance a man loses the sight of one eye, he need not have any pain; and were he originally blind the possession of even one eye would have been thought a priceless blessing. Again, however great may be the sufferings of life, they cannot be as great as its *joys*, since nearly everyone wishes to go on living. While it is undeniable that human pain, like that of animals, is most useful, serving to warn men of dangers and diseases, which would otherwise lead to their destruction.

Moreover, in a material world like ours, if the forces of nature act according to fixed laws, a certain amount of suffering seems *inevitable*. If, for example, the force of gravity always acts as it does, it will occasionally cause a tower to fall and injure someone. Such an event could only be avoided by God's continually interfering with these forces. But this would render all human life a hopeless confusion. While, at present, owing to these forces being invariable, a great deal of the evil which might otherwise result from them can be foreseen and avoided. If, however, men will not avoid it,—if, for instance, in spite of the numerous eruptions of Vesuvius, they still choose to go and live on its slopes,—it is hard to see how they can blame anyone but themselves. In the same way, if a man chooses to sit on the safety valve of an engine, it is his own fault if he gets blown up.

And even in other cases, when the evil cannot be foreseen, as in an unexpected earthquake, it is at least open to doubt whether it is any worse for a number of men to die like this, suddenly and together, than that they should all die in the usual way, slowly, one by one, and often after a long illness. It of course appeals more to the imagination, but it probably involves less suffering.

Thus we may say that human suffering, excluding that due to man himself, is by no means so great as it seems; that it is, as a rule, more than counterbalanced by human happiness; and that a certain amount seems not only useful, but in a world like ours inevitable. But though all these considerations are undoubtedly true, and undoubtedly lessen the difficulty, they do not remove it altogether.

The following appears to be the true explanation: that though God foreknew all this suffering when He created the world, and in this sense *designed* it, He need not have *desired* it, but may have desired something else, for the attainment of which, this suffering was a necessary condition. And this *something else* must obviously have been the training and perfecting of man's character; for which, some kind of suffering seems essential.

For if there were no suffering in the world, there could be no fortitude, no bravery, no patience, no compassion, no sympathy with others, no self-sacrifice for their good—nothing, in fact, that constitutes the highest type of man. In other words, a being such as man, can only be made perfect through suffering. Therefore this suffering implies no defect in God's design. It is a means, and, as far as we can judge, the only possible means for developing the highest and noblest character in man, such a character indeed as alone makes him worthy of admiration. Moreover, a man's character can only be formed by himself, it cannot be given him ready-made, for then it would not be *his* character at all; and it can only be formed gradually, it cannot be done all at once. Therefore, if God wishes a man to have the special character acquired by constantly bearing suffering, it can only be obtained by constantly giving him suffering to bear.

Here, then, we have the most probable explanation of the physical evils which man endures. Their object is to develop and perfect his character; and as this is a good object, and as it cannot be obtained in any other way, they may well have been designed by a good God.

**(3.) Moral evil in man.**

But we now come to the most difficult part of the subject, the existence of *moral evil* in man. This, as before said, is the chief cause of human misery, and might it not have been avoided? In other words, could not all *sin* have been excluded from the world? But assuming man to be a *free being*, it could not have been avoided, for freedom is always liable to abuse. Therefore, if God decided that man was to be free in some cases to act right or wrong, it necessarily follows that he may act wrong. No Omnipotence could possibly alter this without destroying man's freedom. Hence, though God designed all the moral evil in the world, He need not have desired it, but (as before) may have desired some totally different object, for the attainment of which, this evil was a necessary condition.

Nor, again, is it difficult to suggest what this object may have been. For unless man is a free being, he can be little better than a machine—a correctly-behaved machine, no doubt, and one able to talk and think, but still only a machine. And God may not have wished that man, who is, as far as we know, His highest and noblest work, should be only a machine. Indeed, the superiority of free men who act right, though they might act wrong, to mere machines is obvious to everyone; and it may far outweigh the disadvantage that some of them should act wrong. Therefore, though we have to pay dearly for freedom, it is well worth the price; and the *infinite value of goodness*, as it is called, may justify, though nothing else could, the risks involved in giving man a free will.

Nor is there anything unlikely in the Creator thus caring about the conduct of His creatures. We certainly should not admire an earthly ruler who regarded traitors to his cause, and his most faithful adherents with the same indifference; or an earthly parent who did not care whether his children obeyed him or not. Why, then, should we think that God, Who has not only given us free will, but also a conscience by which to know what is right (*i.e.*, what is *His* will), should yet be indifferent as to whether we do it or not? Everything points the other way, that God, Who is a Moral Being, and Who has made us moral beings also, wishes us to freely act right. Therefore He allows us to act wrong, with all the misery it involves, in order to render possible our thus freely choosing to act right.

Or to put the argument in other words, a free being is far higher than a being who is not free, and yet a free being cannot exist without the possibility of his acting wrong. So, however strange the conclusion appears, moral evil, or at least its possibility, is essential to the universe, if it is to be worthy of its Creator, if, that is, it is to contain beings of the highest order—*persons* and not *things*. Or, to put it still shorter, if God is good, it is only natural that He should create beings capable of goodness, and therefore of necessity capable of badness, for the two must go together.

And if it be still urged that, as God foreknew how men would use their freedom, He need not have created those who would habitually use it wrongly; in other words, there might be no *wicked men* in the world, the answer is obvious. Wicked men are as necessary as any other form of evil to test a man's character, and to develop moral perfection. For just as physical evil, pain, suffering, etc., can alone render possible certain physical virtues, such as fortitude and patience; so moral evil, or sin, can alone render possible certain moral virtues.

If, for instance, there were no sin in the world there could be no forbearance with the faults of others, no moral courage in standing alone for an unpopular cause, no forgiveness of injuries, nor (what is perhaps the highest of all virtues) any rendering good for evil. These require not merely the possibility, but the actual existence of sin, and they would all be unattainable if we had nothing but physical evils to contend with, and there were only good men in the world. The case then stands thus. Evil men are essential to an evil world. An evil world is essential to proving a man's character. Proving a man's character is essential to his freely choosing to serve God; and his freely choosing to serve God seems essential to his being such a servant as God would care to have.

One other point should be noticed before we conclude. It is that with regard to the conduct of free beings, *foreknowing* is not the same as *foreordaining*. God may have foreknown how a man would use or misuse his freedom, but without foreordaining or compelling him to do either. In the same way, in human affairs it is possible in some cases, and to some extent, to foreknow what a man will do, but without in any way compelling him to do it. This is a most important distinction, and we have no reason for thinking that God foreordained any man to misuse his freedom, though He may have foreknown that he would do so.[7]

[7] Of course if God creates a man, *foreknowing* how he will act, He may, in a certain sense, be said to *foreordain* it as well; compare Rom. 8. 29. "Whom He foreknew, He also foreordained."


## (*D.*) CONCLUSION.

We may now sum up the argument in this chapter. We first showed that God is not only able to take an interest in man's welfare; but that the marks of beneficent design afford abundant evidence that He actually does so. On the other hand, the so-called *insignificance of man* is more apparent than real, since his position at the end of evolution shows his great importance; while his mind and spirit fully account for this, and prove him to be an altogether unique being, certainly in regard to this earth, and perhaps in regard to the universe.

And as to the *existence of evil*, it is undeniable that God must have foreknown all the evil in the world when He created it; and in this sense He designed it. But He may also have foreknown that it is only temporary, and that it will lead to a more than compensating permanent good, which could not be obtained in any other way. For the evils in this world need not be *ends*, but may be only *means* to ends; and, for all we know, they may be the very best means for obtaining the very best ends. Indeed, as before said, they seem to be not only the best, but the only possible means for developing all that is highest and noblest in man. We conclude, then, that though God designed both the evil and the good in the world, He need not have desired both: and there are indications in nature sufficient to show that the good is what He desired, and the evil is only its inevitable companion.

This conclusion is often expressed by saying that *Goodness* is an attribute of God; and the word may certainly be admitted. Indeed if God is not *good*, He has made a being, in this respect, nobler than Himself; since some men, in spite of their faults, are undoubtedly good. But it is important to notice the sense in which the word is used, and in which alone it is true.

By God's *goodness*, then, or by His taking an interest in man's welfare, is not meant a mere universal beneficence, or wishing to make everyone as happy as possible, without regard to his conduct. The existence of evil seems fatal to such a theory as this. But rather God wishes to promote man's welfare in the truest and best way, not by giving him everything he likes, but by training and developing his character. God is thus not only *beneficent*, but *righteous* also. And He therefore wishes man to be not only happy, but righteous also. And He therefore of necessity (as a man cannot be made righteous against his will) gives him *free* will, with the option of being unrighteous, and consequently unhappy. So this view of God's character, combining beneficence with righteousness, not only accounts for the marks of beneficent design all through nature, but also for the existence of evil, especially moral evil, in man, and seems the only way of reconciling them. In short, beneficence and righteousness are both good, and the Goodness of God includes both.

Now if we admit that goodness is an attribute of God, the analogy from His other attributes would show that He possesses it in its highest perfection. He is thus a Being not only of infinite *Power* and *Wisdom*, but also of perfect *Goodness*—the word 'perfect' being obviously more suitable for a moral quality like goodness, than 'infinite' would be. And it will be noticed that these three great attributes of God correspond to the three chief arguments for His existence. The first, or that from the universe requiring an adequate Cause, proves an All-Powerful Creator; the second, or that from its having been designed, proves that He is All-Wise; and the third, or that from human nature, proves that He is All-Good. They also correspond to some extent to the three aspects under which we considered man's character in the last chapter; so we arrive at the grand conclusion that God is physically *All-Powerful*, mentally *All-Wise*, and morally *All-Good.*

# CHAPTER VI.
## THAT GOD MIGHT MAKE SOME REVELATION TO MAN.

This depends chiefly on man's future destiny.

(*A.*) THE IMMORTALITY OF MAN.

By this is meant the personal immortality of man's spirit, and there are four chief arguments in its favour:

(1.) From his unique position.

(2.) From his unjust treatment.

(3.) From his vast capabilities.

(4.) From his inherent belief.

(5.) Counter-arguments.

(*B.*) THE PROBABILITY OF A REVELATION.

(1.) From God's character; since He would be likely to benefit man.

(2.) From man's character; since he desires it, and his unique position makes him not altogether unworthy of it.

(3.) Two difficulties: a revelation is said to be unjust, if only given to certain men; and anyhow incredible unless quite convincing. But neither of these can be maintained.

We decided in the last two chapters that man is a free and responsible being, and that God takes an interest in his welfare. We now come to the subject of a *Revelation*, by which is meant any superhuman knowledge directly imparted by God to man. And by *superhuman* knowledge is meant any knowledge which man could not obtain for himself; such as God's object in creating him, His wishes in regard to his conduct, or any past or future events of which he would otherwise be ignorant. And that God could, if He chose, impart such knowledge, either by visions, or dreams, or in some other way, can scarcely be disputed. Nor will anyone affirm (least of all an Agnostic) that we know enough about God to be quite sure that He never would choose to do so. Therefore a revelation is certainly *possible*; but is it at all *probable*? This is what we have to examine. And as the answer to it will depend to a great extent on man's future destiny, we will first consider the question of his *Immortality*, and then the probability, or otherwise, of God's making a *Revelation* to him.

## (*A.*) THE IMMORTALITY OF MAN.

By this is meant the immortality of man's *spirit*. And if we admit (as was admitted in IV.) that man is a compound being, consisting of a free and partly supernatural spirit, his real *self*, which controls his body and mind; what becomes of this spirit at death? We know what becomes of the body: the various molecules are arranged in other groups, and the natural forces are changed into other natural forces. Nothing is lost or annihilated. But what becomes of the spirit? If this is a free supernatural force, the idea that it should perish altogether, when the accompanying natural forces are re-arranged at death, is most unlikely. Indeed the apparent indestructibility of matter points to a corresponding immortality of spirit.

No doubt God could, *if He chose*, destroy either, just as He could create either; but without some supernatural interference, the creation or destruction of either seems incredible. Yet if a man's spirit is not destroyed, it must survive; for it does not seem to have any separate parts into which it can be split up like a man's body. Therefore, as it cannot undergo the only kind of death of which we have any knowledge (which is this re-arrangement of separate parts), it may survive for ever. And there are four chief arguments in favour of this personal immortality of man;—those derived from his *unique position*; his *unjust treatment*; his *vast capabilities*; and his *inherent belief*. We will consider each in turn, and then see what can be said on the other side.

### (1.) From his unique position.

The first argument is from man's *unique position*, more especially when we regard him as the last and noblest result of the vast scheme of evolution, which has been in progress here for so many thousands of years. For such a vast scheme, like everything else, requires not only a *cause*, but a *purpose*; and however much evolution can explain, it cannot explain itself. Why should there have been any evolution at all? Why should a universe of dead matter have ever produced life? There must have been some motive in all this, and what adequate motive can be suggested?

We can only look for an answer in *man*, who is not only the highest creature on this planet, but as far as we know on any planet; so here if anywhere we must find the explanation. Evolution would then have *God* for its Cause, and *man* for its purpose—an undoubtedly adequate *Cause*, but is it an adequate *purpose*? For the human race cannot exist for ever as it is. Everything points to this earth sooner or later falling into the sun, when all forms of life must cease. Therefore, if man is not immortal, the whole of evolution which has led up to him as its final end will still have had no *permanent* result. And no result which is not permanent seems altogether worthy of the Eternal God, the Author of this evolution.

But if, on the other hand, man is immortal; and if this earth, with its strange mixture of good and evil, is a suitable place in which to test and form his character; and if perhaps God wishes hereafter to be surrounded by men who have stood the test, and have formed their character in accordance with His Will; then it may lead to a *permanent* result. And then its creation would not be such a hopeless mystery as on the opposite theory; for the perfecting of immortal beings seems an object worthy even of God.

Thus if we deny the immortality of man, the whole of evolution becomes meaningless, and nature is a riddle without a solution. But if we admit it, there is at least the possibility of a satisfactory answer. For then, as just said, nature is seen to be only *a means to an end*—a temporary (though perhaps necessary) means to a permanent end—the end being to produce *man* (a free being), and then to provide a suitable place for his moral training. And this will enable him, if he wishes, from being a *free* man, to become also a *righteous* man, that is, a man who acts right, though he might act wrong, and thus to some extent worthy to share in his Maker's immortality. And we must remember, man could not have been created righteous, using the word in its strict sense. He might have been created *perfect* (like a machine), or *innocent* (like a child), but to be *righteous* requires, as just said, his own co-operation—his continually choosing to act right, though he might act wrong. And this of necessity is a slow process, with some failures. But the end aimed at is a permanent, and therefore perhaps an adequate, end; and the present world seems exactly suited to attain this end, as it affords a man boundless opportunities (every day, if he likes to use them) of acting right, though he might act wrong.

We thus seem forced to the conclusion—however strange it may appear—that the gradual training and perfecting of *man* is the only adequate explanation of the world, the real object of its long evolution. Yet, if he is not *immortal*, this object can never be attained, for no one reaches moral perfection here; while even if they did, it would only last for a short time. And we may ask, is it likely that such a vast scheme should end in failure, or at most in only a temporary success? Is it not rather probable that if man is the end of evolution, then God, the Author of evolution, must value him; and if God values him, He is not likely to let him perish for ever. In short (as it has been well put), such vast progress from such small beginnings points to an end proportionately great, and this involves the immortality of man. On the whole, then, we may say in the words of Romanes, one of the great champions of evolution, that 'only by means of this theory of probation is it possible to give any meaning to the world, *i.e.*, any *raison d'être* of human existence.'[8]

[8] Thoughts on Religion, 1895, p. 142.

### (2.) From his unjust treatment.

The second argument is from man's *unjust treatment* in this world. For as we saw in the last chapter, God is a Moral Being, able to distinguish right from wrong; and, as far as we can judge, He is One Who will always act right Himself. Yet His treatment of men in this world seems most unjust. Wicked men are allowed to prosper by their wickedness, good men suffer unjustly, while some men's lives seem to be nothing but suffering; and how is this to be accounted for?

There is here again one, and only one, satisfactory explanation, which is that this life is not the whole of man's existence, but only a preparation for a *future life*—a short trial for a long hereafter. And, looked at from this point of view, the most apparently miserable lives may afford as valuable training, perhaps more so, than the outwardly happy ones. The temptation to dishonesty, for example, can be as well resisted by a poor man who is only tempted to steal sixpence, as by a rich man who is tempted to embezzle a thousand pounds.

And if resisting such a temptation helps to form a man's character, as it certainly does, and hence, perhaps, to fit him for a better life hereafter, this can be as well done in the one case as in the other. And the same principle applies universally; even a child has his temptations, which are very real *to the child*, though they may seem ridiculous to us. So if this life is intended as a time of probation in which to form a man's character, we cannot imagine a better system or one more admirably adapted to the end in view. And we must remember a man's *character* is the thing most worth forming, since (as far as we can judge) it is his only *permanent* possession. All else will be surrendered at death, but his character will last as long as the man himself, and hence perhaps for ever.

Nor is this all, for these trials and sufferings themselves may be the very means of adding to man's future happiness. The joy of having resisted temptation, for instance, would be impossible if men were never tempted; and the joy of rescuing others from suffering and sin, and thus perhaps making everlasting friendships, would be impossible if there were no suffering, and no sin. And the same applies in other cases. So man's probation in this life, with its incessant battle against evil, may (for all we know) increase his future happiness in a way which nothing else could possibly do, and to an extent of which we can form no conception. No pain or suffering, then, can be looked upon as useless, and no position in this world as one to be despised; in short, to anyone who believes in a future state, life is always worth living. And we may be sure that in a future state every injustice will be made good, and all wrongs will be righted.

### (3.) From his vast capabilities.

The third argument is from man's *vast capabilities*. For he does not seem adapted to this life only, but has aspirations and longings far beyond it. His powers seem capable of continual and almost endless development. Nearly all men wish for immortality. This life does not seem to satisfy them entirely. For instance, men, especially scientific men, have a longing after knowledge which can never be fully realised in this world. A man's capacities are thus out of all proportion to his destiny, if this life is all; and to many it seems improbable that the Creator should have endowed men with such needless and useless capacities.

And this is strongly confirmed by the analogy of nature. For example, a bird in an egg shows rudimentary organs which cannot be used as long as it remains in the egg; and this of itself is a proof that it is intended some day to leave the egg. On the other hand, a full-grown bird seems to be entirely adapted to its present state, and not to have any longing after, or capacity for, any higher state; therefore we may infer that no higher state is intended for it. And by the same reasoning we may infer that some higher state is intended for man, as his mental and spiritual nature is not entirely satisfied by his present life. In short, all animals seem made for this world alone, and man is the only unsatisfied being in the universe.

Moreover, the period of preparation in a man's life seems out of all proportion to the time prepared for, if death ends all. The development in a man's moral character often continues till nearly the close of his life. His character has then reached maturity. But for what is it matured? Surely not for immediate destruction. Must not the wise Creator, Who designed everything else with such marvellous skill, have intended something better for His noblest creatures than mere boundless capabilities, unsatisfied longings, and a lifelong preparation all for nothing?

### (4.) From his inherent belief.

The fourth argument is from man's *belief* in immortality. For such a belief has existed among men in nearly every age and country, learned and ignorant, civilised and uncivilised. It was implied by the pre-historic men who buried food and weapons with their dead, and it was maintained by such philosophers as Socrates and Plato, and how are we to account for it? It cannot have arisen from experience; and the attempts to explain it as due to the desire which men have for immortality, or to someone occasionally dreaming that he sees a departed friend, are quite inadequate. Desire is not conviction, and dreams are notoriously untrustworthy. They might account for an individual here and there entertaining this belief, but not for mankind always and everywhere doing so; especially in face of the apparent contradiction afforded by every grave.

The belief, then, seems intuitive, and an inherent part of human nature; and we may ask, is it likely that God should have implanted such a strange belief in man if it were erroneous?

These, then, are the four great arguments in favour of man's immortality—those derived from his unique position; his unjust treatment; his vast capabilities; and his inherent belief. And with the doubtful exception of the second, not one of them applies to animals; so the common objection, that if man is immortal, animals must be so too, is quite untenable.

### (5.) Counter-arguments.

On the other hand, the great and only important argument *against* man's immortality is that his spirit seems to be inseparably connected with his body. As far as we can judge, it is born with the body; it often inherits the moral character of its parents, just as the body inherits bodily diseases; it certainly develops and matures with the body; and in most cases it seems to gradually decay with the body; therefore it is inferred the two perish together.

But this does not follow; since, as said in [Chapter IV.](), it is not the *same* body (in the sense of the same material particles) with which the spirit is united, even in this life. It is united to a continually changing body, yet it always survives. So it is not unlikely that it may survive the still greater change at death. Moreover, it is united to the body as its *master*, not its servant. It is, as already shown, a *free* spirit; and it decides to a great extent what the body shall say, and what it shall do. It thus uses the body as a means, or instrument, by which to act in the outer world; and therefore, of course, when the instrument gets out of order, its actions will become confused, but without implying that the spirit itself is so. In the same way, if we shut up a clerk in a telegraph office, as soon as his instruments get out of order, the messages he sends, which are his only means of communicating with the outer world, will become confused, and finally cease, but without implying that there is anything wrong with the clerk himself.

And this is confirmed by the fact that instances are known in which a man's intellect and will have remained quite vigorous all through a mortal sickness, and up to the very moment of death; so the gradual decay of the body does not necessarily involve that of the mind and spirit. While in states which somewhat resemble death, when, for instance, the body is fast asleep, or rendered unconscious by an accident, the mind and spirit are often peculiarly active, as in dreams. Therefore, when the body is really dead, the spirit may (for all we know) not only survive, but be endowed with still greater powers.

On the whole, then, this is not an insuperable difficulty; while the previous arguments render the idea of a future life *distinctly probable*. And this has, of course, a most important bearing on our next question; indeed, it is scarcely too much to say that the probability of a revelation depends on that of a future life. For if death ends all, man's existence is so short that a revelation can scarcely be thought probable; but if he is to live for ever, the case is very different.

### (*B.*) THE PROBABILITY OF A REVELATION.

Now (assuming man to be immortal) a revelation, from whichever side we regard it, appears to be somewhat *probable*. For God is a Being, Who seems likely to make a revelation; and man is a being exactly fitted to receive one; so we will consider these points first, and then the chief difficulties.

### (1.) From God's character.

Now we have already shown that God takes an interest in man's welfare, being not only beneficent, but *righteous*; and that He apparently wishes to train and develop man's character, so that he may be righteous also. And from this we may infer that if a revelation would benefit man, and thus *help* him to be righteous also, it would not be improbable for God to make one. And that the knowledge given by a revelation might influence him in this way cannot be denied; for, as a matter of fact, such knowledge, either real or pretended, has had precisely this effect on millions of men.

We may also infer from God's methods in nature, which are those of slow development, that if He made a revelation at all it would be done *gradually*. At first it would be very simple, and such as could be transmitted orally. Then when man acquired the art of writing, and could thus hand it on accurately, a more definite revelation might be given. And this again might become more and more perfect, as man himself became more perfect. We obviously do not know enough to speak with confidence, but still God's character, so far as we can judge of it, seems to be in favour of His making some revelation—and that a *progressive* revelation—to man.

### (2.) From man's character.

Passing on now to man's character, we find that he has been given a nature exactly fitted to receive a revelation. For religion of some kind is, and always has been, practically universal; and nearly all important religions have rested on real or pretended revelations from God, and have been accepted in consequence. In other words the nature of man has everywhere led him to seek for, demand, and, if need be, imagine a revelation from God. Nor is this in any way surprising, for a thoughtful man cannot help *wishing* to know why he is placed in this world; why he is given free will; how he is meant to use his freedom; and what future, if any, is in store for him hereafter: in short, what was God's object in creating him. It seems of all knowledge to be the highest, the noblest, the most worth knowing.

And therefore as this result of man's nature was not only brought about by God, but must have been foreknown, and intended by Him, it is not improbable that He should satisfy it; especially as it cannot be satisfied in any other way, for the knowledge being superhuman, is out of man's own reach. And it may be added, the more we realise this, and feel that God is *Unknowable*, in the sense that we can gain no satisfactory knowledge about Him by human science and reasoning, so much the more likely does it seem that He should give us such knowledge by revelation.

And all this is strengthened when we consider man's *unique position* to which we have already alluded. For if we admit that the creation and perfecting of man is the chief object the Creator had in view for so many thousands of years, it does not seem unlikely that He might wish to hold some communication with him. In fact, as the whole of nature shows design or purpose; and as man occupies a special place in nature; we may fairly conclude that God has some special purpose in regard to man, and, for all we know, He may have something special to tell him about it.

We conclude then that man's character, and the unique position he occupies on this earth, is a strong argument in favour of his receiving some revelation from God.

**(3.) Two difficulties.**

But now for the other side. There are two chief difficulties. The first is on the ground of *injustice*; since any revelation, it is said, would imply a partiality to the men or nation to whom it was given, and would therefore be unjust to the rest of mankind. But this is quite untenable, for God's other benefits are not bestowed impartially. On the contrary, pleasure and pain, good and evil, are never equally distributed in this world. What seems to be partiality and favouritism is the rule everywhere, and this without any apparent merit on the part of the men concerned. Moreover, the advantages of a revelation may not concern this world only. And all who believe in a future life are convinced of God's justice, and that men will only be judged according to the knowledge of His Will which they possessed, or might have possessed had they chosen, and not according to any higher standard which was out of their reach.

The other and more important difficulty is, that if God gave a revelation at all, it would be absolutely *convincing*. Everything that God does He does well; and we cannot, it is urged, imagine His making a revelation to man, and yet doing it so imperfectly as to leave men in doubt as to whether He had done it or not. For this would imply that He either could not, or would not, make the evidence sufficient to ensure conviction, neither of which is credible.

Now, though all this seems very probable, a moment's reflection will show that it is not conclusive; for exactly the same may be said in regard to the whole of Natural Religion. Is it likely, for instance, that God should create free and responsible men, and yet give them such insufficient evidence about it, that while many are fully convinced, others deny not only their own freedom and responsibility, but even the existence of the God Who made them? Yet He has done so. Therefore there is nothing improbable in the evidence for a revelation, if one were given, being of a similar character.

Indeed, there is much to be said in favour of its being so, since in most other matters man is left a free choice. He is often able to find out how he ought to think and how he ought to act, but he is not forced to do either. And God may have wished that the same rule should be followed in regard to a revelation, and that man should be left free to believe it or not, just as he is left free to act on it or not, if he does believe it, and just as he is left free to choose right or wrong in other cases. Therefore we cannot say that no revelation can come from God unless the evidence for it is overwhelming. It would doubtless be sufficient to convince a man if he took the trouble to examine it carefully; only it need not be such as to compel conviction. What kind of evidence we may expect will be considered in the next chapter.

Neither of these difficulties, then, is at all serious; and we are forced back to the conclusion that, provided man is immortal, a revelation seems for several reasons to be somewhat probable. To put it shortly, if God is good and really cares for man's welfare, it seems unlikely that He should withhold from him that knowledge which is the highest, the noblest, and the most longed for;— the knowledge of Himself. While, if man is a free and immortal being, occupying a unique position in the world, and intended to live for ever, it seems unlikely that he should be told nothing, and therefore know nothing, as to why he was created, or what is his future destiny. Thus when we consider both God's character and man's character, it seems on the whole to be somewhat *probable*, that God would make a revelation to man; telling him how he ought to use his freedom in this world, and possibly what future is in store for him hereafter.

# CHAPTER VII.
## THAT A MIRACULOUS REVELATION IS CREDIBLE.

A Divine messenger would probably have credentials.

(*A.*) SUPERHUMAN SIGNS.

These include superhuman *knowledge*, afterwards verified (such as prophecy), and superhuman *coincidences*; and there is nothing incredible in either.

(*B.*) SUPERNATURAL SIGNS, or Miracles.

These are 'marvels specially worked by God as signs to confirm a revelation.' This definition is threefold, referring to their outward appearance, cause, and purpose.

(1.) *Miracles as marvels*: though they seem to be contrary to experience, they are not really so, for we have no experience of the proper kind to refer to.

(2.) *Miracles as special works of God*: they only interfere with the uniformity of nature in the same way that human works interfere with it.

(3.) *Miracles as signs*: there is nothing to show that they are inconsistent with God's Character.

We decided in the last chapter that it was somewhat probable for God to make a revelation to man, that is to say, to certain men, for them to make known to others. And if so, it is also probable that these men would have some means of showing that the knowledge had come from God and not from themselves. In other words, if God sends a message to man, it is probable that the messenger would have *credentials*. And this is especially so when we remember that men have often appeared in the world's history who professed to have a revelation from God, and have misled mankind in consequence. Is it not probable, then, that if God really did give a revelation, He would take care that His true messengers should have credentials which would distinguish them from all the others?

These credentials, then, or *signs*, must plainly be such as could not be imitated by man; and must therefore of necessity be *superhuman*, if not *supernatural*. So we may divide them into these two classes; and we have now to consider whether they are *credible*. By this is meant something more than merely possible; for the possibility of such signs follows at once from the existence of God. But are they credible? is there, that is, at least a slight chance that they would occur?

**(*A.*) SUPERHUMAN SIGNS.**

These include, to begin with, superhuman *knowledge*, which can be afterwards verified, such as *prophecy*. And there is no difficulty here, provided we admit a revelation at all. The only possible objection refers to prophecies regarding human conduct; which it may be said would interfere with man's freedom. But this is only part of the more general objection that any foreknowledge on God's part would interfere with man's freedom, which we have already considered in Chapter II.; and there is no special difficulty in regard to prophecies. In every case, as said before, God merely foreknows the use man will make of his freedom. Therefore the event will not occur *because* it was foretold, but rather it was foretold because God knew that it would occur.

Superhuman *coincidences* form another, and very important class of superhuman signs. In these a man's acts or sayings are confirmed by natural events *coinciding* with them in a remarkable manner. For example, suppose a prophet claimed to have a revelation from God; and, as a proof of this, invited the people to witness a sacrifice on a cloudless day. He then killed an animal, and placed it on an altar of stones, but put no fire under it, and even threw water over it. Suddenly, however, a thunderstorm arose, and the sacrifice was struck by lightning. Now the thunderstorm might have arisen and the lightning might have struck on that particular spot, in strict accordance with natural laws. Yet the *coincidence* of this occurring just when and where the prophet wanted it, would tend strongly to show that God, Who must have foreknown and designed the coincidence, meant to confirm what the prophet said.

Or, to put the argument in other words, the lightning would seem to have struck the sacrifice *on purpose*; and therefore such events have been popularly described as *natural forces acting rationally*. Of course, as a rule, the forces of nature do not act rationally. A falling meteorite, for instance, does not go a yard out of its way to kill anyone, or to spare him. Man, on the other hand, does act rationally. His acts are directed for a purpose, and thus show design. And, in the events we are considering, the forces of nature seem also to act with a purpose; and this makes it probable that the Author of these forces was really acting with this purpose. In short, the events seem to have been not only *superhuman*, but *designed* coincidences. And they present no difficulty whatever from a scientific point of view, as they are part of the ordinary course of nature.

Of course, the value of such coincidences varies greatly according to whether the event is of a usual or unusual character. In the latter case, more especially if the event is very unusual or the coincidence very striking, they are popularly called miracles. And they may have considerable value, though there is always a slight chance of the agreement being, as we might say, accidental.

### (*B.*) SUPERNATURAL SIGNS.

We pass on now to supernatural signs or *Miracles* in the strict sense; which we will define as *marvels specially worked by God as signs to confirm a revelation*. This definition has, of course, been chosen so as to suit the miracles recorded in the Bible, and it is really threefold. In the first place, a miracle is described as to its outward *appearance*. It is a marvel—that is to say, a strange and unusual event, which we cannot account for, and which thus attracts attention. Secondly, it is described as to its *cause*. This marvel is said to have been specially worked by God—that is to say, by some action on His part different from His usual action in nature. While, lastly, it is described as to its *purpose*; it is a marvel worked by God as a sign to confirm a revelation.

The first of these aspects is expressed in the Old Testament by the word *wonder*, the second by such phrases as God's *mighty hand* or *outstretched arm*, and the third by the word *sign*; all these terms being often used together. While in the New Testament the words used are *wonders*, *mighty works*, and *signs*, which again exactly correspond to these three aspects of the miracles. And it should be noticed these aspects are not chosen merely to suit the present argument, since other events can and ought to be looked at in the same way, not as mere facts, but also with reference to their alleged cause and purpose. And to show the great importance of this, we will consider an event from modern history; and select the well-known example of the Mont Cenis Tunnel.

Suppose, then, that anyone heard of this as a *marvel* only, the cause and purpose being left out of account. Suppose, that is, he heard that a small straight cavity of uniform size, and several miles long, had been formed under a range of mountains; and that it had begun as two cavities, one from each end, which after years of growth, had exactly met in the middle. He would at once pronounce the event incredible, for the cavity is quite unlike all natural cavities.

But now suppose the next point, as to its *cause*, to be introduced. It is said to be something more than a natural cavity, and to be the work of man. All previous difficulties would now vanish, but fresh ones would arise. For numbers of men must have worked together for years to excavate such a cavity, and from what we know of human nature, men will only do this for commercial or profitable ends, and not for boring useless holes through mountains; so the event is still practically incredible.

But now suppose the last point of *purpose* to be introduced. It is said that this is not a mere useless hole bored through a mountain; but a hole bored for a particular purpose; it is, in fact, a railway tunnel. Then all difficulties would disappear. Of course, whether we believe the tunnel was actually made depends upon what evidence we have; but it is clear that when we consider the *cause* by which, and the *purpose* for which, it is said to have been made, there is nothing incredible about it.

Now a similar method must be adopted in regard to miracles. They must not be regarded simply as *marvels*, but as marvels said to have been brought about by an adequate *cause*, and for a sufficient *purpose*. And it is just these elements of cause and purpose which may make the marvels credible. We will consider these points in turn.

**(1.) Miracles as marvels.**

The first aspect of miracles is that of marvels. As such, they are events which seem to be *contrary to our experience*—contrary, that is, to what our experience of apparently similar events would lead us to expect. Suppose, for instance, it were stated that on one occasion three men were thrown into a furnace, but instead of being burnt to death they walked about, and in a few minutes came out alive and unhurt.

Such a marvel would be contrary to our experience, and that it would be therefore *very improbable* is obvious. But is this improbability sufficient in all cases to make the event incredible, no matter what testimony there may be in its favour? Hume's argument that it is sufficient is well known. He says we can only judge of the probability of anything, whether it be the occurrence of an event, or the truthfulness of the narrator, by *experience*. And as it is contrary to experience for miracles to be true, but not contrary to experience for testimony to be false, the balance of probability must always be against the miracle.

But of course this reasoning, if true, must apply to all alleged events which are contrary to experience; and yet such events have occurred by the thousand. Let us take a single example. Everyone has had some experience as to how far it is possible to hear the human voice distinctly, and till the last half century, the limit has always been fixed at a few hundred yards. Now, suppose anyone were told for the first time that it was possible to speak right across England, he would justly say that it was utterly contrary to experience. No one, he would think, could possibly speak loud enough to be heard even twenty miles away. But ought he to add that it was therefore incredible?

From this it is clear that there must be some flaw in Hume's argument; and it is easily discovered. For the argument regards the event only as a marvel, and *without reference to its cause*. But we have no right to leave this out of account, nor do we in ordinary affairs. When anyone first hears of a marvel, he does not merely compare it with his previous experience, and then come to a decision; in which case, as Hume supposes, it might be always against the marvel. But he first inquires how this strange event is said to have been brought about. For if any cause is stated to have been at work as to the influence of which he knows nothing, then he has no experience of the proper kind to appeal to. There is the testimony in favour of the event as before; and if he disbelieves it, he does so, not because it is contrary to his experience, but because he thinks the supposed cause either did not exist, or would not have had the effect asserted.

A reference to the previous example will make this quite plain. When the man first heard of persons talking across England, instead of at once declaring it incredible, he would, if a reasonable man, inquire as to the *cause* of this. He would then be told that a wire was stretched across England with an instrument called a telephone at each end. Now, as to the possibility or adequacy of such a contrivance he might doubt a good deal; but one thing would be quite clear, that this was a case to which his experience, however large, did not apply.

Here, then, is the explanation of Hume's argument. So long as a marvel, contrary to experience, is regarded *only* as a marvel, the probability must be always against its truth. But if we inquire as to how it was brought about, and find that some *cause* is said to have been at work, as to the influence of which we are ignorant, then the argument is no longer applicable. We have simply no experience of the proper kind to appeal to.

Now this is precisely the case with regard to miracles. As marvels they seem contrary to experience; but they claim to have a special *cause*, to be specially worked by God—that is to say, by some action on His part different from His usual action in nature; and of the influence of this cause we have no experience whatever. We may, of course, deny its existence or doubt its adequacy; but the argument, that the event is contrary to experience, vanishes.

It is clear then that the fact of miracles appearing to be contrary to experience is no reason for disbelieving *them*, though it might be a reason for disbelieving other alleged marvels, because they claim to have a special cause, by which to account for this special character. We have now to examine whether this special cause really existed—that is to say, we pass on to the second aspect of the miracles; our conclusion thus far being that they are credible as *marvels*, if it be credible that they were *specially worked by God.*

**(2.) Miracles as special works of God.**

Now, any special action on God's part is often thought to present great difficulties, as interfering with the uniformity of nature. But, as we shall see, it would only interfere with it in the same way that human action interferes with it. Neither of them violates the laws of nature, though both are able to bring about results which nature of itself could not have brought about.

In the case of human action this is quite obvious. Suppose, for example, a clock with an iron pendulum is placed on a table and keeps perfect time. Suddenly, without anyone touching it, it begins to gain rapidly, and then, after a short time, goes on as before. To anyone unacquainted with the cause, this would appear a *marvel*: and might even be thought incredible, as (assuming the clock to be properly constructed) it would seem to imply some alteration in the laws of motion, or the force of gravity. Yet we know a man can easily produce such a marvel by holding a magnet under the table. The disturbing cause, it will be noticed, was not really the magnet, which always acts according to law; nor the hand which held it; but the action of the *human will* on matter. This took place in the man's brain, and enabled him to move first his hand, and then the magnet. Thus we may say the marvel was produced by *natural means supernaturally applied*; for the magnet was undoubtedly a natural means, yet nature of itself would never have used it in the way described. It required something *above* nature (something *super*-natural) and this was the free will of man.

Now, miracles claim to have been produced in a somewhat similar, though to us unknown, manner by the action of God's Will on matter, that is to say, by natural means supernaturally applied; and, if so, they are certainly credible, under this head. For we know that God has the power of acting on matter, and that He used it once in creating the universe, so He might use it again if He thought fit.

Moreover, God's knowledge of the laws of nature is complete, while man's is only partial. As, then, man, with his limited power over nature and partial knowledge of its laws, can produce marvels so unlike nature's ordinary course (a steam engine, for instance), yet without violating any of its laws; still more can God, Who has complete power over nature, and complete knowledge of its laws. For to deny this would be to deny to God the power which we concede to man; and which we must remember, God Himself has given to man. And this would lead to the strange conclusion that God has enabled man to do what He cannot do Himself. No doubt we cannot imagine *how* God can exert His Will over matter, but neither can we imagine how we can do it ourselves. The difficulty is as great in the one case as in the other.

From this it is clear that miracles need not violate natural laws. And though at first one might be inclined to dispute this with regard to particular miracles; the statement is quite correct, provided we make due allowance for our own ignorance. Take, for example, the supposed case of the men in the furnace. We certainly do not know how their bodies were kept cool, but we cannot say it was impossible. For extreme heat, and even *extreme* cold, may be very close together, as is shown by the well-known experiment of freezing mercury inside a red-hot crucible. As a mere marvel this is quite as wonderful as the men in the furnace; and an ignorant man would probably pronounce both to be equally incredible.

Or, to take another example, suppose it were said that on one occasion a few loaves of bread were miraculously increased so as to feed some thousands of persons: could we say that this must have violated natural laws? Certainly not, for bread is composed of carbon, and other elements, which were in abundance all round. And though we only know one way of forming them into bread, which is by means of a living plant, we cannot say that this is the only method. Indeed, there is nothing incredible in substances like bread being made artificially some day. Of course in all marvels produced by *man*, we know the special cause at work, but this does not justify us in saying that in a miracle, merely because we do not know it, the laws of nature must be violated.

Moreover there is much to be said in favour of what is usually called God's *immanence* in nature, but which would perhaps be better described as *nature's immanence in God*.[9] This means that all natural forces are due to the present and immediate action of God's Will; and if it is correct, it greatly lessens the difficulty as to miracles. For then there would be no interference with nature at all, leave alone violating its laws, God would be working there all the time, only in a miracle He would not be working in exactly the same way as in ordinary events.

[9] Acts 17. 28; Col. 1. 17.

But in any case there is, as we have shown, nothing incredible in the way in which miracles are said to be *caused*, provided it is credible that God should wish to use His power over nature in the assumed manner; for natural forces are anyhow His servants, not His masters. And this brings us to the third aspect of the miracles; for whether God would wish to act in a certain way depends of course on what *purpose* He had in doing so.

### (3.) Miracles as signs.

Now the purpose for which miracles are said to be worked is as *signs to confirm a revelation*. Therefore, since we have already shown that it is somewhat probable that God would make a revelation, we have now only to inquire whether miracles are suitable means for confirming it. And they appear to be the most suitable means possible; for they would both attract men's attention to the revelation, and also convince them of its superhuman character; which are precisely the two points required.

It may still be objected, however, that God's character, as shown by nature, is *Unchangeable*; and therefore it is most improbable that He would at times act in a special manner with regard to natural events. And the more nature is studied the stronger does this objection appear; since there are thousands of cases, such as storms and earthquakes, when it seems to us that a slight interference with nature would be most beneficial to man, yet it never occurs. Or the objection may be otherwise expressed by saying that a miracle would reflect on either the Wisdom or the Power of God; since, if All-Wise, He would have foreseen the occasion, and if All-Powerful, He would have provided for it; so any subsequent interference with nature is something like having to remedy a fault.

This is no doubt the most serious objection to miracles, but it is by no means insuperable. For, to begin with, God is a *Free Being*, Who does not always act the same ([Chapter I.](#)). And when we turn to the only other free being we know of, which is man himself, what do we find? A man may, as a rule, act uniformly, yet on some special occasion, and for some special reason, he may, and often does, act differently; and why should not God do the same? Indeed the only changelessness in a man which we could admire, would be that of *moral character*, always and invariably acting right. And for all we know the changelessness of God may be only of such a kind, and this certainly would not prevent Him from acting in some special manner, in order to obtain some special purpose.

Secondly, in the case before us, it is even probable that He would do so, since the chief object of the miracles could not have been obtained by the ordinary course of nature, though their immediate effects might have been. For example, instead of healing men miraculously, they might be healed naturally; but then there would be no evidence that the healer was sent by God, and was speaking in His name. In short, the messenger would be without *credentials*; and, as we have already shown, this seems unlikely.

Thirdly, though miracles do not show God's changelessness in the same manner as the unchanging course of nature, they are not inconsistent with it. For no one supposes them to be *after-thoughts* with God, but to have been planned from the very beginning. And if God always intended to make a revelation to man, and always intended that when He did so, He would confirm it by miracles, they would involve no inconsistency or change on His part.

Fourthly, there may be some *other* attributes of God which miracles show, and which the ordinary course of nature does not; such as His superiority over nature itself on the one hand, and the interest He takes in man on the other. One object of a revelation might be to convince man that though God was the Ruler of the Universe, He yet cared for man's happiness and valued his affections. And how could such a revelation *as this*, be better confirmed than by an (apparent) interference with nature for the benefit of man. For this would show, as nothing else could show, both that there was a Being *above* nature, and that He cared for man *more* than He cared for nature.

And it entirely agrees with what we decided in the last chapter, that the whole of nature seems to be only a means to an end, the end being the moral training of man, enabling, that is, a free man to become a *righteous* man. And if so, it is out of the question to think that *in order to further this end*—the very end for which nature itself exists—God might not, if He thought fit, interfere with the course of nature. We may therefore answer the objection in one sentence, God is *All-Good*, as well as All-Wise, and All-Powerful; and His Goodness might induce Him to use miracles, though by His Wisdom and Power He might have dispensed with them.

We may now sum up the present argument. We showed that miracles are credible both as *marvels* and as *special works of God*, if it be credible that they were brought about as *signs to confirm a revelation*. And we have now shown that, supposing God to make a revelation, which we have already admitted, there is nothing inconsistent with His character as far as we know it, and therefore nothing in the slightest degree incredible, in His using such signs, as one of the means of confirming its truth. On the whole, then, we conclude that a Miraculous Revelation is certainly *credible*. Whether one has ever been made will be discussed in the following chapters.

# PART II.
## THE JEWISH RELIGION.

| CHAP. | VIII. | THAT THE ACCOUNT OF THE CREATION WAS DIVINELY REVEALED. |
| --- | --- | --- |
| " | IX. | THAT ITS ORIGIN WAS CONFIRMED BY MIRACLES. |
| " | X. | THAT ITS HISTORY WAS CONFIRMED BY MIRACLES. |
| " | XI. | THAT ITS HISTORY WAS ALSO CONFIRMED BY PROPHECIES. |
| " | XII. | THAT THE JEWISH RELIGION IS PROBABLY TRUE. |

# CHAPTER VIII.
## THAT THE ACCOUNT OF THE CREATION WAS DIVINELY REVEALED.

(*A.*) Its General Principles.

(1.) Its pure Monotheism; admittedly true.

(2.) Its seven days need not be taken literally.

(3.) Its gradual development; admittedly true.

(*B.*) Its Detailed Order.

(1.) The earliest state of the earth.

(2.) Light.

(3.) The Firmament.

(4.) Dry Land.

(5.) Vegetation.

(6.) The Sun and Moon.

(7.) Fishes and Birds.

(8.) Land Animals.

(9.) Man.

(*C.*) Conclusion.

The accuracy of the narrative points to its having been Divinely revealed.

Having decided in the previous chapters on the Existence of God, and that it was credible that He might make a miraculous Revelation to man; we pass on now to the *Jewish Religion*, which (as well as the Christian) actually claims to be such a Revelation.

And the first argument we have to consider in its favour is that afforded by the opening chapter of Genesis. It is urged that this account of the Creation must have been *Divinely revealed*, since it contains a substantially correct account of events which could not have been otherwise known at the time. What then we have to examine is, whether this narrative is nearer the truth, as we now know it from geology and other sciences, than could have been the case, if written by a man ignorant of these sciences. And the ancient narratives of Babylonia, India, Persia, and elsewhere, show how far from the truth mere human conjecture on such a subject is likely to be.

While if we admit a revelation at all, there is nothing improbable in some account of the creation of the world having been revealed to man very early in his history, and being accurately preserved by the Jews, while only distorted versions of it occur among other nations. Indeed considering the common custom among ancient nations of worshipping the heavenly bodies, animals, etc., no subject could have been more suited for a first revelation than the statement in simple language that all these were created by one supreme God. We will now consider the *general principles* of the narrative, and then its *detailed order*.

### (*A.*) ITS GENERAL PRINCIPLES.

The most important of these are its pure Monotheism, its seven days, and its gradual development, each of which we will notice in turn.

### (1.) Its pure Monotheism.

This alone renders it almost, if not quite, unique among similar narratives. According to the writer, the whole universe, including sun, moon, and stars, was all due to *one* God. And this is obvious enough now, but it was not so when the narrative was written. For other ancient accounts are either *Pantheistic*, and confuse God with the universe; or *Dualistic*, and assume two eternal principles of good and evil; or *Polytheistic*, and make the universe the work of several gods. The Jewish writer, on the other hand, has kept clear of all these theories; and he is admittedly right and all the others wrong.

### (2.) Its seven days.

Next as to the seven days. Now it is generally assumed, doubtless from their being referred to in the Fourth Commandment, that the writer intended these *days* to be ordinary days of twenty-four hours each, but this is at least doubtful. For ordinary days depend on the *sun*, and would therefore have been impossible before the formation of the sun on the *fourth* day; as the writer himself implies, when he says that the division of time into days and years was due to the sun.

Then there is the difficulty as to the *seventh* day, when God rested from all His work. This, it will be remembered had no close, or *evening*, and it is implied that it has continued ever since. For if God only rested for twenty-four hours, and then set to work again it would not have been a rest from *all* His work. But in this case, the seventh day would represent a long period of time, and if so the other days would probably do the same. Moreover the writer, or compiler, of this very narrative, after describing the creation in six days, says it all occurred in *one* day,[10] so he could scarcely have thought the days to be literal.

[10] Gen. 2. 4.

There are thus great difficulties from the narrative itself in taking the word *day* in its ordinary sense; and it seems better to consider it (like so many terms in the Bible) as a human analogy applied to God. Then God's *days* must be understood in the same way as God's *eyes* or God's *hands*; and this removes all difficulties.

None of these terms are of course literally true, but they represent the truth *to man* in such a way that he can to some extent understand it. For example, the phrase that God gained the victory *by His own right hand* clearly means that He gained it not with the assistance of others, or with the help of weapons, but simply by His own unaided inherent strength. It was such a victory as might *in a man* be described as gained by his own right hand. And the same may be said of the passage, *The eyes of the Lord are over the righteous, and His ears are open unto their prayers*, and many others which occur in the Bible. The terms hands, eyes, and ears, when applied to God, are thus human analogies, which must not be taken literally.

And in one passage at least the word *day* is used in a similar sense; for we read "Hast thou eyes of flesh or seest thou as man seeth? Are thy days as the days of man, or thy years as man's days?"[11] Here it will be noticed *days* and *years* are applied to God in precisely the same manner as *eyes* and *seeing*.

[11] Job 10. 4, 5.

Moreover similar terms occur all through the present narrative. Even the simple words *God said* cannot be taken literally, for there was no one to speak to. They must be meant in the sense that God *thought*, or that God *willed*. And we have no more right to suppose the days to be literal days than to suppose that God literally spoke. What we are to suppose in the one case is that God—the Almighty One, for whom nothing is too hard—created all things in such a way as might *to man* be best represented by a simple word of command. And what we are to suppose in the other case, is that God—the Eternal One, to whom a thousand years are but as yesterday—created all things in such periods of time as might *to man* be best represented by six days. Vast as the universe was, man was to regard it as being to God no more than a week's work to himself. In short, the time of creation, however long in itself, was utterly insignificant in its relation to God; to *Him* each stage was a mere day.

And this it may be added, is not a purely modern theory, made to reconcile the narrative with science; for the Greek Jew, Philo, born about B.C. 20, who knew nothing of geology, ridicules the idea of the days of Genesis being literal, or representing any definite periods of time.[12]

[12] Works of Philo Judæus, First book of Allegories of the Sacred Laws, Yonge's translation, 1854, vol. i., p. 52.

### (3.) Its gradual development.

Next, it must be noticed that, according to Genesis, God did not create a perfect world all at once, but slowly built it up step by step. At first the earth was waste and void, and only after it had passed through several stages did it become fully inhabited. Moreover, at every step (with two exceptions, the firmament and man, noticed later on), God examined the work and pronounced it *good*. He seems thus to have discerned a beauty and excellence in each stage; though it was not till the close of the whole work that He was completely satisfied, and pronounced it all *very* good.

And the narrative appears to be quite correct. For geology shows that the formation of the earth, with its various inhabitants, was a *gradual* process, not accomplished all at once, but slowly step by step, through successive ages. And it also shows that these ages were of such magnitude and importance that we cannot regard them as mere preparations for man's coming, but as having a beauty and excellence of their own, so that they well deserved to be called *good*. But we may ask, how did the writer of Genesis know all this?

And then as to the way in which this development was brought about. According to Genesis, each stage was due to what we may call a *Special Divine force*, represented by a word of command from God. And this also seems correct, for we cannot otherwise account for the first appearance of the various groups, such as plants, animals, and men. It is not disputed that these various stages may have been evolved from the previous ones, *e.g.*, the living from the not-living, which the narrative itself suggests in the words, *Let the earth put forth grass*; and also at its close, when it speaks of *the generations* of the heaven and of the earth; which implies some kind of organic descent, or evolution. Indeed the common expression that God *made*, is probably used in the sense of *evolved*; since the same word is employed in ver. II of fruit-trees *making* fruit (translated *bearing* or *yielding* fruit); yet we know they do not *make* fruit suddenly out of nothing, but slowly produce it.

What is disputed is, that this evolution took place merely under the influence of natural development, and without the additional influence of a new Divine force. And considering that all attempts to effect a similar transition *now* have failed completely, it is not unreasonable to suppose that there was some other and special Cause at work *then*. Nor is it easy to see how some of the changes could have been otherwise produced. Take, for instance, this very subject of the origin of life. As far as we know, the only natural mode in which life can begin is from a living parent, yet there was a time when there were no living parents on this earth. How, then, could it have originated, except by some process other than natural, *i.e.*, supernatural? Or, again, to take another instance, when the first *free being*, whether animal or man, appeared on this planet, a force totally different from all natural forces was introduced, and one which could not have been derived from them alone.

And then there is another, and very interesting point, to notice. It is that according to Genesis, these steps were not all of equal importance. For while it describes most of them by the word *made*, which, as just said, seems to mean here *evolved*; on three occasions, and only three, it uses the word *create*. These refer to the origin of the *universe*, of *animal life* (fishes and birds), and of *man*. And this is very significant, when we remember that these correspond to the beginning of *matter*, *mind*, and *spirit*; and are therefore (as said in Chapter IV.) just the three places where something altogether *new* was introduced; which could not, as far as we can see, have been evolved from anything else. And this double method of producing, partly by *creating*, and partly by *making* or evolving, is again referred to at the close of the narrative, where we read that God rested from all His work, which He had *created and made*. So much for the general *principles* of the narrative, we pass on now to its detailed *order*.

### (*B.*) ITS DETAILED ORDER.

It will be remembered that in Genesis, after describing the earliest state of the earth, there are eight stages in its development; two of which occurred on the third, and two on the sixth, day. We have thus altogether nine subjects to examine.

### (1.) The earliest state of the earth.

Now according to Genesis, the earth was at first *waste and void* and in *darkness*, and apparently surrounded by *the waters*. And if we adopt the usual nebula theory, and refer this to the first period after it became a separate planet, and had cooled so as not to give out any light itself, these statements seem quite correct. For we know from geology that the earth was then waste and void as far as any form of life was concerned, while it was probably surrounded by a dense mass of clouds and vapours sufficient to produce darkness. Genesis then starts from the right starting-point, but again we must ask, how did the writer know this?

### (2.) Light.

The first step in the development of the earth was, we are told, the introduction of *light*. That this is what Genesis means seems plain, for the *light* must refer to the *darkness* of the previous verse, and that referred to the *earth*. As to whether light previously existed in other parts of the universe, Genesis says nothing, it is only concerned with this earth. And in the development of this earth, *light* (which in nature always includes *heat*) must obviously have come first. For on it depend the changes in temperature, which lead to the formation of winds, clouds, and rain; while it also supplies the physical power that is necessary for the life of plants and animals; so in placing *light* as the first step, Genesis is certainly correct. Of course, the *source* of light at this early period was the remainder of the nebula from which our planet was thrown off. It was thus spread over an immense space, instead of being concentrated like that of our present sun; and probably only reached the earth through a partial clearing of the clouds just alluded to.

### (3.) The firmament.

The next step was separating the waters *above* (*i.e.*, these dense clouds) from the waters *below* which are stated to be the seas (v. 9-10) and forming between them a firmament or *expanse* (see margin), that is to say, the *air*. The idea that the writer thought this expanse meant a solid plane holding up the waters above (because it is perhaps derived from a word meaning firm or solid) is scarcely tenable. For the firmament was called *heaven*, and the upper waters, above this *heaven*, must mean the sources from which the *rain* usually comes, since it is called *rain from heaven*.[13] And these sources are easily seen to be *clouds*; and no one could have thought that a *solid* firmament was between the clouds, and the seas.

[13] Deut. 11. 11.

Moreover this same word *heaven* (though used in various senses) is translated *air* later on in this very narrative when it speaks of fowls of the *air* (verses 26-28, 30). And it also occurs in other passages, in some of which it cannot possibly mean anything but the air, *e.g.*, 'any winged fowl that flieth in the *heaven*,' and 'the way of an eagle in the *air*,'[14] which is an additional reason for thinking that it means the air here.

[14] Deut. 4. 17; Prov. 30. 19.

And the omission, before noticed, to say that God saw that the firmament was *good*, is quite natural, if this means only the air, *i.e.*, the space between the clouds and the seas; just as an artist, though he might examine his pictures to see that they were *good*, would not examine the spaces between them. But it is difficult to account for, if it means a *solid* firmament, which would seem to require God's approval like everything else.

On the other side, we have the expression about opening the *windows* of heaven when it rained at the time of the Flood,[15] which is sometimes thought to imply openings in a solid firmament. But it need not be taken literally, any more than that about the *doors* of the sea;[16] especially as in another place the *heavens dropping water* is explained as meaning that the clouds dropped it.[17] And since God promised that in future when a *cloud* was seen it should not cause another *flood*,[18] it is clear that the flood was thought to have come from the clouds, and not from any openings in a solid reservoir in the sky.

[15] Gen. 7. 11; 2 Kings 7. 2; Mal. 3. 10.

[16] Job 38. 8-11.

[17] Judges 5. 4 (R.V.).

[18] Gen. 9. 14.

There is also the passage about the sun and moon being *set in the firmament*. But the writer cannot have meant they were *fastened* to the firmament, since the moon keeps changing its position relatively to the sun, just as a rainbow often does in regard to the cloud in which it is also said to be *set*.[19] Of course their being in the firmament at all, is not correct if this means only the air. But the word may be used here in a wider sense, like the English word *heaven*, to include both the air, and the space beyond. For we speak of the clouds of heaven, and the stars of heaven, and in neither case with any idea of their being *heaved up*, which is said to be the literal meaning of the word. And in its primary sense, as we have shown, the firmament or *expanse* between the upper and lower waters (the clouds and the seas) must mean the *air*. And the order in which this is placed after light, and before plants and animals is obviously correct.

[19] Gen. 9. 13.

**(4.) Dry land.**

We now come to an important point, the appearance of *dry land*. According to Genesis, there was not always dry land on the earth; the whole of it was originally covered by the waters. And science shows that this was probably the case; the earth being at first surrounded by watery vapours, which gradually condensed and formed a kind of universal ocean. And then, when the surface became irregular, through its contracting and crumpling up, the water would collect in the hollows, forming seas, and dry land would appear elsewhere. But how was it possible for the writer of Genesis to know all this? There is nothing in the present aspect of nature to suggest that there was once a time when there was no *dry land*; and if it was a guess on his part, it was, to say the least, a very remarkable one.

**(5.) Vegetation.**

We next come to vegetation; and it is placed in exactly its right position. For it requires four things: *soil*, *air*, *water*, and *light* including heat; and these were the four things which then existed. The narrative, it will be noticed, speaks of three groups, *grass*, *herbs*, and *fruit-trees*; and it seems to imply that they appeared at the same time. But since its general plan is that of a series of events, the other view, that they appeared successively, is at least tenable.

There is, however, this difficulty. None of these groups were complete before the following periods. Some plants, for instance (including both herbs and fruit-trees), appeared long after the commencement of fishes and birds, and similarly some fishes and birds after the commencement of land-animals. But the difficulty is due to the fact that the classes *overlap* to a large extent. And the order given in Genesis is nearer the truth than any other would be. Had the writer, for example, placed them plants, animals, birds, fishes; he would have been quite wrong. As it is, by placing them plants, fishes, birds, animals, he is as near the truth as he can be, if classes which really overlap have to be arranged in a consecutive narrative.

**(6.) The sun and moon.**

We next come to the formation (that is the *making*, or evolving) of the sun and moon. The stars are also mentioned, but it is not said that they were made on the fourth day, and they are not alluded to in the opening command. Now, this alleged formation of the sun *after* that of light is certainly the most striking point in the narrative, and was long thought to be a difficulty. But science has now shown that it is correct. However strange we may think it, light did undoubtedly exist long before the sun. In other words, the original nebula of our solar system was luminous, and lighted the earth, long before it contracted into a body with a definite outline, and producing such an intense and concentrated light, as could be called a sun. And since the earth would cool much quicker than the large nebula from which it was thrown off, vegetation might commence here before the nebula had become a sun, though this latter point is doubtful.

Two objections have now to be noticed. The first refers to the *moon*, which must have been thrown off from the earth long before the dry land and vegetation appeared; and being so small, would have consolidated sooner. But when considered only as *lights*, as they are in the narrative, it is quite correct to place the moon with the sun; since moonlight is merely reflected sunlight, and must obviously have commenced at the same time. The other objection is, that according to Genesis, the earth seems to be the centre of everything, and even the sun exists solely for the sake of lighting the earth. But (as before pointed out) the narrative is only concerned with this earth; and while we know that sunlight is of use to the inhabitants of our planet, we do not know that it serves any other useful purpose.

These, however, are but minor matters; the important point, as before said, is that Genesis places the formation of the sun *after* that of light. This must have appeared when it was written, and for thousands of years afterwards, an obvious absurdity, since everyone could see that the sun was the source of light. We now know that it is correct. But how could the writer have known it, unless it had been divinely revealed?

**(7.) Fishes and birds.**

We next come to fishes and birds, which formed the commencement of animal life, and thus involved the beginning of *mind* in some form; so Genesis (as before said) appropriately uses the word *create* in regard to them. It is not clear whether the narrative means that they appeared at the same time, or successively, though here, as in other cases, the latter is the more probable. And science entirely agrees in thus placing fishes before birds and both of these after plants. This latter point indeed must be obvious to every naturalist, since the food of all animals is derived, either directly or indirectly, from the vegetable world.

And Genesis is equally correct in emphasising the great abundance of *marine* life at this period—the waters were to *swarm with swarms of living creatures* (R.V. Margin), and also in specially alluding to the great *sea-monsters* (wrongly translated *whales* in A.V.), since these huge saurians were a striking feature of the time. The Hebrew word is said to mean *elongated* or stretched-out creatures, and as several of them were over 50 feet long, no more suitable term can be imagined. But again we must ask how did the writer know that such creatures were ever plentiful enough, or important enough, to deserve this special mention?

What are called *invertebrate* animals, such as insects, and shell-fish, do not seem to be included in the narrative. But it never claims to describe everything that was created; and its extreme brevity, combined with the insignificance of these creatures, may well account for their being omitted.

**(8.) Land animals.**

We next come to land animals, which we are told the earth was to *bring forth*. As however it is said in the next verse that God *made* (or evolved) these creatures, this need not mean that they were produced directly from the earth, as in the case of plants. And the position in which they are placed, after fishes and birds and before man, is again correct. It is true that a few animals such as kangaroos, seem to have appeared as early as birds, but land animals as a whole undoubtedly succeeded them. Three classes are mentioned, *beasts of the earth*, *cattle*, and *creeping things*, probably small animals, since another Hebrew word is used for them, later on, which is said elsewhere to include weasels and mice.[20]

[20] Gen. 7. 21; Lev. 11. 29.

**(9.) *Man.***

Last of all we come to the creation of man. Four points have to be noticed here. The first refers to the *time* of man's appearance, which everyone now admits was not till towards the close of the Tertiary or most recent group of strata; so Genesis is quite correct in placing him last of all. As to the actual date, it says nothing; for its chronology only leads back to the creation of *Adam* in chapter 2, and not to that of the *human race* (male and female) in chapter 1. And it is implied in several places, that there were men before Adam[21] and this was in consequence maintained by some writers long before geology was thought of.[22] We need not therefore discuss the difficulties connected with the story of Adam and Eve, as to which the present writer has never seen a satisfactory explanation.

[21] Gen. 4. 13-17, 26; 6. 2-4.

[22] *E.g.*, Peyreyrius, A.D. 1655, quoted in the Speaker's Commentary.

Secondly, the creation of man is represented as of an altogether *higher order*, than any of the previous ones, since God did not say, "Let the earth bring forth a thinking animal" or anything of that kind, but '*Let us make man.*' And this also is quite correct, for man, as we know (Chapter IV.) has a *free will*, which makes him a personal being, and therefore far above everything else on this planet.

And when we consider the vast possibilities, involved in the creation of such a being,—able to act right or wrong, and therefore able, if he wishes, to act in opposition to the will of his Maker, thus bringing sin into the world with all its consequent miseries,—it seems only suitable that such a momentous step should have been taken with apparent deliberation and in a manner different from all the others.

And it explains why no such expression as *after its kind*, which is so frequently used of plants and animals, is ever applied to man; for he is not one of a kind in the same sense. Each man is *unique*, a separate personal being, distinct from all else in the world, and not (like a tree for instance) merely one example of a certain way in which molecules may be grouped.

It also explains why man (unlike plants, animals, etc.) is not said to have been created *good*. For goodness in a free being must include moral goodness, or *righteousness*; and, as explained in Chapter VI., man could not have been *created* righteous. He might have been created *perfect*, like a machine, or *innocent*, like a child, but to be *righteous* requires his own co-operation, his freely choosing to act right, though he might act wrong. No doubt he was made in a condition perfectly suited for the *exercise* of his free choice; but this seems included in God's final approval of the whole creation that it was all *very good*.

Thirdly we are told that man (and man alone) was created *in the image of God*. And once more the narrative is quite correct; for that which distinguishes man from the rest of creation is his *free will*, to which we have just alluded. And that which distinguishes God's action from all natural forces is also His *freedom*, (Chapter I.). So it is perfectly true to say that man was created *in the image of God*, since the special attribute which separates him from all else on this planet is precisely the attribute of God Himself.

And here we may notice in passing, that though God intended man to be both in His image and *likeness*; He only created him in His *image* (vv. 26, 27). And the reason is probably that while image means resemblance in *nature* (possessing free will, etc.), likeness means resemblance in *character*[23] (always acting right). Therefore, of course, though God wished man to be both in His image and likeness, He could only create him in His *image*; the other point, that of *likeness* in character, depending (as just said) on the free will of the man himself.

[23] The Hebrew word appears to be sometimes used in this sense. *E.g.*, Ps. 58. 4; Isa. 13. 4. In one brief reference in Gen. 5. 1-2, when speaking of Adam, *likeness* is used where we should have expected *image*; though even here it is not said that man was *created* in God's likeness, but merely that he was so *made*.

The fourth, and last point is that though the writer assigns to man this unique position, he does not give him, as we might have expected, a *day* to himself, but *connects him with land animals*, as both appearing on the sixth day. And this also seems correct, for in spite of his immense superiority, man, in his physical nature, is closely connected with animals. Therefore the writer appropriately uses both words, *made* and *created*, in regard to him. The former shows that in one respect (as to his body) he was evolved like the rest of nature; the latter, that in another respect (as to his spirit) he was essentially distinct.

## (*C.*) CONCLUSION.

We have now discussed the narrative at some length, and (omitting details) it shows three great periods of life. Each of these has a leading characteristic; that of the third day being vegetation; that of the fifth day fishes and birds, special mention being made of great sea-monsters; and that of the sixth day land animals, and at its close man. And though these groups *overlap* to a large extent, yet speaking broadly, the three periods in Geology have much the same characteristics. The Primary is distinguished by its vegetation (*e.g.*, the coal beds); the Secondary by its saurians, or great sea-monsters; and the

Tertiary by its land animals, and at its close (now often called the Quaternary) by man. The harmony between the two is, to say the least, remarkable.

And the theory of Evolution which like geology, was unknown when the narrative was written, also supports it, as has been admitted by some of its leading exponents. Thus Romanes once said, and as if the fact was undisputed, 'The order in which the flora and fauna are said, by the Mosaic account, to have appeared upon the earth corresponds with that which the theory of Evolution requires, and the evidence of geology proves.'[24] We decide, then, that the order of creation, as given in Genesis, is in most cases certainly, and in all cases probably, correct.

[24] *Nature*, 11th August, 1881.

And this is plainly of the utmost importance, for the points of agreement between Genesis and science are far too many, and far too unlikely to be due to accident. They are far too many; for the chance against eight events being put down in their correct order by guesswork is 40,319 to 1. And they are far too unlikely; for what could have induced an ignorant man to say that light came before the sun, or that the earth once existed without any dry land?

Moreover, the general principles of the narrative, especially its pure Monotheism and its gradual development, are very strongly in its favour. And so are some individual points, such as the idea of creation, in its strict sense, being limited to matter, mind, and spirit. While our admiration for it is still further increased by its extreme conciseness and simplicity. Seldom, indeed, has such a mass of information been condensed into as few lines; and seldom has such a difficult subject been treated so accurately yet in such simple and popular language.

Now what conclusion can be drawn from all this? There seem to be only two alternatives: either the writer, whoever he was, knew as much about science as we do, or else the knowledge was revealed to him by God. And if we admit a revelation at all, the latter certainly seems the less improbable. And this, it may be added, was the opinion of the great geologist Dana, who said (after carefully considering the subject) that the coincidences between the narrative, and the history of the earth as derived from nature, were such as to imply its Divine origin.[25] We therefore conclude that this account of the creation was *Divinely revealed*.

[25] Bibliotheca Sacra, April, 1885, p. 224.

# CHAPTER IX.
## THAT ITS ORIGIN WAS CONFIRMED BY MIRACLES.

Importance of the Pentateuch, as the only record of the origin of the Jewish Religion.

(*A*.) ITS EGYPTIAN REFERENCES.

These are very strongly in favour of its early date;

(1.) In the history of Joseph.

(2.) In the history of Moses.

(3.) In the laws and addresses.

(*B*.) ITS LAWS.

These are also in favour of its early date:

(1.) The subjects dealt with.

(2.) Their connection with the history.

(3.) Their wording.

(*C*.) THE THEORY OF A LATE-DATE.

There are four chief arguments in favour of this, but they are not at all convincing:

(1.) The language of the Pentateuch.

(2.) Its composite character.

(3.) Its laws being unknown in later times.

(4.) The finding of Deuteronomy.

(*D*.) CONCLUSION.

The Pentateuch was probably written, as it claims to be, by Moses; and we must therefore admit the miracles of the Exodus.

We pass on now to the *origin* of the Jewish Religion—that is to say, the events connected with the Exodus from Egypt. And as the only account we have of these is contained in the *Pentateuch*, we must examine this book carefully. Is it a trustworthy, and, on the whole, accurate account of the events which it records? And this depends chiefly on its *date*. Is it a *contemporary* document, written by, or in the time of, Moses? And modern discoveries have at least shown that it may be so. For Egypt was then in such a civilised state, that it is practically certain that Moses, and the other leaders of Israel, could have written had they chosen. And as they somehow or other brought the people out of Egypt, it is extremely probable that they would have recorded it. But did they, and do we possess this record in the Pentateuch?

This is the question we have to decide; and we will first consider the *Egyptian references* in the Pentateuch, and then its *Laws*, both of which are very strongly in favour of an early date. Then we will see what can be said for the opposite theory, or that of a *late-date*; and lastly, the *conclusion* to be drawn from admitting its genuineness.

**(A.) ITS EGYPTIAN REFERENCES.**

Now a considerable part of the Pentateuch deals with Egyptian matters, and it appears to be written with correct details throughout. This would of course be only natural in a contemporary writer living in Egypt, but would be most unlikely for a late writer in Canaan. The question is therefore of great importance in deciding on the date of the book; so we will first consider these *Egyptian references* (as they are called) in the history of Joseph, then in that of Moses, and then in the laws and addresses. They cannot of course be properly appreciated without some knowledge of ancient Egypt, but they are far too important to be omitted. It is disappointing to have to add that the evidence is almost entirely indirect, but up to the present no reference to either Joseph, or Moses, has been found on the Egyptian monuments, and none to the Israelites themselves that are at all conclusive.

**(1.) In the history of Joseph.**

To begin with, there are three cases where it is sometimes said that the writer seems *not* to have been a contemporary, since Egyptian customs are there explained, as if unknown to the reader. These are their eating at different tables from the Hebrews, their dislike of shepherds, and their habit of embalming.[26] But the inference from the first two is extremely doubtful; though that from the third is rather in favour of a late date. There is not, however, a single word here (or anywhere else) which is *incorrect* for Egypt, or which shows that the writer himself was unaware of its customs.

[26] Gen. 43. 32; 46. 34; 50. 3.

On the other hand, there is abundant evidence in favour of a contemporary date. The Pharaoh is generally thought to be Apepi II., who belonged to a *foreign* dynasty of Shepherd Kings, probably Asiatic tribes like the Israelites themselves. And this will explain the evident surprise felt by the writer that one of his chief officers should be an *Egyptian*, which seems so puzzling to the ordinary reader.[27] It will also account for Joseph and his brethren being so well received, and for their telling him so candidly that they were *shepherds*, though they knew that shepherds were hated by the Egyptians. Had the Pharaoh himself been an Egyptian, this was hardly the way to secure his favour.

[27] Gen. 39. 1.

We will now consider a single chapter in detail, and select Gen. 41; nearly every incident in which shows a knowledge of ancient Egypt:

Ver. 1. To begin with, the words *Pharaoh* and *the river* (*i.e.*, the Nile), though they are the proper Egyptian names, seem to have been adopted in Hebrew, and occur all through the Old Testament; so they afford no indication of date.

2-4. The *dreams*, however, are peculiarly Egyptian. Cattle along the river bank, and feeding on the *reed-grass* (an Egyptian word for an Egyptian plant), was a common sight in that country, but must have been almost unknown in Canaan. And their coming up *out of the river* was specially suitable, as they represented the years of plenty and famine, which in Egypt depend entirely on the rise of the Nile.

5-7. In the same way wheat with *several ears* is known to have been produced in Egypt; but is nowhere mentioned as grown in Canaan.

8. Moreover, we know that the Pharaohs attached great importance to dreams, and used to consult their *magicians* and *wise men* when in doubt; both these classes being often mentioned—and mentioned together—on the monuments.

9-12. We also know that there were officials corresponding to the *chief butler* and the *chief baker*. And a reference has even been found to the curious custom of the former giving the King *fresh grape-juice*, squeezed into a cup (Gen. 40. 11), which is not likely to have been known to anyone out of Egypt.

13. And hanging the chief baker evidently means, from Gen. 40. 19, hanging up the dead body, after he had been *beheaded*; which latter was an Egyptian, and not a Jewish, punishment.

14. Next we are told, that when Joseph was hurriedly sent for by Pharaoh, he yet stopped to *shave*. And this was only natural, as the upper class of Egyptians always shaved; but it would scarcely have occurred to anyone in Canaan, as the Israelites always wore beards.[28]

[28] 2 Sam. 10. 5.

35. So again the custom of laying up corn in storehouses, to provide against the frequent famines, and for taxation, was thoroughly Egyptian, the Superintendent of the Granaries being a well-known official. But as far as we know nothing of the kind existed in Canaan.

39. We then come to the promotion of Joseph; and several instances are known of foreigners, and even slaves, being promoted to high offices in Egypt.

40. And the monuments show that it was the regular Egyptian custom to have a Superintendent, who should *be over the house*.

42. Joseph is then given Pharaoh's *signet ring*, the use of which, at this early period, has been fully confirmed by the inscriptions. And he also receives *fine linen* (an Egyptian word being used for this) and a *gold chain about his neck*. This latter was a peculiarly Egyptian decoration, being called *receiving gold*, and is continually alluded to on the monuments. And a specimen may be seen in the Cairo Museum, which happens to date from about the time of Joseph.

43-44. And the apparently insignificant detail that Joseph rode *in a chariot* (implying horses) is also interesting, since, as far as we know, horses had only recently been introduced into Egypt by the Shepherd Kings. And had they been mentioned earlier—as, for instance, among the presents given to Abraham[29]—it would have been incorrect. And the expression *Abrech*, translated *Bow the knee*, is probably an Egyptian word (Margin R.V.).

[29] Gen. 12. 16.

45. We also know that when foreigners rose to great importance in Egypt they were often given a new *name*. And Joseph's new name, Zaphenathpaneah, (probably meaning Head of the College of Magicians, a title he had just earned[30]) as well as Asenath, and Potiphera, are all genuine Egyptian names; though (with the exception of Asenath) they have not at present been found as early as the time of Joseph.

[30] H. E. Naville, Professor of Egyptology, at the University of Geneva, 'Archæology of the Old Testament,' 1913, p. 80.

49. Lastly, the usual Egyptian custom (as shown by the monuments) of having a scribe to *count* the quantity of corn as it is stored, is incidentally implied in the statement that on this occasion, owing to its great abundance, Joseph had *to leave off numbering it*.

Thus everything in this chapter, *and the same may be said of many others*, is perfectly correct for Egypt; though much of it would be incorrect for Canaan, and is not likely to have been known to anyone living there. Yet the writer not only knows it, but *takes for granted that his readers know it too*, as he never explains anything. So the narrative is not likely to have been written after the time of Moses, when the Israelites left Egypt. And this, it may be added, is the opinion of many who have made a special study of ancient Egypt. Thus Prof. Naville declares 'I do not hesitate to say that he (Moses) was the only author who could have written the history of Joseph, such as we have it.'[31]

[31] Transactions of Victoria Institute, vol. xlvii., 1915, p. 355.

There is also evidence of quite another kind that this latter part of Genesis was written in Egypt. This is afforded by six passages, where, after the name of a place, is added some such phrase as *which is in Canaan*.[32] Yet there do not appear to be any other places of the same name liable to be confused with these. When then would it be necessary to explain to the Israelites that these places, Shechem, etc., were in Canaan? Certainly not after the conquest, when they were living there, and it was obvious to everyone; so we must refer them to the time when they were in Egypt.

[32] Gen. 23. 2, 19; 33. 18; 35. 6; 48. 3; 49. 30.

And this is strongly confirmed by a little remark as to the *desert of Shur*, which lies between Egypt and Canaan, and which is described as being *before Egypt as thou goest towards Assyria*.[33] Clearly then this also must have been written in Egypt, since only to a person living there would Shur be on the way to Assyria.

[33] Gen. 25. 18.

And the same may be said of the curious custom of first asking after a person's health, and then, if he is still alive.[34] This was thoroughly Egyptian, as some exactly similar cases have been found in a papyrus dated in the eighth year of Menephthah, generally thought to be the Pharaoh of the Exodus.[35] But it is scarcely likely to have been adopted by a writer in Canaan, as it makes the narrative seem so ridiculous.

[34] Gen. 43. 27-28.

[35] Chabas, Mélanges Égyptologiques, Third Series, vol. ii., Paris, 1873, p. 152.

### (2.) In the history of Moses.

Secondly, as to the history of *Moses*. The name itself is Egyptian;[36] and his being placed in an ark of *papyrus* smeared with bitumen was quite suited to Egypt, where both materials were commonly used, but would have been most unsuitable anywhere else. And several of the words used here, as well as in other parts of the Pentateuch, show that the writer was well acquainted with the Egyptian *language*. In this single verse for instance, there are as many as six Egyptian words, *ark, papyrus, pitch, flags, brick,* and *river*, though some of these were also used in Hebrew.[37] Then as to the Israelites making bricks with *straw*. This is interesting, because we know from the monuments that straw was often used for the purpose, the Nile mud not holding together without it, and that its absence was looked upon as a hardship. So here again the narrative suits Egypt, and not Canaan; where as far as we know, bricks were never made with straw. And it so happens that we have a little direct evidence here. For some excavations were made at Tel-el-Muskhuta in 1883; which turns out to be *Pithom*, one of the *store cities* said to have been built by the Israelites.[38] And nearly its whole extent is occupied by large brick stores; some of the bricks being made with straw, some with fragments of reed or stubble used instead, and some without any straw at all. While, unlike the usual Egyptian custom, the walls are built with mortar; all of which exactly agrees with the narrative.[39]

[36] Driver's Exodus, 1911, p. 11.

[37] Exod. 2. 3.

[38] Exod. 1. 11. Transactions of Victoria Institute, vol. xviii., p. 85.

[39] Exod. 1. 14; 5. 12.

Next, as to the *Ten Plagues*. There is much local colouring here, and hardly one of them would have been suitable in Canaan. Moreover, the order in which they come is very significant, as it makes them agree with the natural calamities of Egypt.

(i.) The water being turned into blood cannot, of course, be taken literally, any more than when Joel speaks of the moon being turned into blood.[40] It refers to the reddish colour, which is often seen in the Nile about the end of June; though it is not as a rule sufficient to kill the fish, or render the water unfit to drink. And the mention of *vessels of wood and stone*[41] is interesting, as it was the custom in Egypt to *purify* the Nile water by letting it stand in such vessels; and the writer evidently knew this, and took for granted that his readers knew it too, though it seems to have been peculiar to that country.

[40] Joel 2. 31.

[41] Exod. 7. 19.

(ii.) Frogs are most troublesome in September.

(iii.) Lice, perhaps mosquitoes or gnats, and

(iv.) Flies, are usually worst in October.

(v.) Murrain among the cattle, and

(vi.) Boils cannot be identified for certain, but their coming on just after the preceding plagues is most natural, considering what we now know, as to the important part taken by mosquitoes and flies in spreading disease.

(vii.) The hail must have occurred about the end of January, as the barley was then in the ear, but the wheat not grown up; and severe hailstorms have been known in Egypt at that time.

(viii.) Locusts are known to have visited Egypt terribly in March, which seems the time intended, as the leaves were then young.

(ix.) The darkness *which might be felt* was probably due to the desert wind, which blows at intervals after the end of March, and sometimes brings with it such clouds of sand as to darken the atmosphere.[42] And curiously enough it often moves in a narrow belt, so that the land may be dark in one place, and light in another close by, as recorded in the narrative.

[42] I have noticed the same in the Transvaal, in particular a sandstorm at Christiana, on 20th October, 1900, which so darkened the sky that for about a quarter of an hour I had to light a candle.

(x.) The death of the *firstborn*, which occurred in April (Abib), was evidently not a natural calamity. But what is specially interesting is the statement *against all the gods of Egypt I will execute judgments*, without any explanation being given of what is meant by this.[43] It refers to the Egyptian custom of worshipping *living* animals, the firstborn of which were also to die; but this would only be familiar to a writer in Egypt, since, as far as we know, such worship was never practised in Canaan. The agreement all through is most remarkable, and strongly in favour of a contemporary date.

[43] Exod. 12. 12; Num. 33. 4.

**(3.) In the laws and addresses.**

And the same familiarity with Egypt is shown in the subsequent laws and addresses of the Pentateuch. Thus we read of laws being written on the doorposts and gates of houses, and on great stones covered with plaster, both of which were undoubtedly Egyptian customs; and the latter was not, as far as we know, common elsewhere.[44] Similarly the Egyptian habit of writing persons' names on sticks, was evidently familiar to the writer.[45] And so was the curious custom of placing food *for the dead*,[46] which was common in Egypt, though it never prevailed among the Israelites.

[44] Deut. 6. 9; 11. 20; 27. 2.

[45] Num. 17. 2.

[46] Deut. 26. 14.

Again the ordinary *food* of the people in Egypt is given as fish, cucumbers, melons, leeks, onions, and garlic, all of which were commonly eaten there.[47] But as the Hebrew names of four out of the five vegetables do not occur elsewhere in the Bible, they could scarcely have been very common in

Canaan; while none of the characteristic productions of that land, such as honey, milk, butter, figs, raisins, almonds, and olives, are mentioned. The list is, as it ought to be, thoroughly Egyptian.

[47] Num. 11. 5.

It must next be noticed that a large part of the *religious worship* prescribed in the Pentateuch was obviously borrowed from Egypt; the most striking instance being that of the *ark*. A sacred ark is seen on Egyptian monuments long before the Exodus, and is sometimes surmounted by winged figures resembling the cherubim.[48] And the *materials* said to have been used for this worship are precisely such as the Israelites might have then employed. The ark, for instance, and also the tabernacle were not made of cedar, or of fir, or of olive, as would probably have been the case in Canaan (for these were the materials used in the Temple)[49] but of shittim, *i.e.*, acacia which is very common near Sinai, though scarcely ever used in Canaan. And the other materials were goats' hair, rams' skins, sealskins (or porpoise skins) from the Red Sea, and gold, silver, brass, precious stones, and *fine linen* from the Egyptian spoils; the latter, as before said, being an Egyptian word.[50] There is no mistake anywhere, such as a late writer might have made.

[48] Comp. Exod. 25. 13-18.

[49] 1 Kings 6. 14-36.

[50] Exod. 25. 3-10.

Moreover, in other places, the writer of the Pentateuch frequently assumes that his readers know Egypt as well as himself. Thus the people are twice reminded of the *diseases* they had in Egypt—'*the evil diseases of Egypt which thou knowest*' or '*which thou wast afraid of*'—and they are warned that if they deserve it, God will punish them with the same diseases again.[51] But such a warning would have been quite useless many centuries later in Canaan; just as it would be useless to warn an Englishman now of the diseases of Normandy, *which thou wast afraid of*, if this referred to some diseases our ancestors had before they left Normandy in the eleventh century. Such words must clearly have been written soon afterwards. Similarly the people are urged to be kind to strangers, and to love them as themselves, because *they knew the heart of a stranger*, having been strangers in the land of Egypt. And this again could scarcely have been written centuries after they left Egypt.[52]

[51] Deut. 7. 15; 28. 60.

[52] Exod. 23. 9; Lev. 19. 34.

Elsewhere the writer describes the climate and productions of Canaan; and with a view to their being better understood, he contrasts them with those of *Egypt*.[53] Obviously, then, the people are once more supposed to know

Egypt, and not to know Canaan. For instance, Canaan is described as a country of hills and valleys, and consequently of running brooks; and not like Egypt where they had to water the land with their *feet*. But no explanation is given of this. It probably refers to the *water-wheels*, which were necessary for raising water in a flat country like Egypt, and which were worked by men's *feet*. But can we imagine a late writer in Canaan using such a phrase without explaining it? On the other hand, if the words were spoken by Moses, all is clear; no explanation was given, because (for persons who had just left Egypt) none was needed.

[53] Deut. 8. 7-10; 11. 10-12.

On the whole, then, it is plain that when Egyptian matters are referred to in the Pentateuch, we find the most thorough familiarity with native customs, seasons, etc., though these are often quite different from those of Canaan. And we therefore seem forced to conclude that the writer was a contemporary who lived in Egypt, and knew the country intimately, and as we have shown, he evidently wrote for persons who had only recently come from there.

**(*B.*) ITS LAWS.**

We pass on now to the Laws of the Pentateuch, which are found in the middle of Exodus, and occupy the greater part of the remaining books. And as we shall see, they also (quite apart from their references to Egypt) bear strong marks of a contemporary origin.

**(1.) The subjects dealt with.**

In the first place several of the laws refer exclusively to the time when the Israelites lived *in the desert*, and would have been of no use whatever after they settled in Canaan. Among these are the laws regarding the *camp* and *order of march*.[54] Full particulars are given as to the exact position of every tribe, and how the Levites were to carry the Tabernacle. And what could have been the object of inventing such laws in later times, when, as far as we know, the people never encamped or marched in this manner?

[54] Num. 1. 47—4. 49.

Then there is the extraordinary law as to the *slaughter of animals*. It is stated in Leviticus that every ox, lamb, or goat, intended for food, was to be first brought to the Tabernacle, as a kind of offering, and there killed. But plainly this could only have been done, when the people were in the desert, living round the Tabernacle. So when the law is again referred to in Deuteronomy, just before they entered Canaan, it is modified by saying that those living at a distance might kill their animals at home.[55]

[55] Lev. 17. 3; Deut. 12. 21.

Moreover, some of the other laws, though applicable to Canaan, are of such a character as to be strongly in favour of an early date. Take, for instance, the remarkable law about *land*, that every person who bought an estate was to restore it to its original owner in the year of Jubilee, the price decreasing according to the nearness of this year.[56] How could anyone in later times have made such a law, and yet assert that it had been issued by Moses centuries before, though no one had ever heard of it?

[56] Lev. 25. 13.

Or take the law about the Levites.[57] They, it will be remembered, had no separate territory like the other tribes, but were given some special cities. And it is scarcely likely that such a curious arrangement could have been made at any time except that of the conquest of Canaan; still less that it could have been made centuries afterwards, and yet ascribed to Moses, without everyone at once declaring it to be spurious.

[57] Num. 35. 1-8.

**(2.) Their connection with the history.**

It must next be noticed that the laws are not arranged in any regular order, but are closely connected with the history; many of them being *dated*, both as to time and place. For instance, 'The Lord spake unto Moses in the Wilderness of Sinai, in the first month of the second year after they were come out of the land of Egypt, saying,' etc.[58] And several others are associated with the events which led to their being made; and these are often of such a trivial nature, that it is hard to imagine their being invented.[59] Thus the Pentateuch shows, not a complete code of laws, but one that was formed *gradually*, and in close connection with the history.

[58] Num. 9. 1; 1. 1; Deut. 1. 3; see also Lev. 7. 38; 16. 1; 25. 1; 26. 46; 27. 34; Num. 1. 1; 3. 14; 33. 50; 35. 1; Deut. 4. 46; 29. 1.

[59] Lev. 24. 15; Num. 9. 10; 15. 35; 27. 8; 36. 8.

And this is confirmed by the fact that in some cases the same laws are referred to both in Leviticus, (near the beginning) and in Deuteronomy (at the end) of the forty years in the Desert, but with slight differences between them. And these *exactly correspond* to such a difference in date. One instance, that referring to the *slaughter of animals*, has been already alluded to. Another has to do with the animals, which might, and might not, be *eaten*. Leviticus includes among the former, several kinds of locusts, and among the latter the mouse, weasel, and lizard; all of which Deuteronomy omits.

Clearly then, when Leviticus was written, the people were in the desert, and there was a lack of animal food, which might tempt them to eat locusts or mice; but when Deuteronomy was written, animal food was plentiful, and laws as to these were quite unnecessary.

In each of these cases, then, and there are others like them, the differences must be due either to the various laws dating from the times they profess to, when all is plain and consistent; or else to the carefully planned work of some late writer, who was trying in this way to pretend that they did.

Still more important is the fact that in several places stress is laid on the people's *personal knowledge* of the events referred to; *e.g.*, 'The Lord made not this covenant with our fathers, but with us, even us, who are all of us here alive this day.'[60] And what is more, this personal knowledge is often appealed to as a special reason for obeying the laws.[61] For instance, 'I speak not with your children which have not known, and which have not seen the chastisement of the Lord, ... but your eyes have seen all the great work of the Lord which He did. *Therefore* shall ye keep all the commandments,' etc. Plainly this would have had no force in later times; indeed it would have provided an excuse for *not* obeying the laws, since the people of those days had no personal knowledge of the events referred to. And we may ask, is it likely that a late author, who falsely ascribed his laws to Moses, in order to get them obeyed, should yet put into the mouth of Moses himself an excuse for not obeying them?

[60] Deut. 5. 3; 24. 9, 18, 22; 25. 17.

[61] Deut. 11. 2-8; 4. 3-15; 29. 2-9.

Moreover, combined with this assumed personal knowledge on the part of the people there is a clear indication of *personal authority* on the part of the writer. The later prophets always speak in God's name, and such expressions as *Thus saith the Lord, Hear ye the word of the Lord,* are extremely common, occurring altogether over 800 times. But in the laws of the Pentateuch nothing of the kind is found. They are delivered by Moses in his own name, often with the simple words, *I command thee,* which occur thirty times in Deuteronomy. And, of course, if the laws are genuine, there is nothing surprising in this, as Moses had been the great leader of the people, for forty years; but a late author would scarcely have adopted a style so different from that of all the other prophets.

### (3.) Their wording.

Lastly we must consider the *wording* of the laws; and this also is strongly in favour of a contemporary origin. Thus, as many as sixteen of them, which have special reference to Canaan, begin with some such phrase as *when ye be come into the land of Canaan,*[62] which plainly supposes that the people were not there already. And the same may be said of numerous other laws, which the people are told to obey when they enter into Canaan; or are even urged to obey in order that they may enter in, both of which again, imply that they were not there already.[63] While several of the laws refer to the *camp*, and sometimes to *tents*, in such a way as to show that when they were written, the people were still living in a camp.[64]

[62] Exod. 12. 25; 13. 11; Lev. 14. 34; 19. 23; 23. 10; 25. 2; Num. 15. 2, 18; 35. 10; Deut. 7. 1; 12. 1, 10, 29; 17. 14; 18. 9; 26. 1.

[63] *E.g.*, Deut. 4. 1, 5, 14; 5. 31; 6. 1, 18; 8. 1.

[64] *E.g.*, Exod. 29. 14; Lev. 4. 12; 6. 11; 13. 46; 14. 3; 16. 26; 17. 3; Num. 5. 2; 19. 3, 14.

The wording, then, of all these laws bears unmistakable signs of contemporary origin. Of course, these signs may have been inserted in later laws to give them an air of genuineness, but they cannot be explained in any other way. Therefore the laws must be either of *contemporary date*, or else *deliberate frauds*. No innocent mistake in ascribing old laws to Moses, can possibly explain such language as this; either it was the natural result of the laws being genuine, or else it was adopted on purpose to mislead.

Nor can the difficulty be got over by introducing a number of compilers and editors. For each individual law, if it falsely *claims* to date from before the conquest of Canaan (and, as we have seen, numbers and numbers of laws do so claim, *When ye be come into the land of Canaan*, etc.), must have been made by *someone*. And this someone, though he really wrote it after the conquest of Canaan, must have inserted these words to make it appear that it was written before.

Practically, then, as just said, there are but two alternatives—that of genuine laws written in the time of Moses, and that of deliberate frauds. And bearing this in mind, we must ask, is it likely that men with such a passion for truth and righteousness as the Jewish prophets—men who themselves so denounced lying and deception in every form[65]—should have spent their time in composing such forgeries? Could they, moreover, have done it so *skillfully*, as the laws contain the strongest marks of genuineness; and could they have done it so *successfully* as never to have been detected at the time? This is the great *moral* difficulty in assigning these laws to a later age, and to many it seems insuperable.

[65] Jer. 8. 8; 14. 14; Ezek. 13. 7.

We have thus two *very strong* arguments in favour of an early date for the Pentateuch: one derived from its *Egyptian references*, the other from its *Laws*. The former shows that no Israelite in later times could have written the book; and the latter that he would not have done so, if he could.

## (*C.*) THE THEORY OF A LATE DATE.

We pass on now to the opposite theory, or that of a *late date*. According to this the Pentateuch, though no doubt containing older traditions, and fragments of older documents, was not written till many centuries after the death of Moses. And the four chief arguments in its favour are based on the *language* of the Pentateuch, its *composite character*, its laws being *unknown* in later times, and the *finding of Deuteronomy* in the reign of Josiah. We will examine each in turn.

**(1.) The language of the Pentateuch.**

Now in general character the language of the Pentateuch undoubtedly resembles that of some of the prophets, such as Jeremiah; so it is assumed that it must date from about the same time. But unfortunately critics who maintain this view do not admit that we have *any* Hebrew documents of a much earlier date, with which to compare it. Therefore we have no means of knowing how much the language altered, so this of itself proves little.

But it is further said that we have three actual *signs of late date*. The first is that the word for *west* in the Pentateuch really means *the sea*, (*i.e.*, the Mediterranean) and hence, it is urged, the writer's standpoint must have been that of Canaan, and the books must have been written after the settlement in that country. But, very possibly the word was in use before the time of Abraham, when the sea actually was to the west. And in later years a Hebrew, writing in Egypt or anywhere else, would naturally use the word, without thinking that it was inappropriate to that particular place. The second expression is *beyond Jordan*, which is often used to denote the *eastern* bank; so here again, it is urged, the writer's standpoint must have been that of Canaan. But this is also untenable. For the same term is also used for the *western* bank in several places,[66] and sometimes for both banks in the same chapter.[67] The third is Joseph's speaking of Canaan as the *land of the Hebrews*, long before they settled there, which is difficult to explain on any theory, but rather in favour of a late date.[68]

[66] *E.g.*, Deut. 11. 30; Josh. 12. 7.

[67] *E.g.*, eastern in Deut. 3. 8; Josh. 9. 10; and western in Deut. 3. 20, 25; Josh. 9. 1.

[68] Gen. 40. 15.

On the other hand, the language contains several *signs of early date*, though most of these can only be understood by a Hebrew scholar, which the present writer does not profess to be. But a couple of examples may be given which are plain to the ordinary reader. Thus the pronoun for *he* is used in the Pentateuch both for male and female; while in the later writings it is confined to males, the females being expressed by a derived form which is very seldom used in the Pentateuch. Similarly, the word for *youth* is used in the Pentateuch for both sexes, though afterwards restricted to males, the female being again expressed by a derived form. These differences, though small, are very significant, and they clearly show that the language was at a less developed, and therefore earlier, stage in the Pentateuch than in the rest of the Old Testament.

**(2.) Its composite character.**

The next argument is that the Pentateuch seems to have had *several authors*; since the same words, or groups of words, occur in different passages all through the book. And this, combined with slight variations of style, and other peculiarities, have led some critics to split up the book into a number of different writings, which they assign to a number of unknown writers from the ninth century B.C. onwards. For instance, to take a passage where only three writers are supposed to be involved, Exod. 7. 14-25. These twelve verses seem to the ordinary reader a straightforward narrative, but they have been thus split up.[69] Verses 19, 22, and parts of 20, 21, are assigned to P, the supposed writer of the Priestly Code of Laws; v. 24 and parts of 17, 20, 21, to E; and the remainder to J; the two latter writers being thus named from their generally speaking of the Deity as *Elohim* and *Jehovah* (translated *God*, and *Lord*) respectively.

[69] Driver's Introduction to Literature of Old Testament, sixth edition, 1897, p. 24. A slightly different division is given in his Exodus, 1911, p. 59.

Fortunately, we need not discuss the minute and complicated arguments on which all this rests, for the idea of any writings being so hopelessly mixed together is most improbable. While it has been shown in recent years to be very doubtful whether these names, *Elohim* and *Jehovah*, occurred in the original Hebrew, in the same places as they do now.[70] And if they did *not*, the theory loses one of its chief supports.

[70] The Name of God in The Pentateuch by Trœlstra; translated by McClure, 1912

And in any case there are at least four plain and simple arguments against it. The first is that the *Egyptian references*, to which we have already alluded extend to all the parts J, E, and P; as well as to Deuteronomy, which these critics assign to yet another author D. They are thus like an Egyptian *water-mark* running all through the Pentateuch. And while it is difficult enough to believe that even one writer in Canaan should have possessed this intimate knowledge of Egypt, it is far more difficult to believe that *four* should have done so.

The second is that all the writers must have been equally *dishonest*, for they all contain passages, which they assert were written by Moses (see further on). And here again it is hard to believe, that even one writer (leave alone four) should have been so utterly unscrupulous.

The third is that the curious custom of God speaking of Himself in the *plural* number, which would be strange in any case, and is especially so considering the strong Monotheism of the Jews, is also common to both J and P.[71] And so is the puzzling statement that it was God Himself Who hardened Pharaoh's heart, which is also found in E.[72]

[71] Gen. 1. 26 (P): 3. 22 (J).

[72] Exod. 4. 21 (E): 7. 3 (P.): 10. 1 (J).

The fourth is that parallel passages to the supposed two narratives of the Flood, ascribed to J and P (and which are thought to occur alternately *nineteen* times in Gen. 7. 8.) have been found *together* in an old Babylonian story of the Flood, centuries before the time of Moses; and also in layers corresponding to J and P.[73] And this alone seems fatal to the idea that J and P were originally separate narratives that were afterward combined in our Genesis.

[73] Sayce's Monument Facts, 1904, p. 20; Driver's Book of Genesis, 1905, pp. 89-95, 107.

Of course those who maintain that Moses wrote the Pentateuch, quite admit that he made use of previous documents, one of which, the book of the *Wars of the Lord*, he actually quotes.[74] Nor is it denied that some *additions* have been made since his time, the most important being the list of kings, who are said to have reigned in Edom *before there reigned any king over the children of Israel*.[75] And this brings the passage down to the time of Saul at least who was Israel's first king. But it is probably a later insertion, since these kings are referred to in a different way from the dukes, who precede and follow them. And the same may be said of a few other passages[76] such as that *the Canaanite was then in the land*, which must clearly have been written after the Israelites conquered the country. But they can all be omitted without breaking the continuity of the narrative.

[74] Num. 21. 14.

[75] Gen. 36. 31-39.

[76] Gen. 12. 6; 13. 7; Exod. 16. 36; Deut. 2. 10-12, 20-23; 3. 14.

**(3.) Its laws being unknown in later times.**

Passing on now to the third argument for a late date, it is urged that the laws of the Pentateuch cannot really have been written by Moses, since, judging from the other Old Testament Books, they seem to have been *unknown* for many centuries after his time. But this is scarcely correct, for even the earliest books, Joshua and Judges contain some references to a *written* law of Moses;[77] while both in Judges and 1 Samuel there are numerous agreements between what is described there, and what is commanded in the Pentateuch.[78] And similar evidence is afforded by the later books, David, for instance, alluding to the *written* law of Moses, as if it was well known.[79] So in regard to the prophets. Two of the earliest of these are Hosea and Amos; and they both contain frequent points of agreement;[80] as well as one reference to a large number of *written* laws.[81]

[77] Joshua 1. 7, 8; 8. 31, 32; 23. 6; 24. 26. Judges 3. 4.

[78] Judges 20. 27, 28; 21. 19; 1 Sam. 2. 12-30; 3. 3; 4. 4; 6. 15; 14. 3.

[79] 1 Kings 2. 3. 2 Kings 14. 6.

[80] Hos. 4. 4-6; 8. 1, 13; 9. 4; 12. 9; Amos 2. 4, 11; 4. 4, 5; 5. 21-25; 8. 5.

[81] Hos. 8. 12 (R.V.).

On the other side, we have the statement in Jeremiah, that God did not command the Israelites concerning burnt-offerings, and sacrifices, when He brought them out of Egypt.[82] But the next verse certainly implies that it was placing these before obedience that God condemned. And Hosea in a similar passage declares this to be the case, and that God's not desiring sacrifice means His not caring so much about it, as about other things.[83] It is also urged that there were practices which are *inconsistent* with these laws; the most important being that the sacrifices were not limited to one place, or the offerers to priests. As to the former, the principle of the law was that the place of sacrifice should be of Divine appointment, *where God had chosen to record His name*, (*i.e.*, where the *ark* was), and not selected by the worshippers themselves.[84] In Exodus it is naturally implied that there should be many such places, as the Israelites were then only beginning their wanderings; and in Deuteronomy that there should be only one, as they were then about to enter Canaan.

[82] Jer. 7. 22.

[83] Hosea 6. 6; 1 Sam. 15. 22.

[84] Exod. 20. 24; Deut. 12. 5.

But for many years, owing to the unsettled state of the country, and the ark having been captured by the Philistines, the law could not be obeyed. When however, the people had rest from their enemies (which was the condition laid down in Deuteronomy) and the temple was built at Jerusalem, the law was fully recognised. After this the worship at *high places* is spoken of as a *sin*, while Hezekiah is commended for destroying these places, and for keeping the commandments *which the Lord commanded Moses.*[85]

[85] 1 Kings 3. 2; 22. 43; 2 Kings 18. 4-6.

The discovery, however in 1907, that there was a Jewish Temple of Jehovah at Elephantine, near Assouan in Egypt, with sacrifices, as early as the sixth century B.C., and that it had apparently the approval of the authorities at Jerusalem, makes it doubtful if the law as to the one sanctuary was ever thought to be absolutely binding.

As to the other point—the sacrifices not being offered only by *priests*—there is an apparent discrepancy in the Pentateuch itself; since Deuteronomy (unlike the other books) seems in one passage to recognise that *Levites* might perform priestly duties.[86] Various explanations have been given of this, though I do not know of one that is quite satisfactory. There are also a few cases, where men who were neither priests, nor Levites, such as Gideon, David, and Elijah, are said to have offered sacrifices.[87] But these were all under special circumstances, and in some of them the sacrifice was directly ordered by God. There is thus nothing like sufficient evidence to show that the laws of the Pentateuch were not known in later days, but merely that they were often not obeyed.

[86] Deut. 18. 6-8.

[87] *E.g.*, Judges 6. 26; 2 Sam. 24. 18; 1 Kings 18. 32.

**(4.) The finding of Deuteronomy.**

Lastly we have the finding of the *Book of the Law* (probably Deuteronomy) when the temple was being repaired in the reign of Josiah, about 621 B.C., which is regarded by some critics as its first publication.[88] But this is a needless assumption, for there is no hint that either the king or the people were surprised at such a book being found, but merely at what it contained. And as they proceeded at once to carry out its directions, it rather shows that they knew there was such a book all the time, only they had never before read it. And this is easily accounted for, as most copies would have been destroyed by the previous wicked kings.[89] On the other hand, an altogether new book is not likely to have gained such immediate and ready obedience; not to mention the great improbability of such an audacious fraud never being detected at the time.

[88] 2 Kings 22.

[89] 2 Kings 21. 2, 21.

Nor is it easy to see why, if Deuteronomy was written at a late date, it should have contained so many obsolete and useless instructions; such as the order to destroy the Canaanites, when there were scarcely any Canaanites left to destroy.[90] Yet the people are not only told to destroy them, but to do it *gradually*, so that the wild beasts may not become too numerous;[91] which shows that the passage was written centuries before the time of Josiah, when there was no more danger from wild beasts than from Canaanites. Nor is it likely, if Deuteronomy was written at that time, when Jerusalem claimed to be the central sanctuary, that the city itself should never once be named in the book, or even alluded to.

[90] Deut. 7. 2; 20. 17.

[91] Deut. 7. 22.

Moreover, discoveries in Egypt have shown that in early times religious writings were sometimes buried in the foundations, or lower walls of important temples; where they were found centuries afterwards when the temples were being repaired; so the account, as we have it in the Bible, is both natural and probable.[92]

[92] E. Naville, Discovery of the Book of the Law, 1911, pp. 4-10.

On the whole, then, none of these arguments for a *late date* are at all conclusive, and we therefore decide that this theory is not only very improbable in any case, but quite untenable in face of the strong evidence on the other side.

### (*D.*) CONCLUSION.

Having thus shown that the Pentateuch appears to date from the time of Moses, it only remains to consider its authorship, and the witness it bears to the miracles of the Exodus.

Now that the greater part should have been written by Moses himself is plainly the most probable view. And this is strongly confirmed by the book itself; for a large part of it distinctly *claims* to have been written by Moses. It is not merely that this title is given in a heading, or opening verse, which might easily have been added in later times. But it is asserted, positively and repeatedly, all through the book itself, both in Exodus, Numbers, and Deuteronomy, that many of the events, and laws referred to (often including several chapters) were actually *written down* by Moses.[93] This is an important point, and it must be allowed great weight.

[93] Exod. 17. 14; 24. 4; 34. 27; Num. 33. 2; 36. 13; Deut. 31. 9, 22, 24. The first two passages in Exod. are assigned to the supposed E, the third to J, those in Num. to P, and those in Deut. to D.

And the first passage, that Moses was to write the threat against Amalek *in a book*, is specially interesting; because we cannot think that the book contained nothing but this single sentence. It evidently means in *the* book (see American R. V.), implying that a regular journal was kept, in which important events were recorded. And this is confirmed by another of the passages, which says that Moses wrote down something that occurred *the same day*;[94] and by another which gives a long and uninteresting list of journeys in the Desert,[95] which certainly looks like an official record kept at the time. While the concluding passage relates how Moses, when he had finished writing the book, gave it to the Levites to keep beside the ark, in order to preserve it, and anything more precise than this can scarcely be imagined.[96]

[94] Deut. 31. 22; comp. Exod. 24. 4.

[95] Num. 33.

[96] Deut. 31. 24-26.

Moreover, the frequent references of Moses to his own exclusion from Canaan, and his pathetic prayer on the subject, have a very genuine tone about them.[97] And his bitter complaint that God had broken His promise, and not delivered the people,[98] could scarcely have been written by anyone but himself; especially after the conquest of Canaan, when it was so obviously untrue.

[97] *E.g.*, Deut. 3. 23-26; 1. 37; 4. 21; 31. 2.

[98] Exod. 5. 23.

And his authorship is further confirmed by the fact that so little is said in his praise. His faults are indeed narrated quite candidly, but nothing is said in admiration of the great leader's courage, and ability, till the closing chapter of Deuteronomy. This was evidently written by someone else, and shows what we might have expected had the earlier part been the work of anyone but Moses himself. Nor is there anything surprising in his writing in the third person, as numbers of other men—Cæsar, for instance—have done the same.

But now comes the important point. Fortunately it can be stated in a few words. If the Pentateuch is a contemporary document, probably written by Moses, can we reject the miracles which it records? Can we imagine, for instance, a *contemporary* writer describing the Ten Plagues, or the Passage of the Red Sea, if nothing of the kind had occurred? The events, if true, must have been well known at the time; and if untrue, no contemporary would have thought of inventing them. We therefore conclude, on reviewing the whole chapter, that the *origin* of the Jewish religion *was confirmed by miracles*.

# CHAPTER X.
## THAT ITS HISTORY WAS CONFIRMED BY MIRACLES.

(*A.*) THE LATER OLD TESTAMENT BOOKS.

(1.) Undesigned agreements; the rebellion of Korah.

(2.) Alleged mistakes; unimportant.

(3.) Modern discoveries; these support their accuracy.

(*B.*) THE OLD TESTAMENT MIRACLES.

(1.) Their credibility; this can scarcely be disputed, if miracles at all are credible; the silence of the sun and moon, two other difficulties.

(2.) Their truthfulness; list of eight public miracles, two examples, Elijah's sacrifice on Mount Carmel, and the destruction of the Assyrian army, considered in detail; conclusion.

Having now examined the origin of the Jewish Religion, we have next to consider its *history*; which also claims to have been confirmed by miracles. So we will first notice (very briefly) the Old Testament *Books*, from Joshua onwards; and then consider some of the *Miracles* which they record.

### (*A.*) THE LATER OLD TESTAMENT BOOKS.

Now, the arguments for, and against the genuineness of these Books need not be discussed at length, since we have already decided in favour of that of the Pentateuch, and most critics who admit the one, admit the other. But a few remarks may be made on three subjects, those of *undesigned agreements*, the importance of which is not obvious at first sight; the *alleged mistakes* in the Old Testament; and the effect of *modern discoveries*.

### (1.) Undesigned agreements.

Now, if we find two statements regarding an event, or series of events, which, though not identical, are yet perfectly consistent, this agreement must be either *accidental* or *not accidental*. And supposing it to be too minute in detail to be accidental it shows that the statements are somehow connected together. Of course, if the events are true, each writer may know them independently, and their statements would thus be in perfect, though unintentional agreement. But if the events are not true, then either one writer must have made his account agree with the other, or else both must have derived their information from a common source. In the former case, there would be intentional agreement between the writers; in the latter, between the various parts of the original account. In any case, there would be designed agreement somewhere; for, to put it shortly, the events, being imaginary, would not fit together of necessity, nor by accident, which is excluded, and hence must do so by design.

This has been otherwise expressed by saying that truth is necessarily consistent, but falsehood is not so; therefore, while consistency in truth may be undesigned, consistency in falsehood can only result from design. And from this it follows that an *undesigned agreement* between two statements—provided of course it is too minute to be accidental—is a sure sign of truthfulness. It shows, moreover, that both writers had independent knowledge of the event, and were both telling the truth. And of course the same argument applies if the two statements are made by the same writer, though in this case there is a greater probability that the agreement is not undesigned.

We will now consider a single example in detail, and select that referring to the rebellion of Korah, Dathan, and Abiram, as it is connected with an important miracle. Korah, we are told,[99] belonged to the family of Kohath and the other two to that of Reuben; and from incidental notices *in another part of the book*, we learn the position of the *tents* of these men. The former was to the south of the central Tabernacle, or Tent of Meeting, on an inner line of tents, while the latter were also to the south, though on an outer line of tents.

[99] Num. 16; 2. 10, 17; 3. 29.

This explains how, when Moses was talking to Korah, he had to *send for* Dathan and Abiram, and how next morning he left the central Tabernacle, where the men had assembled to offer incense, (and where they were afterwards destroyed, probably by lightning) and *went unto* Dathan and Abiram (vv. 8-25). It explains how, later on, the *tents* of Dathan and Abiram are twice mentioned, while that of the leading conspirator, Korah, is strangely omitted. It explains how the *families* of these two were destroyed, though no mention is made of that of Korah; since the destruction was probably limited to the tents of Dathan and Abiram, who were brothers, and the small tabernacle they had erected alongside, and from which alone the people were told to *depart* (vv. 26, 27). We may therefore conclude that Korah's *family* was not destroyed, since their tent was at some distance. And this accounts for what some have thought to be a discrepancy in another passage, where we read that the *sons* of Korah did not die; as well as for Dathan and Abiram, being mentioned alone later on.[100] In fact, the position of these tents is the key to the whole narrative, though we are left to discover it for ourselves.

[100] Num. 26. 11; Deut. 11. 6.

Now if the account is true and written by a contemporary, all is plain; for truth, as said before, is necessarily consistent. But if the story is a late fiction, all this agreement in various places is, to say the least, very remarkable. Can we imagine a writer of fiction *accidentally* arranging these details in different parts of his book, which fit together so perfectly? Or can we imagine his doing so *intentionally*, and yet never hinting at the agreement himself, but leaving it so unapparent that not one reader in a thousand ever discovers it? This single instance may be taken as a sample of numerous others which have been noticed all through the Old Testament; and they certainly tend to show its accuracy.

**(2.) Alleged mistakes.**

We pass on now to the alleged mistakes in the Old Testament, and considering the long period covered, and the variety of subjects dealt with, and often the same subject by various writers, the number of even apparent discrepancies is not very great. And it is beyond dispute that many of these can be explained satisfactorily, and doubtless many others could be so, if our knowledge were more complete. Moreover, they are, as a rule, *numerical* mistakes, such as the incredibly large numbers in some places,[101] and the rather discordant chronology in Kings and Chronicles. But the former may be due to some error in copying, and the latter to the different ways of counting a king's reign.

[101] Num. 26. 11; Deut. 11. 6.

The only mistake of any real importance refers to the large numbers of the Israelites, who are said to have left Egypt,—some 600,000 men, besides children, or probably over two million altogether. For on two subsequent occasions, when the census of the tribes is given, it totals up to about the same number.[102] This is no doubt a serious difficulty; as anyone can see, who will take the trouble to calculate the space they would require on the march, or in camp. If we assume, for instance, that they crossed the arm of the Red Sea in, say, *forty* parallel columns, these would still have to be of enormous length to contain 50,000 persons each, with their flocks and herds.

[102] Exod. 12. 37. Num. 1. 26.

Perhaps the best explanation is that suggested by Professor Flinders Petrie, that the word translated *thousands* should be *families*,[103] so that the tribe of Reuben, for instance,[104] instead of having forty-six *thousand* five hundred men, would have forty-six *families*, (making about) five hundred men. The chief arguments in favour of this are, first, that the same word is used in Judges 6. 15, where it so obviously means family and not thousand, that it is so translated in both the Authorised and Revised Versions.

[103] Egypt and Israel, 1911, p. 43.

[104] Num. 1. 21.

And secondly, it would account for the remarkable fact that though there were twelve tribes, and they were each counted twice, yet the number of the hundreds is never 0, 1, 8 or 9; but always one of the other six digits. It is extremely unlikely (practically incredible)[105] that this would occur in an ordinary census, but the proposed theory explains it at once. For the hundreds could scarcely be 0, or 1, as this would mean too few men in a family; or 8 or 9, which would mean too many; while the other digits always work out to what (allowing for servants) is a reasonable proportion, from 5 to 17. On this theory the number of men would be reduced to 5,600, which is much more intelligible. But some other passages scarcely seem capable of this interpretation, so it must be admitted that the number forms a difficulty, whatever view we adopt.

[105] The chance of its occurring would be only $(6/10)^{24}$ or less than 1 in 200,000.

### (3.) Modern discoveries.

Lastly, as to the effect of modern discoveries on the accuracy of the Old Testament. In the case of the Pentateuch, as we have seen, there is very little *direct* evidence either way; but it is different in regard to some of the later books.

In the first place, and this is very important, modern discoveries have shown that the period of Jewish history from the time of Moses onwards was distinctly *a literary age*. In Egypt, Babylonia, Syria, and elsewhere, it was the custom, and had been for centuries, to record all important events, at least all those that were creditable to the people concerned; so it is almost certain that the Jews, like the surrounding nations, had their historians. In every age conquerors have loved to record their conquests, and why should the Jews alone have been an exception?

Yet the historical books of the Old Testament have no competitors. If, then, we deny that these are in the main a contemporary record, we must either assume that the Jews, unlike the surrounding nations, had no contemporary historians, which is most unlikely; as well as being contrary to the Books themselves, where the *recorders* are frequently mentioned, even by name.[106] Or else we must assume that their works were replaced in later days by other and less reliable accounts, which were universally mistaken for the originals, and this seems equally improbable.

[106] *E.g.*, 2 Sam. 8. 16; 2 Kings 18. 18; 2 Chron. 34. 8.

Passing on now to the evidence in detail, it may be divided into two classes, geographical and historical. In the first place the *geography* of Palestine has been shown to be minutely accurate. But this does not prove the Old Testament Books to be genuine, but merely that they were written by Jews who knew the country intimately. It helps, however, in some cases to remove apparent difficulties. Thus the discoveries at Jericho, in 1908, have shown that the place was merely a small fortified hill, the length of the surrounding wall being about half a mile, so there was no difficulty in the Israelites walking round it seven times in the day.[107] And much the same may be said of the *historical* notices. The monumental records of the Kings of Judah and Israel have not at present been discovered, but we can often check the history by the records of other countries. And these are as a rule in perfect agreement, not only as to the actual facts, but as to the society, customs, and state of civilisation, of the period. Indeed, in some cases where this was formerly disputed, as in the importance assigned to the *Hittites*, it has been fully justified by modern discoveries.[108] But this again does not prove the genuineness of the Books, though it certainly raises a probability in their favour.

[107] Josh. 6. 15.

[108] 1 Kings 10. 29; 2 Kings 7. 6.

Sometimes, however, the evidence is stronger than this, one of the best known instances being Daniel's mention of *Belshazzar*.[109] He states that the last king of Babylon was Nebuchadnezzar's son, or grandson (margin, A.V.) called Belshazzar, who was slain at night when the city was captured (about B.C. 538). But according to Berosus, who wrote about the third century B.C., all this appears to be wrong. The last king of Babylon was a usurper called Nabonidus, and any such person as Belshazzar is quite unknown. And so matters remained till some cuneiform inscriptions were discovered at Mugheir in 1854.

[109] Dan. 5. 1.

From these it appears that Belshazzar was the eldest son of Nabonidus, and was apparently associated with him in the government. And an inscription recently found at Erech shows that this was the case for several years.[110] There is no proof that he ever had the title of *King*, unless he is the same as one *Mardukshazzar*, about this time (not otherwise identified), which is not unlikely, as we know Marduk was sometimes called *Bel*—i.e., Baal, or Lord. And another inscription, somewhat mutilated, seems to show that he was slain at Babylon in a night assault on the city (or some portion of it) as described by Daniel, some months after Nabonidus had been taken prisoner.[111] As to his relationship with Nebuchadnezzar perhaps his mother (or grandmother) was a royal princess. And there certainly seems to have been some connection between the families, as we know from the inscriptions that he had a brother called Nebuchadnezzar.

[110] Expository Times, April, 1915. Comp. Dan. 8. 1.

[111] Transactions of Victoria Institute, vol. xxxviii., 1906, p. 28; vol. xlvi., 1914, p. 14.

Now, of course, if Daniel himself wrote the book, he would have known all about Belshazzar, however soon afterwards it was forgotten. But, if the book is a late fiction, written by a Jew in Palestine about B.C. 160, which is the rationalistic theory, as the wars between Egypt and Syria up to that date are clearly foretold, how did he know the name of Belshazzar at all, or anything about him, when such a person was unknown to previous historians? Plainly then, this is a distinct argument in favour of the contemporary date of the book.[112]

[112] It is worth noting that this rationalistic theory, which was generally accepted by the so-called Higher Critics, has now become so difficult to maintain in the face of archæology that Dr. Pinches, Lecturer in Assyriology at University College, London, said recently 'I am glad to think with regard to the Book of Daniel that the Higher Criticism is in fact buried.' Transactions of Victoria Institute, vol. xlix., 1917, p. 135.

And much the same may be said of Isaiah's mention of *Sargon* of Assyria, who is stated to have taken Ashdod. Yet the very existence of such a king was unknown to secular history, till the last century; when his palace was discovered at Khorsabad, with inscriptions recording, among other things, his capture of Ashdod.[113]

[113] Isa. 20. 1. Orr's Problem of Old Test., 1906, p. 399.

Two other cases are of special interest, because the monuments seemed at first to show that the Bible was wrong. One of these refers to a so-called *Pul*, King of Assyria;[114] but when the list of Assyrian monarchs was discovered, no such king could be found. It looked like a serious discrepancy, and was even spoken of as 'almost the only important historical difficulty' between the Bible and the monuments.[115] But it has now been discovered that *Pulu* was the original name of a usurper, who changed it to Tiglath Pileser III. on ascending the throne; though he was still sometimes called Pulu.[116] This not only removes the difficulty, but tends to show the early date of the narrative; for a late writer would probably have called him by his better-known name.

[114] 2 Kings 15. 19.

[115] Rawlinson, Historical Illustrations of the Old Testament, 1871, p. 121.

[116] Hastings, Dict. of the Bible, vol. iv., p. 761.

The other instance refers to *Jehu*, who is stated in the Assyrian inscriptions to be the son of Omri; though according to the Bible he was no relation whatever. But it has now been shown that the words translated *son of Omri* may only mean *of the land or house of Omri*, which is a common Assyrian name for the kingdom of Israel.[117]

[117] Driver, Schweich Lecture, 1908, p. 17.

As a last example we will take the *dates* given for the Fall of the two capital cities, Samaria and Jerusalem. These were calculated long ago (margin, A.V.) from a number of statements in the Bible, giving the lengths of different reigns, etc., at B.C. 721 and 588 respectively.[118] And now the inscriptions from Assyria and Babylonia fix the former at *B.C.* 722 and the latter at 586.[119] Everyone must admit that these are remarkable agreements, considering the way in which they have had to be calculated.

[118] 2 Kings 17. 6; 25. 3.

[119] Hastings, Dict. of the Bible, vol. i., p. 401.

We have now briefly considered the Books of the Old Testament, both as to their *undesigned agreements*, which are very interesting; their *alleged mistakes*, which are unimportant; and the effect of *modern discoveries*, which has undoubtedly been to support their accuracy. What, then, is the value of the evidence they afford as to the history of the Jewish Religion having been confirmed by miracles?

**(*B.*) THE OLD TESTAMENT MIRACLES.**

We will include under this term superhuman coincidences as well as miracles in the strict sense; and they occur all through the historical books of the Old Testament. A few of them have been already noticed in the last chapter, but we must now discuss them more fully, first considering whether they are credible, and then whether they are true.

**(1.) Their credibility.**

Now this can scarcely be disputed, *provided miracles at all are credible*, which we have already admitted, since scientific difficulties affect all miracles equally; and of course the Superhuman Coincidences have no difficulties of this kind whatever. Among these may be mentioned most of the Ten Plagues, the destruction of Korah, the falling of the walls of Jericho, probably due to an earthquake; the lightning which struck Elijah's sacrifice; and many others.

The *Passage of the Red Sea*, for instance, almost certainly belongs to this class. The water, we are told, was driven back by a strong east wind, lasting all night; and this was doubtless due to natural forces, though, in common with other natural events (such as the growth of grass[120]), it is in the Bible ascribed to God. And the statement, *the waters were a wall unto them*, need not be pressed literally, so as to mean that they stood upright. It may only mean here, as it obviously does in some other cases, that the waters were a defence on each side, and secured them from flank attacks.[121] And as they must have advanced in several parallel columns, probably half a mile wide, this certainly seems the more likely view.

[120] Ps. 147. 8-9.

[121] Exod. 14. 21, 22; Nahum 3. 8; 1 Sam. 25. 16.

And what makes it still more probable is that much the same thing occurred in this very neighbourhood in recent times. For in January, 1882, a large expanse of water, about 5 feet deep, near the Suez Canal, was exposed to such a strong gale (also from the east) that next morning it had been entirely driven away, and men were walking about on the mud, where the day before the fishing-boats had been floating.[122] Moreover, on this theory, the miracle would not lose any of its evidential value. For the fact of such a strip of dry land being formed just when and where the Israelites so much wanted it, and then being suddenly covered again, through the wind changing round to the west (which it must have done for the dead Egyptians to have been cast up on the *east* side)[123], would be a coincidence far too improbable to be accidental.

[122] Transactions of Victoria Institute, vol. xxviii., 1894, p. 268. It is vouched for by Major-General Tulloch, who was there on duty at the time.

[123] Exod. 14. 30.

Another well known miracle, which probably belongs to this class, is the *'silence' (or standing still) of the sun and moon*.[124] This is often thought to mean that the earth's rotation was stopped, so that the sun and moon apparently stood still. But a miracle on so vast a scale, was quite needless for the destruction of a few Canaanites, and there is another, and far better explanation.

[124] Josh. 10. 12-14.

It is that the miracle, instead of being one of prolonged light, the sun remaining visible after it should have set, was really one of prolonged *darkness*. The sun, which had been hidden by thick clouds, was just about to shine forth, when Joshua prayed to the Lord that it might be *silent, i.e.*, remain obscured behind the clouds, which it did during the rest of the day. The Hebrew seems capable of either meaning. For the important word translated *stand still* is literally *be silent* (see margin), both in verses 12 and 13; and while this would be most suitable to the sun's remaining obscured by clouds during the day, it could scarcely be used of its continuing to shine at night.

On the other hand, the rest of the passage seems to favour the ordinary view. But if we admit that this is what Joshua *prayed for*, that the sun and moon should remain *silent* or obscured, the rest of the passage can only mean that this is what took place. And it may be mentioned that, as early as the fourteenth century, a Jewish writer Levi ben Gershon maintained that the words did not mean that the sun and moon literally *stood still*, or in any way altered their motion; though it is only fair to add that this was not the general view.[125]

[125] Numerous quotations are given in 'A Misunderstood Miracle,' by Rev. A. S. Palmer, 1887, pp. 103-107.

Moreover, even if the word did mean *stand still*, Joshua would only be likely to have asked for the sun and moon to stand still, if they were apparently *moving*. And they only move fast enough to be apparent when they are just coming out from behind a dense bank of clouds, due, of course, to the clouds really moving. And to *stand still* in such a case, would mean to stay behind the clouds, and remain *obscured*, the same sense as before. And the words could then have had an *immediate* effect; visible at once to all the people, which certainly seems implied in the narrative, and which would not have been the case on the ordinary view.

Assuming, then, that either meaning is possible, a prolonged darkness is much the more probable for three reasons. To begin with, the miracle must have occurred in the early *morning*, Gibeon, where the sun was, being to the south *east* of Beth-horon, the scene of the incident. And it is most unlikely that Joshua, with the enemy already defeated, and nearly all the day before him, should have wished to have it prolonged. Secondly, just *before* the miracle there had been a very heavy thunderstorm, involving (as here required) thick clouds and a dark sky; and this is stated to have been the chief cause of the enemy's defeat. So Joshua is more likely to have asked for a continuance of this storm, *i.e.*, for prolonged darkness, than for light. Thirdly, the moon is mentioned as well as the sun, and, if Joshua wanted darkness, both would have to be *silent*; but if he wanted light, the mention of the moon was quite unnecessary.

On the whole, then, the miracle seems to have been a superhuman coincidence between a prayer of Joshua and an extraordinary and unique thunderstorm, which caused the sun to remain *silent* or invisible all day. And if the Canaanites were sun-worshippers (as many think probable), it was most suitable that at the time of their great battle with the Israelites, the sun should have been obscured the whole day, and it naturally led to their utter confusion.

Before passing on, we may notice two objections of a more general character, that are often made to the Jewish miracles. The first is that some of them were very *trivial*, such as Elisha's purifying the waters of Jericho, increasing the widow's oil, and making the iron axe-head to float;[126] and hence it is urged they are most improbable. And no doubt they would be so, if we regard them as mere acts of kindness to individual persons. But if we regard them as so many signs to the Israelites (and through them to the rest of the world), that Elisha was God's prophet; and that God was not a far-off God, but One Who knew about and cared about the every-day troubles of His people, they were certainly not inappropriate. Indeed, if this was the end in view, they were just the kind of miracles most likely to attain it.

[126] 2 Kings 2. 22; 4. 6; 6. 6.

The second and more important objection would destroy, or at least lessen, the value of all the miracles. They could not, it is urged, have really confirmed a revelation from God, since the same writers who describe them, also describe *other* miracles, which, they say, were worked in opposition to God's agents. But if we exclude some doubtful cases, we have only one instance to judge by. It is that of the *magicians of Egypt*, who imitated some of the earlier miracles of Moses and Aaron; and here the inference is uncertain. For we are told that this was due to their *enchantments* (or *secret arts*, margin R.V.), a term which might very possibly cover some feat of jugglery; as they knew beforehand what was wanted, and had time to prepare. While the fact that they tried and failed to imitate the next plague, which they frankly confessed was a Divine miracle, makes this a very probable solution.[127]

[127] Exod. 7. 11, 22; 8. 7, 18, 19.

We decide, then, that none of the Jewish miracles can be pronounced *incredible*; though some of them no doubt seem, at first sight, very improbable.

## (2.) Their truthfulness.

Now, of course, the miracles vary greatly in evidential value, the following being eight of the most important:

The destruction of Korah, Num. 16.

The passage of the Jordan, Josh. 3. 14-17.

The capture of Jericho, Josh. 6. 6-20.

Elijah's sacrifice on Mount Carmel, 1 Kings 18. 17-40.

The cure of Naaman's leprosy, 2 Kings 5. 10-27.

The destruction of the Assyrian army, 2 Kings 19. 35.

The shadow on the dial, 2 Kings 20. 8-11.

The three men in the furnace, Dan. 3. 20-27.

We will examine a couple of instances in detail and select first *Elijah's sacrifice on Mount Carmel*. This is said to have occurred on the most public occasion possible, before the King of Israel and thousands of spectators. And as a miracle, or rather *superhuman coincidence*, it presents no difficulty whatever. The lightning which struck the sacrifice was doubtless due to natural causes; yet, as before explained (Chapter VII.), this would not interfere with its evidential value.

Moreover, it was avowedly a test case to definitely settle whether Jehovah was the true God or not. The nation, we learn, had long been in an undecided state. Some were worshippers of Jehovah, others of Baal; and these rival sacrifices were suggested for the express purpose of settling the point. So, if miracles at all are credible, there could not have been a more suitable occasion for one; while it was, for the time at least, thoroughly successful. All present were convinced that Jehovah was the true God, and, in accordance with the national law, the false prophets of Baal were immediately put to death.

Now could any writer have described all this, even a century afterwards, if nothing of the kind had occurred? The event, if true, must have been well known, and remembered; and if untrue, no one living near the time and place would have thought of inventing it. And (what renders the argument still stronger) all this is stated to have occurred, not among savages, but among a fairly civilised nation and in a literary age.

Next as to *the destruction of the Assyrian army*. Here it will be remembered that when Sennacherib came to attack Jerusalem, he publicly, and in the most insulting manner, defied the God of Israel to deliver the city out of his hand (probably about B.C. 701).[128] We then read how Isaiah declared that God accepted the challenge, and would defend Jerusalem, and would not allow it to be destroyed. '*I will defend this city to save it, for mine own sake, and for my servant David's sake.*' And the sacredness of the city is very strongly insisted on.

[128] 2 Kings 18. 28-35; 19. 10, 34.

Now it is inconceivable that this could have been written after Jerusalem had been captured by Nebuchadnezzar in *B.C.* 598; though there is no real inconsistency in God's preserving the city in the one case, and not in the other. For Nebuchadnezzar is always represented as being, though unconsciously, God's servant in punishing the Jews; while Sennacherib openly defied Jehovah.

Then comes the sudden destruction of the Assyrian army, probably by pestilence;[129] and the extreme fitness of this, after Sennacherib's challenge, must be obvious to everyone. Moreover, such a very public event, if untrue, could not have been recorded till long afterwards; yet, as we have seen, the narrative could not have been written long afterwards. Sennacherib does not of course allude to it himself in his inscriptions, for kings never like to record their own defeats; but this is no reason for doubting that it occurred, especially as it is confirmed by the Babylonian historian Berosus.[130] And even Sennacherib himself, though he mentions the campaign, and says that he shut up Hezekiah in Jerusalem, never claims to have taken the city.

[129] Comp. 2 Kings 19. 35; 1 Chron. 21. 12.

[130] Quoted by Josephus, Antiq. x. 1.

We need not examine the other miracles in detail, since the argument is much the same in every case. They are all said to have occurred on important and critical occasions when, if we admit miracles at all, they would be most suitable. They are all said to have been *public* miracles, either actually worked before crowds of persons, or else so affecting public men that their truth or otherwise must have been well-known at the time. And they were all of such a kind that any mistake or fraud as to their occurrence was out of the question. It is, then, on the face of it, most unlikely that miracles, *such as these*, should have been recorded unless they were true. Indeed, if the Old Testament books were written by contemporaries, or even within a century of the events they relate, it is very difficult to deny their occurrence. We decide, therefore, that the *history* of the Jewish Religion was *confirmed by miracles*.

# CHAPTER XI.
## THAT ITS HISTORY WAS CONFIRMED BY PROPHECIES.

(*A.*) GENERAL PROPHECIES.

Three examples considered:

(1.) The desolation of Assyria and Babylonia.

(2.) The degradation of Egypt.

(3.) The dispersion of the Jews, including the Roman siege of Jerusalem.

(*B.*) SPECIAL PROPHECIES.

List of eight important ones: a single example, the destruction of Jerusalem by the Babylonians considered in detail; some general remarks.

(*C.*) CONCLUSION.

The cumulative nature of the evidence.

We pass on now to the Jewish Prophecies. It should be explained at starting that the word *prophecy* is used here in the sense of *prediction*; and not as it often is, in the Bible, to include various kinds of teaching. And the prophecies may be divided into two classes, general and special.

### (*A.*) GENERAL PROPHECIES.

We will consider the General Prophecies first, the most important of which concern the Jews themselves, and their great neighbours Assyria and Babylonia, on the one hand, and Egypt on the other. All these nations had existed for centuries, and there was nothing to indicate what was to be their future; yet the prophets foretold it, and with remarkable accuracy.

### (1.) The desolation of Assyria and Babylonia.

And first as to Assyria and Babylonia. The future of these countries was to be utter *desolation*. The kingdoms were to be destroyed, the land was to become a wilderness, and the cities to be entirely forsaken. We read repeatedly that they were to be desolate *for ever*; and though this cannot be pressed as meaning literally for all eternity, it certainly implies a long duration.[131] A single passage referring to each may be quoted at length.

[131] Isa. 13. 19-22; 14. 22, 23; Jer. 50. 13, 39, 40; 51. 26, 37, 43; Nahum 3. 7; Zeph. 2. 13-14.

Thus Zephaniah says of Assyria, 'And he will stretch out his hand against the north, and destroy Assyria; and will make Nineveh a desolation, and dry like the wilderness. And herds shall lie down in the midst of her, all the beasts of the nations; both the pelican and the porcupine shall lodge in the chapiters thereof [the capitals of the fallen columns]: their voice shall sing in the windows; desolation shall be in the thresholds: for he hath laid bare the cedar work.'

And Isaiah says of Babylon, 'And Babylon, the glory of kingdoms, the beauty of the Chaldean's pride, shall be as when God overthrew Sodom and Gomorrah. It shall never be inhabited, neither shall it be dwelt in from generation to generation; neither shall the Arabian pitch tent there; neither shall shepherds make their flocks to lie down there. But wild beasts of the desert shall lie there; and their houses shall be full of doleful creatures; and ostriches shall dwell there, and satyrs [or goats] shall dance there. And wolves shall cry in their castles, and jackals in the pleasant palaces: and her time is near to come, and her days shall not be prolonged.'

It seems needless to comment on prophecies so plain and straightforward. Nor need we insist at any length on their exact fulfilment; it is obvious to everyone. For two thousand years history has verified them. The utter desolation of these countries is without a parallel: the empires have vanished, the once populous land is deserted, and the cities are heaps of ruins, often the dens of wild beasts,—lions, hyænas, and jackals having all been seen among the ruins of Babylon. In short, the prophecies have been fulfilled in a manner which is, to say the least, very remarkable.

### (2.) The degradation of Egypt.

Next as to Egypt. The future foretold of this country was not desolation but *degradation*. Ezekiel tells us it was to become a *base kingdom*, and he adds, 'It shall be the basest of the kingdoms; neither shall it any more lift itself up above the nations: and I will diminish them, that they shall no more rule over the nations.'[132] And here also prophecy has been turned into history. The permanent degradation of Egypt is a striking fact which cannot be disputed. When the prophets wrote, Egypt had on the whole been a powerful and independent kingdom for some thousands of years: but it has never been so since. Persians, Greeks, Romans, Byzantine Greeks, Saracens, Memlooks, Turks, and we may now add British, have in turn been its masters; but it has been the master of no one. It has never more *ruled over the nations* as it used to do for so many centuries. Its history in this respect has been unique—an unparalleled period of prosperity followed by an unparalleled period of degradation.

[132] Ezek. 29. 15.

With such an obvious fulfilment of the main prophecy, it seems needless to insist on any of its details, though some of these are sufficiently striking. Thus, we are told, *Her cities shall be in the midst of the cities that are wasted.*[133] And though it is doubtful to what period this refers, no more accurate description can be given of the present cities of Egypt, such as Cairo, than that they are in the midst of the cities that are wasted, such as Memphis, Bubastis, and Tanis. While a few verses farther on we read, *There shall be no more a prince out of the land of Egypt*; yet, when this passage was written, there had been independent Egyptian sovereigns, off and on, from the very dawn of history. But there have been none since. Stress, however, is not laid on details like these, some of which are admittedly obscure, such as the forty years' desolation of the land with the scattering of its inhabitants;[134] but rather on the broad fact that Egypt was not to be destroyed like Assyria and Babylonia, but to be *degraded*, and that this has actually been its history.

[133] Ezek. 30. 7, 13.

[134] Ezek. 29. 11-13.

### (3.) The dispersion of the Jews.

Lastly, as to the Jews. Their future was to be neither desolation, nor degradation, but *dispersion*. This is asserted over and over again. They were to be scattered among the nations, and dispersed through the countries; to be wanderers among the nations; sifted among all nations; tossed to and fro among all the kingdoms of the earth; and scattered among all peoples from one end of the earth even unto the other end of the earth.[135]

[135] Ezek. 22. 15; Hos. 9. 17; Amos 9. 9; Deut. 28. 25, 64; see also Deut. 4. 27; Neh. 1. 8; Jer. 9. 16.

Moreover, in their dispersion they were to be subjected to continual *suffering* and *persecution*. They were to become a proverb, and a byword among all people. Their curses were to be upon them, for a sign and for a wonder, and upon their seed for ever. They were to have a yoke of iron upon their necks; and to have the sword drawn out after them in all lands, etc. Yet, in spite of all this, they were not to be absorbed into other nations, but to remain *distinct*. They and their seed *for ever* were to be a separate people, a sign and a wonder at all times; and God would never make a full end of *them*, as He would of the nations among whom they were scattered. Indeed heaven and earth were to pass away, rather than the Jews cease to be a distinct people.[136]

[136] Deut. 28. 37, 46, 48; Lev. 26. 33; Jer. 24. 9; 29. 18; 30. 11; 31. 35-37.

And here again history has exactly agreed with prophecy. The fate of the Jews, since the destruction of Jerusalem in A.D. 70, has actually been *dispersion*, and this to an extent which is quite unique. It has been combined, moreover, with incessant suffering and persecution, yet they have always remained a separate people. The Jews are still everywhere, though the Jewish nation is nowhere. They are present in all countries, but with a home in none, having been literally *scattered among the nations*.

We will now examine a single passage in detail, and select the latter part of Deut. 28. The whole chapter is indeed full of prophecies as to the future condition of the Jews, some of which seem to point to the Babylonian captivity, (*e.g.*, v. 36); but after this we come to another and final catastrophe in v. 49. This evidently begins a fresh subject, which is continued without a break till the end of the chapter. And it is specially interesting because, not only is the world-wide dispersion of the Jews, and their continual sufferings, clearly foretold; but also the *previous war* which led up to it. We have, as is well known, a full account of this in the history of Josephus, and as he never alludes to the prophecy himself (except in the most general terms), his evidence is above suspicion.

Ver. 49. First of all the conquerors themselves are described as a nation *from far, from the end of the earth, as the eagle flieth, a nation whose tongue thou shalt not understand*, etc. And this is very applicable to the Romans, whose general, Vespasian, had come from Britain, and their troops from various countries, who had the eagle as their standard, and whose language, Latin, was unknown to most of the Jews.

50. And the merciless way in which these fierce warriors were to spare neither old nor young was painfully true in their treatment of the Jews.

51. And they also of course destroyed or confiscated their property.

52. Then the war is foretold as one of *sieges* (he shall *besiege* thee in all thy gates), rather than of open battles. And this was certainly the case, since a large number of towns, including Jotapata, Gamala, Masada, and Jerusalem itself, suffered terrible sieges. And these were to be continued *till the high walls came down*, which is very appropriate to the Roman battering rams that were actually used at all these places.

53. Then we have the dreadful famine, due to the severity (or *straitness*) of the siege, evidently the great siege, that of Jerusalem. This is strongly insisted on, being repeated three times, and it was to drive the wretched inhabitants to cannibalism of the most revolting kind, which it actually did.

54. It was also to lead to considerable strife *within the city*; even between members of the same family. And this, though by no means common in all sieges, was abundantly fulfilled in the case of Jerusalem.

55. And they were to grudge their nearest relatives a morsel of food; which again exactly agrees with Josephus, who says that parents would fight with their own children for pieces of food.

56. And all this was to be the fate, not only of the poor; but, what is very remarkable, and perhaps unique in the world's history, of the *wealthy* also. It was even to include one instance at least (perhaps several) of a lady of high

position. She is described as not *setting her foot upon the ground*, which means that she was accustomed to be carried about in a chair, or ride on an ass; and was therefore rich enough to buy anything that could be bought.

57. And she was to *eat her own children secretly*. Here was the climax of their sufferings. Yet this very detail, so unlikely to have occurred, and so unlikely to have been discovered if it did occur (as it was to be done secretly), is fully confirmed by Josephus. For he mentions one instance that actually was discovered, in which a lady *eminent for her family and wealth* (Mary, the daughter of Eleazar) had secretly eaten half her own child.[137]

[137] Wars, vi. 3.

58. And these miseries were to come upon the Jews for their disobedience of God's laws; and again Josephus says that their wickedness at this time was so great that if the Romans had not destroyed their city, he thinks it would have been swallowed up by the earth.[138]

[138] Wars, v. 13.

59. Moreover, the plagues of themselves, and of their seed, were to be *wonderful, even great plagues, and of long continuance*. And no one who has read the account of the siege, and the subsequent treatment of the Jews, will think the description at all exaggerated.

60. And the people are specially threatened with *the diseases of Egypt, which thou wast afraid of*, and this, as said in Chapter IX., implies that the passage was written soon after the people left Egypt, and therefore centuries before any siege or dispersion.

61. And it was to end, as it actually did end, in the destruction of the nation, *until thou be destroyed*.

62. While the Jews that survived were to be left comparatively *few in number*, which was certainly the case, even allowing that the statement of Josephus that 600,000 perished in the siege may be an exaggeration.

63. And these were to be forcibly expelled from the land of Canaan, which they were just about to conquer. And they actually were so expelled by the Romans, partly after this war, and still more so after their rebellion in A.D. 134, when for many centuries scarcely any Jews were allowed to live in their own country, an event probably unique in history.

64. But instead of being taken away to a single nation, as at the Babylonian captivity, they were now to be scattered over the whole world, *among all peoples, from one end of the earth, even unto the other end of the earth*. And how marvellously this has been fulfilled is obvious to everyone. No mention is made of a *king* here, as in ver. 36; so while that suits the Babylonian captivity, this suits the

later dispersion, though in each case there is a reference to their serving other gods, for which it must be admitted there is very little evidence.

65. Then we have the further *sufferings* that the Jews were to undergo in their dispersion. Among these nations they were to find *no ease, nor rest for the sole of their foot*, but were to have *a trembling heart, and failing of eyes, and pining of soul.* And here, again, the event is as strange as the prophecy. Nowhere else shall we find a parallel to it. For centuries the Jews were not only persecuted, but were often expelled from one country to another, so that they found *no rest* anywhere, but were driven from city to city, and from kingdom to kingdom.

66. And their life was to hang in doubt night and day;

67. And they were to be in a continual state of fear and alarm; all of which was completely fulfilled.

68. Lastly, we read, that some of the Jews, instead of being dispersed, were to be *brought to Egypt again with ships*, and to be in bondage there. And this also came true, after the siege, when many of the Jews were sold for slaves, and sent to the mines in Egypt, probably in slave ships.

Everyone must admit that the agreement all through is very remarkable; in fact, the prophecies about the dispersion of the Jews—and we have only examined a single instance in detail—are even more striking than those about the desolation of Assyria and Babylonia, or the degradation of Egypt. And to fully realise their importance, let us suppose that anyone *now* were to foretell the future of three great nations, saying that one was to be utterly destroyed, and the land desolated; another to sink to be a base kingdom; and the third to be conquered and its inhabitants forcibly expelled, and scattered over the whole world. What chance would there be of any one of the prophecies (leave alone all three) coming true, and *remaining true for two thousand years?* Yet this would be but a similar case.

What conclusion, then, must be drawn from all these prophecies, so clear in their general meaning, so distinctive in their character, so minute in many of their details, so unlikely at the time they were written, and yet one and all so exactly fulfilled? There appear to be only three alternatives. Either they must have been random *guesses*, which certainly seems incredible. Or else they must have been due to deep *foresight* on the part of the writers, which seems equally so; for the writers had had no experience of the permanent desolation of great empires like Assyria and Babylonia, while as to the fate of Egypt and the Jews themselves, history afforded no parallel. Or else, lastly, the writers must have had *revealed* to them what the future of these nations would be; in which case, and in which case alone, all is plain.

## (*B.*) SPECIAL PROPHECIES.

We pass on now to the Special Prophecies. These are found all through the Old Testament, the following being eight of the most important.

The fact that David's throne should always be held by his descendants, *i.e.*, till the captivity, about 450 years;[139] and its fulfilment is specially remarkable when contrasted with the rival kingdom of Samaria, where the dynasty changed eight or nine times in 250 years.

[139] 2 Sam. 7. 12-16; 1 Kings 9. 4, 5.

The division of the kingdom into ten and two tribes, evidently announced at the time, since Jeroboam had to go away in consequence, and apparently the reason why the rebels were not attacked.[140]

[140] 1 Kings 11. 31, 40; 12. 24.

The destruction, rebuilding, and final destruction of the Temple; the first of these prophecies being made so publicly that it caused quite a commotion, and nearly cost the prophet his life.[141]

[141] Jer. 26. 8-16; Isa. 44. 28; Dan. 9. 26.

The destruction of the altar at Bethel, which was set up as a rival to that at Jerusalem; publicly announced some centuries before, including the name of the destroyer.[142]

[142] 1 Kings 13. 2; 2 Kings 23. 15, 16.

The destruction of Israel by the Assyrians.[143]

[143] 1 Kings 14. 15; Isa. 8. 4.

The destruction of Jerusalem by the Babylonians.[144]

[144] 2 Kings 20. 17.

The captivity of the Jews, including its duration of seventy years, their most unlikely restoration, and the name of the restorer.[145]

[145] Jer. 29. 10; Isa. 44. 28.

The wars between Syria and Egypt.[146]

[146] Dan. 11.

We will examine a single instance in detail, and select that referring to the *destruction of Jerusalem* by the Babylonians, as this is connected with one of the miracles mentioned in the last chapter, *the shadow on the dial*. Now, it will be remembered that, on one occasion, the Jewish King Hezekiah was seriously ill, and on being told of his unexpected recovery, he naturally asked for a *sign*. And then in accordance with his demand the shadow on his dial went back ten *steps*.[147]

[147] 2 Kings 20. 8-11 (margin, R.V.); Isa. 38. 8.

This *dial* was evidently a flight of steps, with some object on the top, perhaps an obelisk, which threw a shadow on a gradually increasing number of these as the sun set. And a sudden vibration of the ground, due perhaps to an earthquake, and causing the obelisk to slope to one side, would quite account for the shadow *going backward*, and leaving some of the steps which it had covered. And the narrative certainly implies that the effect was sudden, and apparently limited to this one dial.

It seems, however, to have attracted considerable attention; since messengers came from Babylon to *enquire about it*, and to congratulate the King on his recovery.[148] And if the sloping obelisk, and perhaps broken steps, were still visible, this would be much more natural than if there was nothing left for them to see. Though in any case, as they called it the wonder that was done *in the land*, it evidently was not noticed elsewhere, and must have been due to some local cause. And we may ask, how could any writer have asserted all this, even a century afterwards, if no such sign had occurred?

[148] 2 Chron. 32. 24, 31.

We are then told that Hezekiah showed these messengers all his treasures, which leads up to the *prophecy* that the treasures should be carried away and Jerusalem destroyed by these very Babylonians. This is introduced in the most natural way possible, as a rebuke to the king for his proud display; and it is difficult to consider it a later insertion. Yet the event could not have been humanly foreseen. For Babylon was then but a comparatively small and friendly nation, shortly to be absorbed into Assyria (in B.C. 689), and only when it regained its independence nearly a century later did it become strong enough to cause any fear to the Jews.

We need not discuss the other prophecies at length, since that they all refer to the events in question is generally admitted. Indeed, in some cases, owing to the mention of names and details, it can scarcely be denied. Therefore those who disbelieve in prophecy have no alternative but to say that they were all written *after the event*.

At this lapse of time it is difficult to prove or disprove such a statement. But it must be remembered that to say that any apparent prophecies were written after the event is not merely to destroy their superhuman character, and bring them down to the level of ordinary writings, but far below it. For ordinary writings do not contain wilful falsehoods, yet every pretended prophecy written after the event cannot possibly be regarded in any other light. The choice then lies between *real prophecies* and *wilful forgeries*. There is no other alternative. And bearing this in mind, we must ask, is it likely that men of such high moral character as the Jewish prophets would have been guilty of such gross imposture? Is it likely that, if guilty of it, they would have been able to pass it off successfully on the whole nation? And is it likely that they would have had any sufficient motive to induce them to make the attempt?

Moreover, many of these prophecies are stated to have been made *in public*, and to have been talked about, and well known long before their fulfilment. And it is hard to see how this could have been asserted unless it was the case, or how it could have been the case unless they were superhuman.

It should also be noticed that in Deuteronomy the occurrence of some definite and specified event is given as the *test* of a prophet, and one of the later prophets (Isaiah) appeals to this very test. For he challenges the false prophets to foretell future events, and repeatedly declares that this was the mark of a true prophet.[149] And it is inconceivable that men should thus court defeat by themselves proposing a test which would have shown that they were nothing more than impostors. Yet this would have been the case if all their so-called prophecies had been written after the events.

[149] Deut. 18. 22; Isa. 41. 22; 44. 8; 48. 3-5; see also Deut. 13. 1-3.

### (*C.*) CONCLUSION.

In concluding this chapter, we must notice the *cumulative nature* of the evidence. The prophecies we have referred to, like the miracles in the last chapter, are but specimens, a few out of many which might be given. This is very important, and its bearing on our present argument is naturally twofold.

In the first place, it does not increase, and in some respects rather decreases, the difficulty of believing them to be true, for thirty miracles or prophecies, provided they occur on suitable occasions, are scarcely more difficult to believe than three. And the number recorded in the Old Testament shows that, instead of being mere isolated marvels, they form a complete series. Their object was to instruct the Jews, and through them the rest of the world, in the great truths of Natural Religion, such as the existence of One Supreme God, Who was shown to be *All-Powerful* by the miracles, *All-Wise* by the prophecies, and *All-Good* by His rewarding and punishing men and nations alike for their deeds. And when we thus regard them as confirming a

Revelation, which was for the benefit of the whole human race, they lose a good deal of their improbability. Indeed many who now believe Natural Religion alone, and reject all revelation, would probably never have believed even this, but for the Bible.

On the other hand, the number and variety of these alleged events greatly increases the difficulty of any *other* explanation; for thirty miracles or prophecies are far more difficult to *disbelieve* than three. A successful fraud might take place once, but not often. An imitation miracle might be practised once, but not often. Spurious prophecies might be mistaken for genuine once, but not often. Yet, if none of these events are true, such frauds and such deceptions must have been practised, and practised successfully, over and over again. In fact, the Old Testament must be a collection of the most dishonest books ever written, for it is full of miracles and prophecies from beginning to end; and it is hard to exaggerate the immense *moral* difficulty which this involves.

Many of the Jewish prophets, as before said, teach the highest moral virtues; and the Jewish religion, especially in its later days, is admittedly of high moral character. It seems, then, to be almost incredible that its sacred writings

should be merely a collection of spurious prophecies uttered after the event, and false miracles which never occurred. We therefore decide in this chapter that the *history* of the Jewish religion *was confirmed by prophecies*.

# CHAPTER XII.
## THAT THE JEWISH RELIGION IS PROBABLY TRUE.

Only two subjects remain to be discussed.

(*A.*) THE EXISTENCE OF ANGELS.

No difficulty here, nor as to their influence.

(*B.*) THE CHARACTER OF GOD.

The Jewish idea of God often thought to be defective.

(1.) Its partiality; but any revelation must be more or less partial.

(2.) Its human element; we must, however, use analogies of some kind when speaking of God, and human analogies are the least inappropriate.

(3.) Its moral defects; since God is shown as approving of wicked men, ordering wicked deeds, and sanctioning wicked customs; but these difficulties are not so great as they seem.

(4.) Its general excellence. On the other hand, the Jews firmly believed in Monotheism, and had the highest mental and moral conception of God; so that their God was the true God, the God of Natural Religion.

(*C.*) CONCLUSION.

Four further arguments; the Jewish Religion is probably true.

We have been considering in the previous chapters several strong arguments in favour of the Jewish Religion; and before concluding we must of course notice *any* adverse arguments which we have not already dealt with. The only two of any importance refer to the Existence of Angels, and the Character ascribed to God; so we will consider these first, and then conclude with some general remarks.

### (*A.*) THE EXISTENCE OF ANGELS.

Now the Old Testament always takes for granted the existence and influence of angels, yet at the present day this is often thought to be a difficulty. But as to the mere *existence* of angels, there is no difficulty whatever. For the whole analogy of nature would teach us that since there are numerous beings in the scale of life below man, so there would be some beings above man—that is to say, between him and the Supreme Being. And this is rendered still more probable when we reflect on the small intervals there are in the descending scale, and the immense interval there would be in the ascending scale if man were the next highest being in the universe to God.

And that these higher beings should be entirely *spiritual*, *i.e.*, without material bodies, and therefore beyond scientific discovery, is not improbable. Indeed, considering that man's superiority to lower beings lies in this very fact of his having a partly spiritual nature, the idea that higher beings may be entirely spiritual is even probable. And though it is difficult for us to imagine how angels can see, or hear without a material body, it is really no more difficult than imagining how we can do it with a body. Take for instance the case of seeing. Neither the eye nor the brain sees, they are mere collections of molecules of matter, and how can a molecule see anything? It is the *man himself*, the *personal being*, who in some mysterious way sees by means of both eyes and brain; and for all we know he might see just as well without them. And the same applies in other cases.

Then that angels should have as great, if not greater, intellectual and moral faculties than man seems certain; otherwise they would not be higher beings at all. And this necessitates their having *free will*, with the option of choosing good or evil. And that, like men, some should choose one, and some the other, seems equally probable. Hence the *existence* of both good and evil angels presents no difficulty. And that the good angels should have a leader, or captain (called in the Old Testament, Michael), and that the evil angels should have one too (called Satan) is only what we should expect.

Next, as to their *influence*. Now that good angels should wish to influence men for good, and might occasionally be employed by God for that purpose, scarcely seems improbable. While, on the other hand, that evil angels should wish to act, as evil men act, in tempting others to do wrong, is again only what we should expect. And that God should allow them to do so is no harder to believe than that He should allow evil men to do the same.

It may still be objected however that we have no actual *evidence* as to the influence of angels at the present day. But this is at least doubtful. For what evidence could we expect to have? We could not expect to have any physical sensation, or anything capable of scientific investigation, for angels, if they exist at all, are spiritual beings. If, then, they were to influence man, say, by tempting him to do evil, all we could know would be the sudden presence of some evil thought in our minds, without, as far as we could judge, any previous cause for it. And who will assert that this is an unknown experience? Yet if it is known, does it not constitute all the proof we could expect of the action of an evil spirit? And of course the same applies to good spirits. There is thus no difficulty as to the existence, and influence of angels.

## (*B.*) THE CHARACTER OF GOD.

We pass on now to the Character ascribed to God in the Old Testament, first considering its difficulties, under the three heads of its *partiality*, its *human element*, and its *moral defects*; and then what can be said on the other side as to its *general excellence*.

### (1.) Its partiality.

The objection here is that God is the just God of all mankind, and it is therefore incredible that He should have selected a single nation like the Jews to be His special favourites, more particularly as His alleged attempt to make them a holy people proved such a hopeless failure. While it is further urged that the very fact of the Jews believing Jehovah to be their special God shows that they regarded Him as a mere national God, bearing the same relation to themselves as the gods of other nations did to them.

But, as said in Chapter VI., any revelation implies a certain *partiality* to the men or nation to whom it is given; though it is not on that account incredible. And there is certainly no reason why the Jews should not have been the nation chosen, and some slight reason why they should; for their ancestor Abraham was not selected without a cause. He did, partly at least, deserve it, since, judging by the only accounts we have, he showed the most perfect obedience to God in his willingness to sacrifice Isaac. It must also be remembered that God's so-called partiality to the Jews did not imply any indulgence to them in the sense of overlooking their faults. On the contrary, He is represented all along as blaming and punishing them, just as much as other nations, for their sins.

Next, as to God's purpose in regard to the Jews having been a *failure*. This is only partly true. No doubt they were, on the whole, a sinful nation; but they were not worse than, or even so bad as, the nations around them; it was only the fact of their being the chosen race that made their sins so serious. They had free will, just as men have now; and if they chose to misuse their freedom and act wrong, that was not God's fault.

Moreover, the Jewish nation was not selected merely for its own sake, but for the sake of all mankind; as is expressly stated at the very commencement, '*In thee shall all the families of the earth be blessed.*'[150] Thus God did not select the Jews, and reject other nations; but He selected the Jews in order that through them He might bless other nations. The religious welfare of the whole world was God's purpose from the beginning; and the Jews were merely the means chosen for bringing it about. And to a great extent the purpose has been fulfilled; for however sinful the nation may have been, they preserved and handed on God's revelation, and the Old Testament remains, and will always remain, as a permanent and priceless treasure of religion.

[150] Gen. 12. 3.

The last part of the objection may be dismissed at once. For if the Jews regarded Jehovah as their special God, it was merely because He had specially *selected* them to be His people. He must therefore have had a power of choice, and might, if He pleased, have selected some other nation, so He could not have been a mere national God, but the God of all nations with power to select among them. And this is distinctly asserted by many of the writers.[151]

[151] *E.g.*, Exod. 19. 5; Deut. 32. 8; 2 Chron. 20. 6; Isa. 37. 16.

We conclude, then, that God's so-called partiality to the Jews does not, when carefully considered, form a great difficulty. To put it shortly, if a revelation is given at all, some individuals must be selected to receive it; if it is given gradually (and God's methods in nature are always those of gradual development) these men would probably belong to a single nation; and if one nation had to be selected, there is no reason why the Jews should not have been the one chosen. While, if they were selected for the purpose of handing on God's revelation to the world at large, the purpose has been completely successful.

**(2.) Its human element.**

The next difficulty, is that the Jewish idea of God was thoroughly *human*, the Deity being represented as a great *Man*, with human form, feelings, attributes, and imperfections. Thus He has hands and arms, eyes and ears; He is at times glad or sorry, angry or jealous; He moves about from place to place; and sometimes repents of what He has done, thus showing, it is urged, a want of foresight, on His part. And all this is plainly inconsistent with the character of the immaterial, omnipresent, omniscient God of Nature. The answer to this objection is twofold.

In the first place, we must of necessity use analogies of some kind when speaking of God, and *human* analogies are not only the easiest to understand, but are also the least inappropriate, since, as we have shown, man resembles God in that he is a personal and moral being. Therefore likening God to man is not so degrading as likening Him to mere natural forces. Such expressions, then, must always be considered as descriptions drawn from human analogies, which must not be pressed literally.

While, secondly, it is plain that the Jewish writers themselves so understood them, for they elsewhere describe the Deity in the most exalted language, as will be shown later on. And this is strongly confirmed by the remarkable fact that the Jews, unlike other ancient nations, had no material idol or representation of their God. Inside both the tabernacle and the temple there was the holy of holies with the mercy seat, but no one sat on it. An empty throne was all that the shrine contained. Their Jehovah was essentially an invisible God, who could not be represented by any human or other form; and this alone seems a sufficient answer to the present objection.

## (3.) Its moral defects.

Lastly as to the supposed moral defects in God's Character. The three most important are that God is frequently represented as approving of wicked men, as ordering wicked deeds, and even in His own laws as sanctioning wicked customs. We will consider these points in turn.

And first as to God's *approving of wicked men*; that is, of men who committed the greatest crimes, such as Jacob and David. This is easily answered, since approving of a man does not mean approving of *everything* he does. The case of David affords a convincing example of this; for though he is represented as a man after God's own heart, yet we are told that God was so extremely displeased with one of his acts that He punished him for it severely, in causing his child to die. In the same way no one supposes that God approved of Jacob because of his treachery, but in spite of it; and even in his treachery, he was only carrying out (and with apparent reluctance) the orders of his mother.[152] Moreover, in estimating a man's character, his education and surroundings have always to be taken into account. And if the conduct of one man living in an immoral age is far better than that of his contemporaries, he may be worthy of praise, though similar conduct at the present day might not deserve it.

[152] Gen. 27. 8-13.

And if it be asked what there was in the character of these men, and many others, to counterbalance their obvious crimes, the answer is plain; it was their intense belief in the spiritual world. The existence of One Supreme God, and their personal responsibility to Him, were realities to them all through life; so, in spite of many faults, they still deserved to be praised.

Next as to God's *ordering wicked deeds*. In all cases of this kind it is important to distinguish between a man's personal acts, and his official ones. At the present day the judge who condemns a criminal, and the executioner who hangs him are not looked upon as murderers. And the same principle applies universally. Now in the Old Testament the Jews are represented as living under the immediate rule of God. Therefore when a man, or body of men, had to be punished for their crimes, He commanded some prophet or king, or perhaps the whole people, to carry out the sentence. And of course, if they failed to do so they were blamed, just as we should blame a hangman at the present day who failed to do his duty. Thus, in the case of *destroying the Canaanites*, which is the instance most often objected to, the people were told, in the plainest terms, that they were only acting as God's ministers, and that if they became as bad as the Canaanites, who were a horribly polluted race, God would have them destroyed as well.[153]

[153] *E.g.*, Lev. 18. 21-28; Deut. 9. 5.

A more serious objection is that God is occasionally represented as if He Himself *caused* men to do wrong, such as His *hardening Pharaoh's heart*.[154] But, as we shall see later on, the Bible often speaks of everything that occurs, whether good or evil, as being, in a certain sense, God's doing. And since the writer asserts more than once that Pharaoh hardened his own heart, there can be little doubt that he intended the two expressions to mean the same. Indeed the whole narrative represents Pharaoh as extremely obstinate in the matter, refusing to listen even to his own people.[155]

[154] *E.g.*, Exod. 14. 4.

[155] Exod. 8. 15, 32; 9. 34; 10. 3, 7.

Thirdly, as to God's *sanctioning wicked customs*. The most important is that of *human sacrifice*; but it is very doubtful whether the passages relied on do sanction this custom;[156] since it is clearly laid down elsewhere that the firstborn of *men* are never to be sacrificed, but are always to be redeemed.[157] Moreover human sacrifices among other nations are strongly condemned, in one passage Jehovah expressly saying that they were not to be offered to Him.[158] It is, however, further urged that we have two actual instances of such sacrifices in regard to *Isaac* and *Jephthah*.[159] But Jephthah had evidently no idea when he made his vow that it would involve the sacrifice of his daughter; and there is nothing to show that it was in any way acceptable to God.

[156] Exod. 22. 29, 30; Lev. 27. 28, 29.

[157] Exod. 13. 13; 34. 20; Num. 18. 15.

[158] Deut. 12. 31.

[159] Gen. 22; Judg. 11. 39.

In the case of *Isaac* we have the one instance in which God did order a human sacrifice; but then He specially intervened to prevent the order from being carried out. And the whole affair, the command and the counter-command, must of course be taken together. It was required to test Abraham's faith to the utmost, therefore as he most valued his son, he was told to offer him. And since children were then universally regarded as property, and at the absolute disposal of their parents, human sacrifices being by no means uncommon, the command, however distressing to his heart, would have formed no difficulty to his conscience. But when his faith was found equal to the trial, God intervened, as He had of course intended doing all along, to prevent Isaac from being actually slain.

With regard to the other practices, such as *slavery*, and *polygamy*, it is undisputed that they were recognised by the Jewish laws; but none of them were *instituted* by these laws. The Pentateuch neither commands them, nor commends them; it merely mentions them, and, as a rule, to guard against their abuse. Take, for instance, the case of slavery. The custom was, and had been for ages, universal. All that the laws did was to recognise its existence and to provide certain safeguards; making kidnapping, for instance, a capital offence, and in some cases ordering the release of slaves every seventh year.[160]

[160] Exod. 21. 2, 16; Lev. 25. 41.

On the other hand, many *worse customs* existed at the time which the Jewish laws did absolutely forbid;[161] and they also introduced a code of morals, summed up in the Decalogue, of such permanent value that it has been practically accepted by the civilised world. While the highest of all virtues, that of doing good to one's *enemies*, which was scarcely known among other nations, is positively enjoined in the Pentateuch.[162]

[161] *E.g.*, Lev. 18-20.

[162] Exod. 23. 4-5.

**(4.) Its general excellence.**

Having now discussed at some length the alleged difficulties in God's character, it is only fair to see what can be said on the other side. And much indeed may be said; for the Jewish conception of the Deity, when considered as a whole, and apart from these special difficulties, was one of the noblest ever formed by man.

To begin with, the Jews firmly believed in *Monotheism*, or the existence of One Supreme God. This was the essence of their religion. It is stamped on the first page of Genesis; it is implied in the Decalogue; it occurs all through the historical books; and it is emphasised in the Psalms and Prophets; in fact they were never without it. And in this respect the Jews stood alone among the surrounding nations. Some others, it is true, believed in a god who was more or less Supreme; but they always associated with him a number of lesser deities which really turned their religion into Polytheism. With the Jews it was not so. Their Jehovah had neither rivals nor assistants. There were no inferior gods, still less goddesses. He was the one and only God; and as for the so-called gods of other nations, they either did not believe in their existence, or thought them utterly contemptible, and even ridiculed the idea of their having the slightest power.[163] And it may be added, this is a subject on which the Jews have become the teachers of the world, for both the great monotheistic Religions of the present day, Christianity and Mohammedanism, have been derived from them.

[163] Deut. 4. 39; 1 Kings 18. 27; 2 Kings 19. 15-18; Ps. 115. 4-8.

Moreover, the great problem of the *Existence of Evil* never led the Jews, as it did some other nations, into Dualism, or the belief in an independent Evil Power. Difficult as the problem was, the Jews never hesitated in their belief that there was but One Supreme God, and that everything that existed, whether good or evil, existed by His permission, and was in a certain sense His doing.[164] And they gave to Him the very highest attributes.

[164] Isa. 45. 7; Prov. 16. 4; Amos 3. 6.

They described Him as *Omnipotent*; the Creator, Preserver, and Possessor of all things, the Cause of all nature, the Sustainer of all life, Almighty in power, and for Whom nothing is too hard.[165]

[165] Gen. 1. 1; Neh. 9. 6; Gen. 14. 22; Amos 5. 8; Job 12. 10; 1 Chron. 29. 11; Jer. 32. 17.

They described Him as *Omniscient*; infinite in understanding, wonderful in counsel, perfect in knowledge, declaring the end from the beginning, knowing and foreknowing even the thoughts of men.[166]

[166] Ps. 147. 5; Isa. 28. 29; Job 37. 16; Isa. 46. 10; Ezek. 11. 5. Ps. 139. 2.

They described Him as *Omnipresent*; filling Heaven and earth, though contained by neither, existing everywhere, and from Whom escape is impossible.[167]

[167] Jer. 23. 24; 1 Kings 8. 27; Prov. 15. 3; Ps. 139. 7.

They described Him as *Eternal*; the Eternal God, the Everlasting God, God from everlasting to everlasting, Whose years are unsearchable, the First and the Last.[168]

[168] Deut. 33. 27; Gen. 21. 33; Ps. 90. 2; Job 36. 26; Isa. 48. 12.

They described Him as *Unchangeable*; the same at all times, ruling nature by fixed laws, and with Whom a change of purpose is impossible.[169]

[169] Mal. 3. 6; Ps. 148. 6; Num. 23. 19.

And lastly, they described Him as in His true nature *Unknowable*; a hidden God, far above human understanding.[170] This will be enough to show the lofty *mental* conception which the Jews formed of the Deity.

[170] Isa. 45. 15; Job 11. 7.

Now for their *moral* conception. They believed their God to be not only infinite in power and wisdom, but, what is more remarkable, they ascribed to Him the highest moral character. He was not only a *beneficent* God, Whose blessings were unnumbered, but He was also a *righteous* God. His very Name was Holy, and His hatred of evil is emphasised all through to such an extent that at times it forms a difficulty, as in the case of the Canaanites. Thus the *goodness* they ascribed to God was a combination of beneficence and righteousness very similar to what we discussed in Chapter V.

Moreover, in this respect the God of the Jews was a striking contrast to the gods of other nations. We have only to compare Jehovah with Moloch and Baal, or with the Egyptian gods, Ptah and Ra, or with the classical gods, Jupiter and Saturn, and the superiority of the Jewish conception of the Deity is beyond dispute. In particular it may be mentioned that among other nations, even the god they worshipped as Supreme always had a *female companion*. Thus we have Baal and Astaroth, Osiris and Isis, Jupiter and Juno, and many others. It is needless to point out how easily such an idea led to immorality being mixed up with religion, a vice from which the Jews were absolutely free. Indeed, few things are more remarkable, even with this remarkable people, than that in the innermost shrine of their temple, in the ark just below the mercy-seat, there was a code of *moral laws*, the *Ten Commandments*. This was the very centre of their religion, their greatest treasure; and they believed them to have been written by God Himself.

Nor can it be said that this high conception of the Deity was confined to the later period of Jewish history. For the above texts have been purposely selected from all through the Old Testament, and even Abraham, the remote ancestor of the Jews, seems to have looked upon it as self-evident that Jehovah, the *Judge of all the earth*, should *do right*.[171] No wonder, then, believing in such a perfect Being as this, the Jews, in contrast with most other nations, thought that their first and great commandment was to *love* God rather than to *fear* Him, that they were each individually responsible to Him for their conduct, and that every sin was a sin against God, Who was a Searcher of hearts, and the impartial Judge of all men.[172] So much, then, for the Jewish conception of the Deity when considered as a whole and apart from special difficulties.

[171] Gen. 18. 25.

[172] Deut. 6. 5; Eccles. 12. 14; Gen. 39. 9; 1 Chron. 28. 9; Job 34. 19.

And from this it follows that the Jewish God, Jehovah, was the true God, the God of Natural Religion, the Being Who is All-Powerful, All-Wise, and

All-Good. Yet strange to say the Jews were not a more advanced nation than those around them. On the contrary, in the arts both of peace and war they were vastly inferior to the great nations of antiquity, but in their conception of the Deity they were vastly superior; or, as it has been otherwise expressed, they were men in religion, though children in everything else. And this appears to many to be a strong argument in favour of their religion. For unless it had been revealed to them, it is not likely that the Jews alone among ancient nations would have had such a true conception of the Deity. And unless they were in some special sense God's people, it is not likely that they alone would have worshipped Him.

### (*C.*) CONCLUSION.

Before concluding this chapter, we must notice four arguments of a more general character; all of which are undisputed, and all of which are distinctly in favour of the Jewish Religion. The first is that the Jews are all descended from *one man*, Abraham. They have always maintained this themselves, and there seems no reason to doubt it. Yet it is very remarkable. There are now about *sixteen hundred* million persons in the world, and if there were at the time of Abraham (say) *one* million men (*i.e.*, males), each of these would, on an average, have 1,600 descendants now.[173] But the Jews now number, not 1,600, but over 12,000,000. This extraordinary posterity would be strange in any case, but is doubly so, considering that it was foretold. It was part of the great promise made to Abraham, for his great faith, that his seed should be as *the stars of heaven*, and as *the sand which is upon the sea-shore* for multitude.[174]

[173] *I.e.*, descendants in the male line; descendants through daughters are of course not counted.

[174] Gen. 22. 17.

The second is that the Jews are anyhow *a unique nation*. For centuries, though scattered throughout the world, they have been held together by their religion. And according to the Bible, their religion was given them for this very purpose, it was to make them a *peculiar people*, unlike everyone else.[175] If then it was, as far as it went, the true religion, revealed by God, the fact is explicable; but if it was nothing better than other ancient and false religions, it is hopelessly inexplicable.

[175] Deut. 14. 2; 26. 18.

The third is that the early history of the Jews, either real or supposed, has exerted a greater and more beneficial influence on the world for the last thousand years, than that of all the great nations of antiquity put together. Millions of men have been helped to resist sin by the Psalms of David, and the stories of Elijah, Daniel, etc., over whom the histories of Egypt and Assyria, Greece, and Rome, have had no influence whatever. And the *effect* of the Religion being thus unique, makes it probable that its *cause* was unique also; in other words, that it was Divinely revealed.

The fourth is that the Jews themselves always prophesied that their God, Jehovah, would one day be universally acknowledged.[176] And (however strange we may think it) this has actually been the case; and the God of this small and insignificant tribe—*the God of Israel*—is now worshipped by millions and millions of men (Christians) of every race, language, and country, throughout the civilised world. These are facts that need explanation, and the Truth of the Jewish Religion seems alone able to explain them.

[176] *E.g.*, Ps. 22. 27; 86. 9; Isa. 11. 9; Zeph. 2. 11.

In conclusion, we will just sum up the arguments in these chapters. We have shown that there are strong reasons for thinking that the account of the *Creation* was Divinely revealed; that the *origin* of the Jewish religion was confirmed by miracles; and that its *history* was confirmed both by miracles and prophecies. And it should be noticed, each of these arguments is independent of the others. So the evidence is all cumulative and far more than sufficient to outweigh the improbability of the religion, due to its apparent *partiality*, which is the most important argument on the opposite side. Moreover, we know so little as to why man was created, or what future, God intended for him, that it is not easy to say whether the religion is really so improbable after all. On the other hand, the evidence in its favour is plain, direct, and unmistakable. And we therefore decide that the *Jewish Religion is probably true.*

# PART III.
## THE CHRISTIAN RELIGION.

| CHAP. | XIII. | THAT THE CHRISTIAN RELIGION IS CREDIBLE. |
|---|---|---|
| " | XIV. | THAT THE FOUR GOSPELS ARE GENUINE FROM EXTERNAL TESTIMONY. |
| " | XV. | THAT THE GOSPELS ARE GENUINE FROM INTERNAL EVIDENCE. |
| " | XVI. | THAT THE GOSPELS ARE GENUINE FROM THE EVIDENCE OF THE ACTS. |
| " | XVII. | THAT THE RESURRECTION OF CHRIST IS PROBABLY TRUE. |
| " | XVIII. | THAT THE FAILURE OF OTHER EXPLANATIONS INCREASES THIS PROBABILITY. |
| " | XIX. | THAT THE OTHER NEW TESTAMENT MIRACLES ARE PROBABLY TRUE. |
| " | XX. | THAT THE JEWISH PROPHECIES CONFIRM THE TRUTH OF CHRISTIANITY. |
| " | XXI. | THAT THE CHARACTER OF CHRIST CONFIRMS THE TRUTH OF CHRISTIANITY. |
| " | XXII. | THAT THE HISTORY OF CHRISTIANITY CONFIRMS ITS TRUTH. |
| " | XXIII. | THAT ON THE WHOLE THE OTHER EVIDENCE SUPPORTS THIS CONCLUSION. |
| " | XXIV. | THAT THE THREE CREEDS ARE DEDUCIBLE FROM THE NEW TESTAMENT. |
| " | XXV. | THAT THE TRUTH OF THE CHRISTIAN RELIGION IS EXTREMELY PROBABLE. |

# CHAPTER XIII.
## THAT THE CHRISTIAN RELIGION IS CREDIBLE.

By the Christian Religion is meant the Three Creeds, its four great doctrines.

(*A.*) THE TRINITY.

(1.) Its meaning; Three Persons in One Nature.

(2.) Its credibility; this must be admitted.

(3.) Its probability more likely than simple Theism.

(*B.*) THE INCARNATION.

(1.) Its difficulties; not insuperable.

(2.) Its motive; God, it is said, loves man, and wishes man to love Him, not improbable for several reasons.

(3.) Its historical position.

(*C.*) THE ATONEMENT.

The common objections do not apply because of the *willingness* of the Victim.

(1.) As to the Victim; it does away with the injustice.

(2.) As to the Judge; it appeals to His mercy not justice.

(3.) As to the sinner; it has no bad influence.

(*D.*) THE RESURRECTION.

(1.) Christ's Resurrection; not incredible, for we have no experience to judge by.

(2.) Man's resurrection; not incredible, for the same body need not involve the same molecules.

(*E.*) CONCLUSION.

Three considerations which show that the Christian Religion, though improbable, is certainly not incredible.

We pass on now to the Christian Religion, by which we mean the facts and doctrines contained in the *Three Creeds*, commonly, though perhaps incorrectly, called the Apostles', the Nicene, and the Athanasian. And, as these doctrines are of such vast importance, and of so wonderful a character, we must first consider whether they are *credible*. Is it conceivable that such doctrines should be true, no matter what evidence they may have in their favour? In this chapter, therefore, we shall deal chiefly with the difficulties of Christianity. Now its four great and characteristic doctrines are those of the

Trinity, the Incarnation, the Atonement, and the Resurrection. We will examine each in turn, and then conclude with a few general remarks.

## (A.) THE TRINITY.

To begin with, the Christian religion differs from all others in its idea of the nature of God. According to Christianity, the Deity exists in some mysterious manner as a *Trinity of Persons* in a *Unity of Nature*; so we will first consider the meaning of this doctrine, then its credibility, and lastly its probability. It is not, as some people suppose, a kind of intellectual puzzle, but a statement which, whether true or false, is fairly intelligible, provided, of course, due attention is given to the meaning of the words employed.

### (1.) Its meaning.

In the first place, we must carefully distinguish between *Person* and *Substance*; this is the key to the whole question. The former has been already considered in [Chapters III.](#) and [IV.](#), though it must be remembered that this term, like all others, when applied to God, cannot mean exactly the same as it does when applied to man. All we can say is that, on the whole, it seems the least inappropriate word. The latter is a little misleading, since it is not the modern English word *substance*, but a Latin translation of a Greek word, which would be better rendered by *nature* or *essence*.

But though difficult to explain, its meaning is tolerably clear. Take, for instance, though the analogy must not be pressed too far, the case of three men; each is a distinct human *person*, but they all have a common human *nature*. This human nature, which may also be called human substance (in its old sense), humanity, or manhood, has of course no existence apart from the men whose nature it is; it is merely *that* which they each possess in common, and the possession of which makes each of them a man. And hence, any attribute belonging to human nature would belong to each of the three men, so that each would be mortal, each subject to growth, etc. Each would in fact possess the complete human nature, yet together there would not be three human natures, but only one.

Bearing this in mind, let us now turn to the doctrine of the Trinity. This is expressed in vv. 3-6 of the Athanasian Creed as follows:—

3. 'The Catholic Faith is this, that we worship one God in Trinity, and Trinity in Unity.

4. 'Neither confounding the Persons, nor dividing the Substance.

5. 'For there is one Person of the Father, another of the Son, and another of the Holy Ghost.

6. 'But the Godhead of the Father, of the Son, and of the Holy Ghost, is all one, the Glory equal, the Majesty co-eternal.'

Here, it will be noticed, vv. 5 and 6 give the *reasons* for v. 4, so that the Godhead in v. 6 is, as we should have expected, the same as the Divine *Substance* or Nature in v. 4. Thus the meaning is as follows:—

We must worship one God (as to Nature) in Trinity (of Persons) and Trinity (of Persons) in Unity (of Nature); neither confusing the Persons, for each is distinct; nor dividing the Nature, for it is all one.

Thus far there is no intellectual difficulty in the statements of the Creed. We do not mean that there is no difficulty in believing them to be true, or in accurately defining the terms used; but that, as statements, their meaning is quite intelligible.

We now pass on to the following verses which are deductions from this, and show that as each of the three Persons possesses the Divine Nature, all attributes of the Godhead (*i.e.*, of this one Divine Nature) are possessed by each of the three. Each is therefore *eternal*, and yet there is only *one* eternal Nature. But this is expressed in a peculiarly short and abrupt manner. No one, of course, supposes that God is Three *in the same sense* in which He is One, but the Creed does not sufficiently guard against this, perhaps because it never occurred to its author that anyone would think it meant such an obvious absurdity. Moreover, even grammatically the verses are not very clear. For the various terms *uncreate, incomprehensible* (*i.e.*, boundless, or omnipresent), *eternal, almighty, God,* and *Lord* are used as if they were adjectives in the first part of each sentence, and nouns in the latter part.

But we must remember these verses do not stand alone. If they did, they might perhaps be thought unintelligible. But they do not. As just said, they are deductions from the previous statement of the doctrine of the Trinity; and, therefore, they must in all fairness be interpreted so as to agree with that doctrine, not to contradict it. And the previous verses (3-6) show clearly that where *three* are spoken of, it refers to Persons; and where *one* is spoken of, it refers to Substance or Nature.

It must however be admitted that the *names* of these Divine Persons imply some closer union between them than that of merely possessing in common one Divine Nature. For they are not independent names like those of different men or of heathen gods, each of whom might exist separately; but they are all *relative* names, each implying the others. Thus the Father implies the Son, for how can there be a Father, unless there is a Son (or at least a child)? And of course an Eternal Father implies an Eternal Son, so any idea that the Father must have lived first, as in the case of a human father and son, is out of the question. Similarly the Son implies the Father, and the Spirit implies Him whose Spirit He is. And though these names are no doubt very inadequate; they yet show that the three Persons are of the same Nature, which is the important point.

We conclude then that the Doctrine of the Trinity means the existence of three Divine Persons, each possessing in its completeness the one Divine Nature; and closely united together; though in a manner, which is to us unknown.

**(2.) Its credibility.**

Having now discussed the meaning of the Christian doctrine, we have next to consider whether it is credible. It must of course be admitted that the doctrine is very mysterious, and though fairly intelligible as a doctrine, is extremely hard to realise (indeed some might say inconceivable) when we try to picture to ourselves what the doctrine actually means. But we must remember that the nature of God is anyhow almost inconceivable, even as simple Theism. We cannot picture to ourselves a Being Who is omnipresent,—in this room, for instance, as well as on distant stars. Nor can we imagine a Being Who is grieved every time we commit sin, for if so, considering the number of people in the world, He must be grieved many thousands of times *every second*; as well as being glad whenever anyone resists sin, also, let us hope, several thousand times a second. All this may be true, just as the marvels of science—the *ether*, for instance, which is also omnipresent, and has millions of vibrations every second—may be true, but our minds are quite unable to realise any of them.

Thus, as said in Chapter III., though we have ample means of knowing what God is *in His relation to us* as our Creator and Judge, yet as to His real nature we know next to nothing. Nor is this surprising when we remember that the only being who in any way resembles God is *man*; and man's nature, notwithstanding all our opportunities of studying it, still remains a mystery.

Now Christianity does attempt (in its doctrine of the Trinity) to state what God is *in Himself*, and without any reference to ourselves, or to nature; and that this should be to a great extent inconceivable to our minds seems inevitable. For the nature of God must be beyond human understanding, just as the nature of a man is beyond the understanding of animals; though they may realise what he is *to them*, in his power or his kindness. And for all we know, Trinity in Unity, like omnipresence, may be one of the unique attributes of God, which cannot be understood (because it cannot be shared) by anyone else. Therefore the mysteriousness of the Christian doctrine is no reason for thinking it incredible.

Nor is it inconsistent with Natural Religion, for though this shows the *Unity* of God, it is only a unity of *outward action*. It does not, and cannot tell us what this one God is *in Himself*, whether, for instance, He exists as one or more Persons. In the same way (if we may without irreverence take a homely illustration) a number of letters might be so extremely alike as to show that they were all written by one man. But this would not tell us what the man was *in himself*, whether, for instance, he had a free will, as well as a body and mind; or how these were related to one another. Hence Natural Religion can in no way conflict with Christianity.

**(3.) Its probability.**

But we may go further than this, and say that the Christian doctrine of *Three Divine Persons* is (when carefully considered) *less* difficult to believe than the Unitarian doctrine of only *One*. For this latter leads to the conclusion, either that God must have been a solitary God dwelling alone from all eternity, before the creation of the world; or else that the world itself (or some part of it) must have been eternal, and have formed a kind of companion. And each of these theories has great difficulties. Take for instance the attributes of *Power* and *Wisdom*, both of which, as we have seen, must of necessity belong to God. How could a solitary God dwelling alone before the Creation of the world have been able to exercise either His Power or His Wisdom? As far as we can judge, His Power could have produced nothing, His Wisdom could have thought of nothing. He would have been a *potential* God only, with all His capacities unrealised. And such a view seems quite incredible.

Yet the only alternative—that the world itself is eternal—though it gets over this difficulty, is still inadequate. For as we have seen God possesses *moral* attributes as well, such as Goodness. And all moral attributes—everything connected with right and wrong—can only be thought of as existing between two *persons*. We cannot be good to an atom of hydrogen, or unjust to a molecule of water. We can it is true be kind to *animals*, but this is simply because they resemble personal beings in having a capacity for pleasure and pain. But moral attributes in their highest perfection can only exist between two persons. Therefore as the eternal God possesses, and must always have possessed, such attributes, it seems to require some other eternal *Person*.

The argument is perhaps a difficult one to follow, but a single example will make it plain. Take the attribute of *love*. This requires at least two persons— one to love, the other to be loved. Therefore if love has always been one of God's attributes, there must always have been some *other* person to be loved. And the idea that God might have been eternally *creating* persons, like men or angels, as objects of His love, though perhaps attractive, is still inadequate. For love in its perfection can only exist between two beings *of the same nature*. A man cannot love his dog, in the same way that he can love his son. In short, *personality*, involving as it does moral attributes like love, implies *fellowship*, or the existence of other and *similar* persons.

Yet, when we think of the meaning of the term God, His omnipresence and omnipotence, it seems impossible that there can be more than one. We must then believe in at least two Eternal and Divine Persons, yet in but one God; and the Christian doctrine of the Trinity in Unity, with all its difficulties, still seems the *least* difficult explanation.

But this is not all, for Natural Religion itself leads us to look upon God in *three* distinct ways, which correspond to the three chief arguments for His existence. (Chaps. I., II., and V.) Thus we may think of Him as the Eternal, Self-Existent One, altogether independent of the world—the All-Powerful *First Cause* required to account for it. Or we may think of Him in His relation to the world, as its Maker and Evolver, working everywhere, in everything and through everything,—the All-Wise *Designer* required by nature. Or we may think of Him in His relation to ourselves as a Spirit holding intercourse with our spirits, and telling us what is right—the All-Good *Moral* God required by conscience. And how well this agrees with the Christian doctrine scarcely needs pointing out; the Father the Source of all, the Son by Whom all things were made, and the Spirit bearing witness with our spirits; and yet not three Gods, but one God.

On the whole, then, we decide that the Doctrine of the Trinity is certainly credible and perhaps even probable. For to put it shortly, Nature forces us to believe in a personal God; yet, when we reflect on the subject, the idea of a personal God, Who is only one Person, seems scarcely tenable; since (as said above) personality implies fellowship.

### (*B.*) THE INCARNATION.

We next come to the doctrine of the Incarnation; which however is so clearly stated in the Athanasian Creed, that its meaning is quite plain. God the Son, we are told, the second Person of the Trinity, was pleased to become Man and to be born of the Virgin Mary, so that He is now both *God* and *Man*. He is God (from all eternity) of the Substance or Nature of His Divine Father, and Man (since the Incarnation) of the Substance or Nature of His human Mother. He is thus complete God and complete Man; equal to the Father in regard to His Godhead, for He is of the same Nature; and inferior to the Father, in regard to His Manhood, for human nature must be inferior to the Divine. Moreover, though He possesses these two Natures, they are not changed one into the other, or confused together; but each remains distinct, though both are united in His One Person. This is in brief the doctrine of the Incarnation; and we will first consider its difficulties, then its motive, and lastly its historical position.

## (1.) Its difficulties.

The first of these is that the Incarnation would be a *change* in the existence of God, Who is the changeless One. He, it is urged, is always the same, while an Incarnation would imply that at some particular time and place a momentous change occurred, and for ever afterwards God became different from what He had been for ever before.

This is no doubt a serious difficulty, but it must not be exaggerated. For an Incarnation would not, strictly speaking, involve any change in the Divine Nature itself. God the Son remained completely and entirely God all the time, He was not (as just said) in any way changed into a man, only He united to Himself a human nature as well. And perhaps if we knew more about the nature of God, and also about that of man (who we must remember was made to some extent in God's image, and this perhaps with a view to the Incarnation), we should see that it was just as natural for God to become Man, as it was for God to create man. We have really nothing to argue from. An Incarnation seems improbable, and that is all we can say.

But if it took place at all, there is nothing surprising in this planet being the one chosen for it. Indeed, as far as we know, it is the only one that could be chosen, since it is the only one which contains personal beings in whom God could become incarnate. Of course other planets *may* contain such beings; but as said before (Chapter V.) this is only a conjecture, and in the light of recent investigations not a very probable one. While if they do contain such beings, these may not have sinned, in which case our little world, with its erring inhabitants, would be like the lost sheep in the parable, the only one which the Ruler of the Universe had come to save.

The second difficulty is, that the Incarnation would lead to a *compound Being*, who is both Divine and human at the same time, and this is often thought to be incredible. But here the answer is obvious, and is suggested by the Creed itself. Man himself is a compound being; he is the union of a material body and an immaterial spirit, in a single person. His spirit is in fact *incarnate* in his body. We cannot explain it, but so it is. And the Incarnation in which Christians believe is the union of the Divine Nature and the human nature in a single Person. Both appear equally improbable, and equally inconceivable to our minds, if we try and think out all that they involve; but as the one is actually true, the other is certainly not incredible.

The third and last of these difficulties refers to the miraculous *Virgin-birth*. But if we admit the possibility of an Incarnation, no method of bringing it about can be pronounced incredible. The event, if true, is necessarily unique, and cannot be supposed to come under the ordinary laws of nature. For it was not the birth of a *new* being (as in the case of ordinary men), but an already existing Being entering into new conditions. And we have no experience of this whatever. Indeed, that a child born in the usual way should be the Eternal God, is just as miraculous, and just as far removed from our experience, as if He were born in any other way. While considering that one object of the Incarnation was to promote moral virtues in man, such as purity, the virgin-birth was most suitable, and formed an appropriate beginning for a sinless life.

**(2.) Its motive.**

But we now come to a more important point, for the Incarnation, if true, must have been the most momentous event in the world's history; and can we even imagine a sufficient reason for it? God we may be sure does not act without motives, and what adequate motive can be suggested for the Incarnation? Now the alleged motive, indeed the very foundation of Christianity, is that God *loves* man; and as a natural consequence wishes man to love Him. Is this then incredible, or even improbable? Certainly not, for several reasons.

To begin with, as we have already shown, God is a Personal and Moral Being, Who cares for the welfare of His creatures, more especially for man. And this, allowing for the imperfection of human language, may be described as God's *loving* man, since disinterested love for another cannot be thought an unworthy attribute to ascribe to God. On the other hand, man is also a personal and moral being, able to some extent to love God in return. And to this must be added the fact that man, at least some men, do not seem altogether unworthy of God's love, while we certainly do not know of any other being who is more worthy of it.

Moreover, considering the admitted resemblance between God and man, the analogy of human parents loving their children is not inappropriate. Indeed it is specially suitable, since here also we have a relationship between two personal and moral beings, one of whom is the producer (though not in this case the creator) of the other. And human parents often love their children intensely, and will sometimes even die for them; while, as a rule, the better the parents are the more they love their children, and this in spite of the children having many faults. Is it, then, unlikely that the Creator may love His children also, and that human love may be only a reflection of this—another instance of how man was made in the image of God? The evidence we have may be slight, but it all points the same way.

Now, if it be admitted that God loves man, we have plainly no means of estimating the *extent* of this love. But by comparing the other attributes of God, such as His wisdom and His power, with the similar attributes of man, we should expect God's love to be infinitely greater than any human love; so great indeed that He would be willing to make any sacrifice in order to gain what is the object in all love, that it should be returned. Might not then God's love induce Him to become man, so that He might the more easily win man's love?

And we must remember that man's love, like his will, is *free*. Compulsory love is in the nature of things impossible. A man can only love, what he can if he chooses hate. Therefore God cannot force man to love Him, He can only induce him; and how can He do this better than by an Incarnation? For it would show, as nothing else could show, that God's love is a self-sacrificing love; and this is the highest form of love. Indeed, if it were not so, in other words, if God's love cost Him nothing, it would be *inferior* in this respect to that of many men. But if, on the other hand, God's love involved self-sacrifice;—if it led to Calvary—then it is the highest possible form of love. And then we see that God's attributes are all, so to speak, on the same scale; and His Goodness is as far above any human goodness, as the Power which rules the universe is above any human power; or the Wisdom which designed all nature is above any human wisdom. Hence, if the Incarnation still seems inconceivable, may it not be simply because the love of God, like His other attributes, is so inconceivably greater than anything we can imagine?

Moreover a self-sacrificing love is the form, which is most likely to lead to its being returned. And experience proves that this has actually been the case. The condescending love of Christ in His life, and still more in His death, forms an overpowering motive which, when once realised, has always been irresistible.

But more than this. Not only does the Incarnation afford the strongest possible motive for man to love God, but it *enables* him to do so in a way which nothing else could. Man, it is true, often longs for some means of intercourse, or communion with his Maker, yet this seems impossible. The gulf which separates the Creator from the creature is infinite, and can never be bridged over by man, or even by an angel, or other intermediate being. For a bridge must of necessity touch *both sides*; so if the gulf is to be bridged at all, it can only be by One Who is at the same time both God and Man. Thus the Incarnation brings God, if we may use the expression, within man's reach, so that the latter has no mere abstract and invisible Being to love, but a definite Person, Whose Character he can appreciate, and Whose conduct he can to some extent follow. In short, the Incarnation provides man with a worthy Being for his love and devotion, yet with a Being Whom he can partly at least understand and partly imitate. And he is thus able to become in a still truer sense a *child of God*; or, as it is commonly expressed, God became Man in order that man might become as far as possible, like God.

And this brings us to another aspect of the Incarnation. Christ's life was meant to be an *example* to man, and it is clear that a *perfect* example could only be given by a Being Who is both God and Man. For God alone is above human imitation, and even the best of men have many faults; so that from the nature of the case, Christ, and Christ alone, can provide us with a perfect example, for being Man He is capable of imitation, and being God He is worthy of it.

Now what follows from this? If Christ's life was meant to be an example to man, it was essential that it should be one of *suffering*, or the example would have lost more than half its value. Man does not want to be shown how to live in prosperity, but how to live in adversity, and how to suffer patiently. The desertion of friends, the malice of enemies, and a cruel death are the occasional lot of mankind. They are perhaps the hardest things a man has to bear in this world, and they have often had to be borne by the followers of Christ. Is it incredible, then, that He should have given them an example of the perfect way of doing so; gently rebuking His friends, praying for His murderers, and acting throughout as only a perfect man could act? No doubt such a life and death seem at first sight degrading to the Deity. But strictly speaking, suffering, if borne voluntarily and for the benefit of others, is not degrading; especially if the benefit could not be obtained in any other way.

When we consider all this, it is plain that many reasons can be given for the Incarnation. Of course it may be replied that they are not adequate; but we have no means of knowing whether God would consider them adequate or not. His ideas are not like ours; for what adequate motive can we suggest for His creating man at all? Yet He has done so. And having created him and given him free will, and man having misused his freedom, all of which is admitted, then that God should endeavour to restore man cannot be thought incredible. Indeed it seems almost due to Himself that He should try and prevent His noblest work from being a failure. And if in addition to this God loves man still, in spite of his sins, then some intervention on his account seems almost probable.

### (3.) Its historical position.

It may still be objected that if the above reasons are really sufficient to account for the Incarnation, it ought to have taken place near the commencement of man's history. And no doubt when we contemplate the great antiquity of man, this often seems a difficulty. But we have very little to judge by, and that little does not support the objection. For in nature God seems always to work by the slow and tedious process of evolution, not attaining what He wanted all at once, but by gradual development. Therefore, if He revealed Himself to man, we should expect it to be by the same method. At first it would be indistinctly, as in *Natural Religion*; which dates back to pre-historic times, since the burial customs show a belief in a future life. Then it would be more clearly, as in the *Jewish Religion*; and finally it might be by becoming Man Himself, as in the *Christian Religion*.

According to Christianity, the whole previous history of the world was a preparation for the Incarnation. But only when the preparation was complete, *when the fullness of the time came*, as St. Paul expresses it,[177] did it take place. And it has certainly proved, as we should have expected, an epoch-making event. In all probability the history of the world will always be considered relatively to it in years B.C. and A.D. And very possibly it has a significance far beyond man or even this planet. For we must remember, man is not merely a link in a series of created beings indefinitely improving, but, as shown in Chapter V., he is the *end* of the series, the last stage in evolution, the highest organised being that will ever appear on this planet, or, as far as we know, on any planet.

[177] Gal. 4. 4.

Therefore, man's rank in the universe is not affected by the insignificance of this earth. Where else shall we find a personal being with attributes superior to those of man? Where else indeed shall we find a personal being at all? The only answer Science can give is *nowhere*. But if so, man's position in the universe is one of unique pre-eminence. And it is this inherent greatness of man, as it has been called, which justifies the Incarnation. *He is worthy that Thou should'st do this for him.*

Moreover when we consider God the Son as the Divine Person who is specially *immanent* in nature, and who has been evolving the universe through countless ages from its original matter into higher and higher forms of life, there seems a special fitness in its leading up to such a climax as the Incarnation. For then by becoming Man, He united Himself with matter in its highest and most perfect form. Thus the Incarnation, like the Nebula theory in astronomy, or the process of Evolution, if once accepted, throws a new light on the entire universe; and it has thus a grandeur and impressiveness about it, which to some minds is very attractive. On the whole, then, we decide that the doctrine is certainly not incredible, though it no doubt seems improbable.

## (*C.*) THE ATONEMENT.

We pass on now to the doctrine of the Atonement, which is that Christ's death was in some sense a sacrifice for sin, and thus reconciled (or made 'at-one') God the Father and sinful man. And though not actually stated in the Creeds, it is implied in the words, *Was crucified also for us*, and *Who suffered for our salvation*.

The chief difficulty is of course on moral grounds. The idea of atonement, it is said, or of one man being made to suffer as a substitute for another, and thus appeasing the Deity, was well-nigh universal in early times, and is so still among savage nations. Such a sacrifice, however, is a great injustice to the *victim*; it ascribes an unworthy character to God, as a *Judge*, Who can be satisfied with the punishment of an innocent man in place of the guilty one; and it has a bad influence on the *sinner*, allowing him to sin on with impunity, provided he can find another substitute when needed.

The answer to this difficulty is, that it takes no account of the most important part of the Christian doctrine, which is the *willingness* of the Victim. According to Christianity, Christ was a willing Sacrifice, Who freely laid down His life;[178] while the human sacrifices just alluded to were not willing sacrifices, since the victims had no option in the matter. And, as we shall see, this alters the case completely both in regard to the victim himself, the judge, and the sinner.

[178] *E.g.*, John 10. 18.

### (1.) As to the Victim.

It is plain that his willingness does away with the injustice altogether. There is no injustice in accepting a volunteer for any painful office, provided he thoroughly knows what he is doing, for he need not undertake it unless he likes. If, on the other hand, we deny the voluntary and sacrificial character of Christ's death, and regard Him as merely a good man, then there certainly was injustice—and very great injustice too, that such a noble life should have ended in such a shameful death.

### (2.) As to the Judge.

Next as to the Judge. It will be seen that a willing sacrifice, though it does not satisfy his *justice*, makes a strong appeal to his *mercy*; at least it would do so in human cases. Suppose for instance a judge had before him a criminal who well deserved to be punished, but a good man, perhaps the judge's own son, came forward, and not only interceded for the prisoner, but was so devotedly attached to him as to offer to bear his punishment (pay his fine, for instance), this would certainly influence the judge in his favour. It would show that he was not so hopelessly bad after all. Mercy and justice are thus both facts of human nature; and it is also a fact of human nature, that the voluntary suffering, or willingness to suffer, of a good man for a criminal whom he deeply loves, does incline man to mercy rather than justice.

Now, have we any reason for thinking that God also combines, in their highest forms, these two attributes of mercy and justice? Certainly we have; for, as shown in Chapter V., the goodness of God includes both *beneficence* and *righteousness*; and these general terms, when applied to the case of judging sinners, closely correspond to mercy and justice. God, as we have seen, combines both, and both are required by the Christian doctrine. Mercy alone would have forgiven men without any atonement; justice alone would not have forgiven them at all. But God is both merciful and just, and therefore the idea that voluntary atonement might incline Him to mercy rather than justice does not seem incredible.

And this is precisely the Christian doctrine. The mercy of God the Father is obtained for sinful man by Christ's generous sacrifice of Himself on man's behalf; so that, to put it shortly, *God forgives sins for Christ's sake.* And it should be noticed, the idea of sins being *forgiven* which occurs all through the New Testament, and is alluded to in the Apostles' Creed, shows that Christ's Atonement was not that of a mere substitute, for then no forgiveness would have been necessary. If, for example, I owe a man a sum of money, and a friend pays it for me, I do not ask the man to forgive me the debt; I have no need of any forgiveness. But if, instead of paying it, he merely intercedes for me, then the man may forgive me the debt for my friend's sake.

And in this way, though Christ did not, strictly speaking, bear man's *punishment* (which would have been eternal separation from God), His sufferings and death may yet have procured man's *pardon*; He suffered on our behalf, though not in our stead. And some Atonement was certainly necessary to show God's *hatred for sin*, and to prevent His Character from being misunderstood in this respect. And it probably would have been so, if men had been forgiven without any Atonement, when they might have thought that sin was not such a very serious affair after all.

### (3.) As to the sinner.

Lastly, the willingness of the victim affects the sinner also. For if the changed attitude of the judge is due, not to his justice being satisfied, but to his mercy being appealed to, this is plainly conditional on a *moral change* in the sinner himself. A good man suffering for a criminal would not alter our feelings towards him, if he still chose to remain a criminal. And this exactly agrees with the Christian doctrine, which is that sinners cannot expect to avail themselves of Christ's Atonement if they wilfully continue in sin; so that *repentance* is a necessary condition of forgiveness. Therefore instead of having a bad influence on the sinners themselves; it has precisely the opposite effect.

And what we should thus expect theoretically has been amply confirmed by experience. No one will deny that Christians in all ages have been devotedly attached to the doctrine of the Atonement. They have asserted that it is the cause of all their joy in this world, and all their hope for the next. Yet, so far from having had a bad influence, it has led them to the most noble and self-sacrificing lives. It has saved them from *sin*, and not only the penalties of sin, and this is exactly what was required. The greatness of man's sin, and the misery it causes in the world, are but too evident, apart from Christianity. Man is indeed both the glory and the scandal of the universe—the *glory* in what he was evidently intended to be, and the *scandal* in what, through sin, he actually became. And the Atonement was a 'vast remedy for this vast evil.' And if we admit the *end*, that man had to be redeemed from sin, impressed with the guilt of sin, and helped to resist sin; we cannot deny the appropriateness of the *means*, which, as a matter of fact, has so often brought it about.

This completes a brief examination of the moral difficulties connected with the Atonement; and it is clear that the *willingness* of the Victim makes the whole difference, whether we regard them as referring to the Victim himself, the Judge, or the sinner.

### (*D.*) THE RESURRECTION.

The last great Christian doctrine is that of the Resurrection. According to Christianity, all men are to rise again, with their bodies partly changed and rendered incorruptible; and the Resurrection of Christ's Body was both a pledge of this, and also to some extent an example of what a risen body would be like. He was thus, as the Bible says, the *firstborn* from the dead.[179] Now this word *firstborn* implies, to begin with, that none had been so born before, the cases of Lazarus, etc., being those of *resuscitation* and not *resurrection*; they lived again to die again, and their bodies were unchanged. And it implies, secondly, that others would be so born afterwards, so that our risen bodies will resemble His. The Resurrection of Christ is thus represented not as something altogether exceptional and unique, but rather as the first instance of what will one day be the universal rule. It shows us the last stage in man's long development, what he is intended to become when he is at length perfected. We will therefore consider first Christ's Resurrection, and then man's resurrection.

[179] Col. 1. 18; Rev. 1. 5; 1 Cor. 15. 20; Acts. 26. 23.

### (1.) Christ's Resurrection.

Now according to the Gospels, Christ's Risen Body combined material and immaterial properties in a remarkable manner. Thus He could be touched and eat food, and yet apparently pass through closed doors and vanish at pleasure; and this is often thought to be incredible. But strictly speaking it is not *incredible*; since no material substance (a door or anything else) is *solid*. There are always spaces between the molecules; so that for one such body to pass through another is no more difficult to imagine, than for one regiment to march through another on parade. And if a regiment contained anything like as many men, as there are molecules in a door, it would probably look just as solid.

Moreover Christ's risen Body, though possessing some material properties, is represented to have been *spiritual* as well. And the nearest approach to a spiritual substance of which we have any scientific knowledge is the *ether*, and this also seems to combine material and immaterial properties, being in some respects more like a solid than a gas. Yet it can pass through all material substances; and this certainly prevents us from saying that it is incredible that Christ's spiritual Body should pass through closed doors.

Indeed for all we know, it may be one of the properties of spiritual beings, that they can pass through material substances (just as the X-rays can) and be generally invisible; yet be able, if they wish, to assume some of the properties of matter, such as becoming visible or audible. In fact, unless they were able to do this, it is hard to see how they could manifest themselves at all. And a slight alteration in the waves of light coming from a body would make it visible or not to the human eye. And it is out of the question to say that God—the Omnipotent One—could not produce such a change in a spiritual body. While for such a body to become tangible, or to take food, is not really more wonderful (though it seems so) than for it to become visible or audible; since when once we pass the boundary between the natural and the supernatural everything is mysterious.

It may of course be replied that though all this is not perhaps incredible, it is still most improbable; and no doubt it is. But what then? We have no adequate means of judging, for the fact, if true, is, up to the present, unique. It implies a *new* mode of existence which is neither spiritual nor material, though possessing some of the properties of each, and of which we have no experience whatever. So we are naturally unable to understand it. But assuming the Resurrection of Christ to be otherwise credible, as it certainly is if we admit His Incarnation and Death, we cannot call it incredible, merely because the properties of His risen Body are said to be different from those of ordinary human bodies, and in some respects to resemble those of spirits. It is in fact only what we should expect.

**(2.) Man's Resurrection.**

Next as to man's resurrection. The Christian doctrine of the resurrection of the *body* must not be confused with that of the immortality of the *spirit*, discussed in [Chapter VI.](), which is common to many religions, and is certainly not improbable. But two objections may be made to the resurrection of the body.

The first is that it is *impossible*, since the human body decomposes after death, and its molecules may afterwards form a part of other bodies; so, if all men were to rise again at the same time, those molecules would have to be in two places at once. But the fallacy here is obvious, for the molecules composing a man's body are continually changing during life, and it is probable that every one of them is changed in a few years; yet the identity of the body is not destroyed. This identity depends not on the identity of the molecules, but on their relative position and numbers so that a man's body in this respect is like a whirlpool in a stream, the water composing which is continually changing, though the whirlpool itself remains. Therefore the resurrection need not be a resurrection of *relics*, as it is sometimes called. No doubt in the case of Christ it was so, and perhaps it will be so in the case of some Christians, only it *need* not be so; and this removes at once the apparent impossibility of the doctrine.

Secondly, it may still be objected that the doctrine is extremely *improbable*. And no doubt it seems so. But once more we have no adequate means of judging. Apart from experience, how very unlikely it would be that a seed when buried in the ground should develop into a plant; or that plants and trees, after being apparently dead all through the winter, should blossom again in the spring. Thus everything connected with life is so mysterious that we can decide nothing except by experience. And therefore we cannot say what may, or may not happen in some future state, of which we have no experience whatever. Indeed, if man's spirit is immortal, the fact that it is associated with a body during its life on this earth makes it not unlikely that it will be associated with a body of some kind during its future life. And that this body should be partly spiritual, and so resemble Christ's risen body, is again only what we should expect. Thus, on the whole, the doctrine of the Resurrection is certainly credible.

### (*E.*) CONCLUSION.

We have now examined the four great doctrines of Christianity, the others either following directly from these, or not presenting any difficulty. And though, as we have shown, not one of these doctrines can be pronounced *incredible*, yet some of them, especially those of the Incarnation and the Atonement, certainly seem *improbable*. This must be fully and freely admitted. At the same time, it is only fair to remember that this improbability is distinctly lessened by the three following considerations.

First, in regard to all these doctrines we have no *adequate* means of deciding what is or is not probable. Reason cannot judge where it has nothing to judge by; and apart from Christianity itself, we know next to nothing as to what was God's object in creating man. If, then, these doctrines are true, their truth depends not on reason, but on revelation. All reason can do is to examine most carefully the evidence in favour of the alleged revelation. Of this we should expect it to be able to judge, but not of the doctrines themselves. We are hence in a region where we cannot trust to our own sense of the fitness of things; and therefore the Christian doctrines must not be condemned merely because we think them contrary to our reason. Moreover many thoughtful men (including Agnostics) do not consider them so. Thus the late Professor Huxley once wrote, 'I have not the slightest objection to offer *a priori* to all the propositions of the Three Creeds. The mysteries of the Church are child's play compared with the mysteries of Nature.'[180]

[180] Quoted with his permission in Bishop Gore's Bampton Lectures, 1891, p. 247, 1898 edition.

And this brings us to the next point, which is that many *other* facts which are actually true appear equally improbable at first sight; such, for instance, as the existence of the ether, or the growth of plants. Apart from experience, what an overwhelming argument could be made out against such facts as these. Yet they concern subjects which are to a great extent within our comprehension, while Christianity has to do with the nature and character of a God Who is admittedly beyond our comprehension. May not the difficulties in both cases, but especially in regard to the latter, be due to our *ignorance* only? The Christian doctrines, we must remember, do not claim to have been revealed in all their bearings, but only in so far as they concern ourselves.

Thirdly, it should be noticed that, though individually these doctrines may seem improbable, yet, when considered as a whole, as in all fairness they ought to be, there is a complete harmony between them. Their improbability is not *cumulative*. On the contrary, one often helps to explain the difficulties of another. This has been recognised by most writers, including many who can scarcely be called theologians. Thus the great Napoleon is reported to have said, 'If once the Divine character of Christ is admitted, Christian doctrine exhibits the precision and clearness of algebra; so that we are struck with admiration at its scientific connection and unity.'[181]

[181] Beauterne, Sentiment de Napoleon 1er sur le Christianisme, new edition, Paris, 1864, p. 110.

In conclusion, it must be again pointed out that we are only now considering the *credibility* of Christianity, and not trying to make out that it appears a probable religion, at first sight, which it plainly does not. Only its improbability is not so extremely great as to make it useless to consider the evidence in its favour. This is especially so when we remember that this improbability must have seemed far greater when Christianity was first preached than it does now, when we are so accustomed to the religion. Yet, as a matter of fact, the evidence in its favour did outweigh every difficulty, and finally convince the civilised world. What this evidence is we proceed to inquire.

# CHAPTER XIV.
## THAT THE FOUR GOSPELS ARE GENUINE FROM EXTERNAL TESTIMONY.

(*A*.) THE UNDISPUTED TESTIMONY.

End of second century; Irenæus, his evidence of great value.

(*B*.) THE ALMOST UNDISPUTED TESTIMONY.

(1.) Justin Martyr, A.D. 150, refers to some Apostolic *Memoirs*, which were publicly read among Christians; and his quotations show that these were our Four Gospels.

(2.) Tatian, Justin's disciple, A.D. 175, wrote the Diatessaron, or harmony of Four Gospels.

(3.) Marcion, A.D. 140, wrote a Gospel based on St. Luke's.

(*C*.) THE DISPUTED TESTIMONY.

(1.) Papias, mentions the first two Gospels by name.

(2.) Aristides, A.D. 125, alludes to some Gospel as well known.

(3.) The Apostolic Fathers, Polycarp, Ignatius, Clement, Barnabas, and the Teaching of the Twelve, seem to contain references to our Gospels.

Having shown in the last chapter that the Christian Religion is *credible*, we have next to consider what evidence there is in its favour. Now that it was founded on the alleged miracles and teaching of Christ, and chiefly on His Resurrection, is admitted by everyone. So we must first examine whether we have any trustworthy testimony as to these events; more especially whether the Four Gospels, which appear to contain such testimony, are genuine. By the *Four Gospels*, we of course mean those commonly ascribed to SS. Matthew, Mark, Luke, and John; and by their being *genuine*, we mean that they were written, or compiled by those persons. And we will first consider the *external testimony* borne by early Christian writers to these Gospels, leaving *the internal evidence* from the Books themselves for the next chapter.

It may be mentioned at starting that we have no complete manuscripts of the Gospels earlier than the beginning of the fourth century; but there is nothing surprising in this, as for the first two centuries books were generally written on *papyrus*, an extremely fragile material. Therefore, with the exception of some fragments preserved in Egypt, all documents of this period have entirely perished. A much better material, *vellum*, began to take the place of papyrus in the third century; but did not come into common use till the fourth. Moreover, during the persecutions, which occurred at intervals up to the fourth century, all Christian *writings* were specially sought for, and destroyed. So the absence of earlier manuscripts though very unfortunate, is not perhaps unnatural; and it is anyhow no worse than in the case of classical works. I have seen it stated, for instance, that there are no manuscripts of either Cicero, Cæsar, Tacitus, or Josephus, within 800 years of their time.

## (*A.*) THE UNDISPUTED TESTIMONY.

Passing on now to the testimony of early writers; we need not begin later than the end of the second century; since it is admitted by everyone that our Four Gospels were then well known. They were continually quoted by Christian writers; they were universally ascribed to the authors we now ascribe them to; and they were always considered to be in some sense divinely inspired.

As this is undisputed, we need not discuss the evidence; but one writer deserves to be mentioned, which is *Irenæus*, Bishop of Lyons. His works date from about A.D. 185; and he not only quotes the Gospels frequently (about 500 times altogether), but shows there were only *four* of acknowledged authority. Since the fanciful analogies he gives for this, likening the four Gospels to the four rivers in Paradise, and the four quarters of the globe, render it certain that the fact of there being four, neither more nor less, must have been undisputed in his day.

Moreover he had excellent means of knowing the truth; for he was born in Asia Minor, about A.D. 130, and brought up under Polycarp, Bishop of Smyrna. And in later years he tells us how well he remembered his teacher. 'I can even describe the place where the blessed Polycarp used to sit and discourse—his going out, too, and his coming in—his general mode of life and personal appearance, together with the discourses which he delivered to the people; also how he would speak of his familiar intercourse with John, and with the rest of those who had seen the Lord; and how he would call their words to remembrance.'[182]

[182] Irenæus, Fragment of Epistle to Florinus. The translations here and elsewhere are from the Ante-Nicene Christian Library.

The importance of this passage, especially in regard to the Fourth Gospel, can scarcely be exaggerated. For is it conceivable that Irenæus would have ascribed it to St. John, unless his teacher Polycarp had done the same? Or is it conceivable that Polycarp, who personally knew St. John, could have been mistaken in the matter? The difficulties of either alternative are very great; yet there is no other, unless we admit that St. John was the author.

It should also be noticed that Irenæus, when discussing two readings of Rev. 13. 18, supports one of them by saying that it is found *in all the most approved and ancient copies*; and was also maintained by men *who saw John face to face.*[183] He had thus some idea as to the value of evidence; and he is not likely to have written as he did about the Four Gospels, unless he had seen of them equally *approved and ancient* copies.

[183] Irenæus, Bk. 5. 30.

### (*B.*) THE ALMOST UNDISPUTED TESTIMONY.

We next come to the testimony of some earlier writers, which was formerly much disputed, but is now admitted by nearly all critics.

### (1.) Justin Martyr.

By far the most important of these is *Justin Martyr*, whose works—two *Apologies* (or books written in defence of Christianity) and a *Dialogue*—date from about A.D. 145-50. He was no ordinary convert, but a philosopher, and says that before he became a Christian, he studied various philosophical systems and found them unsatisfactory; so we may be sure that he did not accept Christianity without making some inquiries as to the facts on which it rested.[184] And as his father and grandfather were natives of Palestine, where he was born, he had ample means of finding out the truth.

[184] Dial., 2.

Now Justin does not allude to any of the Evangelists by name, but he frequently quotes from the '*Memoirs of the Apostles*,' which he says were sometimes called *Gospels*,[185] and were publicly read and explained in the churches, together with the Old Testament Prophets. And he gives no hint that this was a local or recent practice, but implies that it was the universal and well-established custom. These Memoirs, he tells us,[186] were written *by the Apostles and their followers*, which exactly suits our present Gospels, two of which are ascribed to Apostles (St. Matthew and St. John), and the other two to their immediate followers (St. Mark and St. Luke). And as Justin was writing for unbelievers, not Christians, there is nothing strange in his not mentioning the names of the individual writers.

[185] Apol. 1. 66; Dial., 100.

[186] Dial., 103.

He has altogether about sixty quotations from these Memoirs, and they describe precisely those events in the life of Christ; which are recorded in our Gospels, with scarcely any addition. Very few of the quotations however are verbally accurate, and this used to be thought a difficulty. But as Justin sometimes quotes the same passage differently, it is clear that he was relying on his memory; and had not looked up the reference, which in those days of manuscripts, without concordances, must have been a tedious process. Also when quoting the Old Testament, he is almost equally inaccurate. Moreover later writers, such as Irenæus, who avowedly quoted from our Gospels, are also inaccurate in small details. It is hence practically certain that Justin was quoting from these Gospels.

### (2.) Tatian.

And this is strongly confirmed by Justin's disciple, *Tatian*. He wrote a book about A.D. 175, discovered last century, called the *Diatessaron*, which, as its name implies, was a kind of harmony of *Four* Gospels. It was based chiefly on St. Matthew's, the events peculiar to the others being introduced in various places. And its containing nearly the whole of *St. John's* Gospel is satisfactory; because it so happens that Justin has fewer quotations from that Gospel, than from the other three. We may say then with confidence, that our four Gospels were well known to Christians, and highly valued by them, in the middle of the second century.

### (3.) Marcion.

Another important witness is Marcion. He wrote (not later than A.D. 140), a kind of Gospel, so similar to St. Luke's that one was evidently based on the other. And though his actual work is lost, Tertullian (about A.D. 200) quotes it so fully that it is fairly well-known; and that St. Luke's is the earlier is now admitted by critics of all schools. Therefore as Matthew and Mark are generally allowed to be earlier than Luke, this shows that all these Gospels were in circulation before A.D. 140.

## (*C.*) THE DISPUTED TESTIMONY.

We pass on now to the testimony of still earlier writers, all of which is more or less disputed by some critics.

### (1.) Papias.

And first as to Papias. He was bishop of Hierapolis in Asia Minor (about a hundred miles from Ephesus) early in the second century; and only a few fragments of his writings have been preserved by Irenæus and Eusebius. We learn from the former that he was a disciple of St. John and a companion of Polycarp; and considering that Irenæus was himself Polycarp's pupil, there is no reason to doubt this.[187] Now Papias tells us himself what were his sources of information: 'If, then, anyone who had attended on the elders came, I asked minutely after their sayings,—what Andrew or Peter said, or what was said by Philip, or by Thomas, or by James, or by John, or by Matthew, or by any other of the Lord's disciples: which things Aristion and the presbyter John, the disciples of the Lord, say. For I imagined that what was to be got from books was not so profitable to me as what came from the living and abiding voice.'

[187] Irenæus, Bk. 5. 33.

He had thus very good means of knowing the truth, for though the Apostles themselves were dead, two of Christ's disciples (Aristion and the presbyter John) were still alive when he made his inquiries. And he refers to the first two Gospels by name. He says, 'Matthew put together the oracles in the Hebrew language, and each one interpreted them as best he could.' And 'Mark, having become the interpreter of Peter, wrote down accurately whatsoever he remembered. It was not, however, in exact order that he related the sayings or deeds of Christ. For he neither heard the Lord nor accompanied Him. But afterwards, as I said, he accompanied Peter.'[188]

[188] Eusebius, Hist., iii. 39.

And his testimony in regard to *St. Matthew* is specially important, because in the passage just quoted he says that he had spoken to those who had known St. Matthew personally; and had carefully questioned them about what he had said. And this makes it difficult to believe that he should have been mistaken as to his having written the Gospel. Nor is it likely that the work of St. Matthew known to Papias was different from the Gospel which we now have, and which was so frequently quoted by Justin a few years later. Whether Papias was acquainted with the Third and Fourth Gospels cannot be decided for certain, unless his works should be recovered; but there are slight indications that he knew them.

### (2.) Aristides.

Next as to Aristides. He was a philosopher at Athens, and addressed an Apology to the Emperor, Hadrian, in A.D. 125, which was recovered in 1889. He has no *quotation* from the Gospels, but what is equally important, he gives a summary of Christian doctrine, including the Divinity, Incarnation, Virgin-Birth, Resurrection and Ascension of Christ; and says that it is *taught in the Gospel*, where men can *read* it for themselves. And this shows that some Gospel, containing this teaching, was then in existence, and easily accessible.

### (3.) The Apostolic Fathers.

The last group of writers to be examined are those who lived soon after the Apostles. The chief of these are *Polycarp* of Smyrna, the disciple of St. John, martyred in A.D. 155, when he had been a Christian 86 years; *Ignatius* of Antioch, also martyred in his old age, about A.D. 110; *Clement* of Rome, perhaps the companion of St. Paul;[189] and the writers of the so-called *Epistle of Barnabas*, and *Teaching of the Twelve Apostles*. Their dates are not known for certain, but it is now generally admitted by rationalists as well as Christians that they all wrote before A.D. 120, and probably before 110. Thus the *Encyclopædia Biblica* (article *Gospels*) dates their works, Polycarp 110; Ignatius (7 Epistles) before 110; Barnabas, probably before 100; Clement 95; Teaching 80-100.

[189] Phil. 4. 3.

Now none of these writers mention the Gospels by *name*; but this is no argument to show that they were not quoting them, because the same writers, when admittedly quoting St. Paul's Epistles, also do it at times, without in any way referring to him. And later Christian writers do precisely the same; the Gospels are often not quoted by name, but their language is continually employed, much as it is by preachers at the present day. If, then, we find in these writers passages similar to those in our Gospels, the inference is that they are quoting from them; and, as a matter of fact, we do find such passages, though they are not numerous. A single example may be given from each.

*Polycarp.* 'But being mindful of what the Lord said in His teaching; Judge not, that ye be not judged; forgive, and it shall be forgiven unto you; be merciful, that ye may obtain mercy; with what measure ye mete, it shall be measured to you again; and once more, Blessed are the poor, and those that are persecuted for righteousness' sake, for theirs is the kingdom of God.'[190]

[190] Polycarp, ch. ii.; Luke 6. 36-38; Matt. 5. 3, 10.

*Ignatius.* 'For I know that after His Resurrection also, He was still possessed of flesh, and I believe that He is so now. When, for instance, He came to those who were with Peter, He said to them, "Lay hold, handle Me, and see that I am not an incorporeal spirit."'[191]

[191] Ignatius to Smyrnæans, ch. iii.; Luke 24. 39.

*Barnabas.* 'Let us beware lest we be found, as it is written, Many are called, but few are chosen.'[192]

[192] Barnabas, ch. iv.; Matt. 22. 14.

*Clement.* 'Remember the words of our Lord Jesus Christ, how He said, Woe to that man! It were better for him that he had never been born, than that he should cast a stumbling-block before one of my elect. Yea, it were better for him that a millstone should be hung about (his neck), and he should be sunk in the depths of the sea, than that he should cast a stumbling-block before one of my little ones.'[193]

[193] Clement, ch. xlvi.; Luke 17. 1. 2.

*Teaching.* 'Having said beforehand all these things, baptize ye in the name of the Father, and of the Son, and of the Holy Ghost in living water.'[194]

[194] Teaching, ch. vii.; Matt. 28. 19.

The passage from Barnabas deserves special mention, since here we have words which only occur in our Gospels, introduced with the phrase *as it is written*, which is only used of Scripture quotations. And this shows conclusively that at the time of the writer, some Gospel containing these words must have been well known, and considered of high authority. And the attempts to explain it away as being from the Book of Esdras,[195] where the words are, 'There be many created, but few shall be saved;' or else as an error on the part of the writer, who thought they came somewhere in the Old Testament, are quite inadmissible.

[195] 2 Esdr. 8. 3.

But it may be said, may not all these quotations be from some *Lost Gospel?* Of course they may. It is always possible to refer quotations not to the only book in which we know they do occur, but to some imaginary book in which they might occur. There is, however, no need to do so in this case, as all the evidence points the other way. Though, even if we do, it does not materially affect the argument; for while it weakens the evidence for our Gospels, it increases that for the *facts* which they record; and this is the important point.

Suppose, for instance, the passage in Ignatius was not taken from St. Luke's, but from some *Lost* Gospel. It could not then be quoted to show that St. Luke's Gospel was known to Ignatius. But it would afford additional evidence that Christ really did rise from the dead, that when He appeared to His Apostles, they at first thought He was a spirit; and that He took the obvious means of convincing them, by asking them to handle His Body. All this would then be vouched for, not only by St. Luke's Gospel; but also by some *other* early Christian writing, which as Ignatius quotes it in A.D. 110 must certainly have been written in the first century, and must have been considered by him as conclusive evidence. For he is careful to distinguish between what he thus *knows* (that Christ had a Body after His Resurrection) and what he merely *believes* (that He has one now). And the same applies in other cases.

And if it be further urged that these writers would have referred more frequently to the Gospels, had they really known them, we must remember that their writings are generally short; and while a single quotation proves the previous existence of the document quoted, ten pages without a quotation do not disprove it. Moreover when they refer to the sayings of Christ, or the events of His life, they always do so without the slightest hesitation; as if everyone acknowledged them to be true. And as we have seen, their allusions often begin with the words *remember* or *be mindful of*, clearly showing that they expected their readers to know them already. Hence some books must then have existed which were well known, containing a life of Christ; and the improbability of these having perished, and a fresh set of Gospels having been published in a few years, is very great.

And the evidence in regard to the *Third* Gospel is particularly strong, since it was addressed to Theophilus, who was clearly a prominent convert; and he must have known from whom the book came, even if for some reason this was not stated in the heading. And as he is not likely to have kept it secret, the authorship of the book must have been well known to Christians from the very beginning. Therefore the testimony of early writers, like Irenæus, who always ascribed it to St. Luke, becomes of exceptional value; and makes it almost certain that he was the author.

We may now sum up the *external testimony* to the Four Gospels. It shows that at the *beginning* of the second century they were well known to Christian writers, and this alone would necessitate their having been written in the first century, or at all events before A.D. 110. And thanks to modern discoveries, especially that of the *Diatessaron*, this is now generally admitted. It may indeed be considered as one of the definite results of recent controversies. But if so, it is, to say the least, distinctly probable that they were written by the men to whom they have been universally ascribed. We have thus strong external testimony in favour of the genuineness of the Four Gospels.

# CHAPTER XV.
## THAT THE GOSPELS ARE GENUINE FROM INTERNAL EVIDENCE.

(*A.*) THE FIRST THREE GOSPELS.

(1.) Their general accuracy; this is shown by secular history, where they can be tested.

(2.) Their sources; the triple tradition; other early documents.

(3.) Their probable date; before the destruction of Jerusalem, A.D. 70.

(*B.*) THE FOURTH GOSPEL.

(1.) Its authorship. The writer appears to have lived in the first century, and to have been an eye-witness of what he describes; so probably St. John.

(2.) Its connection with the other Gospels. It was meant to supplement them; and it does not show a different Christ, either in language or character.

(3.) Its connection with the Book of Revelation. This admitted to be by St. John, and the Gospel was probably by the same author.

Having decided in the last chapter that the Four Gospels are probably genuine from *external testimony*, we pass on now to the *internal evidence*, which, it will be seen, strongly supports this conclusion. For convenience we will examine the first Three, commonly called the *Synoptic* Gospels, separately from the Fourth, which is of a different character.

### (*A.*) THE FIRST THREE GOSPELS.

In dealing with these Gospels, we will first consider their general accuracy, then their sources, and then their probable date.

**(1.) Their general accuracy.**

It is now admitted by everyone that the writers show a thorough acquaintance with Palestine both as to its geography, history, and people, especially the political and social state of the country in the half-century preceding the fall of Jerusalem (A.D. 70). The Jewish historian Josephus, who wrote about A.D. 95, gives us a vivid description of this; and everything we read in the Gospels is in entire agreement with it.

In regard to the actual events recorded, we have, as a rule, no other account, but where we have, with the doubtful exception of the enrolment under *Quirinius*, their accuracy is fully confirmed. According to St. Luke[196] this enrolment occurred while Herod was king, and therefore not later than what we now call B.C. 4, when Herod died; but, according to Josephus and other authorities, Quirinius was Governor of Syria, and carried out his taxing in A.D. 6.

[196] Luke 2. 2 (R.V.).

This used to be thought one of the most serious mistakes in the Bible, but modern discoveries have shown that it is probably correct. To begin with, an inscription was found at Tivoli in 1764, which shows that Quirinius was *twice* Governor of Syria, or at least held some important office there. And this has been confirmed quite recently by an inscription found at Antioch, which shows that the former time was about B.C. 7.[197] There is thus very likely an end of that difficulty, though it must be admitted that it would place the birth of Christ a little earlier than the usually accepted B.C. 4, which however some critics think probable for other reasons.

[197] Ramsay, 'Bearing of Recent Discovery on New Testament.' 1915, p. 285-292.

Next it will be noticed that St. Luke says that this was the *first* enrolment, implying that he knew of others; and discoveries in Egypt have confirmed this in a remarkable manner. For they have shown that it was the custom of the Romans to have a *periodical* enrolment of that country (and therefore presumably of the adjacent country of Syria) every fourteen years. Some of the actual census papers have been found for A.D. 20, 48, 62, 76, etc., and it is extremely probable that the system started in B.C. 9-8, though the first enrolment may have been delayed a few years in Palestine, which was partly independent.

And St. Luke's statement that everyone had to go to *his own city*, which was long thought to be a difficulty, has been partly confirmed as well. For a decree has been discovered in Egypt, dated in the seventh year of Trajan (A.D. 104), ordering all persons to return to their own districts before the approaching census,[198] which is worded as if it were the usual custom. The next census in A.D. 6, which is the one referred to by Josephus, is also mentioned by St. Luke;[199] but he knew, what his critics did not, that it was only one of a series, and that the *first* of the series took place at an earlier date.

[198] Ramsay, p. 259.

[199] Acts. 5. 37.

Curiously enough, there used to be a very similar error, charged against St. Luke, in regard to Lysanias; whom he says was tetrarch of Abilene, a district near Damascus, in the fifteenth year of Tiberius, about A.D. 27.[200] Yet the only ruler of this name known to history in those parts was a king, who was killed in B.C. 34. But inscriptions found at Baalbec, and Abila (the latter dating somewhere between A.D. 14-29) show that there was a second Lysanias, hitherto unknown, who is expressly called the *tetrarch* and who is now admitted to be the one referred to by St. Luke.[201] On the whole then, these Gospels, wherever we have any means of testing them by secular history, appear to be substantially accurate.

[200] Luke 3. 1.

[201] Boeckh's Corp. Ins. Gr., No. 4523; Ramsay, 'Bearing of Recent Discovery on New Testament.' 1915, p. 298.

But it may be said, do not the Gospels themselves contradict one another in some places, and if so they cannot all be correct? Now that there are some apparent contradictions, especially in the narratives of the Resurrection (see Chapter XVII.), must of course be admitted; but many of these can be explained satisfactorily, and those which cannot are as a rule quite trivial. For example,[202] St. Matthew relates that at Christ's Baptism the Voice from Heaven said, '*This* is my beloved Son in *whom* I am well pleased;' and the other Evangelists, '*Thou* art my beloved Son, in *thee* I am well pleased.' There is a clear verbal discrepancy, whatever words were used, or in whatever language they were spoken. Again, St. Matthew records the passage about the Queen of the South as being spoken just after, and St. Luke as just before, the similar passage about the men of Nineveh, though both can hardly be correct. Such mistakes as these, however, do not interfere with the substantial accuracy of the narratives.

[202] Matt. 3. 17; 12. 42; Mark 1. 11; Luke 3. 22; 11. 31.

**(2.) Their sources.**

Now the first three Gospels have, as is well known, a number of identical passages, which must plainly be due to *copying* in some form, either two Evangelists copying the third, or all three some earlier document. The portion they have in common (often called the *Triple Tradition*) includes some of the parables of Christ, and several of His miracles, such as calming the storm, feeding the five thousand, curing the man at Gadara, and raising the daughter of Jairus. If, as is probable, it represents the testimony of a single witness, there is little difficulty in identifying him with St. Peter.

But it is *most unlikely* for the *whole* of this earlier document to have been included in three separate Gospels; it is sure to have contained something that was only copied by one or two. Therefore most scholars are now of opinion that the so-called Triple Tradition was merely our St. Mark's Gospel, practically all of which was copied, either by St. Matthew or St. Luke, if not by both. And this is certainly probable, for the many graphic details in this Gospel show that it must date from an extremely early time; so it was most likely known to the other Evangelists. It would also agree with the statement of Papias (quoted in the last chapter) that St. Mark got his information from St. Peter. And as some of it has to do with events, such as the Transfiguration, when St. Peter was present, and St. Matthew was not, there is nothing improbable in St. Matthew (as well as St. Luke) including part of it in his Gospel.

This however is not all; for our first and third Gospels also contain a good deal in common, which is not in Mark, and this looks like another older document, often called 'Q' from the German *Quelle*, meaning '*source*.' It consists chiefly of discourses and parables, though including at least one miracle, that of healing the centurion's servant, and is admitted by most critics to date from before A.D. 50.

But here again, it is unlikely for the *whole* of this earlier document to have been included in two separate Gospels, it is sure to have contained something else besides. Moreover, *as thus restored* (from Matthew and Luke) it is obviously incomplete. It contains scarcely any narrative to explain how the discourses arose, and of necessity it omits everything in Christ's life which is recorded by St. Mark as well, for this has been already assigned to the so-called Triple Tradition. Therefore when it was complete, it must have contained a good deal more, which may well have been the remainder of our St. Matthew's Gospel. St. Luke would then have only included *a part* of what St. Matthew wrote, just as they both only included a part of what St. Mark wrote. And the supposed second document would be our St. Matthew's Gospel, just as the supposed Triple Tradition is now thought to be our St. Mark's Gospel. There are difficulties on every theory, but on the whole this seems as satisfactory as any other, and it accounts fairly well for the first two Gospels.

But the third Gospel requires further explanation, for besides what is copied from the other two, it contains a good deal of additional matter, such as the parable of the Prodigal Son, which St. Luke must have got from some other source. While he expressly says that *many* had written before himself; so there were several such sources in existence. And this was only natural, for the Christian religion spread rapidly, and St. Luke himself shows us what its converts were taught. For he says that he only wrote his Gospel to convince Theophilus of the things about which he had already been instructed.[203] Clearly then the course of instruction must have included what the Gospel included; and this was the whole of Christ's life, from His Virgin-Birth to His Ascension. It is hence probable that from the very first Christian teachers had some account of that life.

[203] Luke 1. 1-4.

And this probability becomes almost a certainty in the light of modern discoveries. For quantities of old *papyri* have been found in Egypt, which show that at the time of Christ, writing was in common use among all classes; soldiers, farmers, servants, schoolboys, were all accustomed to write. Therefore, as it has been well said, 'so far as antecedent probability goes, founded on the general character of preceding and contemporary society, the first Christian account of the circumstances connected with the death of Jesus must be presumed to have been written in the year when Jesus died.'[204] And since St. Luke, when he was at Jerusalem met several of the *elders* there, including Christ's brother, St. James,[205] he probably had access to all existing documents.

[204] Ramsay, Transactions of Victoria Institute, vol. xxxix., 1907, p. 203.

[205] Acts 21. 18.

There is thus no reason to doubt his own statement, that he had ample means of knowing the truth, *from the beginning*. And this, he says, was the very reason why he determined to write; so a more trustworthy historian can scarcely be imagined.[206] Fortunately, however, though dividing the Gospels into their original parts is an interesting study, it is in no way essential to our present argument.

[206] Luke 1. 2-3.

### (3.) Their probable date.

We now come to the *probable date* of the first three Gospels; and there are strong reasons for fixing this before the fall of Jerusalem, in A.D. 70. In the first place several *subjects* are discussed, such as the lawfulness of the Jews paying tribute to Cæsar,[207] which would have had no interest after that event. And that conversations on such subjects should have been composed in later days, or even thought worth recording, is most unlikely. Nor are Christ's instructions as to what persons should do when they bring their gifts to the altar, likely to have been recorded after the altar, and everything connected with it, had been totally destroyed.[208]

[207] Matt. 22. 17.

[208] Matt. 5. 24.

Secondly, nearly all the *parables* of Christ have very strong marks of truthfulness, as they are thoroughly natural in character, and suit the customs and scenery of Palestine. Moreover, they are unique in Christian literature. However strange we may think it, the early Christians never seem to have adopted Christ's method of teaching by parables. Yet, if they had composed these parables, instead of merely recording them, they would doubtless have composed others like them. It is hence probable that these discourses are genuine; and, if so, they must obviously have been written down very soon afterwards.

Thirdly, there are a few passages which deserve special mention. Two of these are Christ's saying that (apparently) there would not be time to go through the cities of Israel before His Second Coming; and that some of His hearers would not die till the end of the world.[209] That such statements should have been composed in later years is out of the question; so we can only conclude that they were actually spoken by Christ. And they show that the Gospels must not only have been written when some of Christ's hearers were still alive, but that they could not have been revised afterwards; or the passages would not have been allowed to remain as they are.

[209] Matt. 10. 23; 16. 28; Mark 9. 1; Luke 9. 27; but some other texts imply the contrary—*e.g.*, Matt. 21. 43; Mark 13. 7, 10; 14. 9; Luke 21. 24.

Another is the statement that the potter's field was called the field of blood *unto this day*;[210] which could scarcely have been written when the whole city was little more than a heap of ruins. Of course, on the other hand, it could not have been written immediately after the time of Christ, but twenty years would probably be a sufficient interval.

[210] Matt. 27. 8; see also 28. 15.

Fourthly, there is the prophetic description of the *fall of Jerusalem* itself, which seems confused by the Evangelists with that of the Day of Judgment, St. Matthew saying, and both the others implying, that the one would immediately follow the other.[211] Had the Gospels been written after the former event, it is almost certain that the writers would have distinguished between the two; indeed, their not doing so is scarcely intelligible, unless we assume that when they wrote, both events were still future.

[211] Matt. 24. 3, 29; Mark 13. 24; Luke 21. 27.

And this is confirmed by the curious hint given to the readers both in Matthew and Mark to *understand*, and act on Christ's advice, and leave the city and go to the mountains, before the siege became too severe.[212] Plainly such a warning could not have been written *after* the siege, when it would have been useless. It must have been written *before*; so if it is a later insertion, as it seems to be, it proves a still earlier date for the rest of the chapter. Moreover, none of the Evangelists have altered the passage, as later writers might have done, to make it agree with the event; since as far as we know, the Christians did not go to *the mountains*, but to Pella, a city in the Jordan valley.[213]

[212] Matt. 24. 16; Mark 13. 14; Luke 21. 21.

[213] Eusebius, Hist., iii. 5.

St. Luke, it will be noticed, omits the hint just referred to, and as his account of Christ's prophecy of the siege is rather more detailed than the others, it is sometimes thought to have been written *after* the event. But this is a needless assumption, for the hint would have been quite useless to Theophilus, to whom the Gospel was addressed; and the prophecy is anyhow no closer than that in Deut. 28., which everyone admits was written centuries before (Chapter XI.).

On the whole, then, everything points to our first three Gospels having been written some years before the destruction of Jerusalem, A.D. 70; and most likely by the Evangelists, to whom they have been universally ascribed.

It may also be added, in regard to the Evangelists themselves, *St. Matthew* the Apostle was a publican or tax-collector, so just the sort of person to keep records, in either Greek or Hebrew.[214] *St. Mark* came of a wealthy family, as his relative, Barnabas, had some property; and his mother, Mary, had a large house at Jerusalem, where Christians used to assemble, and where it has been thought the Last Supper was held.[215] And the *young man* who followed from here to Gethsemane was probably St. Mark himself, or he would not have recorded such a trivial incident.[216]

[214] Matt. 9. 9.

[215] Acts 4. 37; 12. 12; 1. 13; Col. 4. 10.

[216] Mark 14. 51.

And *St. Luke*, as we shall see in the next chapter, was a doctor, who says he got his information from *eye-witnesses*. And if he was the companion of Cleopas, as is perhaps probable (for such a graphic narrative must have come from one who was present, yet the language is thoroughly that of St. Luke), he would also have had some slight knowledge of Christ himself.[217] And in similar cases where St. John speaks of two disciples, but gives the name of only one, it is practically certain that he himself was the other.[218] Moreover St. Luke says that his Gospel, which only goes as far as the Ascension, was about *those matters which have been fulfilled among us*[219] (*i.e.*, which have *occurred* among us), and this implies that it was written in Palestine at a very early date, and that St. Luke himself was there during at least part of the time referred to.

[217] Luke 24. 18; *Expositor*, Feb., 1904.

[218] John 1. 40; 18. 15.

[219] Luke 1. 1. (R.V.). A short paper on *Fulfilled among us*, by the present writer, appeared in the *Churchman*, Aug. 1914.

All three must thus have been well-educated men, and quite in a position to write Gospels if they wanted to. While as none of them seem to have taken a prominent part in the founding of Christianity, there was no reason for ascribing the Gospels to them, rather than to such great men as St. Peter and St. Paul, unless they actually wrote them.

## (*B.*) THE FOURTH GOSPEL.

We pass on now to the Fourth Gospel, and will first examine the internal arguments as to its authorship, which are strongly in favour of its being the work of St. John; and then the two arguments on the opposite side, said to be derived from its connection with the other Gospels, and the Book of Revelation.

### (1.) Its authorship.

To begin with, the writer appears to have lived in the *first century*. This is probable from his intimate acquaintance with Jerusalem, and as before said that city was only a heap of ruins after A.D. 70. Thus he speaks of Bethesda, the pool near the sheep-gate, having five porches; of Solomon's porch; of the pool of Siloam; and of the Temple, with its treasury; its oxen, sheep, and doves for sacrifice; and its money-changers for changing foreign money into Jewish, in which alone the Temple tax could be paid. And his mention of Bethesda is specially interesting as he uses the present tense, *There is in Jerusalem*, etc., implying that the gate and porches were still standing (and therefore the city not yet destroyed) when he wrote.[220]

[220] John 5. 2.

Secondly, the writer appears to have been an *eye-witness* of what he describes. He twice asserts this himself, as well as in an Epistle which is generally admitted to be by the same writer, where he declares that he had both seen, heard, and touched his Master.[221] So, if this is not true, the work must be a deliberate forgery; which is certainly improbable. Moreover, he frequently identifies himself with the Twelve Apostles, recording their feelings and reflections in a way which would be very unlikely for any late writer to have thought of. Would a late writer, for instance, have thought of inventing questions which the Apostles wanted to ask their Master, but were afraid to do so? Or would he have thought it worth repeating so often that they did not understand at the time the real significance of the events they took part in?[222]

[221] John 1. 14; 19. 35; 1 John 1. 1.

[222] *E.g.*, John 2. 17, 22; 4. 27; 13. 28; 16. 17.

The author is also very particular as to times and places. Take, for instance, the passage 1. 29-2. 12, with its expressions *On the morrow*, *Again on the morrow*, *About the tenth hour*, *On the morrow*, *And the third day*, *And there they abode not many days*. It reads like extracts from an old diary, and why should all these insignificant details be recorded? What did it matter half a century later whether it was the same day, or on the morrow, or the third day; or whether they stayed many days in Capernaum, or only a few; as no hint is given as to why they went there, or what they did? The only reasonable explanation is that the writer was present himself (being of course the unnamed companion of St. Andrew); that this was the turning-point in his life when he first saw his Lord; and that therefore he loved to recall every detail.

And it may be noticed in passing that this passage explains an apparent difficulty in the other Gospels, where it is stated that these Apostles were called to follow Christ, after the death of St. John the Baptist; though with a suddenness and ready obedience on their part, which is hard to believe.[223] But we here learn that they had already been with Christ some months before, in company with the Baptist, so they were doubtless prepared for the call when it came. And the passage, like many others, bears internal marks of truthfulness. In particular may be mentioned the words of Nathanael, *Thou art the Son of God, thou art the King of Israel*, implying that the latter title was at least as honourable as the former. No Christian in later times, when Christ was obviously not the King of Israel (except in a purely spiritual sense), and when the title *Son of God* had come to mean so much more than it ever did to the Jews, would have arranged it thus.

[223] *E.g.*, Mark 1. 14-20.

Lastly, if we admit that the writer was an eye-witness, it can hardly be disputed that he was the Apostle *St. John*. Indeed, were he anyone else, it is strange that an Apostle of such importance should not be once mentioned throughout the Gospel. It is also significant that the other John, who is described in the first three Gospels as John the *Baptist*, to distinguish him from the Apostle, is here called merely *John*. No confusion could arise if, and only if, the writer himself were the Apostle John. While still more important is the fact that at the close of the Gospel, we have a solemn declaration made by the author's own friends that he was the *disciple whom Jesus loved* (admitted by nearly everyone to be St. John), that he had witnessed the things he wrote about, and that what he said was true. And testimony more ancient or more conclusive can scarcely be imagined.

With regard to the *date* of the book, we can say little for certain. But the extreme care which is taken in these closing verses to explain exactly what Christ did, and did not say, as to St. John's dying, before His coming again, seems to imply that the matter was still undecided, in other words that St.

John was still alive, though very old, when they were written. And if so the Gospel must have been *published* (probably in some Gentile city, like Ephesus, from the way the Jews are spoken of)[224] towards the close of the first century; though a large part of it may have been *written* in the shape of notes, etc., long before.

[224] *E.g.*, John 2. 13; 5. 1; 6. 4.

### (2.) Its connection with the other Gospels.

But, as before said, there are two arguments against the genuineness of this Gospel. The first is that the Christ of the Fourth Gospel is almost a different person from the Christ of the other three. The *events* of His life are different, His *language* is different, and His *character* is different; while, when the Gospels cover the same ground, there are *discrepancies* between them. But every part of this objection admits of a satisfactory answer.

To begin with, the fact that the Fourth Gospel narrates different *events* in the life of Christ from what we find in the other three must of course be admitted. But what then? Why should not one biography of Christ narrate certain events in His life, which the writer thought important, but which had been omitted in previous accounts? This is what occurs frequently at the present day, and why should it not have occurred then? The Fourth Gospel may have been written on purpose to *supplement* some other accounts.

And there is strong evidence from the book itself that this was actually the case. For the writer refers to many events without describing them, and in such a way as to show that he thought his readers knew about them. He assumes, for instance, that they know about St. John the Baptist being imprisoned, about Joseph being the supposed father of Christ, and about the appointment of the Twelve.[225] It is probable then that the Gospel was written for well-instructed Christians, who possessed some other accounts of Christ's life. And everything points to these being our first three Gospels.

[225] John 3. 24; 6. 42, 70.

Then as to the *language* ascribed to Christ in the Fourth Gospel being different from that in the others. This is no doubt partly true, especially in regard to His speaking of Himself as *the Son*, in the same way in which God is *the Father*. But it so happens that we have in these other Gospels at least three similar passages[226] which show that Christ did occasionally speak in this way. And there is no reason why St. John should not have preserved such discourses because the other Evangelists had omitted to do so. On the other hand, the title *Son of Man* (applied to Christ) occurs repeatedly in all the Gospels, though strange to say only in the mouth of Christ Himself. This is a striking detail, in which St. John entirely agrees with the other Evangelists.

[226] Matt. 11. 25-27; 24. 36; 28. 19; Mark 13. 32; Luke 10. 21, 22.

The next part of the objection is that the *Character* assigned to Christ in the Fourth Gospel is different from that in the other three; since instead of teaching moral virtues as in the Sermon on the Mount, He keeps asserting His own Divine nature. And this also is partly true, for the Fourth Gospel shows the Divinity of Christ more directly than the others, which only imply it (Chapter XXI.). And very probably the writer did so on purpose, thinking that this aspect of Christ's character had not been sufficiently emphasised in the previous accounts. Indeed, he implies it himself, for he says that he omitted much that he might have inserted, and merely recorded what he did in order to convince his readers that Jesus was the Christ, the Son of God.[227]

[227] John 20. 31.

But no argument for a late date can be drawn from this. Because four of St. Paul's Epistles (*i.e.* Rom.; 1 Cor.; 2 Cor.; and Gal.) which have been admitted to be genuine by critics of all schools, describe exactly the same Christ as we find in the Fourth Gospel, speaking of His Divinity, Pre-existence, and Incarnation (Chapter XXI.). And from the way in which St. Paul alludes to these doctrines he evidently considered them the common belief of all Christians when he wrote, about A.D. 55. So the fact of the Fourth Gospel laying stress on these doctrines is no reason whatever against either its genuineness or its early date. Indeed, it seems to supply just those discourses of Christ which are necessary to account for St. Paul's language.

Lastly, as to the *discrepancies*. The one most often alleged is that according to the first three Gospels (in opposition to the Fourth) Christ's ministry never reached Jerusalem till just before His death. But this is a mistake, for though they do not relate His attendance at the Jewish feasts, like St. John does, they imply by the word *often* ('How *often* would I have gathered thy children,'[228] etc.) that He had frequently visited the city, and preached there. And one of them also refers to an earlier visit of Christ, to Martha and Mary, which shows that He had been to Bethany (close to Jerusalem) some time before.[229]

[228] Matt. 23. 37; Luke 13. 34.

[229] Luke 10. 38.

Another difficulty (it is scarcely a discrepancy) is the fact that such a striking miracle as the raising of Lazarus, which is described in the Fourth Gospel, should have been *omitted* in the other three. It is certainly strange, but these Evangelists themselves tell us there were *other* instances of raising the dead, which they do not record,[230] and they probably knew of it, as it alone explains the great enthusiasm with which Christ was received at Jerusalem. This they all relate, and St. Luke's saying that it was due to the *mighty works*, which the people had *seen*, implies that there had been some striking miracles in the neighbourhood.[231]

[230] Matt. 10. 8; 11. 5; Luke 7. 22.

[231] Luke 19. 37.

On the other hand, there are several *undesigned agreements* between the Gospels, which are a strong argument in favour of their accuracy. Take, for instance, the accusation brought against Christ of destroying the Temple, and rebuilding it in three days. This is alluded to both by St. Matthew and St. Mark; but St. John alone records the words on which it was founded, though he does not mention the charge, and quotes the words in quite a different connection.[232]

[232] Matt. 26. 61; Mark 14. 58; John 2. 19.

Or take the Feeding of the five thousand.[233] St. Mark says that this occurred in a desert place, where Christ had gone for a short rest, and to avoid the crowd of persons who were *coming and going* at Capernaum. But he gives no hint as to why there was this crowd just at that time. St. John says nothing about Christ's going to the desert, nor of the crowd which occasioned it; but he happens to mention, what fully explains both, that it was shortly before the Passover. Now we know that at the time of the Passover numbers of people came to Jerusalem from all parts; so Capernaum, which lay on a main road from the north, would naturally be crowded with persons *coming and going*. And this explains everything; even St. Mark's little detail, as to the people sitting on the *green* grass, for grass is only green in Palestine in the spring, *i.e.*, at the time of the Passover. But can anyone think that the writer of the Fourth Gospel purposely made his account to agree with the others, yet did this in such a way that not one reader in a hundred ever discovers it? The only reasonable explanation is that the event was true, and that both writers had independent knowledge of it.

[233] Matt. 14. 13; Mark 6. 31; Luke 9. 10; John 6. 4.

The objection, then, as to the connection of the Fourth Gospel with the other three must be put aside. It was plainly meant to *supplement* them; and it shows not a different Christ, either in *language* or *character*, but merely a different aspect of the same Christ, while the slight *discrepancies*, especially when combined with the undesigned coincidences, rather support its genuineness.

### (3.) Its connection with the Book of Revelation.

We pass on now to the other argument. The Book of Revelation is generally admitted to be the work of St. John, and it is ascribed to him by Justin

Martyr.[234] Its date is usually fixed at A.D. 68; though many critics prefer A.D. 95, which is the date given by Irenæus.

[234] Dial., 81.

Yet it is said it cannot be by the same writer as the Fourth Gospel because the *Greek* is so different, that of the Revelation being very abrupt, with numerous faults of grammar, while the Gospel is in good Greek. Therefore it is urged that a Galilean fisherman like St. John, though he might have been sufficiently educated to have written the former, as his father was well off and kept servants, and he himself was a friend of the High Priest,[235] could scarcely have written the latter. Various explanations have been given of this. Perhaps the best is that the Revelation was written by St. John himself, since he is not likely to have had friends in Patmos; and that when writing the Gospel he had the assistance of a Greek disciple.

[235] Mark 1. 20; John 18. 15.

On the other side, it must be remembered that though the two books are different in language, they are the same in their *teaching*; for the great doctrine of the Fourth Gospel, that of the Divinity of Christ, is asserted almost as plainly in the Revelation. And even the striking expression that Christ is the *Logos*, or *Word*, occurs in both books, though it is not found elsewhere in the New Testament, except in one of St. John's Epistles.[236] And the same may be said of another striking expression, that Christ is the *Lamb*, which also occurs in the Gospel and Revelation, though not elsewhere in the New Testament.[237] This similarity in doctrine is indeed so marked that it strongly suggests the same authorship; and if so, it makes it practically certain that the Fourth Gospel was written by St. John.

[236] John 1. 1; 1 John 1. 1; Rev. 19. 13.

[237] John 1. 29, 36; Rev. 6. 1; 14. 1.

On the whole, then, these objections are not serious; while, as already shown, the Fourth Gospel has very strong internal marks of genuineness. And when we combine these with the equally strong external testimony, it forces us to conclude that St. John was the author. This Gospel, then, like the other three, must be considered *genuine*; indeed, the evidence in favour of them all is overwhelming.

# CHAPTER XVI.
## THAT THE GOSPELS ARE GENUINE FROM THE EVIDENCE OF THE ACTS.

Importance of the Acts, as it is by the writer of the Third Gospel.

(*A.*) ITS ACCURACY.

Three examples of this:

(1.) The titles of different rulers.

(2.) The riot at Ephesus.

(3.) The agreement with St. Paul's Epistles.

(*B.*) ITS AUTHORSHIP.

The writer was a companion of St. Paul, and a medical man; so probably St. Luke.

(*C.*) ITS DATE.

There are strong reasons for fixing this at the close of St. Paul's imprisonment at Rome, about A.D. 60; and this points to an earlier date for the first three Gospels.

We have next to consider an argument of great importance derived from the Acts of the Apostles. This book is universally admitted to be by the same writer as the Third Gospel, as is indeed obvious from the manner in which both are addressed to Theophilus, from the *former treatise* being mentioned in the opening verse of the Acts, and from the perfect agreement in style and language. Hence arguments for or against the antiquity of the Acts affect the Third Gospel also, and therefore, to some extent, the First and Second as well. So we will consider first its *accuracy*, then its *authorship*, and lastly its *date*.

### (*A.*) ITS ACCURACY.

Now, this book, unlike the Gospels, deals with a large number of public men and places, many of which are well known from secular history, while inscriptions referring to others have been recently discovered. It is thus liable to be detected at every step if inaccurate; yet, with the doubtful exception of the date of the rebellion of Theudas, and some details as to the death of Herod Agrippa, no error can be discovered. As this is practically undisputed, we need not discuss the evidence in detail, but will give three examples.

### (1.) The titles of different rulers.

We will commence with the *titles* given to different rulers. As is well known, the Roman provinces were of two kinds, some belonging to the Emperor, and some to the Senate. The former were governed by *prprætors*, or when less important by *procurators*, and the latter by *proconsuls*, though they frequently changed hands. Moreover, individual places had often special names for their rulers; yet in every case the writer of the Acts uses the proper title.

For example, the ruler at Cyprus is rightly called *proconsul*.[238] This used to be thought a mistake, but we now know that it is correct; for though Cyprus had previously belonged to the Emperor, it had been exchanged with the Senate for another province before the time in question. And an inscription[239] found there at Soli has the words in Greek, *Paulus proconsul*, probably the Sergius Paulus of the Acts. Cyprus, it may be added, subsequently changed hands again.

[238] Acts. 13. 7.

[239] Cyprus, by Cesnola (London, 1877), p. 425.

In the same way Gallio is correctly described as *proconsul* of Achaia.[240] For though this province belonged to the Emperor for some years before A.D. 44, and was independent after A.D. 66, it belonged to the Senate in the interval, when the writer referred to it. And an inscription, recently found at Delphi, shows that Gallio was proconsul in A.D. 52, which agrees well with the chronology of the Acts.[241] Equally correct is the title of *governor* or *procurator*, applied to both Felix and Festus.[242] While it is satisfactory to add that the title *lord*, addressed to the Emperor Nero, which used to be thought rather a difficulty, as it was not known to have been adopted till the time of Domitian (A.D. 81-96), has now been found in papyri of the age of Nero.[243]

[240] Acts 18. 12.

[241] Palestine Exploration Quarterly, July, 1913.

[242] Acts 19. 38; 23. 26; 26. 30.

[243] Acts 25. 26; Deissman, New Light on the New Testament, 1907, p. 80.

Again, Herod (*i.e.*, Agrippa I.) shortly before his death, is styled *king*.[244] Now we learn from other sources that he had this title for the last three years of his government (A.D. 41-44), though there had been no king in Judæa for the previous thirty years, nor for many centuries afterwards.

[244] Acts 12. 1; Josephus, Antiq., xviii. 6, xix. 5.


Moreover, his son is also called *King* Agrippa, though it is implied that he was not king of Judæa, which was governed by Festus, but of some other province. Yet, strange to say, he seems to have held some official position in regard to the Jews, since Festus *laid Paul's case before him*, as if he were in some way entitled to hear it.[245] And all this is quite correct; for Agrippa, though King of Chalcis, and not Judæa, was yet (being a Jew) entrusted by the Emperor with the management of the Jewish Temple and Treasury, and the choice of the High Priests, so he was a good deal mixed up in Jewish affairs.[246] And this, though only a trifle, is interesting; because a late writer, who had taken the trouble to study the subject, and find out the position Agrippa occupied, is not likely to have shown his knowledge in such a casual way. Scarcely anyone notices it. And equally correct is the remarkable fact that his sister *Bernice* used to act with him on public occasions.[247]

[245] Acts 25. 13, 14.

[246] Josephus, Antiq., xx., 1, 8, 9.

[247] Acts 25. 23; Josephus, Wars, ii. 16; Life, xi.

Again at Malta we read of the *chief-man* Publius; the accuracy of which title (for it is a *title*, and does not mean merely the most important man) is also proved by inscriptions, though as far as we know it was peculiar to that island.[248] At Thessalonica, on the other hand, the magistrates have the curious title of *politarchs*, translated 'rulers of the city.'[249] This name does not occur in any classical author in this form, so the writer of the Acts used to be accused of a blunder here. His critics were unaware that an old arch was standing all the time at this very place, the modern Salonica, with an inscription containing this very word, saying it was built when certain men were the politarchs. The arch was destroyed in 1876, but the stone containing the inscription was preserved, and is now in the British Museum.[250] And since then other inscriptions have been found, showing that the term was in use all through the first century.

[248] Acts 28. 7; Boeckh's Corp. Ins. Lat. X., No. 7495; Corp. Ins. Gr., No. 5754.

[249] Acts 17. 6.

[250] In the Central Hall, near the Library.

Nor is this accuracy confined to well-known places on the coast; it extends wherever the narrative extends, even to the interior of Asia Minor. For though the rulers there are not mentioned, the writer was evidently well acquainted with the places he refers to. Take *Lystra*, for instance.[251] According to the writer, it was a city of Lycaonia, though the adjacent town of Iconium was not, and this has been recently proved to be correct. And it is interesting, because many classical authors wrongly assign Iconium to Lycaonia; while Lystra, though belonging to that province in the first century, was separated from it early in the second; so a late writer, or one ignorant of the locality, might easily have made a mistake in either case. And an inscription found near Lystra, in 1909, shows that the two gods, Jupiter and Mercury (*i.e.*, Zeus and Hermes) were commonly associated together by the inhabitants, as they are represented to be in the Acts.

[251] Acts 14. 1-12; Ramsay, Bearing of Recent Discovery on New Testament, 1915, pp. 48-63.

### (2.) The riot at Ephesus.

As a second example we will take the account of the *riot at Ephesus*. All the allusions here to the worship of Diana, including her image believed to have fallen from heaven (perhaps a meteorite roughly cut into shape), her magnificent shrine, the small silver models of this, her widespread worship, and the fanatical devotion of her worshippers, are all in strict agreement with what we know from other sources.

Moreover, inscriptions discovered there have confirmed the narrative to a remarkable extent. They have shown that the *theatre* was the recognised place of public meeting; that there were certain officers (who presided at the games, etc.) called *asiarchs*; that another well-known Ephesian officer was called the *town-clerk*; that Ephesus had the curious designation of *temple-keeper* of Diana (long thought to be a difficulty); that *temple-robbing* and *blasphemy* were both crimes which were specially recognised by the Ephesian laws; and that the term *regular assembly* was a technical one in use at Ephesus.[252] The reference to the *town-clerk* is particularly interesting, because what is recorded of him is said to agree with the duties of the town-clerk at Ephesus, though not with those of the same official elsewhere.[253] All this minute accuracy is hard to explain unless the narrative came from one who was present during the riot, and recorded what he actually saw and heard.

[252] *Comp.* Acts 19. 29-39; with inscriptions found in the Great Theatre. Wood's Discoveries at Ephesus, 1877, pp. 43, 47, 53, 51, 15, 39.

[253] Harnack, The Acts of the Apostles, translated by Wilkinson, 1909, p. 63.

### (3.) The agreement with St. Paul's Epistles.

Our third example shall be of a different kind. It is that if we compare the biography of St. Paul given in the Acts with the letters of that Apostle, many of them written to the very Churches and persons described there, we shall find numerous *undesigned agreements* between them. And these, as before explained (Chapter X.) form a strong argument in favour of the accuracy of both. Take, for instance, the Epistle to the Romans. Though not dated, it was evidently written at the close of St. Paul's second visit to Greece; and therefore, if mentioned in the Acts, it would come in at Chapter 20. 3. And the following are two, out of the numerous points of agreement.

The first is St. Paul's saying that he was going to Jerusalem, with alms from Macedonia and Achaia for the poor in that city. Now in the Acts it is stated that St. Paul had just passed through these provinces, and was on his way to Jerusalem, though there is no mention about the alms there. But it happens to be alluded to some chapters later, without, however, mentioning then where the alms came from.[254] The agreement is complete though it is certainly not designed.

[254] Rom. 15. 25, 26; Acts 19. 21; 24. 17.

The other refers to St. Paul's travels, which he says extended from Jerusalem as far as *Illyricum*. Now Illyricum is not once mentioned in the Acts; so there can be no intentional agreement here. And yet there is agreement. For we learn from various places that St. Paul had gone from Jerusalem all through what we now call Asia Minor, and just before the date of this Epistle had passed through Macedonia, which was his limit in this direction. And as this was the next province to Illyricum, it exactly agrees with the Epistle.[255]

[255] Rom. 15. 19; Acts 20. 2.

We may now sum up the evidence as to the accuracy of the Acts. The above instances are only specimens of many which might be given. The writer knew about Jerusalem and Athens just as well as about Ephesus. While his account of St. Paul's voyage from Cæsarea to Italy, including as it does, references to a number of places; to the climate, and prevailing winds of the Mediterranean; and to the phrases and customs of seamen, is so accurate, that critics of all schools have admitted that he is describing a voyage he had actually made. In short, the Book of the Acts is full of correct details throughout, and it is hard to believe that anyone but a contemporary could have written it.

### (*B.*) ITS AUTHORSHIP.

Now if we admit the general accuracy of the book, there is little difficulty in deciding on its *authorship*. As is well known, certain portions of it (describing some of St. Paul's travels, including his voyage to Italy) are written in the first person plural, and are commonly called the "*We*" sections.[256] This shows that the writer was a *companion* of St. Paul at that time; and then the great similarity in *language*, between these sections and the rest of the book, shows that they had the same author. For they are both written in the same style, and they both contain over forty important words and expressions, which do not occur elsewhere in the New Testament, except in the Third Gospel. This is indeed so striking that it practically settles the point.[257]

[256] Acts 16. 9-40; 20. 5-21. 18; 27. 1-28. 16.

[257] Harnack, Luke the Physician, translated by Wilkinson, 1907, p. 53.

But there are also slight *historical* connections between the two portions. For example, in the earlier chapters some incidents are recorded, in which a certain Philip (one of the *Seven*) was concerned; and why should these have been selected? The writer was not present himself, and many far more important events must have occurred, of which he gives no account. But a casual verse in the *We* sections explains everything: the writer, we are told, stayed *many days* with Philip, and of course learnt these particulars then. And as it seems to have been his rule only to record what he knew for certain, he might well have left out other and more important events, of which he had not such accurate knowledge.[258] And the earlier reference, which ends with the apparently pointless remark that *Philip came to Cæsarea*, without saying why or wherefore, is also explained, since this was the place where the writer afterwards met him. It is then practically certain that the whole book was written by one man, and that he was a companion of St. Paul in many of his travels.

[258] Acts 6. 5; 8. 5, 26, 40; 21. 10.; Luke 1. 3.

It is also practically certain that he was a *medical man*. The evidence for this is overwhelming, but as the fact is generally admitted, we need not discuss it at length. All we need say is that 201 places have been counted in the Acts, and 252 in the Third Gospel, where words and expressions occur which are specially, and many of them exclusively, used by Greek medical writers, and which, with few exceptions, do not occur elsewhere, in the New Testament.[259] For instance, we read of the many proofs of the Resurrection; the word translated *proofs* being frequently used by medical writers to express the infallible symptoms of a disease, as distinct from its mere signs, which may be doubtful, and they expressly give it this meaning. And we read of the restoration of all things; the word translated *restoration* being the regular medical term for a complete recovery of a man's body or limb.[260]

[259] Hobart's Medical Language of St. Luke (1882); some of his examples are rather doubtful.

[260] Acts 1. 3; 3. 21.

We conclude then, from the book itself, that the writer was an intimate friend of St. Paul and a medical man; and from one of St. Paul's Epistles we learn his name, *Luke the beloved physician*.[261] And this is confirmed by the fact that both this Epistle and that to Philemon, where St. Paul also names Luke as his companion, appear to have been written from Rome, when, as we know, the writer of the Acts was with him. And he seems to have remained with him to the last, *only Luke is with me.*[262] Yet this beloved and ever-faithful friend of St. Paul is not once named in the Acts, which would be most unlikely unless he were the author.

[261] Col. 4. 14; Philemon 24.

[262] 2 Tim. 4. 11.

## (*C.*) ITS DATE.

The *date* of the book can also be fixed with tolerable certainty. It is implied in its abrupt ending. The last thing it narrates is St. Paul's living at Rome, two years before his expected trial (A.D. 58-60).[263] It says nothing about this trial, nor of St. Paul's release, nor of his subsequent travels, nor of his second trial and martyrdom (probably under Nero, A.D. 64); though had it been written after these events, it could hardly have failed to record them. This is especially the case as the martyrdom of St. Peter and St. Paul, which, according to early authorities, occurred together at Rome, would have formed such a suitable conclusion for a work chiefly concerned with their labours.

[263] Rackham's Commentary on the Acts, 1901, p. lxvii; many place it a year or two later, some a little earlier.

On the other hand, the abrupt ending of the book is at once accounted for if it was written at that time, about A.D. 60, by St. Luke, who did not relate anything further, because nothing further had then occurred. And it is obvious that these two years would not only have formed a most suitable period for its compilation, but that he is very likely to have sent it to his friend Theophilus just before the trial, perhaps somewhat hurriedly, not knowing whether it might not involve his own death, as well as that of St. Paul.

This would also account for the great prominence given to the events of the immediately preceding years in Chapters 20. to 28., which is quite unintelligible, unless the book was written soon afterwards. They were nothing like as important as the events of the next few years, about which the writer says nothing. And why should he go through the earlier stages of St. Paul's arrest and trial, so carefully, step by step, from Lysias to Felix, from Felix to Festus, and then to Agrippa, and on to Rome; and then when he comes to the crisis, and the Apostle is about to appear before Cæsar, suddenly break off, without giving a hint as to which way it was decided? Everyone must feel how tantalising it is; and how unlikely he is to have stopped here, if he could have gone on.

This abrupt ending, then, is the great argument for dating the book about A.D. 60; but it is supported by several others. In the first place, the journey to Rome itself, especially the shipwreck, is described with such minute and graphic details, that it seems likely to have been written down very soon afterwards, probably in that city.

Secondly, the Roman judges and officials are always represented as treating the Christians with fairness, and even kindness; and the writer leaves St. Paul appealing to Cæsar, with every hope of a favourable verdict. There is no sign of bitterness or ill-feeling anywhere. And all this would have been most unlikely after the great persecution in A.D. 64; when Christians regarded Rome with the utmost horror.[264] Compare the somewhat similar case of the Indian Mutiny. Can we imagine an Englishman in India writing soon after the Mutiny a history, say of Cawnpore, up to 1854, and then closing it, without ever letting a hint fall that he was aware of the terrible tragedy which happened in 1857, or showing the slightest ill-feeling towards its perpetrators? The only reasonable conclusion would be that such a history must have been written *before* the Mutiny. In the same way the Acts must have been written *before* Nero's great persecution.

[264] *E.g.*, Rev. 17. 6.

Thirdly, the same sort of argument is afforded by the destruction of Jerusalem in A.D. 70. Had the book been written after this, it is strange that the writer should seem to be entirely unaware of it; more especially as it had so close a bearing on the events described in the Acts, such as the Jewish law not being binding on Gentile Christians. And it is the more significant, because he records the prophecy of the event in his Gospel,[265] but nowhere hints that the prophecy had been fulfilled.

[265] Luke 19. 43.

Lastly, an early date is implied by the passage, where St. Paul tells his friends near Ephesus, that they would not see him again. It was quite natural for him to have said so at the time, as his feelings were very despondent; but no one, writing many years later, would have recorded it *without comment*; since it is almost certain that St. Paul, after his release from Rome, did revisit Ephesus.[266]

[266] Acts 20. 25, 38; 2 Tim. 4. 20.

On the whole, then, there is very strong evidence in favour of the Acts of the Apostles having been written by St. Luke about A.D. 60; and this of course proves an earlier date for *St. Luke's Gospel*. And this again proves a still earlier one for *St. Mark's Gospel*, which is now generally admitted to have been written before St. Luke's; and probably for *St. Matthew's* as well. The evidence of the Acts, then, while confirming our previous conclusion that the first three Gospels were certainly written before A.D. 70, enables us to add with some confidence that they were also written before A.D. 60. And, it may be added, Prof. Harnack, who long maintained the opposite view, has at last accepted this early date for all these Gospels.[267] The book has of course no direct bearing on the date of St. John's Gospel.

[267] Date of Acts, and Synoptic Gospels, translated by Wilkinson, 1911, pp. 99, 133, 134. Some writers would place them still earlier. Thus Canon Birks, dates them all between A.D. 42-51, and he gives strong reasons for thinking that St. Luke, and his Gospel, are referred to in 2 Cor. 8. 18. (Horæ Evangelicæ, 1892, edit., pp. 259, 281, 293); and Archdeacon Allen places the second Gospel, about A.D. 44, and the first about A.D. 50. (Introduction to the Books of the New Testament, 1913, p. 13.)

# CHAPTER XVII.
## THAT THE RESURRECTION OF CHRIST IS PROBABLY TRUE.

(*A.*) ITS IMPORTANCE.

The third day, the empty tomb.

(*B.*) THE NARRATIVES.

The various accounts, table of Christ's appearances, the three groups, the double farewell.

(*C.*) THEIR DIFFICULTIES.

(1.) Discrepancies; often due to the appearances being placed together; the disciples going to Galilee.

(2.) Omissions; the Gospels only record selected instances, and St. Paul refers to them in groups.

(*D.*) THEIR TRUTHFULNESS.

(1.) Agreements; very important.

(2.) Mutual explanations; very numerous.

(3.) Signs of early date; very interesting.

Conclusion, the narratives appear to be thoroughly trustworthy.

We decided in the previous chapters that the Four Gospels, and also the Acts of the Apostles, were *genuine*; that is to say, they were written by the persons to whom they are commonly ascribed. And to these may be added the four great Epistles of St. Paul, and the Revelation of St. John, which, as before said, are admitted to be genuine by critics of all schools. We have thus direct testimony as to the life of Christ, that is to say, the testimony of contemporaries, some of whom must have known Him well. St. Matthew and St. John were two of His Apostles; St. Mark and St. Luke had exceptionally good means of knowing the truth, and may perhaps have had some slight knowledge of Christ themselves, as had also St. Paul.[268] We have now to examine the value of this testimony, more especially as to the *Resurrection of Christ*. So in the present chapter we will consider the *importance* of the Resurrection, and the *narratives* we have of it; both as to their *difficulties*, and their *truthfulness*; and in the next the various alternative theories.

[268] 2 Cor. 5. 16.

## (A.) ITS IMPORTANCE.

In the first place, we cannot overestimate the importance of the Resurrection, for this fact, either real or supposed, was the foundation of Christianity. This is plain not only from the Gospels, but still more from the Acts, where we have numerous short speeches by the Apostles, given under various circumstances, and to various audiences, including Jewish Councillors, Greek philosophers, and Roman governors. And in nearly all of them the Resurrection of Christ is not only positively asserted, but is emphasised as a fact established by indisputable evidence and as being the foundation of Christianity.[269] It is even said that it was the special duty of an apostle to bear witness to it; and St. Paul seems to have been aware of this, since, when claiming to be an apostle, he is careful to show that he was thus qualified. And for himself he makes it the basis of all his teaching, *if Christ hath not been raised, then is our preaching vain*.[270] It is certain, then, that the first preachers of Christianity preached the Resurrection of Christ.

[269] Acts 2. 24; 4. 10; 5. 30; 10. 40; 13. 30; 17. 31; 26. 23.

[270] Acts 1. 22; 1 Cor. 9. 1; 15. 14-17.

It is equally certain that they preached that it occurred on the *third day*, counting from the Crucifixion.[271] This also is stated not only in the Gospels, but by St. Paul; who in one place bases his whole argument on the fact that the Body of Christ (unlike that of David) *saw no corruption*, a point also alluded to by St. Peter, and implying a Resurrection in a few days.[272] While if further evidence is required, the fact that this third day (the first day of the week) became *the Lord's Day*—the Christian Sunday—seems to put the matter beyond dispute.

[271] Sometimes described as *after three days*, but that the two expressions are intended to mean the same is clear from Matt. 27. 63-64, where Christ's saying that He would rise again *after three days* is given as the reason for guarding the sepulchre *until the third day*. In the same way *after eight days* evidently means *on the eighth day* (John 20. 26).

[272] 1 Cor. 15. 4; Acts 13. 35-37; 2. 31.

Once more it is certain that the Christians believed that this Resurrection was one of Christ's *Body*, not His *Spirit*. This again is clear not only from the Gospels, which all speak of the *empty tomb*; but also from St. Paul's Epistles. For when he says that Christ *died*, and was *buried*, and was *raised on the third day*, and *appeared* to Cephas, etc., he must mean Christ's *Body* (for a Spirit cannot be *buried*); and he must mean that it was the *same* Body that died and was buried, that was afterwards raised, and appeared to them, including himself.[273] Christ's being *raised*, it will be noticed, was distinct from, and previous to, His *appearing* to anyone, just as in the Gospels the empty tomb is always mentioned *before* any of the appearances.

[273] 1 Cor. 15. 3-5.

And even in the one case, where St. Paul alludes to what he saw as a *heavenly vision*, he refers to it in order to prove that it is not incredible that God should *raise the dead*,[274] which again shows that he thought it was a *Body*, for a *Spirit* cannot be raised from the *dead*. And his specifying *the third day* makes this (if possible) still plainer, for the life of the spirit after death does not commence on the third day; nor would it have prevented Christ's Body from seeing corruption.

[274] Acts 26. 19, 8.

From all this it is abundantly clear that St. Paul, like the Four Evangelists, and the other Apostles, believed in what is called the *physical* Resurrection, in the sense that Christ's Body was restored to life, and left the tomb. Though like them, he also believed that it was no longer a *natural* body, bound by the ordinary laws of nature, but that it had been partly changed as well, so that it shared to some extent the properties of spirits.

Nor is his statement that *flesh and blood* cannot inherit the Kingdom of God, opposed to this.[275] For when he uses the same expression elsewhere (*e.g.*, *I conferred not with flesh and blood*)[276] it is evidently not used in a literal sense. It does *not* mean flesh and blood, in the same way in which we might speak of bones and muscles. It means *men*. So his meaning here is probably that mere men—human beings as such—cannot inherit the future life of glory. Their bodies will first have to be changed, and made incorruptible; but they will still be *bodies*. And as just said, St. Paul is quite definite as to its being the Body of Christ that was *buried*, that was afterwards raised on the third day.

[275] Cor. 15. 50.

[276] Gal. 1. 16; Eph. 6. 12; comp. Matt. 16. 17.

We may say, then, with confidence, that wherever the Resurrection was believed, the fact that it occurred on the third day, and the fact that it was a physical Resurrection, involving the empty tomb, was believed also. The three invariably went together. But was this belief justified? This is the question we have to discuss.

## (*B*.) THE NARRATIVES.

Now we have five different accounts of the Resurrection; and these are so thoroughly independent that not one of them can be regarded as the source of any of the others. Little stress, however, can be laid on the latter part of St. Mark's account, as the genuineness of the last twelve verses is doubtful;

but it anyhow represents a very early Christian belief, Aristion being sometimes named as the author. And even the earlier part is conclusive as to the empty tomb, and the promised appearance in Galilee. On the other hand, St. Paul's account, which is perhaps the strongest, is universally allowed to have been written within thirty years of the event; the most probable date for which is A.D. 29 or 30, and for the Epistle A.D. 55. And it should be noticed that St. Paul reminds the Corinthians that what he here says about the Resurrection is what he preached to them on his first visit (about A.D. 50), and that as they had *received* it from him, so he had himself *received* it from others at a still earlier date.[277]

[277] 1 Cor. 15. 1-3.

And we can even fix this date approximately, for two of the appearances he records were to St. Peter and St. James; and he happens to mention elsewhere[278] that these were the two Apostles he met at Jerusalem, three years after his conversion (A.D. 35, or earlier); so he doubtless heard the whole account then, even if he had not heard it before. And this was certainly within *ten years*—probably within *seven* years—of the Crucifixion. More ancient testimony than this can scarcely be desired. And if anything could add to its importance it would be St. Paul's own statement that in this respect his teaching was the same as that of the original Apostles: *Whether then it be I or they, so we preach and so ye believed.*[279]

[278] Gal. 1. 19.

[279] 1 Cor. 15. 11.

We need not quote the various accounts here, but the accompanying table gives them in a convenient form for reference. Altogether Christ seems to have been seen on thirteen different occasions; and there may have been others, which are not recorded, though they are perhaps hinted at.[280]

[280] Acts 1. 3; 13. 31; John 20. 30.

It is doubtful however if the eighth appearance was separate from the ninth, for St. Matthew says that when the Eleven saw Him, on the mountain in Galilee, as He had appointed, *they* worshipped Him, but *some* doubted. This *some* can scarcely mean some of the Eleven, who had just worshipped. It probably refers to some others who were present (*i.e.*, some of the five hundred) who doubted at first if it was really He, as He was some way off, and it was before He *came* to them. And since the command to preach the Gospel to all the world, which St. Matthew records, was probably addressed to the Eleven only, it will account for his not mentioning that others were present. In the same way St. Luke relates the Ascension, as if only the Eleven were there, though it is clear *from his own narrative* that he knew there were others with them; since he afterwards records St. Peter as saying so.[281]

[281] Acts 1. 1-13; 22-23.

On the other hand, the appearance to the five hundred must have been on a *mountain*, or some other open space, as a room would not have been large enough. It must have been in *Galilee*, as there were not so many disciples in Jerusalem.[282] It must have been *by appointment*, as they could hardly have come together by accident; and they are not likely to have come together at all unless the *Eleven* had collected them. And all this is an additional reason for identifying it with that recorded by St. Matthew.

[282] Acts 1. 15.

It must next be noticed that the appearances form *three groups*. First a group in or near Jerusalem, which was chiefly to the Twelve Apostles, and extended over eight days. Secondly a group in Galilee, the most important being that to the five hundred, which was a sort of *farewell* to His Galilean disciples. And thirdly to a group back again at Jerusalem, chiefly to the Twelve, but including others, and ending with the Ascension, or *farewell* to His Judæan disciples.

## TABLE OF CHRIST'S APPEARANCES.

|  | *1 Cor.* | *Matt.* | *Mark.* | *Luke.* | *John.* |
|---|---|---|---|---|---|
| Empty tomb visited by women | .. | 28. 1-8 | 16. 1-8 | 24. 1-11, 22-23 | 20. 1-2 |
| And by Apostles | .. | .. | .. | 12, 24 | 3-10 |
| An appearance in Galilee foretold | .. | 7 | 16. 7 | .. | .. |
| Then Christ was seen *In or near Jerusalem, by* | | | | | |
| (i.) Mary Magdalene | .. | .. | 9-11 | .. | 11-18 |
| (ii.) The two Marys | .. | 9-10 | .. | .. | .. |
| (iii.) St. Peter | 15. 5 | .. | .. | 34 | .. |
| (iv.) Cleopas and another, perhaps St. Luke, at Emmaus. | .. | .. | 12-13 | 13-35 | .. |

| (v.) The Apostles and others (without St. Thomas) | 5 | .. | 14 | 36-43 | 19-25 |
| (vi.) The Apostles (with St. Thomas) | .. | .. | .. | .. | 26-29 |
| *In Galilee, by* | | | | | |
| (vii.) Seven Apostles on the Lake. | .. | .. | .. | .. | 21. 1-23 |
| (viii.) The Apostles on the mountain | .. | 16-20 | 15-18 | .. | .. |
| (ix.) Over 500 persons | 6 | .. | .. | .. | .. |
| (x.) St. James | 7 | .. | .. | .. | .. |
| *Back at Jerusalem, by* | | | | | *Acts.* |
| (xi.) The Apostles at Jerusalem | .. | .. | .. | 44-49 | 1. 4-5 |
| (xii.) The Apostles and others at Bethany | 7 | .. | 19-20 | 50-53 | 6-11, 22 |
| (xiii.) St. Paul | 8 | .. | .. | .. | 9. 3-9 |

And though this *double* farewell is sometimes thought to be a difficulty, yet as Christ's Resurrection was meant to be the proof of His mission, it seems only natural that He should have appeared again to *all* His disciples, and have taken leave of them; both those in Galilee, and those at Jerusalem, the Apostles themselves being of course present on each occasion. And as the words *when they were come together* imply that the meeting in Jerusalem, like that in Galilee, had been previously announced, all the Judæan disciples may well have been there; and this we know was the case with Matthias, Justus, and others.[283]

[283] Acts 1. 6, 22.

### (*C.*) THEIR DIFFICULTIES.

Passing on now to the difficulties in the narratives; they may be conveniently placed under the two heads of *discrepancies* and *omissions*.

### (1.) Discrepancies.

These seem to be chiefly due to two of the Evangelists, St. Mark and St. Luke, recording separate appearances as if they were continuous. But it so happens that they do much the same in the rest of their Gospels, often recording separate sayings of Christ as if they were one discourse; and even in closely-connected passages a break has sometimes to be assumed.[284]

While in these very narratives, St. Luke describes an appearance at Jerusalem in Acts 1. 4, and continues without any change of place till v. 12, when he says *they returned to Jerusalem*. Plainly he is here grouping together words spoken on different occasions.

[284] *E.g.*, in Luke 14. 21-22.

Therefore he may have done the same at the end of his Gospel. Indeed, it is almost certain that he did, otherwise we should have to place the Ascension in the middle of the night, which is scarcely probable. Moreover, in the Acts he expressly says that the appearances lasted *forty days*; and he quotes St. Paul, as saying that they lasted *many days*.[285] He seems to have thought it unnecessary in his Gospel to explain that they were at different times; and if St. Mark did the same, it would account for most, though not all, of the discrepancies between them.

[285] Acts 1. 3; 13. 31.

These discrepancies, however, are often much exaggerated. Take for instance the fifth appearance in the previous list. St. Luke and St. John evidently refer to the same occasion, as it was on the evening of Easter Day; yet one says the Apostles were *terrified*, and thought they saw a spirit; while the other says they were *glad*. Can both be true? Certainly they can, if we assume (as is most natural) that the Apostles were *at first* terrified, and thought they saw a spirit; but were afterwards glad, when on Christ's showing them His hands and side, they were convinced that it was really Himself. And He may then have reproached them for their unbelief as recorded by St. Mark.

Or take the case of the Angels at the Tomb. These are referred to by every Evangelist, though some call them men (in white or dazzling apparel) and others angels. But as St. Luke uses both words,[286] and as angels are not likely to have appeared in any but a human form, there is no real difficulty here. While if the second angel was not always visible, it would account for some of the Evangelists speaking of only one. And it may be mentioned in passing, that one of the angels is said to have been seen by the Roman soldiers as well, who went and told the Jews about it.[287] And this is not likely to have been asserted within twenty years unless it had been the case, as the Jews would have contradicted it. Yet if it was the case, it affords an additional argument for the Resurrection, and one derived from Christ's enemies, not His friends.

[286] Luke 24. 4, 23. Similarly Gabriel is called a *man* in Dan. 9. 21, and an *angel* in Luke 1. 25.

[287] Matt. 28. 4, 11.

A more important difficulty is caused by Christ's command to the women, that they and the Apostles were to proceed to Galilee to meet Him, when, as He knew, He was going to appear to them in Jerusalem the same day. The most probable explanation is that the meeting in Galilee was the one *intended* all along, in fact we are definitely told so.[288] But when the women, in consequence of the Angel's message, and after they had recovered from their fright (which at first made them run away and say nothing to anyone),[289] went and told the Apostles to go there, they were *disbelieved*.[290] This naturally made the women doubt too, so they returned to the grave to make further inquiries, none of them having the slightest intention of going to Galilee.

[288] Mark 14. 28.

[289] Mark 16. 8.

[290] Luke 24. 11.

Under these circumstances, something more was necessary, so Christ appeared first to Mary Magdalene, and then to her with the other Mary, when He told them Himself to warn the Apostles to proceed to Galilee, which they again did, and were again *disbelieved*.[291] Then He appeared to the two disciples on the way to Emmaus, and when they came back, and told the rest, they were also at first *disbelieved*; the Apostles, though now admitting that Christ had been seen by St. Peter, still denying such a bodily resurrection (able to eat food, etc.) as they described.[292]

[291] Mark 16. 11.

[292] Mark 16. 13; Luke 24. 34.

After this there was nothing for it, but for Christ to appear to the Apostles Himself, and convince them personally by eating food in their presence, which He did, when most of them were assembled together the same evening. And He may then have told them to remain in Jerusalem till they were *all* convinced, as they could scarcely have been expected to collect the five hundred for the meeting in Galilee, so long as they kept disputing among themselves as to whether He had really risen. And it was thus another week before the last sceptic (St. Thomas) was convinced, and they finally started for Galilee. These discrepancies then are not nearly so serious as is commonly supposed.

### (2.) Omissions.

With regard to the *omissions*, none of our lists are at all complete, and this is often thought to be a difficulty. But as far as the *Gospels* are concerned, the writers nowhere profess to give a complete list of Christ's appearances, any more than of His parables, or His miracles; they only record (as one of them tells us)[293] *selected instances*. And in the present case their choice is quite intelligible. Thus St. Matthew closes his Gospel, which is concerned chiefly with the Galilean ministry, with the farewell meeting in Galilee; St. John, whose Gospel is concerned chiefly with the Judæan ministry, ended his (before the last chapter was added, which seems a sort of appendix) with some of the appearances in Jerusalem. While St. Luke, who was more of an historian, and wrote everything *in order*,[294] though he describes most in detail the appearance to the two disciples at Emmaus (which is only natural if he was one of them), is yet careful to carry his narrative right on to the Ascension. Therefore, though they only record certain appearances, they may well have known of the others; and there can be little doubt that they did.

[293] John 20. 30.

[294] Luke 1. 3.

Thus, St. Matthew speaks of the Eleven meeting Christ by *appointment*, so he must have known of some interview when this appointment was made, (perhaps the one on the Lake), as the messages to the women did not fix either the time or place.[295] In the same way St. Mark must have known of a meeting in Galilee, as he refers to it himself, and St. Luke of an appearance to St. Peter.[296] While St. John, though he does not record the Ascension, must certainly have known of it, as he refers to it twice in the words, *if ye should behold the Son of Man ascending*, and *I ascend unto My Father*, the former passage clearly showing that it was to be a visible ascent, and that the Apostles were to see it.[297] Plainly, then, the Evangelists did not relate every appearance they knew of, and the objection as far as they are concerned, may be dismissed at once.

[295] Matt. 28. 16, 7, 10.

[296] Mark 16. 7; Luke 24. 34.

[297] John 6. 62; 20. 17.

On the other hand, *St. Paul's list* certainly looks as if it were meant to be complete; and this is no doubt a real difficulty. Surely, it is said, if the other appearances had occurred, or were even supposed to have occurred, when St. Paul wrote, he would have heard of them; and if he had heard of them, he would have mentioned them, as he was evidently trying to make out as strong a case as he could. He might perhaps have omitted the appearances to *women*, as their testimony was not considered of much value at the time; and they were not witnesses of the Resurrection, in the sense he alludes to—*i.e.*, persons who went about preaching it;[298] but why should he have omitted the rest?

[298] 1 Cor. 15. 11.

There is however a fairly good explanation. The appearances it will be remembered form *three groups*. Now St. Paul mentions two appearances to individual Apostles—St. Peter and St. James; and this was doubtless because he had had such vivid accounts of them from the men themselves, when he met them at Jerusalem. For we may be sure that if they had not told him, he would not have accepted it from anyone else. But he seems to refer to the others *in these groups*, first to the Twelve (at Jerusalem), then to the five hundred (in Galilee), and then to all the Apostles, evidently meaning more than the Twelve (back again at Jerusalem). But by so doing, he does not limit it to only one appearance in each group. In the same way a man might say that on returning to England he saw first his parents, then his brothers, then his cousins; though he had seen his parents on two days a week apart, his brothers for only a few hours, and his cousins for several successive days.

And the fact that St. Paul, in one of his speeches in the Acts,[299] expressly says that Christ was seen for *many days* at Jerusalem, strongly confirms this view. We conclude, then, that in his Epistle he is mentioning the appearances by groups, rather than every single one; wishing to emphasise the number of men who had seen Christ, rather than the number of times they had seen Him; and if so it does away with the difficulty. None of these objections, then, are of much importance.

[299] Acts 13. 31.

### (*D.*) THEIR TRUTHFULNESS.

Turning now to the other side, the narratives bear abundant marks of truthfulness. These we will consider under the three heads of *agreements*, *mutual explanations*, and *signs of early date*.

### (1.) Agreements.

In the first place it is important to notice that in spite of the discrepancies and omissions just alluded to, there is an extraordinary amount of *agreement* in the narratives. For all the more important points—the third day, the empty tomb, the visit of the women, the angelic message, the first appearance being in Jerusalem, the incredulity of some of the disciples, and Christ's not only appearing, but speaking as well, and this in the presence of all the Apostles— are *all* vouched for by *every* Evangelist.

They also agree in saying that the Apostles *remained in Jerusalem* after Christ's arrest, and did not as we might have expected return at once to Galilee? For the last two Gospels expressly state that they were in Jerusalem on Easter Day; and the first two imply it, or how could the women have been told to take them a message to *go* to Galilee?

Further they all agree in *not* giving (what imaginary accounts might well have contained) any description of the Resurrection itself, any appearance of Christ to His enemies; or any information as to the other world, though this last would have been so eagerly welcomed, and could have been so easily invented.

Moreover the *order* in which the appearances are placed is also the same in every account, that to Mary Magdalene for instance (wherever it occurs) being, always placed first, that to St. Peter next, that to Cleopas next, then that to the Twelve, etc. And this is the more remarkable because the narratives are so obviously independent, and the order is not at all a likely one. Writers of fiction, for instance, would never have made Christ first appear to so little known a person as Mary Magdalene, rather than to His Mother or His Apostles.

Once more the narratives all agree in the extreme *calmness* with which they are written. One would have thought it almost impossible for anyone after relating the story of the Cross, to have avoided some word of triumph, or exultation, in regard to the Resurrection and Ascension. But nothing of the kind is found. The writers record them, like the rest of the history, as simple matters of fact, apparently regarding them as the natural close for such a Life, and calling for no comment. How unlikely this would be in legendary accounts scarcely needs pointing out.

It may also be added (though it does not concern these actual narratives) that the Evangelists all agree in saying that Christ had *prophesied* His own Resurrection.[300] And while this does not of course prove it to have been true, it yet forms a difficulty on any other theory.

[300] *E.g.*, Matt. 16. 21; Mark 9. 31; Luke 18. 33; John 2. 19-21.

**(2.) Mutual explanations.**

In the next place it is surprising to find how often a slight remark in one of the narratives will help to explain some apparent improbability, or difficulty in another. And since, as just said, the narratives are quite independent, and were certainly not written to explain one another; such indications of truthfulness are of great value. We will therefore consider several examples.[301]

[301] These and some others are discussed in a paper in the *Expositor*, May, 1909, by the present writer.

To begin with, St. John records Mary Magdalene as visiting the empty Tomb, and then telling the disciples *we know not where they have laid Him*. But to whom does the *we* refer, as she was apparently alone all the time? St. John does not explain matters; but the other Evangelists do. For they say that though Mary

Magdalene was the leader of the party, and is always named first, yet as a matter of fact there were other women with her; and this accounts for the *we*. Later on no doubt she was alone; but then she uses the words *I know not*.[302]

[302] John 20. 2, 13.

Secondly, St. Luke says that *Peter* was the disciple who ran to the tomb on hearing of the Angel's message, without however giving any reason why he should have been the one to go. But St. Mark, though he does not mention the visit of Peter, records that the message had been specially addressed to him; and St. John says that Mary Magdalene had specially informed him; and this of course explains his going. St. Luke, it may be added, in the subsequent words, *certain of them that were with us*,[303] implies that at least one other disciple went with him, which agrees with St. John.

[303] Luke 24. 24.

St. Luke then says that when Peter arrived at the tomb, he saw the linen cloths *by themselves*, and went home *wondering*. This seems only a trifle, but what does it mean? St. Luke does not explain matters, but St. John does; for he describes how the cloths were arranged. This was in a way which showed that the Body could not have been hurriedly stolen, but had apparently vanished without disturbing them. It convinced St. John that the disappearance was supernatural, and would quite account for St. Peter's wondering.[304]

[304] Luke 24. 12; John 20. 6-8.

Again, St. Matthew narrates that when Christ appeared to Mary Magdalene, and the other Mary, He was at once recognised, held by the feet, and worshipped. And they do not seem to have been at all surprised at meeting Him near the tomb, in spite of the Angel's message that they should go to Galilee to see Him. Evidently something must have occurred between, making a break in the narrative after v. 8, which is quite possible, for the words, *And behold* (Rev. Vers.) do not always imply a close connection.[305] And from the other Evangelists we learn what this was. For St. John describes an appearance to Mary Magdalene *alone*, when she was rebuked for wishing to touch Him, apparently in the old familiar way, and without any act of reverence; and St. Mark says this was the *first* appearance. If then a few minutes later, she, in company with the other Mary, saw Christ again, it would quite account for their not being surprised at meeting Him, and also for their altered behaviour in prostrating themselves to the ground, and being in consequence permitted to hold Him by the *feet*, and worship Him.

[305] *E.g.*, Matt. 2. 1.

Once more St. Luke says that when Christ appeared to the Apostles in the evening, He was mistaken for a *spirit*; but he gives no reason for this, and it was apparently the only occasion on which it occurred. St. John however, though he does not mention the incident, fully explains it; for he says that *the doors were shut* for fear of the Jews; and obviously if Christ suddenly appeared within closed doors, it would account for their thinking that He must be a spirit. On the other hand, St. John speaks of Christ's showing them His hands (and also His side) though without giving any reason for this. But St. Luke's statement that they at first took Him for a spirit, and that He did this to convince them of His identity, quite accounts for it; so each of the narratives helps to explain the other.

But this is not all, for St. Luke then adds that as they still disbelieved, Christ asked if they had anything to eat (*i.e.*, if they would give *Him* something to eat) and they at once offered Him a piece of broiled fish. But he gives no hint as to why they happened to have any fish ready. St. Mark however, though he does not mention either the request, nor its response, fully explains both; for he says they were *sitting at meat* at the time, probably just concluding their evening meal. And all this still further explains St. John's narrative, that Christ said to them *again*, the second time, *Peace be unto you*; which would be much more natural if something had occurred between, than if (as St. John implies) it was just after the first time.

Again, St. Mark records Christ as saying, after His command to preach the Gospel to all the world, 'He that believeth *and is baptised* shall be saved,' though without any previous reference to baptism. But St. Matthew says the command was not only to make disciples of all nations, but to *baptise* them as well, and this of course explains the other passage, though curiously enough St. Matthew himself does not refer to it.

And then as to the appearance to the five hundred recorded by St. Paul. None of the Evangelists mention this, but it explains a good deal that they do mention. Thus St. John alludes to the Apostles being in *Galilee*, (instead of staying in Jerusalem) after the Resurrection, but he gives no hint as to why they went there. Nor do St. Matthew and St. Mark, who say Christ told them to go there, give any hint as to why He told them; but this appearance to the five hundred, who had to be collected in Galilee, explains everything. It also accounts for St. Matthew's curious remark (before noticed) that when the Eleven saw Christ in Galilee, *they worshipped Him, but some doubted*. And it probably explains St. Luke's omission of Galilee among the places where the Apostles themselves had to preach the Resurrection; as there were so many witnesses there already.[306]

[306] Acts 1. 8.

Now of course too much stress must not be laid on small details like these, but still the fact that such short and independent accounts should explain one another in so many ways is a distinct evidence of truthfulness. Legendary accounts of fictitious events would not be likely to do so.

**(3.) Signs of early date.**

In conclusion, it is interesting to note that these accounts, especially those in the first three Gospels, show signs of an extremely early, if not a *contemporary* date. Thus St. Peter is still called by his old name of *Simon*,[307] and it is the last occasion when that name is used, without explaining to whom it refers; St. Paul, some years later, though alluding to this same appearance, calling him by what was then his usual name of Cephas or Peter. Whilst St. John, writing many years afterwards, though he is equally accurate as to Simon being the name in use at the time, thinks it necessary to explain who was meant by it ('Jesus saith to Simon *Peter*, Simon son of John, lovest thou Me?').[308]

[307] Luke 24. 34.

[308] John 21. 15; comp. Acts. 15. 7, 14.

Similarly the Apostles are still spoken of as *the Eleven*, though they could only have had this title for *just these few weeks*.[309] And the fact of their having had it seems to have been soon forgotten. For St. Paul even when alluding to this very time prefers to call them by the familiar title of *the Twelve*, which was equally correct, as we are specially told that St. Matthias, who was afterwards chosen as the twelfth, had been with them all along.[310]

[309] Mark 16. 14; Luke 24. 9, 33.

[310] Acts 1. 22; 1 Cor. 15. 5.

There are also some incidental remarks in the narratives, which seem so natural, and yet so unlikely to have been invented. Thus we read that on one occasion after Christ appeared to the Apostles, they still disbelieved *for joy*; and on another, that though they knew it was the Lord, they yet wanted to ask Him *Who art Thou?*[311] Such bewildered feelings are quite intelligible at the time, but are not likely to have been thought of afterwards.

[311] Luke 24. 41; John 21. 12.

Moreover the *kind* of Resurrection asserted (though no doubt presenting great difficulties) is strongly in favour of a contemporary date. For it was not (as said in Chapter XIII.) a mere resuscitation of Christ's natural body, but His rising again in a body which combined material and spiritual properties in a remarkable manner. And there was nothing in the Old Testament, or anywhere else, to suggest such a Resurrection as this; it was quite unique. Indeed the *combination* of these properties—and they occur in the same Gospel—is so extremely puzzling, that it is hard to see how anything but actual experience (or what they believed to be such) could ever have induced men to record it. And much the same may be said of their ascribing an *altered appearance* to Christ's Body, so that He was often not recognised at first. Late writers are not likely to have imagined this.

Lastly, the utter absence of any attempt at harmonising the narratives, or avoiding the apparent discrepancies between them, also points to their extreme antiquity. The writers in fact seem to narrate just what they believed to have happened, often mentioning the most trivial circumstances, and without ever attempting to meet difficulties or objections. And while such disconnected accounts might well have been written by the actual witnesses of a wonderful miracle, they are not such as would have been deliberately invented; nor are they like subsequent legends and myths.

These narratives then appear throughout to be thoroughly trustworthy; and we therefore decide that the *Resurrection of Christ is probably true*. In the next chapter we will consider the various alternative theories.

# CHAPTER XVIII
## THAT THE FAILURE OF OTHER EXPLANATIONS INCREASES THIS PROBABILITY.

The first witnesses of the Resurrection. The value of all testimony depends on four questions about the witnesses, and here the denial of each corresponds to the four chief alternative theories.

(*A.*) THE FALSEHOOD THEORY.

This would be to deny their *veracity*, and say that they did not speak the truth, as far as they knew it. But it is disproved by their motives, their conduct, and their sufferings.

(*B.*) THE LEGEND THEORY.

This would be to deny their *knowledge*, and say that they had not the means of knowing the truth. But amply sufficient means were within their reach, and they were quite competent to use them.

(*C.*) THE VISION THEORY.

This would be to deny their *investigation*, and say that they were too excited to avail themselves of these means. But this theory has immense difficulties.

(1.) Arguments in its favour.

(2.) Arguments against it.

(3.) Its failure to account for the facts.

(4.) The theory of real visions.

(*D.*) THE SWOON THEORY.

This would be to deny their *reasoning*, and say that they did not draw the right conclusion, since Christ's appearances were due to His not having died. But this theory also has immense difficulties.

(*E.*) CONCLUSION.

The alleged difficulties of the Christian Theory, extremely strong argument in favour of the Resurrection.


We decided in the last chapter that the Resurrection of Christ was *probably true*; that is to say, we carefully examined the various narratives, and came to the conclusion that they had every appearance of being candidly and truthfully written. We have now to consider, more in detail, *the testimony of its first witnesses*. And, as we shall see, this affords strong additional evidence in its favour; since all attempts to account for this testimony, without admitting its truth, fail hopelessly.

By the *first witnesses*, we mean those persons who saw, or said they saw, Christ alive after His Crucifixion. This will include the twelve Apostles, and over 500 other Christians, most of whom St. Paul says were still alive when he wrote. It will also include two persons, who at the time were *not* Christians,— St. Paul himself, an avowed enemy, and St. James who, though he was Christ's brother, does not seem to have believed in Him.[312]

[312] John 7. 5.

And before discussing the value of their testimony, it may be well to glance at some general rules in regard to all testimony. If, then, a person plainly asserts that a certain event took place, before we believe that it did take place, we must inquire first as to his *Veracity*: did he speak the truth as far as he knew it? Next as to his *Knowledge*: had he the means of knowing the truth? Next as to his *Investigation*: did he avail himself of those means? And lastly, as to his *Reasoning*: did he draw the right conclusion? And all possible ways of denying the truth of a man's statement can be brought under one or other of these heads. For if it is not true, it must be either:—

| Intentionally false | | | | = want of Veracity. |
|---|---|---|---|---|
| or | | | | |
| Unintentionally false, in which case he either | had not the means of knowing the truth | | | = want of Knowledge. |
| | or | | | |
| | had the means, and either | did not use them | | = want of Investigation. |
| | | or | | |
| | | used them wrongly | | = want of Reasoning. |

From this it is clear that for anyone to deny a man's statement, without disputing either his veracity, knowledge, investigation, or reasoning, is very like denying that one angle is greater than another, without disputing that it is neither equal to it, nor less than it. We have now to apply these general rules to the testimony in favour of the Resurrection of Christ. And, as we shall see, the denial of these four points corresponds to the four chief alternative theories, which, may be called the *Falsehood*, the *Legend*, the *Vision*, and the *Swoon* Theory.

## (A.) THE FALSEHOOD THEORY.

We will begin with the Falsehood Theory. This would be to deny the *veracity* of the witnesses, and say that though they asserted that Christ rose from the dead, and appeared to them, they did not really believe it. In other words they were deliberate impostors, who, knowing that their Master did not rise from the dead, yet spent their whole lives in trying to persuade people that He did. And, as we shall see, their *motives*, their *conduct*, and their *sufferings*, are all strongly opposed to such a theory.

And first as to their *motives*, had they any interest in asserting that Christ rose from the dead unless they really believed it? Clearly they had *not*, for they were so few or so faint-hearted that they could not prevent their Master being crucified. What chance was there then of persuading the world that He had risen from the dead, and why should they have embarked on such a hopeless scheme? Nothing indeed but the most firm conviction of their Lord's Resurrection, and therefore of supernatural assistance, would ever have induced men to have ventured on it. If they believed the Resurrection to be true, then, and only then, would they have had any motive whatever for preaching it.

Next as to their *conduct*, did this show that they really believed what they preached? And here also the evidence is overwhelming. When their Master was crucified His followers were naturally filled with gloom and despair; but in a few days this was changed to intense joy and confidence. They preached the Resurrection in the very place where He was crucified, and boldly went forth to convert the world in His name. It is clear that before such a marvellous change could take place they must at least have thought they had, what St. Luke asserts they actually did have, *many proofs* of the Resurrection.[313] To them, at all events, the evidence must have seemed conclusive, or Christianity would have perished on Calvary.

[313] Acts 1. 3.

Lastly as to their *sufferings*. This is the most important point, since voluntary suffering in any form, but especially in its extreme form of martyrdom, seems conclusive as to a man's veracity. Persons do not suffer for what they believe to be false; they must have believed it to be true, though this does not of course prove that it actually was true. And here is the answer to the common objection, that since all religions have had their martyrs, this kind of evidence proves nothing. On the contrary, it does prove something, though it does not prove everything. It does not prove that what the man died for was true, but it does prove that he believed it to be true. It is therefore a conclusive test as to his *veracity*.

What evidence have we, then, that the first witnesses suffered for the truth of what they preached? And once more the evidence is complete and overwhelming, both from the Acts and St. Paul's Epistles. We need only refer to these latter, as their genuineness is undisputed. St. Paul then, in one place, gives a list of the actual sufferings he had undergone; he alludes to them in numerous other places, and often as if they were the common experience of all Christians at the time; and in one passage he expressly includes the other Apostles with himself in the long list of sufferings he describes. While he elsewhere declares that at a still earlier time, before his conversion, he himself persecuted the Christians *beyond measure*.[314]

[314] 2 Cor. 11. 24-27; Rom. 8. 35; 1 Cor. 4. 9-13; Gal. 1. 13.

There can thus be no doubt as to the continual sufferings of the first witnesses, and, as just said, it is a decisive proof of their veracity. We conclude therefore that when they asserted that Christ rose from the dead, they were asserting what they honestly believed whether rightly or wrongly, to be true. And as this belief was due, simply to the witnesses believing that they saw Christ alive after His death; we must further conclude that they honestly believed in the appearances of Christ as recorded by themselves, and their friends, in the New Testament. In other words, these accounts are not *intentionally* false.

So much for the *veracity* of the witnesses. It is not, as a rule, denied by modern opponents of the Resurrection; but in early times, when men ought to have known best, it was evidently thought to be the only alternative. St. Paul declares emphatically that unless Christ had risen, he and the other Apostles were *false witnesses*, in plain words *liars*.[315] That was the only choice. They were either saying what they knew to be true, or what they knew to be false. And the idea of there being some *mistake* about it, due to visions, or swoons, or anything else, never seems to have occurred to anyone.

[315] 1 Cor. 15. 15.

### (*B.*) THE LEGEND THEORY.

We pass on now to the Legend Theory. This would be to deny the *knowledge* of the witnesses: and say that our Gospels are not genuine, but merely record subsequent legends; so we cannot tell whether the first witnesses had, or had not, the means of knowing the truth. But if we admit the genuineness of our Gospels, and the veracity of their writers (both of which have been admitted), the Legend Theory is out of the question.

They asserted, it will be remembered, that Christ's *Body*, not His Spirit, appeared to them, after the crucifixion; and from their own accounts it is clear that they had ample means of finding out if this was true. Whether they used these means, and actually did find out, is, of course, another question; but as to sufficient means being available, and their being quite competent to use them if they liked, there can be no doubt whatever. As has been well said, it was not one person who saw Him, but many; they saw Him not only separately, but together; not only for a moment, but for a long time; not only by night, but by day; not only at a distance, but near; not only once, but several times. And they not only saw Him, but they touched Him, walked with Him, conversed with Him, ate with Him, and examined His Body to satisfy their doubts. In fact, according to their own accounts, Christ seems to have convinced them in every way in which conviction was possible that He had really risen from the dead.

And even apart from our Gospels, the Legend Theory is still untenable. For St. Paul mentions several of the appearances, and as this was within a few years of the events, there was no time for the growth of legends. Moreover he heard of them direct from those who saw them, St. Peter, St. James, etc., so he must have known the circumstances under which they occurred, and, being an educated man, is not likely to have been taken in by any imposture. While his saying that some of the five hundred had died, though most of them were still alive when he wrote, implies that he had also made some enquiries about that appearance. His testimony is thus very valuable from every point of view, and absolutely fatal to the Legend Theory.

### (*C.*) THE VISION THEORY.

We now come to the Vision Theory. This would be to deny the *investigation* of the witnesses; and say that they were so excited, or so enthusiastic, or perhaps so stupid, that they did not avail themselves of the ample means they had of finding out the truth. In other words they so expected their Lord to appear to them after His death, and kept so dwelling on the thought of Him, as though unseen, yet perhaps very near to them, that after a time they fancied they actually saw Him, and that He had risen from the dead. The wish was, in fact, father to the thought; so that when a supposed appearance took place, they were so filled with joy at their Master's presence, that they neglected to ascertain whether the appearance they saw was real, or only due to their own fancy.

Such is the theory; though it is often modified in regard to particular appearances, by ascribing them to dreams, or to someone being mistaken for Christ. And as it is at present the favourite one with those who reject the Resurrection, we must examine it carefully; first considering the arguments in its favour, then those against it, then its failure to account for the facts recorded, and lastly what is known as the theory of real visions.

### (1.) Arguments in its favour.

Now we must at once admit that it is possible for an honest man to mistake a phantom of his own brain, arising from some diseased state of the mind or body, for a reality in the outer world. Such *subjective* visions, as they are called, are by no means unheard of, though they are not common. And of course the great, if not the only argument in its favour is that it professes to account for the alleged Resurrection, without on the one hand admitting its truth, or on the other that the witnesses were deliberate impostors. Here, it is urged, is a way of avoiding both difficulties, by allowing that the witnesses honestly believed all they said, only they were *mistaken* in supposing the appearances to be real, when they were merely due to their own imagination. And undoubtedly the fact that men have often thought they saw ghosts, visions, etc., when there was really nothing to see, gives it some support.

### (2.) Arguments against it.

Let us now consider how this Vision Theory would suit the accounts of the Resurrection written by the witnesses themselves, and their friends. As will be seen, we might almost imagine that they had been written on purpose to contradict it.

To begin with, the writers were not unacquainted with visions, and occasionally record them as happening to themselves or others. But then they always use suitable expressions, such as falling into a trance.[316] No such language is used in the Gospels to describe the appearances of Christ, which are always recorded as if they were actual matters of fact. While as to St. Paul, he never confuses the revelations and visions, which he sometimes had, with the one great appearance of Christ to him near Damascus, which qualified him to be an Apostle.[317]

[316] *E.g.*, Acts 10. 10; 9. 10; 16. 9.

[317] 1 Cor. 9. 1; 15. 8; Gal. 1. 16-17.

Secondly, the appearances did not take place (as visions might have been expected to do, and generally did)[318] when the disciples were engaged in prayer, or in worship. But it was during their ordinary everyday occupations; when for instance they were going for a walk, or sitting at supper, or out fishing. And they were often simple, plain, and almost trivial in their character, very different from what enthusiasts would have imagined.

[318] *E.g.*, Acts 10. 30; 11. 5; 22. 17.

Thirdly, subjective visions due to enthusiasm, would not have started so soon after the Crucifixion as the *third* day. It would have required a much longer time for the disciples to have got over their utter confusion, and to have realised (perhaps by studying the old prophecies) that this humiliation was, after all, part of God's scheme, and was to be followed by a Resurrection. Nor again would such visions have only lasted for a short time; yet with the single exception of that to St. Paul, they were all over in a few weeks, though the enthusiasm of the witnesses lasted through life.

Fourthly, it is plain from all the accounts that the Apostles did not *expect* the Resurrection, and were much surprised at it, though they afterwards remembered that Christ had foretold it. This is shown, not only by the Christians bringing spices, to embalm the Body, and persons do not embalm a body unless they expect it to remain in the grave; but also by the account of the appearances themselves. For with the exception of the two farewell meetings (and possibly that to the two Marys), Christ's appearance was wholly unexpected. No one was looking for it, no one was anticipating it. When for instance Mary Magdalene found the tomb empty, it never even occurred to her that He had come to life again, she merely thought the Body had been removed.

Fifthly, and this is very remarkable, when Christ did appear, He was often *not recognised*. This was the case with Mary Magdalene, with Cleopas and his companion, and with the disciples at Tiberias. But it is plain that, if they so hoped to see their risen Master, that they eventually fancied they did see Him, they would at once have recognised Him; and their not doing so is quite inconsistent with the Vision Theory.

Sixthly, we are repeatedly told that at first some of the disciples *disbelieved* or *doubted* the Resurrection.[319] This is an important point, since it shows that opinions were divided on the subject, and therefore makes it almost certain that they would have used what means they had of finding out the truth. And a visit to the grave would have shown them at once whether the Body was there, or not: and they are not likely to have preached the Resurrection, without first ascertaining the point. Moreover, some of them remained doubtful even after the others were persuaded, St. Thomas in particular requiring the most convincing proof. His state of mind was certainly not that of an enthusiast, since, instead of being so convinced of the Resurrection as to have imagined it, he could with great difficulty be got to believe it. Indeed, according to these accounts, scarcely one of the witnesses believed the Resurrection till the belief was almost forced on him.

[319] Matt. 28. 17; Mark 16. 11-14; Luke 24. 11, 37; John 20. 25.

Seventhly, subjective visions do not occur to different persons *simultaneously*. A man's private illusions (like his dreams) are his own. A number of men do not simultaneously dream the same dream, still less do they simultaneously see the same subjective vision—at least a vision like that here referred to, of a person moving about among them, and speaking to them. This is quite different from Constantine's army thinking that they saw a luminous cross in the sky, or a body of Spanish troops that they saw their patron (St. James) riding at their head, or anything of that kind; several instances of which are known. But a subjective vision, at all resembling what is described in the Gospels, is extremely rare. It may perhaps happen to one person in ten thousand once in his life. It is difficult to believe that even two persons should have such an experience at the same time, while the idea that a dozen or more men should simultaneously see such a subjective vision is out of the question. And the Gospels, it may be added, always imply that Christ was visible *to all present* (though some of them doubted as to His identity), which was not, as a rule, the case in other alleged visions.

Eighthly, how are we to account for visionary *conversations*? Yet these occurred on *every* occasion. Christ never merely appeared, and then vanished. He always spoke, and often for a considerable time, giving detailed instructions; and can we imagine anyone believing a mere vision to have done all this? Is it possible, for instance, for St. Thomas to have believed that Christ conversed with him, and for the other Apostles, *who were all present*, to have believed it too, if the whole affair was only a vision? Indeed, conversations *in the presence of others* seem peculiarly hard to explain as visions, yet they are mentioned more than once.

For all these reasons then—because the appearances are not described in suitable language, did not occur on suitable occasions, began and ended too soon, were not expected, were not recognised, were not believed, occurred simultaneously, and always included conversations as well—the Vision Theory is to say the least extremely improbable.

### (3.) Its failure to account for the facts.

But this is not all; the Theory is not only improbable, it does not account for the actual *facts* recorded—facts concerning which, unless the writings are intentionally false, there could be no doubt whatever. A vision, for instance, could not have rolled away the stone from the door of the tomb, yet this is vouched for by *every* Evangelist. Again, persons could not have honestly believed that they went to the tomb, and found it empty, if the Body was there all the time. And this also is vouched for by *every* Evangelist. Nor could they have thought that they *touched* their Master, *i.e.*, took hold of His feet, if He existed only in their imagination; for the attempt to touch Him would at once have shown them their mistake.[320] Nor could they have seen Him *eat food*, for a vision, like a dream, would not explain the disappearance of the food. Nor again could a mere vision take bread, and on another occasion bread and fish, and give it them to eat.[321] In regard to all these particulars, then, the Vision Theory is hopelessly untenable.

[320] Matt. 28. 9.

[321] Luke 24. 30, 43; John 21. 13; Acts 10. 41.

There is also the great difficulty as to what became of the *dead Body* of Christ. For if it was still in the grave, the Jews would have produced it, rather than invent the story about its being stolen; and if it was not in the grave, its removal could not have been due to visions. With regard to this story it may be noticed that St. Matthew says it was *spread abroad* among the Jews; and Justin Martyr, himself a native of Palestine, also alludes to it. For he says that the Jews sent men all over the world to proclaim that the disciples *stole* the Body at *night*;[322] so there can be no doubt that some such story existed.

[322] Matt. 28. 15; Justin, Dial., 108.

But its weakness is self-evident. For if the soldiers (who were probably posted on the Saturday evening, and thus not known to the women) were, as they said, *asleep* at the time, how could they tell whether the disciples had stolen the Body, or whether Christ had come forth of His own accord? Moreover that Roman soldiers, with their strict discipline, who were put there on purpose to keep the Body, should really have gone to sleep, and allowed it to be stolen, is *most improbable*. And though it seems unlikely that they could have been bribed to say they were asleep, if they were not, as it was a capital offence; we must remember that they were *already* liable to death; since they had left the tomb, and the Body was gone. So whether they were asleep, or awake, at the time mattered little. And in any case, the fact of their having left it (which is plain from all the accounts) shows that something very extraordinary must have happened.

All, then, that the story proves is this (but this it does prove unquestionably), that though the Body was guarded, yet when it was wanted it was gone, and could not be found. And this is a strong argument not only against the Vision Theory, but against every theory except the Christian one. For when the Resurrection was first announced, the most obvious and decisive answer would have been for the Jews to have produced the dead Body; and their not doing this strongly supports the Christian account. Indeed, the *empty tomb*, together with the failure of all attempts to account for it, was doubtless one of the reasons why the Apostles gained so many converts the first day they preached the Resurrection.[323]

[323] Acts 2. 41.

Lastly, we must remember that this gaining of converts, *i.e.*, the *founding of Christianity*, is, after all, the great fact that has to be explained. And even if the Vision Theory could account for the Apostles themselves believing that they had seen Christ, it would not account for their being able to convince others of this belief, especially if the Body was still in the tomb. For a mere vision, like a ghost story, would begin and end in nothing; and if the Resurrection also began in nothing, how are we to account for its ending in so much?

Summing up these arguments, then, we conclude that the Vision Theory is most improbable in any case; and can only be accepted at all by admitting that nearly the whole of our accounts are not only untrue, but intentionally so. But then it is quite needless. Its object was to explain the alleged Resurrection without disputing the *veracity* of the writers, and this it is quite unable to do. In short, if the writers honestly believed the accounts as we have them, or indeed any other accounts at all resembling them, the Vision Theory is out of the question.

It does not even account satisfactorily for the one appearance, that to St. Paul, which it might be thought capable of explaining. For his *companions* as well as himself saw the Light and (apparently) heard the Voice, though not the actual words.[324] And how could a subjective vision of St. Paul have thus affected all his companions? Moreover physical blindness does not result from such a vision, and to say that in his case the wish was father to the thought, and that his expectation and hope of seeing Christ eventually made him think that he did see Him, is absurd. For even when he did see Him, he did not recognise Him; but had to ask *Who art Thou, Lord?* Here then was the case of an avowed enemy, and a man of great intellectual power, who was converted, and that against his will, solely by the appearance of Christ. And as he had access to all existing evidence on both sides, and had everything to lose and nothing to gain from the change, his conversion alone is a strong argument in favour of the Resurrection, more especially as the fact itself is beyond dispute.

[324] Acts 9. 7; 22. 9; 26. 13, 14.

### (4.) The Theory of real visions.

Before passing on, we must just glance at a modification of the Vision Theory, that has been suggested in recent years; which is that the Apostles saw *real* visions, miraculously sent by God, to persuade them to go on preaching the Gospel. And no doubt this theory avoids many of the difficulties of the ordinary Vision Theory, especially in regard to the appearances beginning so soon as the third day, their not being expected, and their occurring simultaneously. But it has even greater difficulties of its own. For it admits the supernatural, and yet these divinely sent visions were such as to *mislead* the Apostles, and to make them think that Christ's Body had risen from the grave, and saw no corruption, when in reality it was still decaying in the tomb.

And this alone is fatal to the theory. For if God gave a supernatural vision, it would certainly be to convince men of what was true, not of what was false. And even a real miracle is easier to believe, than that God should found His Church on a false one. Moreover supernatural visions are just as unable as natural ones to account for the facts recorded, such as the rolling away of the stone, the empty tomb, the holding of Christ by His feet, or the disappearance of the food. While the great difficulty as to what became of the dead Body, applies to this as much as to the ordinary Vision Theory.

### (*D.*) THE SWOON THEORY.

Lastly we come to the Swoon Theory. This would be to deny the *reasoning* of the witnesses; and say that though they saw Christ alive after His Crucifixion, they did not draw the right conclusion in thinking that He had risen from the dead, since as a matter of fact He had never died, but had only fainted on the Cross.

And in support of this, it is urged that death after crucifixion did not generally occur so quickly, since Pilate *marvelled if He were already dead*; and that He might easily have been mistaken for dead, as no accurate tests were known in those days. While the blood coming out of His side is also appealed to, because blood does not flow from a dead body. Moreover, as He was then placed in a cool rock cave, with aromatic spices, He would probably recover consciousness; when He would come forth and visit His friends, and ask for something to *eat*: which is what He did according to St. Luke. And they, superstitious men, looking upon their Master as in some sense Divine, and perhaps half expecting the Resurrection, would at once conclude that He had risen from the dead; especially if they had already heard that the tomb was empty.

And the chief argument in favour of the theory is, of course, the same as that in favour of the Vision Theory. It professes to account for the recorded appearances, without admitting either the truth of the Resurrection, or deliberate falsehood on the part of the witnesses; who, according to this theory, were themselves mistaken in thinking that Christ had risen from the dead, when in reality He had never died. They could not therefore have helped in restoring Him; He must have recovered by Himself. This is essential to the theory; so it is quite unlike a case recorded by Josephus, where a man who had been crucified, and taken down alive, was gradually restored by a doctor.[325]

[325] Josephus, Life, 75.

How then would this theory suit the facts of the case? While admitting its possibility, it is hard to find words to express its great *improbability*. It has immense difficulties, many of them peculiarly its own. And first as to Christ Himself. He must have been extremely exhausted after all the ill-treatment He had received, yet He is supposed not only to have recovered consciousness, but to have come out of the tomb by Himself, rolling away the large stone. And then, instead of creeping about weak and ill, and requiring nursing and medical treatment, He must have walked over twelve miles—and this with pierced feet[326]—to Emmaus and back. And the same evening He must have appeared to His disciples so completely recovered that they, instead of looking upon Him as still half-dead, thought that He had conquered death, and was indeed the Prince of Life. All this implies such a rapid recovery as is quite incredible.

[326] The feet being pierced is often disputed, but St. Luke (who probably knew more about crucifixion than we do) evidently thought they were; for he records Christ as saying, *See my hands and my feet that it is I myself*, which implies that His hands and feet would identify Him.

Next as to the piercing of His side with a spear.[327] This is recorded by an eye-witness, and would doubtless of itself have caused death, though St. John's statement that He was dead already seems the more probable. Nor did the blood coming out, in any way, disprove this. For blood (as long as it remains liquid) will of course flow out *downwards* from any body, just as other liquids would do. Only when a person is alive, the action of the heart will make it flow out upwards as well.

[327] John 19. 34.

Again, it is most unlikely that so many persons, both friends and foes, should have mistaken Christ for dead. Yet according to this theory the *soldiers* entrusted with the execution, who must have had a good deal of experience in such matters; the *centurion*, who was sent for by Pilate on purpose to ascertain this very point; the *Christians*, who took down the Body and wrapped it in linen cloths; and the *Jews*, who are not likely to have left their Victim without making sure of the fact, must all have honestly believed that Christ was dead when He was not. Moreover, the tomb was carefully guarded by His enemies for the express purpose of securing the Body. How then did they let it escape? If they were not asleep at the time, they must either have done this *willingly*, because they were bribed; or *unwillingly*, because they could not help it, being overcome by some supernatural Power; and either alternative is fatal to the Swoon Theory.

This theory also requires not only that the Apostles should have been mistaken in thinking that Christ had risen from the dead, but that Christ Himself should have countenanced the mistake; or He would have explained the truth to His disciples. He is thus made to be a deceiver instead of His Apostles, which all will admit to be most improbable.

And then, what became of Him afterwards? If He died again within a few weeks, His disciples could scarcely have thought Him the Prince of Life, who had the keys of Death and of Hades;[328] and if He continued to live, where did He go to? Moreover He must have died again at some time, and His real tomb is sure to have been much venerated by His followers; and it would have prevented any belief in the Ascension. Yet as said before (Chapter XV.), this seems to have formed a part of Christian instruction from the very first.

[328] Acts 3. 15; Rev. 1. 18.

But perhaps the chief argument against this theory is that it does not account for many of the actual *facts* recorded; such as Christ passing through closed doors, His vanishing at pleasure, and His Ascension. These details present no difficulty on the Vision Theory, nor on that of deliberate falsehood; but they are inconsistent with the present one. And though it accounts to some extent for the empty tomb; it does not account for the *angels* being there, announcing the Resurrection.

Nor does it account for the *grave-clothes* being so carefully left behind. For if Christ had come out of the tomb by Himself, He could scarcely have left His clothes behind; not to mention the difficulty of taking them off, caused by the adhesive myrrh, which would have stuck them together, and to the Body. These grave-clothes are thus fatal to this, as to every other theory, except the Christian one; yet it was a simple matter of fact, as to which there could be no possible *mistake*. Either the clothes were there, or else the persons who said they saw them were telling a falsehood. Moreover, in any case Christ could not have walked to Emmaus and back, or appeared to the Apostles, or to anyone else, in His *grave-clothes*, so He must have obtained some others, and how did He get them? His enemies are not likely to have supplied them, and if His friends did, they must have been aware of the fraud.

On the whole then, we decide that the *Swoon Theory*, like the Vision Theory, is very improbable in any case, and only tenable at all by supposing a large part of our narratives to be intentionally false. But then it is quite needless.

## (*E.*) CONCLUSION.

Before concluding this chapter a few remarks may be made on the alleged difficulties of the *Christian* theory. There are only two of any importance. The first is that the Resurrection would be a *miracle*, and probably nine out of ten men who disbelieve it, do so for this reason. It is not that the evidence for it is insufficient (they have perhaps never examined it) but that no conceivable evidence would be sufficient to establish such an event. Miracles, they say, are incredible, *they cannot happen*, and that settles the point; for it is of course easier to believe *any* explanation, visions, swoons, or anything else, than the occurrence of that which cannot happen.

But we have already admitted, in Chapter VII., that miracles are *not* incredible. And though no doubt, *under ordinary circumstances*, a dead man coming to life again would be so *extremely* improbable as to be practically incredible; yet these were not ordinary circumstances, and Christ was not an ordinary man. On the contrary, as we shall see, He was an absolutely unique Man, claiming moreover to be Divine, and having a mass of powerful evidence both from His own Character, from previous Prophecies, and from subsequent History, to support His claims. Therefore that He should rise from the dead, as a proof that these claims were well-founded, does not seem so very improbable after all.

The other difficulty refers to Christ's not appearing *publicly* to the Jews. Why, it is asked, did He only appear to His own disciples? Surely this is very suspicious. If He really did rise from the dead, and wished the world to believe it, why did He not settle the point by going publicly into Jerusalem?

But we cannot feel sure that this would have *settled the point*. No doubt the Jews who saw Him would have been convinced, but the nation as a whole might, or might not, have accepted Christianity. If they did *not*, saying for instance it was due to a pretender, it would have been worse than useless. While if they did, the Romans would very likely have looked upon it as a national insurrection, and its progress would have been more than ever difficult. It would also have greatly weakened the force of *Prophecy*; since, in the absence of ancient manuscripts, people might think that the old Jewish prophecies had been tampered with, to make them suit their Christian interpretation. But now these prophecies, having been preserved by men who are opposed to Christianity, are above suspicion.

Moreover, to get the world to believe in the Resurrection required not only evidence, but *missionaries*, that is to say, men who were so absolutely convinced of its truth, as to be willing to spend their whole lives in witnessing for it, in all lands and at all costs. And the chief object of the appearances may have been to produce such men; and it is obvious that (apart from a miraculous conversion like St. Paul's) there could not have been more than a few of them.

For only a *few* could have conversed with Christ, and eaten with Him after His death, so as to be quite certain that He was then alive; only a *few* could have known Him so intimately before, as to be quite certain that it was really He, and only a *few* had loved Him so dearly as to be willing to give up everything for His sake. In short, there were only a few *suitable* witnesses available. And Christ's frequently appearing to these few—the *chosen witnesses* as they are called[329]—in the private and intimate manner recorded in the Gospels, was evidently more likely to turn them into ardent missionaries (which it actually did) than any public appearance. Indeed it so often happens that what everybody should do, nobody does; that it may be doubted whether Christ's publicly appearing to a number of persons in Jerusalem would have induced even one of them to have faced a life of suffering, and a death of martyrdom, in spreading the news. This objection, then, cannot be maintained.

[329] Acts 10. 41.

In conclusion, it seems scarcely necessary to sum up the arguments in this chapter. We have discussed at some length the veracity, knowledge, investigation, and reasoning of the *first witnesses* of the Resurrection; and as we have seen, not one of these points can be fairly doubted. In fact the evidence in favour of each is overwhelming. Therefore the alternative theories—the Falsehood, the Legend, the Vision, and the Swoon Theory—which are founded on denying these points, are all untenable. And this greatly supports the conclusion we arrived at in the last chapter; so that combining the two; we have an *extremely strong* argument in favour of the Resurrection of Christ.

# CHAPTER XIX.
## THAT THE OTHER NEW TESTAMENT MIRACLES ARE PROBABLY TRUE.

(*A.*) THEIR CREDIBILITY.

They present few difficulties; the casting out of evil spirits.

(*B.*) THEIR TRUTHFULNESS.

(1.) General marks of truthfulness.

(2.) Special marks of truthfulness.

(*C.*) THEIR PUBLICITY.

(1.) They occurred in public.

(2.) They were publicly appealed to.

(3.) They were never disputed.

(4.) The silence of classical writers.

(*D.*) CONCLUSION.

Futile attempts to explain them away, the subject of modern miracles.

Having discussed in the last two chapters the Resurrection of Christ, we pass on now to the other New Testament miracles, and will consider in turn their *credibility*, their *truthfulness*, and their *publicity*.

### (*A.*) THEIR CREDIBILITY.

Now with one exception, the casting out of evil spirits, the miracles present scarcely any difficulty provided miracles at all are credible, which we have already admitted. Most of them, especially those of healing, were very suitable from a moral point of view, while that they were meant to confirm Christ's teaching and claims is beyond dispute. Not only do all the Evangelists declare this, but Christ Himself though He refused to work a miracle when challenged to do so—He would not work one *to order*, as we might say—yet appealed to His *public* miracles in the most emphatic manner.

Thus, when St. John the Baptist sent messengers to inquire whether He was the Messiah, His only answer was, 'Go your way, and tell John the things which ye do hear and see; the blind receive their sight, and the lame walk, the lepers are cleansed, and the deaf hear, and the dead are raised up,'[330] etc. And this is specially important because Christians would not have *invented* an incident which shows that Christ's own messenger had (apparently) lost faith in Him. Yet it is not easy to separate his question from the reply which it received; while if we admit that Christ gave this reply, it seems to settle the question as to His working miracles.

[330] Matt. 11. 4; Luke 7. 22; see also Mark 2. 10; John 5. 36.

And He afterwards condemned Chorazin, and other cities, in the strongest terms, because, although He had done so many miracles there, they had not repented; which again shows both the publicity of the miracles, and their intended evidential value.[331] And this passage also is very important, since its genuineness is confirmed by the fact that not a single miracle is recorded as having been worked at Chorazin. Yet, if the Evangelists (or anyone else) had invented the saying, they would surely have invented some miracles there to justify it. If on the other hand, they did not invent it, and the words were actually spoken by Christ, is it conceivable that He should have blamed these cities for not believing on Him in spite of His miracles, if He had done no miracles?

[331] Matt. 11. 21-24; Luke 10. 13-15. Both this passage, and the last, belong to Q, the supposed earliest source of our Gospels.

We pass on now to the *casting out of evil spirits*, which implies that persons may sometimes be *possessed* by such spirits, and this is often thought to be a difficulty. But though our ignorance on the subject is undoubtedly great, there is nothing incredible here. For we have already admitted the *influence* of such spirits (Chapter XII.), and what is called *possession* is merely an extreme form of influence. Indeed, the accounts of mesmerism at the present day, though they cannot always be trusted, seem to show that even one man may so entirely *possess* the mind and will of another as to make him do whatever he wishes. And it is certainly no more difficult to believe that this power may in some cases be exercised by an evil spirit. With regard to the outward symptoms mentioned in the Gospels, they seem to have resembled certain forms of madness; though, as the patients are now kept under restraint in civilised countries, they have not the same notoriety.

But it may be said, why ascribe this madness to an evil spirit? But why not? Madness often follows the frequent yielding to certain temptations, such as drunkenness or impurity; and that it may really be due to the action of an evil spirit (an *unclean* spirit is the significant term used in the Gospels) and be the appropriate punishment for yielding to *his* temptation, is certainty not incredible. And if so, considering the immoral state of the world at the time of Christ, we cannot be surprised at such cases being far more common then than now. And the writers, it may be added, do not (like some early nations) attribute *all* maladies to evil spirits, for we read of men having fever and palsy, as well as being blind, lame, deaf, and dumb, without any hint of its being due to an evil spirit; so they were quite able to distinguish between the two.

There is, however, one instance—the swine at Gadara—of *animals* being thus afflicted,[332] which undoubtedly forms a difficulty, and I have never seen a satisfactory explanation of it. But still our ignorance about animals, combined with the fact that they resemble man in so many respects, prevents us from saying that it is absolutely incredible. And as to the alleged *injustice* of the miracle (which is often objected to) we must remember that if Christ were the Divine Being He claimed to be, the world and all it contained belonged to Him; so His allowing the swine to be destroyed by evil spirits was no more unjust to their owners, than if He had allowed them to die by disease.

[332] Matt. 8. 30-32; Mark 5. 11-13; Luke 8. 32-33.

Lastly, all the Christian miracles lose a great deal of their improbability when we consider the *unique position of Christ*. And what would be incredible, if told of another man who had done nothing to alter the history of the world, may easily be credible of *Him*. We decide, then, that all the New Testament miracles are *credible*: we have next to consider whether they are *true*.

**(*B*.) THEIR TRUTHFULNESS.**

Now the testimony in favour of these miracles is very similar to that in favour of the Resurrection of Christ. They are recorded by the same writers and in the same books, and everything points to these accounts being trustworthy. To put it shortly, the writers had no motive for recording the miracles unless they believed them to be true, and they had ample means of finding out whether they were true or not; while many of them are such as cannot possibly be explained by want of investigation, or an error in reasoning. Moreover, as we shall see, they contain numerous marks of truthfulness. These may be divided into two classes, *general*, or those which concern the miracles as a whole; and *special*, or those which concern individual miracles, or sayings about them; and we will consider each in turn.

**(1.) General marks of truthfulness.**

Among these we may notice first the extremely *simple and graphic* way in which many of the miracles are described, such as the curing of the man who was born blind, with the repeated questioning of the man himself.[333] Then there is the raising of the daughter of Jairus, and the curing of the man who was deaf and had a difficulty in speaking, both of which are described with the most minute details, including the actual Aramaic words spoken by Christ.[334] It is difficult to think that they do not come from eye-witnesses. And the same may be said of a large number of the miracles.

[333] John 9. 8-34.

[334] Mark 5. 41; 7. 34.

Secondly, the *kind* of miracles ascribed to Christ seem (as far as we can judge) to be worthy of Him. They were not for His own benefit, but for that of other people, and they are a great contrast to the imaginary miracles ascribed to Him in the Apocryphal Gospels, most of which are extremely childish. When for instance Christ was a boy, we read of His making clay birds fly; of His turning children into kids for refusing to play with Him; and of His cursing another boy who had run against Him, and who in consequence fell down dead.[335] How different such miracles are from those in our Gospels scarcely needs pointing out. Nor is the case of the *barren fig-tree*, so often objected to, an exception. For the tree itself could have felt no injury, and as far as we know, its destruction injured no one else.

[335] Gospel of the Infancy, chapters xv., xvii., xix.

Thirdly, the miracles are closely connected with the *moral teaching* of Christ, and it is difficult either to separate the two, or to believe the whole account to be fictitious. His wonderful works, and His wonderful words involve each other, and form together an harmonious whole, which is too life-like to be imaginary. Indeed, a life of Christ without His miracles would be as unintelligible as a life of Napoleon without his campaigns. And it is interesting to note in this connection that our earliest Gospel, St. Mark's, contains (in proportion to its length) the most miracles. As we should expect, it was Christ's miracles, rather than His moral teaching, which first attracted attention.

Fourthly, the miracles were as a rule miracles of *healing*: that is to say, of restoring something to its natural state, such as making blind eyes see; and not doing something unnatural, such as giving a man a third eye. Miracles of either kind would of course show superhuman power; but the former are obviously the more suited to the God of Nature. And this *naturalness* of the miracles, as we may call it, seems to many a strong argument in their favour.

Fifthly, there were an immense *number* of miracles, the ones recorded being mere *examples* of those that were actually worked. Thus in St. Mark's Gospel we are told that on one occasion, Christ healed *many* who were sick with *divers* diseases; on another that He had healed so *many*, that those with plagues pressed upon Him to touch Him; and on another that everywhere He went, into the villages, cities, or country, the sick were laid out, so that they might touch His garment, and *as many as touched Him were made whole*.[336]

[336] Mark 1. 34; 3. 10; 6. 56

Sixthly, there was a great *variety* in the miracles. They were of various kinds, worked in various places, before various witnesses, and with various details and characteristics. They occurred in public as well as in private; in the towns as well as in the country; at sea as well as on land; in groups as well as singly;

at a distance as well as near; after due notice as well as suddenly; when watched by enemies as well as among friends; unsolicited as well as when asked for; in times of joy, and in times of sorrow. They were worked on the blind as well as the deaf; the lame as well as the dumb; the leprous as well as the palsied; the dead as well as the living. They concerned men as well as women; the rich as well as the poor; the educated as well as the ignorant; the young as well as the old; multitudes as well as individuals; Gentiles as well as Jews; nature as well as man—in fact, according to our accounts, it is difficult to imagine any miracles that could have been more absolutely convincing.

Seventhly, the miracles of Christ were (with trifling exceptions) worked *suddenly*. They were not like gradual cures, or slow recoveries, but they were done in a moment. The blind man *immediately* received his sight; the palsied *immediately* took up his couch: the leper was *straightway* cleansed; the infirm was *straightway* made whole; the dead *immediately* rose up, etc.[337] This was evidently a striking feature in the miracles, and the Evangelists seem to have been much impressed by it.

[337] Luke 18. 43; 5. 25; Mark 1. 42; Matt. 8. 3; John 5. 9; Luke 8. 55.

Eighthly, many of the miracles were of a *permanent* character, and such as could be examined again and again. When, for instance, a man who had long been lame, or deaf, or blind, was restored to health, the villagers, as well as the man himself, could certify to the cure for years to come. And miracles such as these are obviously of much greater value than what we may call *momentary* miracles (such as Christ's calming the storm) where the only possible evidence is that of the actual spectators.

Lastly, and this is very remarkable, the Evangelists nearly always relate that Christ worked His miracles *by His own authority*: while the Old Testament prophets, with scarcely an exception, worked theirs by calling upon God. Take for instance the similar cases of raising a widow's son.[338] Elijah prays earnestly that God would restore the child to life; Christ merely gives the command, *I say unto thee, Arise*. The difference between the two is very striking, and is of itself a strong argument in favour of Christ's miracles; for had the Evangelists invented them, they would certainly have made them resemble those of the Old Testament. But instead of this, they describe them as worked in a new and unprecedented manner, and one which must at the time have seemed most presumptuous.

[338] 1 Kings 17. 21; Luke 7. 14.

The Gospel miracles then, from the simple and graphic way in which they are described; their not containing anything childish or unworthy; their close connection with the moral teaching of Christ; their naturalness; their number; their variety; their suddenness; their permanence; and above all from the authoritative way in which they are said to have been worked; have every appearance of being truth fully recorded.

## j(2.) Special marks of truthfulness.

Moreover several individual miracles, and sayings about them, are of such a kind as could scarcely have been invented. Take, for instance, the raising of the daughter of Jairus.[339] Now of course anyone, wishing to magnify the power of Christ, might have invented this or any other miracle. But if so, he is not likely to have put into the mouth of Christ Himself the words, *The child is not dead but sleepeth*. These words seem to imply that Christ did not consider it a miracle; and though we may be able to explain them, by the similar words used in regard to Lazarus,[340] they certainly bear the marks of genuineness.

[339] Mark 5. 39.

[340] John 11. 11.

We are also told, more than once, that Christ's power of working miracles was *conditional* on the faith of the person to be healed, so that in one place He could do scarcely any miracles *because of their unbelief*.[341] This is not the sort of legend that would have grown up round a glorified Hero; it bears unmistakably the mark of truthfulness. But then if the writer had good means of knowing that Christ could do no miracles in one place, because of their unbelief; had he not equally good means of knowing that Christ could, and did, do miracles in other places?

[341] Matt. 13. 58; Mark 6. 5-6; Luke 18. 42.

And what shall we say of Christ's frequent commands to keep His miracles *secret*?[342] There were doubtless reasons for this in every case; but Christ's followers, who presumably recorded the miracles in order to get them known, are not likely to have invented, and put into His mouth the command to keep them secret. Nor is Christ likely to have given it, had there been no miracles to keep secret. Nor again is anyone likely to have added, unless it was the case, that the command was generally *disobeyed*. This seems surprising, yet it is very true to human nature that a man who had been suddenly cured of a long complaint, should insist on talking about it.

[342] *E.g.*, Mark 3. 12; 5. 43; 7. 36.

In the same way the discussions about working miracles *on the Sabbath Day* have a very genuine tone about them and it is difficult to imagine them to be inventions.[343] Yet such discussions could not have arisen, if there had been no miracles on the Sabbath, or any other day.

[343] Mark 3. 1-5; Luke 13. 10-17; John 5. 9-16; 9. 14-16.

Then there is the striking passage where Christ warned His hearers that even working miracles in His name, without a good life, would not ensure their salvation.[344] This occurs in one of His most characteristic discourses, the Sermon on the Mount, and it is hard to doubt its genuineness. But even if we do, it is not likely that Christ's followers would have invented such a warning, if as a matter of fact no one ever did work miracles in His name.

[344] Matt. 7. 22.

And much the same may be said of another passage where Christ is recorded as saying that *all* believers would be able to work miracles.[345] If He said so, He must surely have been able to work them Himself; and if He did not say so, His followers must have been able to work them, or their inventing such a promise would merely have shown that they were not believers. On the whole, then, as said before, the accounts of the New Testament miracles have every appearance of being thoroughly truthful.

[345] Mark 16. 17.

## (*C.*) THEIR PUBLICITY.

But the most important point has still to be noticed, which is the alleged *publicity* of these miracles; and as this renders the testimony in their favour peculiarly strong, we must examine it at some length.

### (1.) They occurred in public.

To begin with, according to our Gospels, all the miracles of Christ occurred during His *public ministry*, when He was well known, that at Cana being definitely called the first.[346] And as they were meant to confirm His teaching and claims, it was only natural for them to begin when His teaching began. But if they had been invented, or had grown up as legends, some at least would have been ascribed to His earlier years (as they are in the Apocryphal Gospels) when there was less chance of their being disputed.

[346] John 2. 11.

Moreover, many of them are stated to have been worked openly, and before crowds of people, including Scribes, Pharisees, and lawyers.[347] And the *names* of the places where they occurred, and even of the persons concerned, are given in some cases. Among these were *Jairus*, a ruler of the synagogue; *Lazarus*, a well known man at Bethany; *Malchus*, a servant of the High Priest; and the *centurion* at Capernaum, who, though his name is not given, must have been well known to the Jews, as he had built them a synagogue. While the miracles recorded in the Acts concern such prominent persons as the *proconsul*, Sergius Paulus, at Cyprus, and the *chief man*, Publius, at Malta. And it is hard to overestimate the immense difficulty of thus asserting *public* miracles, with the names of persons, and places, if none occurred; yet the early Christians asserted such miracles from the very first.

[347] *E.g.*, Luke 5. 17-21.

Take for instance the feeding of the five thousand, near the Lake of Galilee. This is recorded in the earliest Gospel, St. Mark's, and must therefore have been written down very soon after the event, when a large number of the five thousand were still alive. Now is it conceivable that anyone would have ventured to make up such an account, even twenty years afterwards, if nothing of the kind had occurred? And if he had done so, would not his story have been instantly refuted? Or take the case of healing the centurion's servant at Capernaum. This, as before said, belongs to Q, the supposed source common to Matthew and Luke, and admitted by most critics to date from before A.D. 50. And how could such a story have been current within twenty years of the event, if nothing of the kind had occurred?

It is also declared that the miracles were much talked about at the time, and caused widespread astonishment. The people *marvelled* at them, they *wondered*, they were *amazed*, they were *beyond measure astonished*, there had been nothing like them *since the world began*.[348] The miracles were in fact the talk of the whole neighbourhood. And we are told that in consequence several of those which occurred at Jerusalem were at once officially investigated by the Jewish rulers, who made the most searching inquiries about them;[349] and in two instances, at least, publicly admitted them to be true.[350] And this also is not likely to have been asserted, unless it was the case; and not likely to have been the case, if there had been no miracles.

[348] Matt. 9. 33; 15. 31; Mark 5. 42; 7. 37; John 9. 32.

[349] *E.g.*, John 9. 13-34; Acts 4. 5-22.

[350] John 11. 47; Acts 4. 16.

**(2.) They were publicly appealed to.**

Moreover, these public miracles were *publicly appealed to* by the early Christians. According to the *Acts*, this was done in the very first public address, that at Pentecost, by St. Peter, who reminds his hearers that they had themselves seen the miracles (*even as ye yourselves know*), as well as in one other speech at least.[351] And this is important, because even those critics, who deny the genuineness of the Acts, yet admit that these speeches date from a very early time. And if so, it shows conclusively that some of Christ's immediate followers not only believed themselves that He had worked miracles, but spoke as if their opponents believed it too.

[351] Acts 2. 22; 10. 38.

That they are not more frequently alluded to in the Acts is not surprising, when we remember that, according to the writer,—and he was an *eye-witness* in some cases, as they occur in the *We* sections,[352]—the Apostles themselves worked miracles. There was thus no occasion for them to appeal to those of Christ as proving the truth of what they preached; their own miracles being quite sufficient to convince anyone who was open to this kind of proof. But still the important fact remains that in the first recorded Christian address the public miracles of Christ were publicly appealed to. And this was within a few months of their occurrence; and at Jerusalem, where the statement, if untrue, could have been more easily refuted than anywhere else.

[352] Acts 16. 18, 26; 28. 6, 8-9.

Passing on to *St. Paul's Epistles*, it is true that they do not contain any reference to Christ's miracles, except of course the Resurrection. But as they were not written to convert heathens, but to instruct those who were already Christians, there is nothing surprising in this; and they do not mention any of His parables either. On the other hand, they do contain direct reference to *Apostolic* miracles. St. Paul in two of his undisputed Epistles positively asserts that he had worked miracles himself; and he uses the same three words, *signs, wonders,* and *mighty works,* which are used in the Gospels to describe the miracles of Christ.[353]

[353] Rom. 15. 18, 19; 2 Cor. 12. 12.

The second passage is extremely important, since he speaks of them as the *signs of an apostle*; and calls upon his opponents at Corinth to admit that he was an apostle *because* he had worked these miracles. And this implies not only that the miracles were done in public, but that his readers as well as himself believed that the power of working miracles belonged to all the Apostles. And it will be noticed that he is addressing the very persons among whom he declares he had worked the miracles; which makes it almost inconceivable that his claim was unfounded, quite apart from the difficulty of believing that such a man as St. Paul would wilfully make a false statement.

From all this it follows that the first preachers of Christianity not only appealed to Christ's miracles; but also to their own, in support of their claims. And, as just said, how they could have done so, if they worked no miracles, is not easy to understand.

We next come to a class of writings where we should expect to find Christ's miracles alluded to, and these are the first Christian *Apologies*. Nor are we disappointed. The three earliest, of which we have any knowledge, were by

Quadratus, Aristides, and Justin; the first two being presented to the Emperor Hadrian, when he visited Athens, A.D. 125.

*Quadratus*, in a passage preserved by Eusebius, lays stress on what we have called the *permanent* character of Christ's miracles. He says: 'The works of our Saviour were always conspicuous, for they were real; both they that were healed and they that were raised from the dead were seen, not only when they were healed or raised, but for a long time afterwards; not only whilst He dwelt on this earth, but also after His departure, and for a good while after it, insomuch that some of them have reached to our times.'[354]

[354] Eusebius, Hist., iv. 3.

*Aristides* bases his defence of Christianity on its moral character, and does not appeal to any public miracles, though as before said (Chapter XIV.) he asserts the Divinity, Incarnation, Virgin-birth, Resurrection, and Ascension of Christ.

Lastly, *Justin*, about A.D. 150, not only specifies many of Christ's miracles; but also says in general terms that He 'healed those who were maimed, and deaf, and lame in body from their birth, causing them to leap, to hear, and to see by His word. And having raised the dead, and causing them to live, by His deeds He compelled the men who lived at that time to recognise Him. But though they saw such works, they asserted it was magical art.'[355] Justin, however, does not base his argument on miracles, but on prophecy, because, as he tells us again, the former might be ascribed to magic.

[355] Dial., 69; Apol. 1. 30.

But still, the actual occurrence of the miracles, he evidently thought to be indisputable. He even says that the Emperor and Senate can learn for themselves that Christ worked miracles (healing the lame, dumb, and blind, cleansing the lepers, and raising the dead) by consulting the *Acts of Pilate*.[356] And this certainly implies that such a document, whether genuine or not, then existed in Rome; and that it contained an account of the miracles. Thus two out of the three earliest writers in defence of Christianity appealed to Christ's miracles, in the most public manner possible, when addressing the Emperor.

[356] Apol. 1. 48, 35.

## (3.) They were never disputed.

But now comes another important point. Though these public miracles were publicly appealed to by the early Christians, and though written accounts of them were in circulation very soon after they are stated to have occurred; yet, as far as we know, they were *never disputed*. And this is the more remarkable, since they are said to have been worked among enemies as well as friends.

They were thus peculiarly open to hostile criticism; and we may be sure that the bitter opponents of Christ, who had brought about His death, would have exposed them if they could. Yet, as just said, they were never disputed, either by Jews or Gentiles; though, of course, they both denied their evidential value.

The *Jews*—that is to say the Scribes and Pharisees—did this, by ascribing them to the Evil One. And though this was a very strange expedient, as their effect was obviously good, and not evil, they had really no alternative. The common people were much impressed by the miracles, and were anxious to welcome Christ as their Messiah;[357] yet the Pharisees decided that such a man as this—so unlike what they expected—could not possibly be their Messiah. They had then to explain away the miracles somehow. And since they denied that they were worked by God, they were bound to ascribe them to the Devil, for these were the only supernatural powers they believed in; though of course both of these had subordinate angels under them. But we may ask, would the Jews have adopted such an expedient had there been any possibility of denying that the miracles occurred? Yet that they did adopt it can scarcely be disputed. It is positively asserted in each of the first three Gospels;[358] and Christians are not likely to have reported such a horrible suggestion as that their Master was an agent of the Evil One, unless it had been made.

[357] John 6. 15; Mark 11. 10.

[358] Matt. 9. 34; 12. 24; Mark 3. 22; Luke 11. 15.

The *Gentiles* on the other hand, believed in a variety of gods, many of whom were favourable to mankind, and could be invoked by *magic*; so they could consistently ascribe the miracles to some of these lesser deities; or, in popular language, to magic. And we have abundant evidence that they did so. As we have seen, it is expressly asserted by Justin, who in consequence preferred the argument from prophecy; and Irenæus did the same, and for avowedly the same reason.[359]

[359] Bk. ii. 32.

Moreover, *Celsus*, the most important opponent of Christianity in the second century, also adopted this view. His works are now lost, but Origen in answering him frequently and positively asserts it; saying that he often spoke of the miracles as *works of sorcery*.[360] And though Celsus lived some years after the time in question, it is most unlikely, if the early opponents of Christianity had denied that the miracles occurred, that its later opponents should have given up this strong line of defence, and have adopted the far weaker one that they did occur, but were due to magic. We are quite justified, then, in saying that Christ's miracles were not disputed at the time, and considering their alleged publicity, this is a strong additional argument in their favour.

[360] Origen cont. Cels., i. 38; ii. 48.

**(4.) The silence of classical writers.**

All that can be said on the other side is from the *silence* of classical writers. Had the miracles really occurred, it is said, especially in such a well-known place as Palestine, the writers of the day would have been full of them. Yet, with the single exception of Tacitus, they do not even allude to Christianity; and he dismisses it with contempt as a *pernicious superstition*.[361]

[361] Tacitus Annals. Bk. xv., ch. 44.

Now these words of Tacitus show that he had never studied the subject, for whatever may be said against the religion, it certainly was not pernicious; so he must have rejected Christianity *without examination.* And if the other classical writers did the same, there is nothing remarkable in their not alluding to it. Alleged marvels were common enough in those days, and they probably did not think the Christian miracles worth inquiring about. But we do not know of any writer who did inquire about them, and was not convinced of their truth.

It may, of course, be replied that some of the events ought anyhow to be alluded to, such as the *darkness over all the land* at the time of the Crucifixion. And if this extended over the whole of Palestine, it is certainly strange that it should not be noticed. But it may only refer to the neighbourhood of Jerusalem. Compare the expression *all the country of Judæa*[362] (when referring to the people being baptized) which is evidently not meant to be taken literally. And if the darkness was limited to the neighbourhood of Jerusalem, there is nothing surprising in its not being recorded by any except Christians, for whom of course it had a special significance.

[362] Mark 1. 5.

It should also be noticed that in some respects the testimony of Christian writers is *more* valuable than that of either Jews or Gentiles: since none of the writers of that country were brought up as Christians. They were all unbelievers before they were believers; and if such testimony from unbelievers would be valuable, it is still more so from those who showed how thoroughly convinced they were of its truth by becoming believers. Indeed, the best Jewish or Gentile evidence conceivable is that of well-educated men, like St. Paul and St. Luke, who, on the strength of it, became Christians.

Lastly, it must be remembered that the argument from silence is proverbially unsound. We have, for instance, over two hundred letters of the younger Pliny, and in only one of these does he mention Christianity. Suppose this one had been lost, what a strong argument could have been formed against the spread of Christianity from the silence of Pliny, yet this one shows its marvellous progress (see Chapter XXII.). This objection, then, is quite insufficient to outweigh the positive testimony in favour of the miracles, to which we have already alluded.

## (*D.*) CONCLUSION.

In conclusion we must notice certain rationalistic explanations which have been given of the miracles. It was hardly to be expected that, with such strong evidence in their favour, the modern opponents of Christianity would merely assert that the accounts were pure fiction from beginning to end. Attempts have of course been made to explain the miracles in such a way that, while depriving them of any supernatural character, it may yet be admitted that some such events occurred, which gave rise to the Christian accounts.

The miracles of *healing* are perhaps the easiest to explain in this way, as some wonderful instances of sudden, though natural, cures have been known. But it is doubtful whether any of Christ's miracles were of such a kind, for St. Paul is careful to distinguish between *gifts of healing* and *working of miracles*.[363] Both were evidently known to the early Church, and known to be different.

[363] 1 Cor. 12. 9-10, 28.

And of course no such explanations will apply to most of the miracles, which have to be got rid of in various other ways. Thus Christ's walking on the sea is explained as His walking on a ridge of sand or rock running out just under the water; the raising of Lazarus as his having had himself buried alive, so that when Christ came, there might be a pretended miracle;[364] and feeding the five thousand as nothing more than the example of Christ and His friends, who so freely shared their small supply with those around them, that others did the same, and thus everyone had a little. It seems scarcely necessary to discuss these theories in detail, as they are all most improbable.

[364] This extraordinary theory was maintained by Rénan in the earlier editions of his *Life of Jesus*, though he afterwards abandoned it.

Moreover, their difficulties are all *cumulative*. The Christian explanation has but *one* difficulty for all the miracles, which is that they *are* miracles, and involve the supernatural. Once admit this, and twenty miracles (provided they occur on suitable occasions) are no more difficult to believe than two. But the difficulties of these explanations are all cumulative. If for instance, the raising of Lazarus is explained by his having been buried alive, it does not account for Christ's walking on the sea. If this is explained by the supposed ridge of sand, it does not account for feeding the five thousand, etc. Thus each difficulty has to be added to all the others, so taken together they are quite insuperable.

One other point has still to be considered, which is the subject of modern miracles. Why, it is said, are there no miracles *now*, when they could be properly tested? If they were really employed by God as helps to the spread of His religion, why should they not have accompanied it at intervals all along, as it is said they did the Jewish religion? They are surely wanted for the support of Christianity at the present day; and if God were, *after due warning*, to work a public and indisputable miracle every half-century, all the other evidences of Christianity might be dispensed with.

The answer to this objection is that the Christian revelation does not claim to be a gradual one, like the Jewish; but a final and complete revelation, made once for all through Christ and His Apostles. Therefore, as there is to be no fresh revelation, there can be no fresh miracles to confirm it. The question of *other* miracles, such as those which are said to have been worked by Christians at various periods, need not be considered here. If *true*, they would of course tend to prove the New Testament ones; while, if *untrue*, they would not disprove them, any more than imitation diamonds would disprove the existence of real diamonds.

Of course, it may be replied that God might still work a miracle now by a man, who stated that it was not to confirm anything that he said himself, but merely what the Founder of Christianity had said; and this is no doubt possible. But it would be a different method from that recorded in the Bible, where a messenger from God always brings his own credentials, even though, as in the case of a prophecy, they may not be verified till afterwards. And what reason have we for thinking that God would change His method now? It is also very doubtful whether a public miracle at the present day, would convince everybody.

This objection, then, must be put aside, and we therefore conclude, on reviewing the whole subject, that the New Testament miracles are not only *credible*, but that there is extremely strong evidence in their favour. Indeed their marks of *truthfulness*, combined with their alleged *publicity*, form together a very powerful argument. And it is rendered all the stronger by their having been so thoroughly successful. Their object was to establish the truth of Christianity, and this is precisely what they did. The evidence they afforded was so decisive, that a hostile world found it irresistible.

Moreover it is doubtful whether any other religion, except, of course, the Jewish, has ever claimed to have been confirmed by public miracles. Christianity thus rests upon a unique foundation. Unlike other religions, it appealed at first not to abstract reasoning, or moral consciousness, or physical force, but to miraculous events, of the truth or falsehood of which others could judge. They did judge, and they were convinced. We decide, then, that the New Testament miracles are probably true.

# CHAPTER XX.
## THAT THE JEWISH PROPHECIES CONFIRM THE TRUTH OF CHRISTIANITY.

(*A.*) Isaiah's Prophecy of the Lord's Servant.

(1.) The historical agreement, very striking.

(2.) The doctrinal agreement, equally so.

(3.) The modern Jewish interpretation, quite untenable.

(*B.*) The Psalm of the Crucifixion.

(1.) Its close agreement, all through.

(2.) Two objections, unimportant.

(*C.*) The Divinity of the Messiah.

At least three prophecies of this; it is also involved in some hints as to the Doctrine of the Trinity.

(*D.*) Conclusion.

Why are not the prophecies plainer? Cumulative nature of the evidence.

We propose to consider in this chapter what is called the argument from *Prophecy*, using the word, as we did in Chapter XI., in the sense of *prediction*. Now it is a remarkable and undisputed fact that for many centuries before the time of Christ, it was foretold that a member of the Jewish nation—small and insignificant though it was—should be a blessing *to all mankind*. This promise is recorded as having been made both to Abraham, to Isaac, and to Jacob;[365] and as a matter of fact, Christianity was founded by a Jew, and has undoubtedly been a blessing to the human race. This is at least a remarkable coincidence. And as we proceed in the Old Testament, the statements about this future Messiah become clearer and fuller, till at last, in the Prophets, we find whole chapters referring to Him, which Christians assert were fulfilled in Christ.

[365] Gen. 22. 18; 26. 4; 28.14.

This argument is plainly of the utmost importance. Fortunately it is much simplified by the question of *dates* being altogether excluded. As a rule, the most important point in an alleged prophecy is to show that it was written before its fulfilment. But here this is undisputed, since everyone admits that the whole of the Old Testament, except some of the apocryphal books, was written before the time of Christ. And as the writings have been preserved by the Jews themselves, who are opposed to the claims of Christianity, we may be sure that not a single alteration in its favour has been made anywhere.

We will now examine a few of the strongest prophecies, avoiding all those that were only fulfilled in a figurative, or spiritual sense; and selecting whole passages rather than single texts. For though many of these latter are very applicable to Christ, they might also be applicable to someone else. So we will first discuss somewhat fully Isaiah's prophecy of the Lord's Servant, and the Psalm of the Crucifixion; and then examine more briefly a group of prophecies referring to the Divinity of the Messiah.

## (A.) ISAIAH'S PROPHECY OF THE LORD'S SERVANT (52. 13-53. 12).

It may be pointed out at starting that no one denies the antiquity of the passage, even if it was not written by Isaiah. And it forms a complete whole, closely connected together and not mixed up with any other subject. So in regard to its fulfilment, most of the details mentioned occurred within a few hours. We will consider first the historical, and then the doctrinal agreement.

### (1.) The Historical Agreement.

With regard to this, the following is the translation from the Revised Version, together with the corresponding events. It will be observed that the sufferings of the Servant are usually expressed in the past tense, and his triumph in the future, the prophet placing himself, as it were, between the two. But the Hebrew tenses are rather uncertain, and what is translated as *past* in the Revised Version is translated as *future* in the Authorised (*e.g.*, 53. 2).

| | |
|---|---|
| 52. 13. 'Behold, my servant shall deal wisely, he shall be exalted and lifted up, and shall be very high. | The excellence of Christ's teaching and conduct is now generally admitted; while as to His exalted position, He is worshipped by millions of men. |
| 14. 'Like as many were astonied at thee (his visage was so marred more than any man, and his form more than the sons of men) so shall he sprinkle many nations; | Yet at the time of His death, which was public so that *many* saw Him, the cruel treatment He had received must have terribly disfigured His face and body. |
| 15. 'Kings shall shut their mouths at him: for that which had not been told them shall they see; and that which they had not heard shall they understand. | But now even Kings are silent with reverence,[366] when contemplating such a wonderful life. |

| | |
|---|---|
| 53. 1. 'Who hath believed our report? | Indeed what the prophet is about to declare, is so marvellous that it can scarcely be believed. |
| 'and to whom hath the arm of the Lord been revealed? | The Arm of the Lord evidently means some instrument, or Person, which God uses for His work, as a man might use his arm.[367] And here it must be a *Person*, from the following words, 'For *he* grew up,' etc. It is thus a most suitable term for the Messiah, who was to be recognised by hardly anyone. |
| 2. 'For he grew up before him as a tender plant, and as a root out of a dry ground: | This was because He lived at a place (Nazareth) which was always regarded as *dry ground* so far as anything good was concerned.[368] |
| he hath no form nor comeliness; and when we see him, there is no beauty that we should desire him. | Moreover, His appearance was humble, and when at His trial, Pilate presented Him to the people, they did not desire Him. |
| 3. 'He was despised, and rejected of men; a man of sorrows, and acquainted with grief: and as one from whom men hide their face he was despised, and we esteemed him not. | But they at once rejected Him as they had done often before. |
| 4. 'Surely he hath borne our griefs, and carried our sorrows: yet we did esteem him stricken, smitten of God, and afflicted. | While His life was not only one of grief and sorrow, but such a death seemed to show that He was accursed of God, for the Jews so regarded anyone who was crucified.[369] |
| 5. 'But he was wounded for our transgressions, he was bruised for our iniquities: the chastisement of our peace was upon him; and with his stripes we are healed. | The scourging and other ill-treatment is here referred to; including probably the nails, and spear, for the word translated *wounded* is literally *pierced*. |
| 6. 'All we like sheep have gone astray; we have turned every | |

| | |
|---|---|
| one to his own way; and the Lord hath laid on him the iniquity of us all. | |
| 7. 'He was oppressed, yet he humbled himself and opened not his mouth; as a lamb that is led to the slaughter, and as a sheep that before her shearers is dumb; yea, he opened not his mouth. | Christ, who is sometimes called the Lamb of God, not only bore His ill-treatment patiently, but refused to plead at either of His trials (the verse repeats twice *He opened not His mouth*) to the utter astonishment of His judges.[370] |
| 8. 'By oppression and judgment he was taken away; and as for his generation, who among them considered that he was cut off out of the land of the living? for the transgression of my people was he stricken. | He was not killed accidentally, or by the mob, but had a judicial trial; and was most unjustly condemned. While few, if any, of His contemporaries understood the real meaning of His death. |
| 9. 'And they made his grave with the wicked, and with the rich in his death (i.e., *when he was dead*. Comp. Ps. 6. 8); | He was appointed to die between two robbers, and would doubtless have been buried with them, had not Joseph of Arimathea intervened; when, in strange contrast with His ignominious death, He was honourably buried, with costly spices, and in a rich man's tomb. |
| although he had done no violence, neither was any deceit in his mouth. | Although His judge repeatedly declared that He was innocent. |
| 10. 'Yet it pleased the Lord to bruise him; he hath put him to grief: when thou shalt make his soul an offering for sin, he shall see his seed, he shall prolong his days, and the pleasure of the Lord shall prosper in his hand. | Yet after His death He was to see His seed, and *prolong His days, i.e.*, rise again from the dead. The word *seed* cannot mean here, actual children,[371] since He was to obtain them by His death. But it may well refer to the disciples, whom Christ saw after His Resurrection, and called His *children*.[372] |
| 11. 'He shall see of the travail of his soul, and shall be satisfied: by his knowledge shall my righteous servant | And this is confirmed by their being spoken of as *the travail of His soul*, not body. While the latter expression also implies that He had had some intense mental struggle comparable to the |

| | |
|---|---|
| justify many: and he shall bear their iniquities. | bodily pains of childbirth; which is very suitable to His mental agony in the Garden and on the Cross. |
| 12. 'Therefore will I divide him a portion with the great, and he shall divide the spoil with the strong; | His subsequent triumph in the Christian Church is here alluded to. |
| because he poured out his soul unto death, | This implies that His sufferings were of some duration; and is thus very appropriate to a lingering death like crucifixion. |
| and was numbered with the transgressors: yet he bare the sin of many, and made intercession for the transgressors.' | While the closing words exactly agree with His dying a shameful death between two robbers; yet praying for His murderers, 'Father, forgive them.' |

[366] *Comp.* Job 29. 9.

[367] *Comp.* Isa. 40. 10; 51. 9.

[368] John 1. 46.

[369] Deut. 21. 23; Gal. 3. 13.

[370] Matt. 26. 62; 27. 14.

[371] *Comp.* Isa. 1. 4.

[372] Mark 10. 24; John 21. 5.

It seems hardly necessary to insist on the agreement shown above; it is indisputable. The sufferings and the triumph of the Lord's Servant are foretold with equal confidence and with equal clearness, though they might well have seemed incompatible.

**(2.) The Doctrinal Agreement.**

But the significance of the passage does not depend on these prophecies alone, though they are sufficiently remarkable, but on the *meaning* which the writer assigns to the great tragedy. It is the Christian doctrine concerning Christ's death, and not merely the events attending it, which is here insisted on. This will be best shown by adopting the previous method of parallel columns, showing in the first the six chief points in the Christian doctrine, and in the other the prophet's words corresponding to them.

| | |
|---|---|
| All mankind are sinners. | 'All we like sheep have gone astray.' |
| Christ alone was sinless. | 'My righteous servant.' 'He had done no violence, neither was any deceit in his mouth.' |
| He suffered not for His own sins, but for those of others. Nor was this the mere accidental suffering of an innocent man for a guilty one; it was a great work of *atonement*, an offering for sin. This is the central feature of the Christian doctrine, and it is asserted over and over again in the prophecy, which is above all that of a *Saviour*. | 'Surely he hath borne our griefs, and carried our sorrows.' 'He was wounded for our transgressions, he was bruised for our iniquities; the chastisement of (*i.e.*, which procured) our peace was upon him; and with his stripes we are healed.' 'The Lord hath laid on him the iniquity of us all.' 'For the transgression of my people was he stricken.' 'Thou shalt make his soul an offering for sin.' 'He shall bear their iniquities.' 'He bare the sin of many.' |
| And this Atonement was the fulfilment of the old Jewish sacrifices; especially that of the Paschal Lamb; so there was a special fitness in Christ's being put to death at the time of the Passover. | This is shown by the language employed, the *offering for sin* being the same word as that used for the old *guilt-offering*.[373] And the curious expression *So shall he sprinkle many nations* evidently refers to the sprinkling of the blood in the Jewish sacrifices, as the same word is used, and means cleansing them from sin.[374] |
| Yet it availed not only for the Jews, but for all mankind. | The *many nations* must include Gentiles as well as Jews. |
| Lastly, Christ's sacrifice was *voluntary*; He freely laid down His life, no one took it from Him (John 10. 18). | 'He poured out his soul unto death,' implies that the act was *voluntary*, and this is rendered still clearer from the context; for it was *because* He did this that He was to divide the spoil, etc. And the words *He humbled Himself*, also imply that the humiliation was voluntary. |

[373] *E.g.*, Lev. 7. 1.

[374] *E.g.*, Lev. 16. 19.

All this, it is plain, exactly suits the Christ in whom Christians believe; and it does not and cannot suit anyone else, since several of the Christian doctrines are quite unique, and do not occur in the Jewish or any other religion. This is indeed so striking, that if anyone acquainted with Christianity, but unacquainted with Isaiah, came across the passage for the first time, he would probably refer it to one of St. Paul's Epistles. And every word of it might be found there with perfect fitness.

**(3.) The modern Jewish interpretation.**

Now, what can be said on the other side? Many of the ancient Jews interpreted the passage as referring to their future Messiah;[375] but the modern Jews (and most critics who disbelieve in prophecy) refer it to the Jewish nation, or to the religious part of it, which they say is here personified as a single man, the Servant of the Lord. And it must of course be admitted that Isaiah does frequently speak of the Jews as God's *servant* (*e.g.*, 'But thou Israel, my servant, and Jacob whom I have chosen,')[376] though he nowhere else uses the term 'my *righteous* servant,' which he does here, and which would have been inapplicable to the nation.

[375] References are given in Edersheim's 'Life and Times of Jesus the Messiah,' 1901, vol. ii., p. 727.

[376] Isa. 41. 8.

But it is important to remember that this prophecy does not stand alone, and a little before, we read in a similar passage, 'It is too light a thing that thou shouldest be my servant to raise up the tribes of Jacob, and to restore the preserved of Israel: I will also give thee for a light to the Gentiles, that thou mayest be my salvation unto the end of the earth. Thus saith the Lord, the Redeemer of Israel, and his Holy One, to him whom man despiseth, to him whom the nation abhorreth, to a servant of rulers: Kings shall see and arise; princes, and they shall worship.'[377]

[377] Isa. 49. 6-7; comp. 42. 1-6.

Here it will be noticed the Lord's *servant* is clearly distinguished from both Jacob and Israel, and evidently means the Messiah. While His bringing salvation to the Gentiles, as well as to the Jews; His humiliation in being despised by men and hated by the Jewish nation; and His subsequent triumph, even Kings submitting themselves to Him; are all alluded to, much as they are in the present passage.

No doubt there is a difficulty in the prophet thus passing from one meaning of the word *servant* to another (especially, in a closely connected passage),[378] and various attempts have been made to explain it; but it does not alter the fact that he does so. Perhaps the best explanation is that Israel was *intended* to be God's Servant, but owing to their sins became unfitted; when God promised in the future to raise up a *righteous* servant, who should do all His pleasure and atone for Israel's failure. And, it may be added, the term *Servant* is applied to the Messiah both by Ezekiel and Zechariah, as well as in the New Testament.[379]

[378] Isa. 49. 3, 5.

[379] Ezek. 34. 23; Zech. 3. 8; Acts 3. 13 (R.V.).

Moreover, the Jewish interpretation not only leaves all the details of the prophecy unexplained and inexplicable, but ignores its very essence, which, as before said, is the atoning character of the sufferings. No one can say that the sufferings of the Jews were voluntary, or that they were not for their own sins, but for those of other people, which were in consequence atoned for. Or, to put the argument in other words, if the *He* refers to the Jewish nation, to whom does the *our* refer in such sentences as *He was wounded for our transgressions*? While v. 8 expressly says that the Jews (God's people) were not the sufferers, but those for whom He suffered. (For the transgression of *my people* was *he* stricken.) This interpretation then is hopelessly untenable, and the passage either means what Christians assert, or it means nothing.

In conclusion, it must be again pointed out that all these minute historical details attending Christ's death, and all these remarkable Christian doctrines concerning it, are all found within fifteen verses of a writing many centuries older than the time of Christ. It would be hard to over-estimate the great improbability of all this being due to chance; indeed, such a conclusion seems incredible.

### (*B.*) THE PSALM OF THE CRUCIFIXION (PS. 22).[380]

[380] This is discussed more fully in an article in the *Churchman*, April, 1912, by the present writer.

We pass on now to another most remarkable prophecy; for this well-known Psalm describes what can only be regarded as a *crucifixion*. The decisive verse is of course, *They pierced my hands and my feet*; but even apart from this, the various sufferings described cannot all be endured in any other form of death, such as stoning or beheading. And the Psalm agrees with the Death of Christ, both in its numerous details, and in its whole scope and meaning. We will therefore consider this close agreement first, and then some of the objections.

### (1.) Its close agreement.

We need not quote the Psalm, as it is so well known; but will point out the agreement verse by verse.

Ver. 1. His feeling forsaken by God, and using these actual words: 'My God, my God, why hast thou forsaken me?'

2. as well as praying for deliverance during the previous night;

3. though in spite of His sufferings, He casts no reproach upon God.

4. His belonging to God's chosen people, the Jews, so that He could speak of *our* fathers;

5. who had so often been helped by God before.

6. His pitiable condition in being exposed to the scorn and reproach of men, and despised by the people.

7. His being lifted up to die in public, so that those who passed by could see Him; and the way in which they mocked Him, shaking their heads, etc.

8. The exact words they used: *He trusted on the Lord that He would deliver him, let Him deliver him seeing He delighteth in him* (margin). These words show that the speakers themselves were Jews, and that He was thus put to death among His own nation. And the last clause can only be meant ironically in the sense that the Sufferer *claimed* that God delighted in him, claimed, that is, in some special sense to be beloved by God.

9. And, as a matter of fact, God had always watched over Him, and had saved Him in His infancy from being slain by Herod.

10. And in return His whole life had been dedicated to God; so that He could say that God had been *His* God, even from His birth.

11. His being abandoned by His disciples, and left without a helper;

12. though surrounded by His enemies, described as *bulls of Bashan*. This curious term is used elsewhere for the unjust rulers of the people,[381] and was therefore very applicable to the chief priests and rulers, who had so unjustly condemned Him, and now stood round the Cross reviling Him.

[381] Amos. 4. 1.

13. And they continually insulted Him, *gaping with the mouth* being a common expression of contempt;[382] *ravening* appropriate to the way in which they had thirsted for His blood before Pilate; and *roaring* to the great noise and tumult made at the time.

[382] *E.g.*, Job 16. 10.

14. His side being pierced, so that there poured out a quantity of watery fluid (mixed with clots of blood), the probable cause of this—the rupture of the heart[383]—being also hinted at; while His bones were nearly out of joint, through the weight of the suspended Body.

[383] See 'The Physical Cause of the Death of Christ,' by Dr. Symes Thompson, 1904.

15. His suffering extreme weakness, and extreme thirst, immediately before His death.[384]

[384] Lam. 4. 4; John 19. 28-30.

16. His being crucified (*i.e.*, His hands and feet being pierced), the men who did this being here called *dogs*. They seem to have been a special set of men, different from the Jews who had before been mocking Him. And as this was the very term used by Christ Himself for the Gentiles, in distinction to the Jews,[385] it was peculiarly appropriate to the Gentile (Roman) soldiers who crucified Him.

[385] Matt. 15. 26.

17. And they also exposed and stretched out His Body, so that the bones stood out in relief. And they then stood watching Him;

18. and divided His garments among them, casting lots for one of them.

19. Then follows a short prayer.

20. The term *sword*, like the *dog*, the *lion's mouth*, and the *wild oxen*, need not be pressed literally; but may be used here (as in other places)[386] for any violent death. And in the New Testament it seems employed for all punishments, including probably a death by crucifixion (St. Peter's).[387]

[386] *Comp.* 2 Sam. 11. 24; 12. 9.

[387] Rom. 13. 4; Matt. 26. 52.

21. Yet in spite of His troubles, and even death, He feels sure of deliverance.

22. And now the strain suddenly changes, the Sufferer is restored to life and freedom and at once declares God's name unto His brethren. And this exactly agrees with Christ's now declaring for the first time God's complete *Name* of, Father, Son, and Holy Ghost, unto His *brethren*, as He calls them, the Apostles.[388] While if we identify this appearance with that to the five hundred, it was literally *in the midst of the congregation*—in the presence, that is, of the first large Christian assembly.

[388] Matt. 28. 10, 19.

23. Moreover, His deliverance is of world-wide significance, and great blessings are to follow from it. These commence with the Jews, who were to *praise* and glorify God; though with a strange feeling of *awe* and fear; all of which was exactly fulfilled.[389]

[389] Acts 2. 43-47.

24. And the blessings are somehow connected with God's not having despised, but having accepted, His sufferings.

25. And they include a reference to some *vows* (meaning uncertain);

26. and to a wonderful feast generally thought to refer to the Holy Communion.

27. And the blessings then extend to the Gentile nations also, even to the most distant parts of the world, who are now to become worshippers of the true God, Jehovah. And, as a matter of fact, Christians exist in all known countries, and wherever there are Christians, Jehovah is worshipped.

28. To Whom the whole earth, both the Jewish kingdom and the Gentile nations, really belongs.

29. And to Whom everyone will eventually bow down.

30. After this we read of a *seed* serving Him, probably used here, as in Isaiah, for disciples, each generation of whom is to tell of this wonderful deliverance to the next. And this they have been doing for eighteen centuries.

31. And so they will continue doing to generations that are yet unborn. While the closing words, *He hath done it* (R.V.) are often taken as referring to the whole Psalm, meaning that the work of suffering and atonement was now complete, *It is done*;[390] and they would thus correspond to Christ's closing words on the Cross, *It it finished*.

[390] Hengstenberg, Commentary on Psalms, 1867, vol. i., 396.

Everyone must admit that the agreement all through is very remarkable; though there are two slight objections.

### (2.) Two objections.

The first is that there is nothing to show that the writer meant the Psalm to refer to the Messiah at all, though, strange to say, some of the Jews so interpreted it;[391] therefore if there is an agreement, it is at most only a chance coincidence. But the idea of *all* these coincidences being due to chance is most improbable. And there certainly is some indication that it refers to the Messiah, since, as we have seen, it leads up to the conversion of the Gentiles, which the other Jewish prophets always associate with the times of the Messiah.

[391] Edersheim, 1901, vol. ii., 713.

Moreover, if the Psalm does not refer to Christ, it is difficult to see to whom it does refer, since it is quite inapplicable to David, or Hezekiah, or anyone else at that time; as crucifixion was not a Jewish punishment, though dead bodies were sometimes hung on trees. Yet, as just said, verses 7-8 show that the Sufferer was put to death among his own nation. This strange anomaly of a Jew being put to death among Jews, though not in the Jewish manner by stoning, but by crucifixion, exactly suits the time of Christ, when Judæa was a Roman province, and crucifixion a Roman punishment.

Many of the *details* also are quite inapplicable. David, for instance, never had his garments divided among his enemies; yet (even apart from our Gospels) there can be little doubt that the garments of Christ were so divided, as the clothes of a prisoner were usually taken by the guard who executed him.

And any such reference (to David, etc.) is rendered still more improbable, because the sufferer appears to have no sense of *sin*, and never laments his own wickedness, as the writers so frequently do when speaking about themselves. And here also the Psalm is entirely applicable to Christ, since (as we shall see in the next chapter) His sinlessness was a striking feature in His character. Nor again did the deliverance of David in any way lead to the *conversion of the Gentiles*, which, as just said, is the grand climax of the Psalm, and excludes all other interpretations.

But in any case this objection (which is also made to other Old Testament prophecies) cannot be maintained; for *who*, we must ask, was their real author? Was it the human prophet, or was it God Who inspired the prophet to write as he did? And the prophets themselves emphatically declared that it was the latter. The word of the Lord came unto them, or a vision was granted unto them, and they had to proclaim it, whether they liked it or not. In fact, as St. Matthew says, it was not really the prophet who spoke, but God, who spoke *through the prophet*.[392] There is thus no reason for thinking that they either knew, or thought they knew, the whole meaning of their prophecies; and the objection may be dismissed at once.

[392] *E.g.*, Matt. 1. 22.

The second objection is, that some of the events fulfilling this, and other Old Testament prophecies, never occurred, but were purposely invented. This, however, destroys altogether the moral character of the Evangelists, who are supposed to tell deliberate falsehoods, in order to get a pretended fulfilment of an old prophecy. And the difficulty of admitting this is very great. Moreover, such explanations can only apply to a very few cases; since, as a rule, the events occurred in *public*, and must therefore have been well known at the time.

And even in those cases where the event was so trivial, that it might possibly have been invented, such an explanation is often untenable. Take, for example, the manner in which Christ on the cross was mocked by His enemies, who said, 'He trusted in God, let him deliver him now if he desireth him.'[393] A more probable incident under the circumstances can scarcely be imagined, the chief priests quoting the familiar language (just as men sometimes quote the Bible now) without thinking of its real significance. But, supposing the words were never uttered, is it conceivable that the Evangelist (or anyone else) would have invented them in order to get a pretended fulfilment of this Psalm, where the Crucified One is mocked with almost identical words; yet have never pointed out the fulfilment himself, but have trusted to the chance of his readers discovering it?

[393] Matt. 27. 43.

Neither of these objections, then, is of much importance; while the agreement of the Psalm with the events attending the death and Resurrection of Christ, seems, as in the previous case, to be far too exact to be accidental.

### (*C.*) THE DIVINITY OF THE MESSIAH.

Our last example shall be of a different kind from the others. It is that the Old Testament contains several passages which show that the future Messiah was to be not only Superhuman, but Divine. And considering the strong Monotheism of the Jews this is very remarkable. The following are three of the most important:—

'For unto us a child is born, unto us a son is given; and the government shall be upon his shoulder: and his name shall be called Wonderful, Counsellor, Mighty God, Everlasting Father, Prince of Peace.'[394] Here we have a plain statement of the Divinity of One Who should be born a child. The two words translated *Mighty God* are incapable of any other translation, and no other is suggested for them in the margin of either the Authorised or Revised Version; while the same two words occur in the next chapter, where they plainly mean *Mighty God* and nothing else. Moreover, the term *Everlasting Father* is literally *Father of Eternity* (see margin) and means the Eternal One. This is another divine title, and does not conflict with the Christian doctrine that it was the Son, and not the Father, Who became Incarnate. While the following words, that of the increase of His government *there shall be no end*, and that it should be established *for ever*, also point to a Divine Ruler, in spite of the reference to David's throne. And it is significant that a few verses before it is implied that the Ministry of this future Messiah should commence in the land of Zebulon, and Naphtali, by the Sea of Galilee; where, as a matter of fact, Christ's Ministry did commence.

[394] Isa. 9. 6; 10. 21; 9. 1-2.

'But thou, Bethlehem Ephrathah, which art little to be among the thousands of Judah, out of thee shall one come forth unto me that is to be ruler in Israel; whose goings forth are from of old, from everlasting.'[395] Here we have a prophecy of the birth of One who had existed *from everlasting*; thus showing the Pre-existence and apparent Divinity of the Messiah, who was to be born at Bethlehem, where, again, as a matter of fact, Christ actually was born.

[395] Mic. 5. 2.

'Awake, O sword, against my shepherd, and against the man that is my fellow, saith the Lord of hosts.'[396] The word translated *fellow* is only found elsewhere in Leviticus, where it is usually translated *neighbour*, and always implies an equality between the two persons.[397] Thus God speaks of the Shepherd who was to be slain with the sword (a term, as before said, used for any violent death), as equal with Himself, and yet at the same time Man; so no one but a Messiah who is both God and Man—*Fellow-God* as well as *fellow-man*—can satisfy the language.

[396] Zech. 13. 7.

[397] Lev. 6. 2; 18. 20; 19. 11, 15, 17; 24. 19; 25. 14, 15, 17.

And here again the reference to Christ is confirmed by the fact that several incidents in His Passion are alluded to, in some of which His Divinity is likewise asserted. The most important are the way in which He (the Just Saviour) rode into Jerusalem on an ass; and the rejoicing with which He was received, when the people welcomed Him as their *King*. And the fact that He (the Lord Jehovah) should be sold for thirty pieces of silver, the money being cast down in the House of the Lord, and afterwards given to the potter; and also that He (again the Lord Jehovah) should be pierced.[398] These are, it is true, expressed in figurative language, and often mixed up with other subjects; so no instance by itself, affords a strong argument. But still their all occurring so close together, and all leading up to the violent death of a *man*, who was yet the *fellow*, or *equal*, with God, can scarcely be accidental. While the prophecy, like so many others, ends with the conversion of the Gentiles, the Lord Jehovah being recognised as King over all the earth; which seems to place the Messianic character beyond dispute.

[398] Zech. 9. 9; 11. 12-13; 12. 10; 14. 9; Luke 19. 37-38.

The Divinity of the Messiah is also involved in some hints which occur in the Old Testament as to the doctrine of the *Trinity*. For instance, the Hebrew word for God, *Elohim*, is a plural word, though, strange to say, it generally takes a singular adjective, and verb. Thus if we tried to represent it in English, the first verse of the Bible would read, 'In the beginning the Gods, He created the heaven and the earth.' Attempts have of course been made to reduce the significance of this by pointing out that a few other Hebrew words, such as *lord* and *master*, sometimes do the same; or by regarding it as a survival from some previous polytheistic religion; or else as being what is called the plural of Majesty, a sort of royal *We*. This, however, does not seem to have been in use in early times, and never occurs in the Bible, where kings always speak of themselves in the singular.[399] Anyhow it is very remarkable that the Jews should have used a plural word for God with a singular verb; especially as the same word, when used of false gods, takes a plural verb.

[399] *E.g.*, Gen. 41. 41; Ezra 6. 12; 7. 21; Dan. 4. 6.

Moreover, God is at times represented as speaking in the plural,[400] saying, for instance, *Let us make man in our image*, as if consulting with other Divine Persons; since it is obvious that the expression cannot refer to angels, who are themselves created, and not fellow Creators. Yet just afterwards we read, 'God created man in *his* own image,' thus implying that there is still but one God. Another and even more remarkable expression is, *Behold, the man is become as one of us*. This cannot possibly be the plural of Majesty; for though a king might speak of himself as *We* or *Us*, no king ever spoke of himself as *one of Us*. Such an expression can only be used when there are other persons of similar rank with the speaker; therefore when used by God, it shows conclusively that there are other Divine Persons. So again when God says, 'Whom shall *I* send, and who will go for *us*?' it implies that He is both one, and more than one; which the previous *thrice* Holy, points to as being a Trinity.[401] The existence of such passages seems to require some explanation, and Christianity alone can explain them.

[400] Gen. 1. 26; 3. 22; 11. 7.

[401] Isa. 6. 8.

## (*D.*) CONCLUSION.

Before concluding this chapter there is still one objection to be considered. Why, it is said, if these prophecies really refer to Christ, are they not plainer? Surely if God wished to foretell the future, He would have done it better than this: and a few words added here and there would have made the reference to Christ indisputable. No doubt they would; but possibly God did not wish to make the reference indisputable. Moreover, if the prophecies had been plainer, they might have prevented their own fulfilment. Had the Jews known for certain that Christ was their Messiah, they could scarcely have crucified Him; and it seems to many that the prophecies are already about as plain as they could be without doing this. The important point, however, is not whether the prophecies might not have been plainer, but whether they are not already too plain to be accidental.

Lastly, we must notice the cumulative nature of the evidence. We have only examined a few instances, but, as said before, Messianic prophecies of some kind more or less distinct, occur at intervals all through the Old Testament. And though some of those commonly brought forward seem weak and fanciful, there are numbers of others which are not. And here, as elsewhere, this has a double bearing on the argument.

In the first place, it does not at all increase the difficulty of the *Christian* interpretation; for twenty prophecies are practically no more difficult to admit than two. Indeed, the fact that instead of being a few isolated examples, they form a complete series, rather lessens the difficulty than otherwise.

On the other hand, it greatly increases the difficulty of *any other* interpretation; for twenty prophecies are far more difficult to deny than two. If one is explained as a lucky coincidence, it will not account for the next; if that is got rid of by some unnatural interpretation of the words, it will not account for the third, and so on indefinitely. The difficulties are thus not only great in themselves, but are all cumulative; and hence together they seem insuperable. Anyhow, it is clear that these Prophecies form another strong argument in favour of Christianity.

# CHAPTER XXI.
## THAT THE CHARACTER OF CHRIST CONFIRMS THE TRUTH OF CHRISTIANITY.

The character of Christ can only be deduced from the New Testament, any other Christ being purely imaginary.

(*A.*) THE TEACHING OF CHRIST.

(1.) Its admitted excellence.

(2.) Two objections.

(3.) His sinlessness.

(*B.*) THE CLAIMS OF CHRIST.

(1.) His claim to be Superhuman—declaring that He was the Ruler, Redeemer, and final Judge of the world.

(2.) His claim to be Divine—declaring His Equality, Unity, and Pre-existence with God.

(3.) How these claims were understood at the time, both by friends and foes.

(*C.*) THE GREAT ALTERNATIVE.

Christ cannot, therefore, have been merely a good man; He was either *God*, as He claimed to be, or else a *bad* man, for making such claims. But the latter view is disproved by His Moral Character.

In this chapter we propose to consider the Character of Christ, and its bearing on the truth of Christianity. Now our knowledge of Christ's character can only be derived from the four Gospels; indeed, a Christ with any other character assigned to Him is a purely imaginary being, and might as well be called by some other name. Taking, then, the Gospels as our guide, what is the character of Christ? Clearly this can be best deduced from His own *teaching* and *claims*, both of which are fortunately given at some length; so we will consider these first, and then the *great alternative* which they force upon us.

### (*A.*) THE TEACHING OF CHRIST.

Under this head, we will first notice the admitted excellence of Christ's teaching, then some objections which are often made, and lastly His sinlessness.

**(1.) Its admitted excellence.**

To begin with, the excellence of Christ's moral teaching hardly needs to be insisted on at the present day, and rationalists as well as Christians have proclaimed its merits. For instance, to quote a few examples:—

'Religion cannot be said to have made a bad choice in pitching on this man as the ideal representative and guide of humanity; nor even now would it be easy, even for an unbeliever, to find a better translation of the rule of virtue from the abstract into the concrete, than to endeavour so to live that Christ should approve our life.'—*J. S. Mill*.[402]

[402] Nature, the Utility of Religion and Theism, 2nd edit., 1874, p. 255.

'Jesus remains to humanity an inexhaustible source of moral regenerations.' And again, 'In Him is condensed all that is good and lofty in our nature.'— *E. Renan*.[403]

[403] Life of Jesus, translated by Wilbour, New York, 1864, pp. 370, 375.

'It was reserved for Christianity to present to the world an ideal character, which, through all the changes of eighteen centuries, has inspired the hearts of men with an impassioned love; has shown itself capable of acting on all ages, nations, temperaments, and conditions; has been not only the highest pattern of virtue, but the strongest incentive to its practice; and has exercised so deep an influence that it may be truly said that the simple record of three short years of active life has done more to regenerate and to soften mankind than all the disquisitions of philosophers, and all the exhortations of moralists.'—*W. E. H. Lecky*.[404]

[404] History of European Morals, 3rd edit., 1877, vol. ii., p. 8.

These quotations are only examples of many which might be given; but it is practically undisputed that the morality taught by Christ is the best the world has ever seen. It is also undisputed that His life was in entire harmony with His teaching. He lived, as far as we can judge, a holy and blameless life, and His character has never been surpassed either in history or fiction.

**(2.) Two objections.**

There are, however, two slight objections. The first is that Christ's teaching was not *original*; and, strictly speaking, this is perhaps true. Something similar to all He taught has been discovered in more ancient times, either in Egypt, India, China, or elsewhere. But this hardly affects the argument. An unlearned Jew living at Nazareth cannot be supposed to have derived his teaching from these sources; and it is a great improvement on all of them put together. The important point is, that there was nothing among the Jews of His own time which could have produced, or even have invented, such a character. He was immeasurably better than His contemporaries, and all of them put together have not exerted an influence on the world a thousandth part that of Christ.

The second objection refers to *certain portions* of Christ's teaching. For example, He urges men not to resist evil, and seems to place virginity above marriage to an exaggerated extent.[405] I have never seen a satisfactory explanation of the latter passage; but it is obvious on the face of it that it cannot be meant for universal application, or it would lead to the extinction of the human race.

[405] Matt. 5. 39; 19. 12.

Again, several of the *parables* are said to be unjust such as that of the workmen in the vineyard, the unrighteous steward, and the wedding garment. But parables must not be pressed literally, and very different interpretations have been put on these. However, we will consider the two last, which are those most often objected to.

With regard to the *Unrighteous Steward*, though apparently he had been guilty of dishonesty, we are told that his lord *commended* him, because he had done wisely.[406] But no one can think that his lord commended him, because he had just cheated him. So if his conduct was really dishonest (about which scholars are by no means agreed) we can only suppose that *in spite of this*, his lord commended him, because of his wisdom. In the same way, if an ingenious robbery were committed at the present day, even the man robbed, might say that he could not help admiring the scoundrel for his cleverness. The meaning then appears to be that *wisdom* is so desirable that it is to be commended even in worldly matters, and even in a bad cause; and therefore of course still more to be aimed at in religious matters, and in a good cause.

[406] Luke 16. 8.

Next as to the *Wedding Garment*. It is distinctly implied that there was only *one* man without it,[407] so obviously the first point to determine is how the other men got their garments. They could not have had them out in the roads, and there was no time to go home and get them, even if they possessed any. It follows then that they must each have been provided with a suitable garment (probably a cloak, worn over their other clothes) when they reached the palace. This appears to have been an eastern custom,[408] and if one of them refused to put it on, he would certainly deserve to be excluded from the feast. Thus the object of the parable seems to be to show that God's blessings can only be obtained on God's terms (*e.g. forgiveness* on *repentance*), though there is no hardship in this, as He has Himself given us grace to comply with these terms, if we like. Neither of these objections, then, is of much importance.

[407] Matt. 22. 11.

[408] Archb. Trench, Notes on the Parables, 1870, p. 234.

**(3.) His sinlessness.**

A most remarkable point has now to be noticed. It is that, notwithstanding His perfect moral teaching, there is not in the character of Christ the slightest consciousness of *sin*. In all His numerous discourses, and even in His prayers, there is not a single word which implies that He thought He ever had done, or ever could do, anything wrong Himself. He is indeed most careful to avoid implying this, even incidentally. Thus He does not tell His disciples, 'If *we* forgive men their trespasses,' etc., but 'If *ye*,' as the former might imply that He, as well as they, had need of the Father's forgiveness.[409] Nor did He ever regret anything that He had done, or ever wish that He had acted otherwise. And though He blamed self-righteousness in others, and urged them to repentance, He never hinted that He had any need of it Himself; in fact, He expressly denied it, for He said that He *always* did those things that were pleasing to God.[410]

[409] Matt. 6. 14.

[410] John 8. 29.

And this is the more striking when we reflect that good men are, as a rule, most conscious of their faults. Yet here was One who carried moral goodness to its utmost limit, whose precepts are admittedly perfect, but who never for a moment thought that He was not fulfilling them Himself. Such a character is absolutely unique in the world's history. It can only be explained by saying that Christ was not merely a good man, but a *perfect* man, since goodness without perfection would only have made Him more conscious of the faults He had. Yet if we admit this, we must admit more; for perfection is not a human attribute, and a *sinless life* needs a good deal to account for it.

**(*B.*) THE CLAIMS OF CHRIST.**

We pass on now to the *claims* of Christ; and His high moral character would plainly lead us to place the utmost confidence in what He said about Himself. And as we shall see He claimed to be both *Superhuman* and *Divine*; and this is how all His contemporaries, both friends and foes, understood Him. And though it is impossible to add to the marvel of such claims, yet the fact that nothing in any way resembling them is to be found among the Jewish Prophets helps us, at least, to realise their uniqueness. Many of them are spoken concerning the *Son of Man*; but there can be no doubt whatever that by this title Christ means Himself.[411]

[411] *E.g.*, Matt. 16. 13, 16.

**(1.) His Claim to be Superhuman.**

This is shown by three main arguments, for Christ declared that He was the Ruler, Redeemer, and final Judge of the world. In the first place, He claimed to be the *Ruler* of the world, saying in so many words that all things had been delivered unto Him, and that He possessed all authority, both in heaven and on earth.[412] Moreover, His dominion was to be not only universal, but it was to last for ever; since after this world had come to an end, the future Kingdom of Heaven was still to be *His* Kingdom, its angels were to be *His* angels, and its citizens *His* elect.[413]

[412] Matt. 11. 27; 28. 18; Luke 10. 22.

[413] Matt. 13. 41; 24. 31.

Secondly, Christ claimed to be the *Redeemer* of the world. He distinctly asserted that He came to give His life a ransom for many, and that His blood was shed for the remission of sins. And the importance He attached to this is shown by the fact that He instituted a special rite (the Holy Communion) on purpose to commemorate it.[414]

[414] Matt. 20. 28; 26. 28; Mark 10. 45; 14. 24; Luke 22. 19.

Thirdly, Christ claimed to be the final *Judge* of the world. This tremendous claim alone shows that He considered Himself quite above and distinct from the rest of mankind. While they were all to be judged according to their works, He was to be the Judge Himself, coming in the clouds of heaven with thousands of angels. And His decision was to be final and without appeal. Moreover, this astonishing claim does not depend on single texts or passages, but occurs all through the first three Gospels.[415] During the whole of His Ministry—from His Sermon on the Mount to His trial before Caiaphas—He persistently asserted that He was to be the final Judge of the world. It is hardly credible that a mere man, however presumptuous, should ever have made such a claim as this. Can we imagine anyone doing so at the present day? and what should we think of him if he did?

[415] Matt. 7. 22; 10. 32; 13. 41; 16. 27; 19. 28; 24. 30; 25. 31-46; 26. 64; and similar passages in the other Gospels.

**(2.) His Claim to be Divine.**

Like the preceding, this is shown by three main arguments; for Christ declared His Equality, Unity, and Pre-existence with God. In the first place, Christ claimed *Equality* with God. He said that the same honour should be given to Himself as to God the Father; that men should believe in Him as well as in God; that He and the Father would together dwell in the souls of men; and that He, like the Father, had the power of sending the Holy Spirit of God.[416] He also commanded men to be baptized into His Name as well as into that of the Father; and promised that whenever and wherever His disciples were gathered together, He would be in the midst of them, even unto the end of the world, which, cannot be true of anyone but God.[417]

[416] John 5. 23; 14. 1, 23; 16. 7.

[417] Matt. 18. 20; 28. 19, 20.

Secondly, Christ claimed *Unity* with God. He did not say that He was another God, but that He and the Father were *One*; that He was in the Father, and the Father in Him; that whoever beheld Him beheld the Father; that whoever had seen Him had seen the Father.[418] These latter texts cannot, of course, be pressed literally, as few would maintain that Christ was really God *the Father*. But just as if a human father and son were *extremely* alike, we might say that if you had seen the son, you had seen the father; so if Christ was truly God—God the Son—the *very image* of His Father,[419] the same language might be used. It would at least be intelligible. But it would be quite unintelligible, if Christ had been merely a *good man*. Can we imagine the best man that ever lived saying, If you have seen me, you have seen God?

[418] John 10. 30; 17. 21; 12. 45; 14. 9.

[419] Heb. 1. 3.

Thirdly, Christ claimed *Pre-existence* with God. He said that He had descended out of heaven; that He had come down from heaven; that He came out from the Father and was come into the world; and that even before its creation He had shared God's glory.[420] While in another passage, '*Before Abraham was, I am*,'[421] He not only said that He existed before Abraham, but by using the words *I am* instead of *I was*, He seemed to identify Himself with Jehovah, the great *I am*, of the Old Testament.[422]

[420] John 3. 13; 6. 38; 16. 28; 17. 5.

[421] John 8. 58.

[422] Exod. 3. 14.

Turning now to the other side, there are four passages in which Christ seems to *disclaim* being Divine. The most important is where He says that the Son (*i.e.* Himself) does not know the time of the future Judgment;[423] and the present writer has never seen a really satisfactory explanation of this. But it may be pointed out that if we admit that Christ was both Divine and human, it is only fair to refer any particular statement to that nature, to which it is applicable; even though the wording seems to suggest the opposite. In the same way, the passage, that the *Lord of Glory* was crucified[424] can only refer to Christ in His *human* nature, and not in His Divine nature, as the Lord of Glory. And in His human nature Christ may have been ignorant of the time of the future Judgment, just as in His human nature He increased in wisdom and stature.[425]

[423] Mark 13. 32.

[424] 1 Cor. 2. 8.

[425] Luke 2. 52.

Then we have the passage where a ruler addresses Christ as '*Good* Master,' and Christ demurs to this, saying that the word was only applicable to God.[426] And how, it is asked, could He have done so, if He had been both good and God? The best explanation seems to be that among the Jews, it was the custom never to address a Teacher (or Rabbi) as *Good*. They said God was 'the *Good One* of the world'; it was one of *His* titles.[427] Therefore as the ruler had no means of knowing that Christ was God, he was not justified in thus addressing Him as *Good*.

[426] Mark 10. 18.

[427] Edersheim's Life and Times of the Messiah, vol. ii., p. 339.

The remaining two passages, 'I go unto the Father; for the Father is greater than I'; and 'I ascend unto my Father and your Father, and my God and your God,'[428] are easier to explain, since here it is obvious that they refer to Christ's *human* nature alone, as it was in His human nature alone that He was ever absent from the Father. And even here He carefully distinguishes His own relationship to God from that of His disciples. For though He teaches them to say *our Father*, yet when including Himself with them, He does not here or anywhere else say *our* Father, or *our* God; but always emphasises His own peculiar position. While we may ask in regard to the first passage, would anyone but God have thought it necessary to explain that God the Father was greater than Himself? Anyhow, these passages do not alter the fact that Christ did repeatedly claim to be both superhuman and Divine.

[428] John 14. 28; 20. 17.

**(3.) How these Claims were understood at the time.**

We have now to consider how these claims were understood at the time. And first, as to *Christ's friends*. We have overwhelming evidence that after His Resurrection all the disciples and early Christians believed their Master to be both superhuman and Divine. And to realise the full significance of this, we must remember that they were not polytheists, who did not mind how many gods they believed in, and were willing to worship Roman Emperors or anyone else; but they were strict monotheists. They firmly believed that there was only one God, yet they firmly believed that Christ was Divine. This is shown throughout the New Testament.

Thus the writers of the *first three Gospels*, though they usually record the events of Christ's life without comment, yet in one passage identify Him with the God of the Old Testament, referring the prophecy about the messenger of the *Lord our God* to the messenger of *Christ*.[429] And as to the *Fourth Gospel*, it begins with asserting Christ's Divinity in the plainest terms, saying that *the Word*, who afterwards became flesh, *was God*. And it appropriately ended, before the last chapter was added, with St. Thomas declaring this same belief, when he addressed Christ as *my Lord and my God*, which titles He fully accepted.[430] Yet immediately afterwards, the author says he wrote his Gospel to convince men that Jesus was the Christ, the Son of God. Evidently then this expression, *the Son of God*, meant to him, and therefore presumably to other New Testament writers, who use it frequently, that Christ was truly God—God the Son—*my Lord and my God*—in the fullest and most complete sense.

[429] Isa. 40. 3; Matt. 3. 3; Mark 1. 3; Luke 3. 4.

[430] John 1. 1; 20. 28.

With regard to the *Acts* an argument on the other side is sometimes drawn from St. Peter's speaking of Christ as 'a *man* approved of God unto you by mighty works,' thus implying, it is urged, that St. Peter did not know Him to be more than man.[431] But since he says he was only appealing to what his *hearers* knew to be true (*even as ye yourselves know*), how else could he have put it? His hearers did not know that Christ was God; they did know that He was *a man approved of God* by many wonderful miracles, because they had seen them. Moreover, in other places the Acts bear strong witness to the Divinity of Christ, as for instance when St. Paul speaks *of the Church of God which He purchased with His own blood*, or St. Stephen says *Lord Jesus receive my spirit*; or when the Apostles are represented as working their miracles, not in the name of God the Father, but in that of Christ.[432]

[431] Acts 2. 22.

[432] Acts 20. 28; 7. 59; 3. 6; 4. 10.

Next, as to the Book of *Revelation*. The evidence this affords is important, because nearly all critics admit that it was written by St. John. And if so, it shows conclusively that one at least of Christ's intimate followers firmly believed in His Divinity. For he not only speaks of Him as being universally worshipped both in heaven and on earth, but describes Him as *the First and the Last*, which is a title used by God in the Old Testament, and is plainly inapplicable to anyone else.[433] And we may ask, is it conceivable that an intimate friend of Christ should have believed Him to be the Everlasting

God, unless He had claimed to be so Himself, and had supported His claim by working miracles, and rising from the dead? Is it not, rather, certain that nothing but the most *overwhelming* proof would ever have convinced a Jew (of all persons) that a fellow Man, with whom he had lived for years, and whom he had then seen put to death as a malefactor, was Himself the Lord Jehovah, *the First and the Last?*

[433] Rev. 5. 11-14; 1. 17, 18; 2. 8; 22. 13; Isa. 44. 6.

But it is urged on the other side, that the writer also calls Him *the beginning of the Creation of God*, as if He had been merely the first Being created.[434] But the previous passages clearly show that this was not his meaning. It was rather that Christ was the *beginning* of creation, because He was its Source and Agent; He by whom, as the same writer declares, *all things were made*. And elsewhere a similar title is given Him for this identical reason, as He is called *the first-born of all creation*, because *all things have been created through Him*.[435]

[434] Rev. 3. 14;

[435] John 1. 3; Col. 1. 15, 16.

Equally important evidence is afforded by *St. Paul's Epistles*. For though he is not likely to have known Christ intimately, he must have been acquainted with numbers who did, including, as he says, *James the Lord's brother*.[436] And his early conversion, before A.D. 35, together with the fact that he had previously persecuted the Church at Jerusalem, and afterwards visited some of the Apostles there, must have made him well acquainted with the Christian doctrines from the very first. Moreover he tells us himself that the faith which he taught was the same as that which he had previously persecuted; and that when he visited the Apostles he *laid before them* the Gospel he preached, evidently to make sure that it agreed with what they preached.[437]

[436] Gal. 1. 19.

[437] Gal. 1. 23; 2. 2.

There can thus be no doubt that the Christianity of St. Paul was the same as that of the Twelve. And all through his Epistles he bears witness to the *superhuman* character of Christ; declaring, among other things, His sinlessness, and that He is the Ruler, Redeemer, and final Judge of the world.[438]

[438] 2 Cor. 5. 21; Rom. 14. 9; 1 Cor. 15. 3; 2 Cor. 5. 10.

He also bears witness to His *Divine* character, saying in so many words that He is over all, God blessed for ever; that we shall all stand before the Judgment-seat of God, which elsewhere he calls the Judgment-seat of Christ; that He was originally in the form of God (*i.e.*, in a state of Deity), and on an equality with God, before He became incarnate, and took the form of Man;

that in Him dwells all the fullness of the Godhead bodily; that He is our great God and Saviour Jesus Christ, Who gave Himself for us; and that the Psalmist prophesied of Him when he said, 'Thy throne, O God, is for ever and ever.'[439] This last passage, from the *Hebrews*, was perhaps not written by St. Paul, but this makes it all the more valuable, as the Epistle is generally dated, from internal evidence, before the destruction of Jerusalem, A.D. 70; and we have thus *another* early witness to the Divinity of Christ.

[439] Rom. 9. 5; 14. 10; 2 Cor. 5. 10; Phil. 2. 6; Col. 2. 9; Titus 2. 13; Heb. 1. 8.

The most important text on the other side is where St. Paul says there is *one God the Father*, and *one Lord Jesus Christ*,[440] which is quoted in the Nicene Creed. But though the statement is a difficult one, it cannot be pressed as implying that Christ is not *God*; for if so it would equally imply that the Father was not *Lord*, which few would contend was St. Paul's meaning.

[440] 1 Cor. 8. 6; *Comp.* Eph. 4. 4-6.

With regard to the above passages, it is important to notice that the allusions are all incidental. St. Paul does not attempt to prove the superhuman and Divine character of Christ, but refers to it as if it were undisputed. He evidently believed it himself, and took for granted that his readers did so too. And his readers included not only his own converts at Corinth and elsewhere, but the converts of other Apostles at Rome, which was a place he had not then visited, and a strong party of opponents in Galatia, with whom he was arguing. It is clear, then, that these doctrines were not peculiar to St. Paul, but were the common property of all Christians from the earliest times. And when combined with the previous evidence, this leaves no doubt as to how Christ's *friends* understood His claims. Whatever they may have thought of them before the Resurrection, that event convinced them that they were true, and they never hesitated in this belief.

Next as to *Christ's foes*. The evidence here is equally convincing. In St. John's Gospel we read that on several occasions during His life, when Christ asserted His superhuman and Divine character, the Jews wanted to kill Him in consequence; often avowing their reason for doing so with the utmost frankness. 'For a good work we stone thee not, but for blasphemy and because that thou, being a man, makest thyself God.'[441] And in thus doing they were only acting in accordance with their law, which commanded a blasphemer to be stoned.[442]

[441] John 10. 33; 5. 18; 8. 59; 11. 8.

[442] Lev. 24. 16.

In none of these instances did Christ repudiate the claims attributed to Him, or say He had been misunderstood. In fact, only once did He offer any explanation at all. He then appealed to the passage in the Old Testament, 'I said, Ye are gods,'[443] and asserted that He was much better entitled to the term, since He was sent into the world by the Father, and did the works of the Father. After which He again asserted His unity with the Father, which was the very point objected to by the Jews.

[443] Ps. 82. 6.

Moreover, not only during His life did Christ make these claims to be Divine, but He persevered with them even when it brought about His death. It is undisputed that the Jews condemned Him for *blasphemy*, and for nothing else. This is the teaching not of one Gospel alone, but of each of the four.[444] Every biography of Christ that we possess represents this as the real charge against Him; though, of course, when tried before the Roman governor that of disloyalty to Cæsar was brought forward as well.

[444] Matt. 26. 65; Mark 14. 64; Luke 22. 71; John 19. 7.

There is only one conclusion to be drawn from all this. It is that Christ did really claim to be both superhuman and Divine; that He deliberately and repeatedly asserted these claims during His life; that this provoked the hostility of the Jews, who frequently wanted to kill Him; that He never repudiated these claims, but persevered with them to the end; and was finally put to death in consequence.

## (*C*.) THE GREAT ALTERNATIVE.

We pass on now to the *great alternative*, which is forced upon us by combining the teaching and the claims of Christ. Before pointing out its importance we must notice a favourite method of trying to get out of the difficulty, which is by saying that the teaching of Christ occurs in the *first three Gospels*, and the claims in the *Fourth*; so if we deny the accuracy of this single Gospel the difficulty is removed. But unfortunately for this objection, though the Divine claims occur chiefly in the Fourth Gospel, the superhuman ones are most prominent in the other three; and we have purposely chosen all the passages illustrating them from these Gospels *alone*. And what is more, they occur in all the supposed *sources* of these Gospels—the so-called Triple Tradition, the source common to Matthew and Luke, etc. Everywhere from the earliest record to the latest, Christ is represented as claiming to be superhuman. And such claims are equally fatal to His moral character if He were only a man. For no good man, and indeed very few bad ones, could be so fearfully presumptuous as to claim to be the absolute Ruler of the world, still less to be its Redeemer, and, least of all, to be its one and only Judge hereafter.

This objection, then, cannot be maintained, and we are forced to conclude that the perfect moral teaching of Christ was accompanied by continual assertions of His own superhuman and Divine character. And as this was a point about which He must have known, it is clear that the statements must have been either true or intentionally false. He must, therefore, have been Divine, or else a deliberate impostor. In other words, the Christ of the Gospels—and history knows of no other—could not have been merely a good man. He was either *God* as He claimed to be, or else a *bad man* for making such claims. This is the *Great Alternative*.

Moreover, it is absolutely unique in the world's history. Nowhere else shall we find a parallel to it. In Christ—and in Christ alone—we have a Man Whose moral character and teaching have fascinated the world for centuries; and yet Who, unless His own claims were true, must have been guilty of the greatest falsehood, and blasphemy. This is the only logical conclusion to be drawn from the facts we have been considering, and all attempts to avoid it fail hopelessly.

Now what effect has this on our present inquiry as to the truth of Christianity? Plainly it forms another strong argument in its favour. For the moral teaching of its Founder is shown to be not only the most perfect the world has ever seen, but it is combined with a sense of entire sinlessness which is absolutely unique among men. Both of these, however, are also combined with claims to a superhuman and Divine character, which, if they are not correct, can only be described as impious, and profane. Therefore, unless Christianity is true, its Founder must have been not only the very *best* of men; but also one of the very *worst*; and this is a dilemma from which there is no escape.

# CHAPTER XXII.
## THAT THE HISTORY OF CHRISTIANITY CONFIRMS ITS TRUTH.

(*A.*) Its Early Triumphs.

(1.) Its immense difficulties.

(2.) Its marvellous success.

(3.) The so-called *natural* causes of success: they all imply the truth of the Religion.

(4.) Contrast with Mohammedanism.

(*B.*) Its Later History.

(1.) Its vitality in the past; very remarkable.

(2.) Its effect at the present; very beneficial.

(3.) Its prospects in the future; very hopeful.

(4.) The spread of *Rationalism*; but this is no new difficulty, while it shows the strength of Christianity, and being only destructive, can never take its place.

(*C.*) Conclusion.

The history of Christianity, which seems to have been foreknown to its Founder, forms another strong argument in its favour.

The argument we have next to consider is that derived from the *History of Christianity*. This religion, it must be remembered, originated, spread over, and finally conquered the civilised world in an historical age. And since the fact of this conquest can neither be disputed nor ignored, it must be accounted for. How is it that an obscure Jewish Peasant, who was crucified as a malefactor, some nineteen centuries ago, should now be worshipped, by over five hundred million persons, including all the most civilised nations of the world? As a mere historical problem, this requires some solution, for an effect in history, as elsewhere, must have an adequate cause. And it is scarcely too much to say that this is the most remarkable effect in the history of mankind. Here, then, is the subject we have to discuss; and we will first consider the *early triumphs* of Christianity, and then its *later history*.

### (*A.*) Its Early Triumphs.

Now it seems hard to exaggerate either the immense difficulties the religion had to overcome, or its marvellous success in overcoming them.

**(1.) Its immense difficulties.**

In the first place, we must consider the immense difficulties of founding such a religion as Christianity. Our familiarity with the subject prevents us from fully realising this, so perhaps an analogy will help to make it clear. Suppose, then, that missionaries *now* appeared in the cities of Europe, in London and Edinburgh, for example, and preached that an obscure peasant, who had been put to death somewhere in Persia as a malefactor, had risen from the dead, and was the God of heaven and earth. What chance would they have of making a single convert? Yet the first preaching of Christianity at Rome or Athens must have been very similar to this, only far more dangerous. Indeed, it is hard to over-estimate the difficulties of founding a religion, the principal doctrine of which,—and one that the Christians so boldly proclaimed,—was that of a crucified Saviour.[445]

[445] 1 Cor. 1. 23.

And all this took place among civilised nations, and in a literary, one might almost say a rationalistic, age; when the old pagan religions were being abandoned, because men could no longer believe in them. What, then, must have been the difficulty of introducing a new religion, which was (apparently) more absurd than any of them, and which worshipped One Who had been crucified? Christianity had, of course, many other difficulties to contend with especially in regard to its absolute claims; for it was a religion which could stand no rival, and its success meant the destruction of every heathen altar. But these sink into insignificance, compared with the great difficulty of the Cross.

**(2.) Its marvellous success.**

Yet, in spite of every difficulty, Christianity prevailed. The new religion spread with great rapidity. This we learn not only from Christian writers, who might be thought to exaggerate; but from impartial men such as *Suetonius* and *Tacitus*. The former says that in the reign of Claudius (A.D. 41-54) the Jews in Rome, *stirred up by one Chrestus* (*i.e.*, Christian Jews), were so numerous that the Emperor thought it expedient to banish them; and the latter that at the time of the great fire (A.D. 64) *large numbers* of Christians were discovered at Rome. While some years later *Pliny*, one of the Roman governors in Asia Minor, complained to the Emperor Trajan that the Christians were so numerous that the temples had long been deserted, though at the time he wrote (A.D. 112) they were being frequented again. He also bears witness to the exemplary lives of the Christians, their steadfastness in their religion, and the divine worship they paid to Christ. And as the religion did not originate in either Rome or Asia Minor, Christians were presumably as numerous elsewhere.

Nor can it be said that they were only to be found among the poor and ignorant. For Pliny himself admits that they included men of *every rank* in life; and the undisputed Epistles of St. Paul, such as that to the Romans (about A.D. 55), show that he thought his readers well educated, and quite able to follow a difficult argument. Moreover, according to the Acts, the people were by no means willing to accept Christianity without inquiry; and St. Paul was obliged in consequence to have long discussions on the subject. This was especially the case at Ephesus, where he *reasoned daily* in one of the schools, for about *two years*,[446] which does not look as if his followers were only among the poor and ignorant. While elsewhere we have the names of some eminent converts.

[446] Acts 19. 9-10; 17. 17.

Among these may be mentioned *Erastus* the treasurer of the city at Corinth; and *Crispus*, the ruler of the Synagogue there; *Dionysius*, the Areopagite at Athens; *Manaen*, the foster-brother of Herod the tetrarch; *Apollos*, a learned Jew of Alexandria, who had made a special study of the Scriptures; and *Theophilus*, a man of high rank (as is shown by the title *Most excellent*), none of whom are likely to have accepted the religion of the Crucified, without very strong evidence.[447] And recent discoveries in the catacombs have made it probable that a distinguished Roman lady, Pomponia Græcina (wife of the General Aulus Plautius) who Tacitus says was accused in A.D. 57 of having adopted a *foreign superstition*, was also a Christian.[448]

[447] Rom. 16. 23; Acts 18. 8; 17. 34; 13. 1; 18. 24; 1. 1; *comp.* 23. 26; 24. 3.

[448] J. Orr, Hist. and Lit. of early Church, 1913, p. 43. Tacitus, Annals, Bk. xiii., ch. 32.

Now what was the cause of this wonderful progress? It is easy to say what was *not* its cause. Physical force and the authority of the Government had nothing to do with it. Its missionaries did not preach with sword in hand, nor were they backed up by the civil power. All they did, all they could do, was to appeal to man's reason and conscience, and this appeal was successful. And we learn from the Christians' themselves, *e.g.*, in the Acts, that there were two main reasons for this. The first was the confident appeal to the facts of Christianity, such as the Resurrection of Christ, as undisputed and indisputable; and the second was the occasional aid of miracles. And the more we reflect on the subject, the more difficult it is to account for it, without at least one of these causes. For the spread of Christianity was not like that of a mere philosophy, or system of morals. It depended entirely on certain alleged *matters of fact*, which facts were quite recent at the time of its origin, occurred at the very place where it was first preached, and were open to the hostile criticism of an entire nation. This, it is needless to say, is without a parallel in history.

But it may be said, notwithstanding this rapid progress at first, Christianity took nearly three centuries to conquer the civilised world. Undoubtedly it did, but the significance of the conquest is not diminished by this. It is rather increased when we remember that at intervals all through this period the Religion suffered the fiercest persecution. That it should have survived such a fearfully prolonged struggle, and have finally conquered, does but show its inherent strength. We may look in vain for anything like this in the rest of history. No other religion has ever withstood such persistent attacks; no other religion has ever obtained such a complete and almost incredible triumph, the Emperor of the civilised world being brought to worship One Who had been put to death as a malefactor. In short, the progress of Christianity was as unique as its origin, and can only be satisfactorily accounted for by its truth.

### (3.) The so-called natural causes of success.

We must next glance at some natural causes which have been alleged as accounting for the wonderful spread of Christianity. Those brought forward by Gibbon in his *Decline and Fall of the Roman Empire* (Chapter XV.) are five in number. The first is the *intense zeal* of the early Christians. And doubtless this was a most important element in spreading their religion. But what gave them this intense zeal? What was it that made them so fearfully in earnest about their new religion, that they faced a life of suffering, and a death of martyrdom in preaching it? There can be but one answer. It was because they were so absolutely convinced of its truth. It was vouched for by what they considered overwhelming evidence, so they willingly risked everything for it. Their zeal, then, is but evidence for their conviction, and their conviction is but evidence for the truth of what they were convinced of; and valuable evidence too, for they plainly had much better means of knowing about it, than any that we can have.

Secondly, there is the doctrine of a *future life*; and doubtless this also had much to do with the success of Christianity. A longing for immortality seems inherent in man, and the vague guesses of philosophers were quite unable to satisfy this. It *might* be true that men should live again, but that was all they could say. Christianity alone, resting on the actual fact of Christ's Resurrection, said it *was* true; so here men found the assurance they wanted. But is it likely that Christianity should have so thoroughly satisfied them in this respect, had there been any real doubt as to Christ's Resurrection?

Thirdly, we have the *miracles* ascribed to the early Christians. Gibbon's argument here is more difficult to follow. Of course if these miracles were true, they would have greatly assisted the new religion; but then they would have been, not a natural but a supernatural cause of success. If on the other hand, the miracles were false, it is hard to see how the early Christians could have helped their religion by claiming miraculous powers which they did not possess, and which their contemporaries must have known that they did not possess.

Fourthly, we have the *pure morality* taught and practised by the early Christians. And no doubt this had something to do with helping their religion. But again we must ask, what was it that enabled the Christians alone in that age of vice and wickedness to lead pure lives? They ascribed it themselves to the example and power of their Founder, and nothing else can account for it. Christian morality cannot be a stream without a source, and no other source can be assigned to it. But could a mere human Teacher have had this more than human influence over thousands of converts, most of whom had never seen him?

Lastly, comes the *union* and *discipline* of the early Church. This may have helped Christianity in the later stages of the struggle, but could obviously have been of little use at the commencement. Moreover, why should Christians of various nations and classes have been so thoroughly united on this one subject, unless they were convinced of its overwhelming importance? On the whole, then, these so-called natural causes of success are at most only *secondary* causes; the truth of the religion is what they all imply, and this is the real cause which alone can account for its success.

A better way of explaining the spread of Christianity, which is now often adopted, is by saying that it arose *at a favourable crisis*. The dispersion of the Jews throughout the known world would, it is urged, have facilitated the spread of a religion founded by Jews. The speculations of the Greeks as to a Divine Word, or *Logos*, would have prevented the doctrines of the Trinity, and the Incarnation, from forming any great difficulty to the learned classes. While the mass of the people were disgusted with the old mythologies of Greece and Rome. These were dying out, because they failed to satisfy human nature, and men were longing for something better. They wanted, as men always will want, a religion; but they wanted it free from the absurdities and immoralities of Pagan worship. Christianity then appeared, and as it was found by many to meet the demand, it naturally succeeded.

In answer to this it must be remembered that Christianity was not a religion founded at Rome or Athens, in which case it might perhaps be said that the demand caused the supply; but it arose as a small Jewish sect in Palestine. While the fierce persecutions it had to endure show that it did not obviously meet the requirements of the day, even apart from the tremendous difficulties involved in the worship of the Crucified. But now suppose, for the sake of argument, that this had been otherwise, and that the world was so suited to receive Christianity as to account for its rapid spread; would the inference be against its Divine origin? Certainly not; for the agreement in this case would be far too close to be accidental. It must have been *designed*. And it would thus show that the God Who rules in history, is also the God Who introduced Christianity. So here again the proposed explanation, even if admitted, does but imply the truth of the religion.

### (4.) Contrast with Mohammedanism.

And this conclusion is rendered still stronger when we contrast the progress of Christianity with that of Mohammedanism. For here we have the one example that history affords of the spread of a religion which can be compared with that of Christianity. Yet the contrast between the two is very marked, whether we consider the means by which they were spread, or their alleged evidence of truthfulness. For Mohammed did not appeal to reason, but to *force*, and all we have to account for is that he should be able to collect an army, that this army should conquer, and that the conquered should adopt the religion of their conquerors, about which they were often given no option. In the spread of Christianity, on the other hand, no force whatever was employed, and it had immense difficulties to contend with. In fact it carried a cross instead of a sword. Thus the contrast between the two is just what we should expect between the natural and the supernatural spread of a religion, the one advancing by worldly power, the other in spite of it.

But an even greater contrast has still to be noticed, which is that Mohammed did not appeal to any *miracles* in support of his claims—that is, to outward matters of fact which could be judged of by other people. And this is the more remarkable since he refers to the miracles of previous prophets, including those of Christ, as authentic,[449] but never claims to have worked any himself. The obvious conclusion is that he felt, as all men must feel, the overwhelming difficulty of asserting public miracles if none occurred, and he therefore appealed to force, because he had nothing better to appeal to. Yet, as we have seen, the early Christians asserted such miracles from the first. They were not advocates of a creed, but witnesses for certain facts, such as the Resurrection and other miracles which they believed they actually saw; and there is nothing corresponding to this in regard to Mohammedanism, or any other religion. It may of course be said that Mohammedanism shows that a religion can make rapid progress without miracles. No doubt it does; and so does Buddhism, which also spread rapidly. But it does not show that a religion which, like Christianity, claims to rest on miracles, can make its way if those miracles are false.

[449] Koran, Sura v.

## (*B.*) ITS LATER HISTORY.

We pass on now from the early triumphs of Christianity to its later history, and will consider in turn its past vitality, its present effect, and its future prospects.

### (1.) Its vitality in the past.

To begin with, a strong argument in favour of Christianity is its vitality. It has survived in spite of external assaults and internal divisions; and its spread and continuity can only be satisfactorily accounted for by its truth. This is an argument the force of which increases as times goes on, and fresh difficulties are encountered and overcome. Moreover, the social state of the world has changed immensely, yet Christianity has always kept in touch with it. It has shown itself suitable for different ages, countries, and social conditions; and, unlike other religions, is still in sympathy with the highest forms of civilisation. In short, Christianity has kept possession of the civilised world for sixteen centuries, and is as vigorous in its age as in its youth.

Its long reign is indeed so familiar to us that there is a danger of not noticing its importance. Can we imagine a man *now* who should found a religion, which nearly two thousand years hence should be still flourishing, still spreading, and still recognising him not only as its founder but its God? Yet this would be but a similar case to that of Christianity. Amid all the changes in history it alone has remained unchanged. Its doctrines, at least the essential ones, contained in the Creeds, have been the same, century after century, and its Founder is still worshipped by millions.

### (2.) Its effect at the present.

In close connection with the history of Christianity comes its effect on the world. A religion which has reigned so long, and over the most civilised nations, must of necessity have had some influence for good or evil. And with regard to Christianity there can be little doubt as to the answer. The present state of the civilised world is a standing witness to its benefits, since nearly all our moral superiority to the nations of old is due to this religion.

For example, it has entirely altered the position of *women*, who are no longer looked down upon as they used to be. It has also altered the position of *children*, who were formerly considered as property, and at the disposal of their parents, infanticide being of course common. Again, it has changed our ideas as to the *sick*, a hospital being almost entirely a Christian institution. It has also changed our ideas about *work*. In all the nations of antiquity, and in heathen countries at the present day, a workman is looked down upon. But to Christians, who believe that God Himself worked in a carpenter's shop, all work is ennobled. Once more, it has created a respect for *human life* as such, and apart from the position of the individual person, which was unknown in ancient times. In short, our acknowledgement of what are called the *rights of man* is almost entirely due to Christianity. Nor is there anything surprising in this; for the common Fatherhood of God and the common love of Christ naturally afford the strongest argument for the common rights of man. In Christ, as St. Paul expresses it, there can be *neither bond, nor free, male nor female*; for all are equal.[450] The good which Christianity has done is thus indisputable.

[450] Gal. 3. 28.

But it may be said, has it not also done some *harm*? What about the religious wars and persecutions in the Middle Ages? With regard to the wars, however, religion was, as a rule, the excuse rather than the cause; for had Christianity never been heard of, there would doubtless have been wars in the Middle Ages, as in all other ages. With regard to the persecutions, they must be both admitted and deplored; but we may ask, what religion except Christianity could have been mixed up with such persecutions, and yet have escaped the odium of mankind? Christianity has done so, because men have seen that it was not the religion itself, but its false friends who were responsible for the persecutions. The important point is that the New Testament, unlike the Koran,[451] does not authorise, still less command, the employment of force in gaining converts.

[451] Koran, Sura viii. 12; ix. 5; xlvii. 4.

We now turn to another aspect of the subject. Not only has Christianity done much good in the past, but it is doing much good at the present. This also is beyond dispute; anyone can verify the fact for himself. Thousands of men and women spend their lives in self-sacrifice among the poor and sick solely for the sake of Christ. Of course, it may be said that all this is folly and that we ought to try and benefit our fellow-men for their own sake or for the sake of the State. But, whether folly or not, the fact remains. The vast majority of those who visit the poor and sick (Sisters of Mercy for instance) do not do so for the sake of the State, or even mainly for the sake of the poor themselves, but from avowedly Christian motives. They believe that Christ loves these poor, and therefore they love them too, and willingly spend their lives in trying to help them.

It is also a fact that this strange *attraction* which Christ exercises, over the hearts of men is unique in history. Can we imagine anyone spending his life in visiting the sick in some large town, and saying that he is doing it for the love of David, or of Plato, or of Mohammed? Yet all through the civilised world thousands are doing it for the love of Christ. And this influence, be it observed, is not like that of other great men, local and temporary, but worldwide and permanent. Christ is thus not only, as we saw in the last chapter, the *holiest* of men, but the *mightiest* of men also; the Man in short who has most influenced mankind. And, with trifling exceptions, few will dispute that this influence has been wholly for good. So judged by its fruits, Christianity is a religion which might very reasonably have had a Divine origin.

On the other hand, it must be admitted that though Christianity has done so much good, it has not entirely reformed the world,—it has not even stopped wars among Christian nations—and its failure to do this, after trying for so many centuries, is thought by some to be adverse to its claims. But others think that its partial success and partial failure are just what we should expect if it were true. And what is more to the point, this seems to have been expected by its Founder, for He always implied that the good and the evil—the wheat and the tares—were to be mixed together until the end of the world. Moreover, its failure has been due almost entirely to the *inconsistency* of its adherents. If all men were Christians, and all Christians lived up to the religion they professed, there would be little to complain of, even in this imperfect world.

On the whole, then, the *effect* of Christianity is distinctly in its favour. It has done much good, and will probably do more as time goes on; though it has not entirely reformed the world, and probably never will. But the good it has done is an actual fact which cannot be disputed, while the argument that it ought to have done more good is at least open to doubt.

**(3.) Its prospects in the future.**

Lastly, the spread of Christianity seems likely to continue, and some day we may expect to see it universally professed in the world, as it is in Western Europe at the present time, though, of course, there will always be individuals who dissent from it. The reasons for this confident hope are, that, speaking broadly, Christian nations alone are extending their influence. Japan may, of course, be quoted as an exception, but strange to say Japan seems to be becoming Christian.

And to this must be added the fact that Christian *missions* are now being revived to a large extent; and, though they are not always successful, yet, taken together, they secure a good many converts. Moreover, there is no other side to this argument. It is not that Christianity is being adopted in some countries but renounced in others. The gains, whether great or small, are all *net profits*. With one exception, there is not a single instance for many centuries of a nation or tribe which once adopted Christianity changing its religion to anything else. And the exception, that of France at the time of the Revolution, strikingly proves the rule; for the change could not be maintained, and in a few years Christianity again asserted itself throughout the country.

## (4.) The spread of Rationalism.

But an important objection has now to be examined. It is said that even in Christian countries an increasingly large number of men either openly reject Christianity, or give it at most a mere nominal approval. This may be called the objection from the spread of *Rationalism*, and it is an important one, because it is an attempt to meet Christianity with its own weapons, by appealing to reason. Of course it must be remembered that a great deal of the infidelity of the present day is not due to reasoning at all, but to the want of it; and it is hopeless to argue against this. For how can men be convinced of Christianity, or anything else, if they will not take the trouble to examine its claims?

But putting aside this class, there are still many men who may fairly be called Rationalists—men, that is, who have studied *both* sides of the subject, and whose reasoning leads them to reject Christianity. They admit that there is evidence in its favour, but they say that it is far from convincing. And it is believed by many that Rationalism is spreading at the present day, and will eventually become common among thoughtful men. Now, of course, the whole of this *Essay* is really an attempt to meet this objection, and to show that, when carefully considered, the arguments in favour of Christianity far outweigh those against it. But three additional remarks may be made here.

The first is, that this is no *new* difficulty. Rationalism has existed ever since the Middle Ages, and was most aggressive and most confident in the eighteenth century, as a single quotation will show. Bishop Butler in the preface to his *Analogy of Religion*, 1736, says, 'It has come, I know not how, to be taken for granted, by many persons, that Christianity is not so much as a subject of inquiry, but that it is now at length discovered to be fictitious. And accordingly they treat it as if, in the present age, this were an agreed point among all people of discernment; and nothing remained but to set it up as a principal subject of mirth and ridicule, as it were by way of reprisals for its having so long interrupted the pleasures of the world.' It is now nearly two centuries since these words were written, and Christianity is still flourishing! Therefore, as all previous attacks have proved futile, there is no reason to believe that the present one will be more successful.

Secondly, these continued assaults on Christianity afford in one respect additional evidence in its favour; since they show, as nothing but repeated attacks could show, its *indestructibility*. Had Christianity never been assailed, its strength would never have been apparent; but now we know that, try as men will for centuries, they cannot get rid of this religion.

Thirdly, it must be remembered that Rationalism is all destructive and not constructive. It can show many reasons for *not* believing in Christianity, but it can give the world nothing which can in any way take its place. It has no satisfactory solution for the great problems of life. Why does man exist at all? Why has he got free will? What is the meaning of sin? Is there any forgiveness for sin? What is the meaning of death? Is there any life beyond death? Is there a judgment? Can we dare to face it? Shall we recognise those whom we have loved on earth? In short, what is man's destiny here and hereafter? These are the questions which always have interested, and always will interest, mankind. Rationalists may say that the Christian answer to them is incorrect; but they can offer no other which is worth a moment's consideration.

## (*C.*) CONCLUSION.

Before concluding this chapter one other point of some importance has to be noticed. It is that the early history of Christianity with its continual triumph amidst continual persecution, seems to have been foreknown to its Founder; as well as His own marvellous influence in the world.

These *prophecies* of Christ concerning His own religion are certainly very striking. We find, on the one hand, a most absolute conviction as to the triumph of His Church. It was to spread far and wide; its missionaries were to go into *all the world* and make disciples *of all the nations*, and its enemies would never *prevail against it.*[452] And on the other, there is an equally certain conviction as to the constant sufferings of its members, who were to expect life-long persecution and the universal hatred of mankind.[453]

[452] Mark 16. 15; Matt. 28. 19; 16. 18.

[453] *E.g.*, Matt. 10. 17, 22.

Yet these strange prophecies of continual success amidst continual suffering were for three centuries as strangely fulfilled, including even the little detail that Christ's followers were to be hated for His *name's* sake.[454] Since as a matter of fact they were often persecuted for the mere *name*, and it was this that made them so indignant. Thus Justin says, 'You receive the *name* as proof against us.... If any deny the *name* you acquit him as having no evidence against him.'[455] As Christ foretold, it was literally for His *name's* sake.

[454] Mark 13. 13.

[455] Justin, Apol. 1. 4; 1 Peter 4. 14.

Moreover, Christ's assertions regarding His own influence in the world are equally remarkable. We will give but two examples.[456] He said, *And I, if I be lifted up from the earth, will draw all men unto Myself.* He was lifted up on the cross, and, however strange we may think it, millions of men have in consequence been drawn to Him with passionate devotion. Again, He said, *I am the light of the world.* And now, after nearly nineteen centuries, both friends and foes admit that His is the teaching which has enlightened and purified mankind.

Had He been a mere Jewish peasant, His making such prophecies as these seems almost as incredible as their fulfilment. But what shall we say when they were both made *and* fulfilled? Have we not here a powerful argument in favour of Christianity? Nor can we get out of the difficulty by denying the genuineness of the passages; for they would be quite as remarkable if invented by an evangelist, as if spoken by Christ Himself.

[456] John 12. 32; 8. 12.

We may now sum up this chapter on the *History of Christianity*. We have considered in turn, both its early triumphs, and its later history; and each of these is, strictly speaking, unique, and each is inexplicable on purely natural grounds. But undoubtedly the more important is the marvellous success of Christianity at first, in spite of the immense difficulties it had to encounter; and, as we have seen, all natural explanations of *this* fail hopelessly.

The historical argument, then, leads us back to *miracles*; for every other explanation of the first triumph of Christianity is found to be inadequate. While, on the other hand, the establishment of the Christian religion is just what we should expect if the miracles were true. And of course true miracles, not false ones, are required to account for it. The most holy and the most powerful religion the world has ever seen cannot have been founded on falsehood or fable. In other words, if we deny that the Christian miracles occurred, and take from Christ all that is superhuman, we cannot imagine Him as the Founder of Christianity. There would be an obvious want of proportion between cause and effect. And, as a matter of fact, it was not a natural Christ, but a supernatural Christ—*the Christ of the Gospels*—who won the heart of mankind, and conquered the world. We seem thus forced to the conclusion that the only thing which can account for the history of Christianity is its *truth*. Anyhow, it is plain that its *History* forms another strong argument in its favour.

# CHAPTER XXIII.
## THAT ON THE WHOLE THE OTHER EVIDENCE SUPPORTS THIS CONCLUSION.

Additional arguments for and against Christianity.

(*A.*) CHRISTIANITY AND PRAYER.

Its universality. There are, however, three difficulties:

(1.) Scientific difficulty; said to be incredible, as interfering with the course of nature.

(2.) Moral difficulty; said to be wrong, as inconsistent with the power, wisdom, and goodness of God.

(3.) Practical difficulty; said to be useless, as shown by observation; but none of these can be maintained.

(*B.*) CHRISTIANITY AND HUMAN NATURE.

It is adapted to human nature; for it meets to a great extent the inherent cravings of mankind, especially in regard to sorrow and sin, death and eternity. The objection as to selfishness.

(*C.*) CHRISTIANITY AND OTHER RELIGIONS.

Their comparative study; the Krishna myth; the Horus myth. Conclusion.

We propose in this chapter to consider some of the remaining arguments for and against Christianity. Fortunately, there are only three of anything like sufficient importance to affect the general conclusion. These arise from the relation of Christianity to prayer, to human nature, and to other religions; and we will examine each in turn.

We need not discuss mere *Bible difficulties*, as they are called; for though some of these are fatal to the theory of Verbal Inspiration, or that every word of the Bible is true; this is now held by scarcely anyone. And if the Book is as trustworthy a record of the facts it relates, as an ordinary History of England, that is amply sufficient to prove Christianity.

Nor, on the other hand, need we discuss further evidence in favour of the Bible. But as we considered what it says about the creation of the world, we may just notice in passing what it says about its end. There will be a *great noise*, the elements will be *dissolved with fervent heat*, and the earth, and all it contains will be *burned up*.[457] Everyone now admits that this is true, for our planet will, sooner or later, fall into the sun, when all these results will follow. But (apart from Revelation) how could the writer have known it? There is nothing in the present aspect of the earth to suggest that it will one day be *burned up*, and considering the amount of water it contains, the idea might well seem incredible. We pass on now to the subject of Prayer.

[457] 2 Peter 3. 10.

### (*A.*) CHRISTIANITY AND PRAYER.

Now the Christian, in common with most other religions, asserts the value of prayer not only for obtaining what are called spiritual blessings, but also as a means of influencing natural events. Yet prayer with such an object is said by many to be scientifically *incredible*, morally *wrong*, and practically *useless*. So we will first glance at the universality of the custom, and then consider these difficulties.

Now, prayer of some kind is, and always has been, the universal rule in almost every religion. It is found wherever mankind is found. No one can point to its inventor, no one can point to a time when men did not pray. Missionaries have not to teach their converts to pray, but merely to *Whom* to pray. In short, prayer of some kind seems universal, just as man's sense of right and wrong is universal, though each is capable of being trained and perfected. Nor is it in any way like an animal's cry of pain when hurt, which, though universal, means nothing; for this of course resembles a man's cry of pain, and has no connection with prayer whatever.

If, then, prayer is a delusion, it is to say the least a very remarkable one, especially as in most ancient religions prayer was made to false gods who could not answer it; yet in spite of every failure, the belief in prayer has always remained. Men have always preferred to think that the failure was due to their own unworthiness, rather than give up the belief in a God Who answers prayer. And this *universality* of the custom is a strong argument in its favour; for it seems most unlikely that God should have implanted in mankind a universal habit of asking if He never intended to answer. We pass on now to the difficulties.

### (1.) Scientific difficulty.

In the first place, it is said that answers to prayer are scientifically *incredible*, since they would involve God's interfering with the course of nature, or, in popular language, working miracles. The most probable explanation is, that they are only a particular class of *superhuman coincidences* (Chapter VII.). According to this theory, God, knowing beforehand that the prayer would be offered, arranged beforehand to answer it. Thus the prayer was not a direct cause of the event which fulfilled it, but it may still have been an indirect cause. For had the man not prayed, God, foreknowing this, might not have arranged for the event to have happened.

And the same is true even when the prayer is made *after* the event. Suppose, for instance, a man heard of the loss of a ship in which his son was travelling, and prayed for his safety. That safety, as far as the shipwreck was concerned, must have been decided before the father prayed. Yet, as everything was foreknown to God, his subsequent prayer might not have been useless; since, if God had not known that the father would have prayed, He might not have brought about the son's safety.

Of course, it may be said that this is making the cause come after the effect, and is therefore absurd. No doubt it would be so if merely physical forces were involved; but when we are dealing with personal beings, able to foresee and act accordingly, there is nothing impossible in a cause happening after what was in a certain sense its effect. For instance, my going for a holiday next week may be the cause of my working hard this; though, strictly speaking, it is my *foreknowledge* of the intended holiday, that leads to my working hard. So in the case before us. It is God's *foreknowledge* that the prayer will be offered, that leads Him to answer it; but for all practical purposes this is the same as if the prayer itself did so.

Therefore this theory does not detract from the value and importance of prayer any more than God's foreknowledge in other respects makes human conduct of no importance. In every case God foreknows the result, not in spite of, but because He also foreknows, the man's conduct on which it depends. While if we admit what is called God's *Immanence* in nature, and that everything that occurs is due to the present and immediate action of His Will (Chapter VII.), it greatly lessens any remaining difficulty there may be in regard to prayer.

From this it is plain that answers to prayer may, without losing their value, be regarded as superhuman coincidences; and, if so, they do not involve any interference with the ordinary course of nature, and all scientific difficulties are at an end.

### (2.) Moral difficulty.

In the next place, prayer is said to be morally *wrong*, since it is inconsistent with each of the three great attributes of God. It is inconsistent with His *Power*, by implying that He is partly under the control of men; with His *Wisdom*, by implying that He has to be informed of what we want; and with His *Goodness*, by implying that He cannot be trusted to act for the best, without our interference.

But with regard to God's *Power*, no one who prays supposes that God is under the control of his prayers, but merely that He may freely choose to be influenced by them. Insignificant as man is in comparison with his Maker, we have already shown that God takes an interest in his welfare. And admitting this, there is nothing improbable in His being influenced by a man's prayer. Nor is this in any way trying to persuade Him to change His Will, since as everything was foreknown to God, the prayer with all it involved, may have been part of His Will from all eternity. Nor does it reflect on His *Wisdom*, for no one who prays supposes that prayer is for the information of God, but merely that it is the way in which He wishes us to show our trust in Him.

And then, as to God's *Goodness*. As a matter of fact, God does not wait for us to pray before sending most of His blessings; but a few of them are said to be conditional on our praying. And this is quite consistent with perfect goodness. Human analogy seems decisive on the point. A father may know what his child wants, may be quite willing to supply that want, and may yet choose to wait till the child asks him. And why? Simply because supplying his wants is not the whole object the father has in view. He also wishes to train the child's character; to teach him to rely upon and trust his father, and to develop his confidence and gratitude. And all this would be unattainable if the father supplied his wants as a machine would do; in which case the child might perhaps forget that his father was not a machine.

Now, for all we know, precisely the same may be the case with regard to prayer. God may wish not only to supply man's wants, but also to train and develop his character. Indeed, as shown in Chapter V., the existence of evil seems to force us to this very conclusion. And if so, it is out of the question to say that His not giving some blessings till they are asked for is inconsistent with perfect goodness. It may be a very proof of that goodness. For, as already said, God's goodness does not consist of simple beneficence, but also of righteousness. And, as a general rule, it certainly seems right that those who believe in God, and take the trouble to ask for His blessings, should be the ones to receive them.

And here we may notice another moral difficulty, which is sometimes felt in regard to prayers *for others*. They are said to be *unjust*, since one man's success would often mean another's failure. Suppose, for instance, a man is going in for a competitive examination, say a scholarship or a clerkship; and a friend of his prays that he may get it. Of course in most cases this will not affect the issue; but all who believe in the power of prayer must admit that in *some* cases it will. Yet is not this hard on the next competitor, who loses the scholarship in consequence?

It certainly seems so. But it is only part of a more general difficulty. For suppose the man's friend instead of praying for him, sent him some money to enable him to have a tutor. Is not this equally hard on the other man? Yet no one will say that his having the tutor could not affect the result; or that his friend acted unfairly in sending him the money. So in regard to prayer.

Indeed of all ways of helping a friend, praying for him seems the fairest; since it is appealing to a Being, Who we know will always act fairly; and will not grant the petition, unless it is just and right to do so. The objection, then, that prayer is morally wrong cannot be maintained from any point of view.

It is, however, only fair to add that a certain class of prayers would be wrong. We have no right to pray for *miracles*, *e.g.*, for water to run uphill, or for a dead man to come to life again; though we have a right to pray for any ordinary event, such as rain or recovery from sickness. The reason for this distinction is obvious. A miracle is, in popular language, something contrary to the order of nature; and as the order of nature is merely the Will of Him who ordered nature, it would be contrary to God's Will. And we must not ask God to act contrary to what we believe to be His Will.

Of course it may be said that to pray for rain, when otherwise it would not have rained, really involves a miracle. But here everything depends on the words *when otherwise it would not have rained*. If we knew this for certain, it would be wrong to pray for rain (just as it would be wrong for the father to pray for his son's safety after hearing that he had been drowned) not knowing it for certain, it is not wrong. Therefore as we do know for certain that water will not run uphill without a miracle, it is always wrong to pray for that. In the same way we may pray for fruitful crops, because it is plainly God's Will that mankind should be nourished; but we may not pray to be able to live without food, since this is plainly not God's Will. No doubt, in the Bible, miracles were sometimes prayed for, but only by persons who acted under special Divine Guidance; and this affords no argument for our doing so.

**(3.) Practical difficulty.**

Lastly, it is said, even admitting that prayers might be answered, yet we have abundant evidence that they never are; so that prayer at the present day is *useless*. But several points have to be noticed here; for no one asserts that *all* prayers are answered. Various conditions have to be fulfilled. A person, for instance, must not only believe in God, and in His power and willingness to answer prayers; but the answer must be of such a kind that it would be right to pray for it. Moreover, he must be trying to lead such a life as God wishes him to lead; and also be honestly exerting himself to gain the required end, for prayer cannot be looked upon as a substitute for work.

And this prevents our deciding the question by *experiment*, as is sometimes urged. Why not, it is said, settle the question once for all by a test case? But this is impossible, since in the vast majority of cases we cannot say whether the above conditions are fulfilled or not; and even if we could, it would still be impracticable. For prayer is the earnest entreaty that God would grant something we earnestly desire; and if used as an experiment, it ceases to be genuine prayer altogether.

But it is further urged that though we cannot decide by experiment we can by *observation*. The facts, however, can be explained on either theory. Suppose, for instance, an epidemic breaks out, and prayer is at once made that it may cease; but instead of ceasing, it continues for a week, and kills a hundred persons. How do we know that but for the prayers it might not have continued for a month and killed a thousand? And the same argument applies in other cases.

Against these various objections we must remember that an immense number of men of many ages and countries, and of undoubted honesty and intelligence have asserted that their prayers have been answered; and the cumulative value of this evidence is very great. While, to those who possess it, the conviction that certain events happened, not accidentally, as we might say, but in answer to some prayer, is absolutely convincing.

None of these difficulties, then, can be maintained. There is nothing *incredible* in prayers being answered, they are not *wrong*, and many of those who ought to know best (*i.e.*, those who pray) assert that they are not *useless*.

## (*B.*) CHRISTIANITY AND HUMAN NATURE.

The next subject we have to consider is a very important one, the *adaptation* of Christianity to human nature. To begin with, it is undeniable that Christianity appeals very strongly to some, at least, among every class of men. The poor value it as much as the rich, the ignorant as much as the learned; children can partly understand it, and philosophers can do no more. And this is not only the case at the present time, but it has been so among all the changing conditions of society for eighteen centuries.

Now, when we inquire into the reason of this powerful hold which Christianity has on so many men, we find it is because it meets certain inherent cravings of human nature. Some of these, such as man's belief in prayer, and his sense of responsibility, are of course satisfied by any form of Theism. So also is his idea of justice, which requires virtue and vice to be suitably rewarded hereafter, since they are not here. But man's nature has many other cravings besides these; yet Christianity seems to satisfy it everywhere.

We will consider four points in detail and select *Sorrow* and *Sin*, *Death* and *Eternity*. The first three, and possibly the fourth, all have to be faced; they are the common heritage of all mankind. And while Rationalism does not help us to face any of them, and Natural Religion leaves much in uncertainty, Christianity meets the needs of mankind throughout, or at all events far better than any other religion.

And first, as to *Sorrow*. It is indisputable that in this life man has to bear a great deal of sorrow and suffering; and it is also indisputable that when in sorrow he longs for someone who can both sympathise with him, and help him. An impersonal God can, of course, do neither; indeed, we might as well go for comfort to the force of gravity. And though a personal God can help us, we do not feel sure that He can sympathise with us. On the other hand, fellow-men can sympathise, but they cannot always help. In Christ alone we have a Being Who entirely satisfies human nature; for being Man, He can sympathise with human sorrow, and being God, He can alleviate it. So here Christianity supplies a universal want Of course, the doctrine of the *Incarnation* also satisfies mankind in other respects, especially in presenting him with a worthy Being for his affections, and with a perfect Example; but these points have been already noticed in Chapter XIII.

Next, as to *Sin*. Here again the facts are practically undisputed. Man's sense of sin is universal, so also is his belief in the justice of God; and therefore in all ages man has longed for some means of appeasing the Deity. The widespread custom of sacrifice is a conclusive proof of this. Yet, wherever Christianity has been accepted, such sacrifices have been abandoned. It is scarcely necessary to point out the reason for this. The Christian doctrine of the *Atonement* entirely satisfies these cravings of mankind. It admits the fact of sin; it provides a sufficient Sacrifice for sin, which man could never provide for himself, and it thus assures him of complete forgiveness. Yet, as shown in Chapter XIII., it does all this without in any way lessening the guilt of sin, or allowing man to sin on with impunity; for it makes *repentance* an essential condition of forgiveness.

Moreover, Christianity proves that sin is not a necessity in human nature; for it alone of all religions can point to One Who, though tempted as we are, was yet without sin. And Christ's temptations were probably greater than any that we can have. For it is only when a man *resists* a temptation that he feels its full force, just as only those trees that were *not* blown down, felt the full force of the gale. Therefore Christ alone, because He was sinless, can have felt the full force of every temptation. And Christians assert, and they surely ought to know best, that this example of Christ is a strong help in enabling them to resist temptation.

Next, as to *Death*. Here again the facts are undisputed. Few persons like to contemplate their own death, yet it is the one event to which we may look forward with certainty. But is there a life after death? Most men long for it, and most religions have tried to satisfy this longing in one way or another, but only with partial success. The higher nature of man revolts against any mere material or sensual heaven, while a purely spiritual heaven does not satisfy him either; for a man longs to know that he will be able to recognise again those whom he has loved on earth. This is indeed one of our deepest, strongest, and most universal longings (who is there that has not felt it?), yet there must always be some doubt as to recognising a spirit.

And here again the Christian doctrine of the *Resurrection of the Body* alone satisfies the cravings of mankind; for all doubt is now at an end. The risen body will define and localise man's spirit then, just as the natural body does now; and though there will be a great change, it will not prevent recognition. Even the Apostles, though unprepared for it, and though themselves unaware of what a risen body was like, were soon able to recognise Christ after His Resurrection.

There is, of course, the well-known difficulty as to the *period of life* of the risen body. A man, it is said, would only be recognised by his grandfather, if he remained a child; and by his grandson, if he were an old man. But the difficulty is not so great as it seems; for in this life a man who has not seen his son, since he was a child, may not be able to recognise him in later years, in the sense of knowing him by sight. But he may be immensely pleased to meet him again, and live near him, especially if in the meanwhile the son had done well, and been a credit to his father. Moreover, the risen body will show us, for the first time, what a man really is, when his accidental surroundings, such as wealth or poverty, have been removed; and his character is at length perfected. And perhaps we shall then see that all that is best in the various states in which he has lived here—the affection of childhood, the activity of boyhood, and the mature judgment of manhood—will be combined in the risen body.

And though it is somewhat tantalising not to know more about this future life, very possibly we are not told more, because we should not be able to understand it if we were. Even in this world it is doubtful if a savage or a young child could understand the intellectual life of a civilised man, however carefully it might be explained to him; and practically certain that an ape could not. And for all we know our own future life may be as far beyond our present understanding. It is the *Great Surprise* in store for us all. But however much we may be changed, our personal identity will still remain, *I shall be I, and you will be you*, with much the same characters as we have at present. This is the important point, and of this we may be quite sure.

Lastly, as to *Eternity*. Christianity, it is true, can say little here, but that little is full of hope. It opens up boundless possibilities, far more than any other religion. For by the Incarnation human nature has been united to the Divine, and thus raised to a position second only to that of God Himself. No destiny, then, that can be imagined is too great for man. Created in the image of the Triune God, with a supernatural freedom of choice; his nature united to God's by the Incarnation; his sins forgiven through the Atonement; his body purified and spiritualised at its Resurrection—surely the end of all this cannot be any mere monotonous existence, but rather one of ceaseless joy and activity. Heaven has been called the *last act* in God's drama of the universe. And considering the magnitude of the previous acts—the formation of the solar system, the development of organic life, etc.—we should expect this last act to be on a scale equally vast and magnificent, and as far above anything we can imagine as the life of a butterfly is above the imagination of a chrysalis.

Now the conclusion to be drawn from all this is quite plain. Christianity is so adapted to man's nature that it probably came from the Author of man's nature; just as if a complicated key fits a complicated lock, it was probably made by the same locksmith. And since Christianity is meant for all mankind, and the vast majority of men have neither time nor ability to examine its proofs, the fact of its thus appealing direct to human nature is certainly a strong argument in its favour.

But we must now consider an objection. It is, that Christianity is really a *selfish* religion, looking only for future rewards, and teaching men to follow virtue, not for virtue's sake, but solely with a view to their own advantage. But this is an entire mistake, though a very common one. The Christian's motive, in trying to lead such a life as God wishes him to lead, is simply *love*. He has, as already said, an overwhelming sense of God's love to him. And though, doubtless, leading a good life will bring with it some future reward, yet this is not the true motive for leading it. Compare the case of a young child trying to please his parents simply because he loves them. It would be unjust to call this selfishness, though it may be quite true that the parents will do much for the child later on in life, which they would not have done had the child never shown them any affection.

Nor, to take another example, is it selfishness for a young man to put aside a certain amount of his earnings for his old age, when he will be unable to work, though it will certainly be to his own advantage. Selfishness is having regard to one's self, *at the expense of other people*. But this does not apply to a Christian striving after his own salvation. The *Great Ambition*, as it is called, is one which all may entertain, all may work for, and all may realise.

Still, it may be asked, is not the hope of future reward meant to influence men at all? No doubt it is to some extent. But what then? Hope is undoubtedly a powerful motive in human nature, and therefore Christianity, by partly appealing to this motive, does but show how fully adapted it is to human nature. It provides the highest motive of *love* for those able to appreciate it; the lower motive of *hope* of future reward for the many who would not be reached by the former; and we may add, the still lower motive of *fear* of future punishment for those who could not be otherwise influenced. This objection, then, as to selfishness is quite untenable.

## *(C.)* CHRISTIANITY AND OTHER RELIGIONS.

We have lastly to consider the relation in which Christianity stands to other religions; since an argument against Christianity is often drawn from their *comparative study*. In far more ancient religions, it is alleged, we find similar doctrines to those of the Trinity, the Incarnation, the Atonement, and the Resurrection; and this is fatal to the claim of Christianity to be the one and only true Religion.

But as to the doctrine of the *Trinity*, it is really unique. Some other religions, it is true, had a group of three gods; but this was merely a form of Polytheism. And though these gods were often addressed by the same titles, there does not appear to have been anything resembling the Christian idea of the Triune God.

Next, as to the *Incarnation*. This is said to resemble similar doctrines of other ancient religions, more especially the incarnation of *Krishna*. For though he was not (as is sometimes asserted) born of a virgin, being the eighth son of his parents;[458] he is yet believed to have been in some sense an incarnation of the supreme god Vishnu. And he is recorded to have worked various miracles similar to those of Christ, and to have claimed an equally absolute devotion from his followers. Most scholars, however, now place these legends some centuries later than the Christian era; and considering the early spread of Christianity in India, and the similarity in name between Krishna and Christ, they may be only distorted versions of the Gospel story.

[458] Tisdall, Christianity and Other Faiths, 1912, p. 89.

But even were they earlier than Christianity, it seems impossible for them to have influenced it. For not only is India many hundreds of miles from Palestine, but there is also a great moral difficulty. Since the miracles and occasional lofty teaching of Krishna are associated all along with a most immoral character. In the Gospels, on the other hand, they occur among suitable surroundings, and form perfect parts of a perfect whole. A single example will illustrate this difference. On one occasion, Krishna is related to have healed a deformed woman, very similar to the story in Luke 13. But it is added he made her beautiful as well as whole, and subsequently spent the night with her in immorality. Few will contend that this was the origin of the Gospel story; and it is but one instance out of many.[459]

[459] Transactions of Victoria Institute, vol. xxi., p. 169.

Any resemblance, then, there may be between the Incarnation of Krishna and that of Christ cannot be due to Christianity having borrowed from the other religion. A far better explanation is to be found in the fact that man has almost always believed that God takes an interest in his welfare. And this inherent belief has naturally led him to imagine an incarnation, since this was the most fitting method by which God could make Himself known to man. And then this supposed incarnation was of course attended by various miracles of healing, somewhat similar to those of Christ, though often mixed up with immoral ideas, from which the Christian doctrine is entirely free.

Next, as to the *Atonement*, especially the position of Christ, as the *Mediator* between God and man. This also is said to resemble far older legends, such as the *Horus* myth of ancient Egypt. The leading idea here seems to have been that Horus was the only son of the supreme God Osiris, and came on earth long ago, before the time of man. He was always looked upon as the champion of right against wrong, and nothing but lofty and noble actions are ascribed to him. With regard to mankind, he became their deliverer and justifier. The soul after death was supposed to pass through a sort of Purgatory; where various dangers were overcome by the help of Horus; and finally, when judged before Osiris, he interceded for the faithful soul and ensured its salvation. And what makes the resemblance to Christianity all the more striking are the titles ascribed to Horus; such as *the Only Begotten Son of the Father*, *the Word of the Father*, *the Justifier of the Righteous*, and *the Eternal King*. But the titles of Horus are very numerous, and very contradictory; therefore, while some of them bear such a striking resemblance to those of Christ, others do not; and many of them are also applied to the other gods.[460]

[460] Transactions of Victoria Institute, vol. xii., p. 52.

But still the position of Horus, as a mediator between God and man, undoubtedly resembles that of Christ. But what is the cause of this similarity? Not surely that the Christian doctrine was founded on that of Horus. As in the previous case, there is another and far better solution. For what was the origin of the Egyptian doctrine itself? It was simply this. The ancient Egyptians firmly believed in the *justice* of God; the *immortality* of man; his *responsibility*, involving a future judgment; and his *sinfulness*, which naturally made him long for some mediator with the just Judge he would have to face hereafter. Given these four ideas—and they all belong to Natural Religion—and Horus was merely an imaginary being, who was thought to satisfy them. Hence, if these ideas are true, and if Christianity is the true religion, which really does satisfy them, that Horus should to some extent resemble Christ seems inevitable. Thus the Horus myth only proves how deeply rooted in the human mind is the idea of a *mediator* between God and man.

Lastly, as to the doctrine of the *Resurrection*, more especially that of Christ. Numerous analogies have been suggested for this, but none of them are at all satisfactory. Thus the Egyptian god Osiris is recorded as doing a great deal after his death; but he is only supposed to have done this by living on in the *spirit*, and there is no hint that his *body* was restored to life, in the sense in which Christ's was; and the same may be said in other cases.[461] While the way in which the educated Athenians (who must have known a good deal about heathen religions) treated St. Paul, when he proclaimed the Resurrection of Christ, shows how absolutely novel they considered the doctrine.[462]

[461] Tisdall, Christianity and Other Faiths, 1912, p. 153.

[462] Acts 17. 19, 32; 26. 8.

We must also remember that the Christian doctrines of the Incarnation, the Atonement, and the Resurrection, were not slowly evolved, but were essential features in Christianity from the very first. They are all strongly insisted on by St. Paul. And this alone seems fatal to the idea of their having been derived from the myths of India, Egypt, and elsewhere.

On the whole, then, it is evident that the *comparative study* of religions, instead of being against Christianity, is distinctly in its favour; for it shows, as nothing but a comparative study could show, its striking superiority. Human nature is always the same, and in so far as other religions have satisfied human nature, they have resembled Christianity. On the other hand, Christianity differs from them in being free from their various absurdities and contradictions, as well as from their tendency to degenerate; and having instead a moral character of admitted excellence, and powerful evidence by which to establish its actual truth. In short, other religions are *human*; and therefore, as man is a mixture of good and evil, they contain some good (what we now call Natural Religion) and some evil. But Christianity is *superhuman*; and therefore contains all the good they do, with much more besides, and with none of their evil. This completes a brief examination of the more important additional arguments for and against Christianity.

# CHAPTER XXIV.
## THAT THE THREE CREEDS ARE DEDUCIBLE FROM THE NEW TESTAMENT.

Only three Doctrines can be disputed.

(*A.*) THE DOCTRINE OF THE TRINITY.

In addition to belief in God the Father, the New Testament teaches—

(1.) The Divinity of Christ.

(2.) The Divinity of the Holy Spirit; so there are

(3.) Three Divine Persons and yet but One God.

(*B.*) THE FINAL STATE OF THE WICKED.

The only alternatives are:

(1.) Their endless misery: very strong texts in favour of this; its difficulties considered.

(2.) Their endless happiness: most improbable.

(3.) Their destruction: more likely than the last, but still improbable. On the whole the statement of the Creed seems fully justified.

(*C.*) THE IMPORTANCE OF A TRUE BELIEF.

This is strongly insisted on in the warning clauses of the Athanasian Creed.

(1.) Their meaning.

(2.) Their truthfulness: they merely repeat similar warnings in the New Testament.

(3.) The objection as to dogmatism.

We have now reached the last stage in our inquiry. We have shown in the previous chapters that there is very strong evidence in favour of what may be called in a general sense, Christianity or the Christian Religion—*i.e.*, the Religion founded by Christ and taught in the New Testament. We have, lastly, to inquire, is this Religion correctly summarised in the doctrines and statements of the *Three Creeds*? And the only doctrines that can be disputed, are found in the Athanasian Creed, and refer to the *Trinity*; the *Final State of the Wicked;* and the importance of a *True Belief:* each of which we will examine in turn.

## (A.) THE DOCTRINE OF THE TRINITY.

Now, although there are no statements in the New Testament identical with those in the Creed, yet the latter are merely logical deductions from the former. For the New Testament asserts that, besides God the Father, there are two other Divine Persons, Christ and the Holy Spirit, and yet but one God.

### (1.) The Divinity of Christ.

This has already been discussed in Chapter XXI., where we showed that Christ claimed to be not only Superhuman, but Divine; and that this is how His contemporaries, both friends and foes, understood Him. The doctrine is also asserted by St. Paul, as well as by St. John, who in the opening verse of his Gospel, states it very concisely, saying that the Word (*i.e.*, Christ) *was with God*, implying a distinction of Persons, and *was* God, implying a unity of Nature; which is the exact doctrine of the Creed.

### (2.) The Divinity of the Holy Spirit.

This also follows at once from the New Testament. For the Holy Spirit is called by Divine names, such as God and Lord; He is given Divine attributes, such as Eternity and Omniscience; and He is identified with Jehovah, the Lord of Hosts, of the Old Testament.[463]

[463] Acts 5. 3, 4; 2 Cor. 3. 17; Heb. 9. 14; 1 Cor. 2. 10; Acts 28. 25; Isa. 6. 5-10.

And yet, He is a distinct *Person*: for, to quote a decisive text,[464] Christ prays the Father to send His disciples *another* Comforter when He goes away; thus showing that the Holy Spirit is a different Person, both from the Father and the Son. And elsewhere we are told that the Spirit *makes intercession for us*, which again shows that He must be a different Person from the Father, with Whom He intercedes.[465] While in another passage blasphemy against the Holy Ghost is said to be the worst of all sins;[466] which shows both that He is a *Person*, or He could not be blasphemed; and that He is *God*, or blasphemy against God would be a greater sin.

[464] John 14. 16, 26; 15. 26.

[465] Rom. 8. 26.

[466] Matt. 12. 31, 32; Mark 3. 28, 29.

No doubt the actual word *Person* is not applied to the Holy Spirit in the New Testament, just as it is not applied to either the Father or the Son, but it cannot be thought inappropriate, provided it is not taken in a literal, or human sense. For the relations between Them closely *resemble* those between human persons, as They love one another, speak to one another, and use the personal pronouns I, Thou, He, and We.

**(3.) Three Divine Persons and yet but One God.**

It is clear, then, from the New Testament, that the Father, the Son, and the Holy Spirit are all Persons, and all Divine; and yet the fact of there being but one God is at times plainly asserted.[467] Now the only means of reconciling all this is by the doctrine of the Trinity in Unity. And this is plainly hinted at in the New Testament itself, for the Three Persons are often closely associated together, as for instance in the text just alluded to, where *Christ* prays *the Father* to give His disciples *another Comforter.*

[467] Mark 12. 29; 1 Cor. 8. 4.

Quite naturally, then, just before His Ascension, Christ completed this earlier teaching by finally, and for ever, joining the Three Persons together, when He commanded Christians to be baptized *into the name of the Father, and of the Son, and of the Holy Ghost.*[468] And this alone is sufficient to prove the doctrine, for it shows that there are *Three* distinct Persons, and that each is *Divine*, for who but God could be thus associated with God? While the expression into the *name* and not *names*, implies a unity in this Trinity.

[468] Matt. 28. 19.

And we happen to have indirect evidence from the *Acts*, that baptism was administered in this way. For when St. Paul found some disciples, who said they knew nothing about the Holy Ghost; he at once asked, 'Into what then were ye *baptized*?'[469] Obviously, then, the baptism to which St. Paul was accustomed must have been into the name of the Holy Ghost, as well as into that of Christ; and the Father's name could scarcely have been omitted. Yet immediately afterwards we are told that they were baptized *into the Name of the Lord Jesus*. In the same way the 'Teaching of the Twelve' once speaks of baptism as *into the Name of the Lord*; and twice as *into the Name of the Father, and of the Son, and of the Holy Ghost.*[470] The former seems to have been only a short way of describing Christian baptism, (in distinction from that of the Jews, or of St. John the Baptist), while the latter represented the actual words used.[471]

[469] Acts 19. 3.

[470] Teaching, chaps. vii. and ix.

[471] *Comp.* Acts 2. 38; 8. 16; 18. 25; I Cor. 10. 2.

Similarly St. Paul sometimes closes his Epistles with the shorter form of blessing. *The grace of the Lord Jesus Christ be with you*; once with an intermediate form, naming the Father and Christ; and once with the longer form, *The Grace of the Lord Jesus Christ, and the love of God, and the communion of the Holy Ghost be with you all.*[472] This latter passage, the genuineness of which is undisputed, is of course extremely important, in fact like the preceding one it is practically conclusive; for again we must ask, who but God could be thus associated with God? If Christ were a mere human prophet, like Isaiah for instance; and the Holy Spirit a mere influence for good; what strange language it would be. Can we imagine anyone blessing his converts with, The grace of Isaiah, the love of God, and the fellowship of a holy influence—God, it will be noticed, being placed *between* the other two, so there can be no ascending or descending scale, they must all be equal?

[472] 1 Cor. 16. 23; Gal. 6. 18; Eph. 6. 23; 2 Cor. 13. 14.

And as St. Paul takes for granted that his readers would understand his meaning, it implies that they had had some previous teaching on the subject, which must clearly have been given them by St. Paul himself on his first visit. And at that early date (about A.D. 50) such teaching could scarcely have originated except from what Christ Himself had taught. This passage, then, implies more than it says, and needs explanation; and as far as we know the former one alone can explain it.

And of course the same is true, though to a lesser degree, of numerous other Trinitarian passages which occur all through the Epistles, including the earliest (1 Thess., about A.D. 50).[473] Nowhere do the writers seem to be explaining anything new to their converts; but merely to be touching on a truth, with which all Christians were of course familiar. Indeed, the very fact of their never attempting to explain or defend the doctrine, shows conclusively that it did not originate with *them*. Persons do not preach a new doctrine without a word of explanation or comment, as if every one already believed it.

[473] *E.g.*, Rom. 15. 30; Eph. 4. 4-6; 1 Thess. 1. 3-5; 1 Peter 1. 2; Jude 20-21.

Thus, to put it shortly, according to the New Testament, there are *Three* distinct Persons; each is God, each is Lord, each is Eternal, each is Omniscient, into the Name of each converts are baptized, each is referred to in Blessing; and yet there is but *One* God. This is what the Bible says, and the Creed says the same, though it says it in more logical language.

### (*B.*) THE FINAL STATE OF THE WICKED.

We pass on now to what is perhaps the most difficult of all subjects, the final state of the wicked. The Creed asserts that all men are to rise again with their bodies, and be judged according to their *works*; and that then, *they that have done good shall go into life everlasting; and they that have done evil into everlasting fire.* This latter expression can scarcely be taken literally, since it is associated in the Bible with another—*the worm that dieth not*—which cannot be literal, as worms do not live for ever, and cannot live at all in fire. While it is said to have been prepared for evil spirits who have no material bodies. Moreover, the joys of heaven are also represented by terms which are clearly not literal; such as attending a wedding, feasting with Abraham, and wearing crowns. Probably we are not at present able to understand the realities in either case, so figures of some kind have to be used; and those associated with gladness and happiness are of course chosen for the one, and those with pain and woe for the other.

But the language certainly implies some form of *endless misery*; and as there are obvious difficulties in accepting such a view, we must discuss the subject carefully. It may be pointed out at starting that we have only three theories to choose from; for unless the wicked are to be in a continual state of change, which seems almost incredible (for a state of change cannot go on for ever, unless it is recurring) they must finally either exist for ever in *misery*, or exist for ever in *happiness*, or be *destroyed*, and not exist for ever.

**(1.) Their endless misery.**

It would be difficult to exaggerate the strength of the texts in favour of this. We are told that the wicked, or at all events some of them, are to awake to shame and everlasting contempt; that they are to be cast into the eternal fire; that they are to depart into the eternal fire prepared for the devil and his angels; that they are to go away into *eternal punishment*; that they are guilty of an eternal sin; that their worm dieth not and the fire is not quenched; and that they are to be cast into the lake of fire, there to be tormented day and night for ever and ever.[474] The fourth of these texts is perhaps the most important, since Christ uses the same word for *eternal* punishment as for *eternal* life; therefore, though the Greek word does not necessarily mean *endless*, it certainly seems to do so here. Similarly in Daniel the same Hebrew word is used for the *everlasting* life of the righteous, as for the *everlasting* contempt of the wicked. Moreover the doctrine is *implied* in numerous other passages;[475] so altogether the New Testament teaching on the subject seems about as plain as it can be.

[474] Dan. 12. 2; Matt. 18. 8; 25. 41, 46; Mark 3. 29; 9. 48; Rev. 14. 11; 20. 15.

[475] *E.g.*, Matt. 7. 13, 23; 8. 12; 10. 33; 12. 32; 13. 42, 50, etc.

Yet everyone must admit that there are great difficulties in accepting it. For the *endless misery* of the wicked appears to be inconsistent with the great attributes of God, especially His power, His justice, and His mercy; as well as with the endless happiness of the righteous. We will consider these points in turn.

And first as to God's *power*. The eternal existence of sinners against God means, it is said, a never-ending conflict between good and evil; and this is most improbable. No doubt it seems so, but then the existence of evil at all is a difficulty; yet as shown in Chapter V. it is essential for free will. And the final state of the wicked is but one out of many difficulties connected with human freedom. That God could create a free man at all; that He could foresee how he would use his freedom; that He should allow him to use it wrongly, thus involving himself and others in misery; and that this misery should last for ever; are all to a great extent beyond our comprehension. But as the first three must be admitted, the last is certainly not incredible.

The second and commonest objection refers to God's *justice*. The suffering, it is said, would be out of all proportion to the offence. Man's life is brief at the most, and every sin in this world cannot deserve countless years of misery in the next. In short, a man's sin here must anyhow be finite, while endless misery, however slight, would be infinite. But very possibly, being sinners ourselves, we do not realise the magnitude of sin, more especially its far-reaching and *permanent* effect on the character of others, who in their turn may influence others also, and so on indefinitely. In this way the consequences of even a single sin may be *endless*, and therefore infinite, and if so its guilt may be infinite too. And this also agrees with the analogy of nature. For in nature nothing is forgotten, and even a small act, like planting a flower has (almost) endless consequences, since the ground will *never* be exactly the same as if it had not been planted.

Moreover, we need not assume that endless misery is for a man's sins here only. Why may not the wicked go on sinning for ever? They must certainly have the power of doing so, for the option of acting, or at all events of thinking right or wrong, is essential to free will; and if we deny them their free will, they are no longer men but mere machines. And it even seems probable that they would do so; for all our experience of human character is that it tends to a final permanence, of good or bad, which nothing can alter. By doing good, men become good—evil gradually loses its influence over them. And then, when their character is fixed, they will cease to be *attracted* by evil; and they will in consequence remain (and this without any effort or struggle on their part) for ever good, and therefore for ever happy. Similarly with regard to the wicked. By committing sin men become sinful, and then, when their character is fixed, they may remain for ever sinful, and therefore for ever miserable. In each case the man's conduct will be always *free*; but his character, and therefore the use which he makes of his freedom, will have become fixed. And perhaps one of the strongest motives for leading a good life here, and thus forming a good character, is the knowledge that, whether good or bad, it will be *our* character for all eternity.

No doubt it is an overwhelming thought that a man's endless happiness, or misery should depend on his short probation in this world; yet as he is given free will with the option of choosing one or the other, there is nothing *unjust* in the results being so permanent. And it entirely agrees with God's methods in nature, where, for instance, the shape of a tree for centuries is fixed during the short time it is growing.

Nor does the fact of God's *foreknowledge* as to how each man will act alter the case or cause any injustice, since, as said in Chapter II., it does not interfere with man's freedom. God merely foreknows the use man will make of his freedom. Therefore His knowing beforehand that a man will commit a murder does not make it unjust to punish him for doing so. And the same rule applies universally; so that although God foreknows that the wicked will be lost, they will not be lost *because* God foreknows it. They will be lost because of their own wilful abuse of their own free will; and God foreknows both this, and its consequences.

The third objection refers to God's *mercy*. Surely, it is said, God would never punish men unless there were a chance of improving them; so it is incredible that He should go on punishing them for ever. But perhaps the future misery of the wicked may not be a punishment at all, in the sense of being inflicted by God; it may be the necessary result of their own acts,—the *consequence* rather than the punishment of sin. Or if we still use the word punishment, we may say that they will be punished, not so much for doing what they have done, as by being what they have become. It will be *according to* their works rather than *because* of them.[476]

[476] Matt. 16. 27; Rom. 2. 6.

And there is much to be said in favour of this view, since it is the way in which God punishes men in this world. Suppose, for instance, a man repeatedly gives way to drink, he will have the natural punishment (which is really God's punishment, Who is the Author of Nature) of being what he has become, an habitual drunkard, and very possibly miserable for the rest of his life. It is the necessary consequence of his sin; and the extent of his misery will, as a rule, be in exact proportion to the extent of his sin. Therefore, if a man is to suffer hereafter for other sins, we should expect this suffering to come in the same way; and to be the natural, and perhaps unavoidable, consequence of the sin itself.

Nor is it difficult to suggest how this may be. For the endless misery of the wicked may be to a great extent mental, rather than bodily—*shame and everlasting contempt*, as Daniel calls it. They may be tormented by remorse and regret at having made themselves unfit to share in the joys of heaven. And until we know the greatness of those joys, we cannot know the greatness of this suffering. But if the joys of heaven are endless, and if the existence of the wicked outside heaven is also endless, it must plainly be an *endless* source of misery. While, in conclusion, the fact that it is the same Christ who has taught us (more than anyone else) the mercy and love of God, who has also taught us the endless misery of the wicked, is an additional reason for thinking that the two cannot really be inconsistent.

The fourth and last objection refers to *man* rather than God. It is that the endless misery of the wicked would destroy the happiness of the righteous; for how could a man enjoy heaven if he knew that his own father and mother were in endless and hopeless misery elsewhere? Of course, if we deny him his memory, and say he does not remember them, it destroys his identity, and for all practical purposes, he is a different man. I have not met with any satisfactory answer to this difficulty. But it may be pointed out that if he knows his parents' fate, he will certainly know their character too, and that their fate was deserved. And this may alter his feelings in regard to them, as it often does now, if we find that one of our friends has behaved in a mean, and disgraceful manner.

Reviewing all these objections, it must be admitted that the endless misery of the wicked seems improbable, but it is certainly not *incredible*. For, to put it shortly, our knowledge of human nature convinces us that, out of a large number of wicked men, some at all events will continue to be wicked, *i.e.* to commit sin as long as they live. Hence, if they live for ever, they will sin for ever. And if they sin for ever, it is not only just, but perhaps inevitable, that they should be miserable for ever. And if so, the endless misery of the wicked does not reflect on either the power, justice, or mercy of God, and, as said above, is certainly not incredible.

## (2.) Their endless happiness.

We pass on now to the next theory, that of their *endless happiness*. According to this, all the wicked (after some suitable punishment) will at last be reconciled to God, and in popular language, go to heaven. And there are several texts which are more or less in favour of this view.[477] But how are we to reconcile these with the far stronger ones before alluded to? The most probable explanation is that they are merely general statements, indicating the final destiny of the vast majority of mankind, but that there are exceptions to this as to most other rules. And the Creed nowhere implies that most men will be lost; it may be only a few obstinate sinners.

[477] *E.g.*, Col. 1. 20; 1 Tim. 4. 10; 1 John 2. 2; Rev. 5. 13.

Moreover, we cannot think that the wicked will be allowed to go on sinning in heaven, so if they go there, they must finally cease to commit sin. Many may do this voluntarily, but what about the remainder? If they *must* finally forsake sin, whether they like it or not, it destroys their free will, and leads to *compulsory goodness*, which is very like a contradiction in terms. For goodness cannot be ascribed to mere machines without free will, which only act under compulsion; yet on this theory the men would be nothing more. In fact, the wicked *men* would in reality have been destroyed, and a good piece of mechanism created instead; which scarcely seems a probable theory.

Then there is this further difficulty: what is to become of the evil angels? If we have to admit endless misery for these, why not for man? Yet the Bible gives no hint that the Devil will in the end be reconciled to God, and go to heaven.

### (3.) Their destruction.

Lastly, as to the other and only possible alternative, the *destruction* of the wicked. This may be better described as their failure to obtain everlasting life; which is here regarded not as the attribute of all men, but as being *conditional* on a man's fulfilling certain duties and developing a certain character in this life. And the wicked, not having done this, will eventually be destroyed and cease to exist. Numerous texts can be quoted in favour of this theory.[478] And it is also supported by the analogy of nature: for if an organism or a species is a failure, it eventually *ceases to exist*; it is not kept alive for ever as a disfigurement to the world.

[478] *E.g.*, John 6. 51; Rom. 6. 23; Matt. 10. 28.

This theory, no doubt, presents less moral difficulties than either of the others, but it is not free from them. For are the wicked to be *punished* after death previous to their destruction? If they are not, justice is not satisfied; and while excessive punishment seems a reflection on God's character, no punishment at all for sinners who have been successful in this world, seems equally so. Yet, on the other hand, any punishment which precedes destruction seems merely vindictive, and of no possible use.

Each of these theories, then, appears improbable, but the *endless misery* of the wicked is scarcely more so than the others, and therefore, as it is the one most strongly supported by the Bible, we seem bound to accept it.

One remark may however be made in conclusion, and it brings a little comfort into this saddest of all truths. It is that whatever doubt may exist as to the future state of the wicked, of one thing we may be quite sure—that their punishment will not be in excess of what they deserve. They will be treated fairly; and every merciful allowance will be made for circumstances, including the inherent weakness of human nature. Christianity indeed seems to emphasise this more than any other religion, since men are to be judged not by the Father, but by the Son; apparently for this very reason that, being Man, He can sympathise with human weakness.[479] And after the judgment, persons will enjoy heaven just in proportion as their lives on earth have rendered them capable of doing so, while the misery of the lost will also be in exact proportion to what they deserve.

[479] John 5. 27.

### (*C*.) THE IMPORTANCE OF A TRUE BELIEF.

The last doctrine to be considered is the importance of a True Belief, that is of believing the *truth* in regard to matters of religion. This is strongly insisted on in the *warning clauses* of the Athanasian Creed; so we will first consider their meaning, then their truthfulness, and lastly, the objection as to dogmatism.

### (1.) Their meaning.

Before discussing this, it may be pointed out that they are often called the *damnatory* or *uncharitable* clauses; but both these terms are somewhat misleading. For the Creed does not condemn anyone by these clauses, it merely declares that certain persons will be condemned by God, which is a very different thing. No one desires their condemnation, but the contrary; therefore, believing the danger to be a fact, it is stated in the hope that persons will in consequence avoid it.

An analogy may help to illustrate this distinction. Suppose a despotic ruler in some island were to put up a notice that anyone walking along a certain part of the coast would be arrested and shot; this might well be called uncharitable. But now, suppose the notice was that, owing to their being quicksands along that part of the coast, anyone walking there would be drowned; this might be untrue, but it could scarcely be called uncharitable. So in regard to the Creed. Its warnings (whether true or false) are in no sense uncharitable; and it no more *consigns men to perdition* (as it is sometimes called) for denying the faith, than a doctor consigns men to die of fever for drinking bad water. In each case they merely state what they believe will (unfortunately) be the result.

Its warnings are also quite different from the *Let him be anathema* of St. Paul, as well as from some of the Psalms, where the writer does not merely state that the wicked will be miserable, but prays that they may be so.[480] This no doubt seems uncharitable, but there is nothing like it in the Creed.

[480] *E.g.*, Gal. 1. 8-9; Ps. 69.

What the Creed says is that holding, or *holding fast*,[481] the Catholic Faith, especially the doctrines of the Trinity and the Incarnation, is necessary to salvation (vv. 1, 28, 29, 42); and that those who do *not* keep (or hold fast) this Faith will *perish* everlastingly (v. 2). The word *keep*, it should be noticed, implies previous possession, since a man cannot keep what he never had; so these verses are inapplicable to heathens, infidels, or even nominal Christians who have never really held the Faith. They refer only to apostates—to those who, having once held the Faith, do not *keep* it.

[481] It is so translated in the revised version, issued in November, 1909, by a Committee, under the Archbishop of Canterbury.

Moreover, there can be little doubt that the apostasy here referred to was not that due to intellectual doubt, but to giving way, *under persecution*. For the Gothic conquerors of Southern Europe, where the Creed was composed about the fifth century, were *Arians*, and they much persecuted the Catholics. So a statement of what the Catholic Faith really was (in opposition to Arianism) might well contain warnings as to the great danger of abandoning it under trial and persecution. In the same way Christ warned His followers that if they denied Him before men, He would also deny them before His Father.

And a time of persecution is distinctly implied in the Creed itself. For in ver. 30 we are told that it is not enough to believe the faith, it must be publicly *confessed*; and even in ver. 1, the *holding* or *holding fast*, suggests a temptation to surrender. Compare the passage: *Thou holdest fast my name, and didst not deny my faith*:[482] where in the Latin translation (the Vulgate) the same word is used for *hold fast*, as occurs in the Creed.

[482] Rev. 2. 13, 25; 3. 11; 2 Tim. 1. 13.

Next as to the meaning of to *perish*. This is no doubt much disputed, both here, and in the similar passage in the Gospel, where Christ says that all who believe on Him shall *not perish, but have eternal (or everlasting) life*; which certainly implies that those who disbelieve, or cease to believe, *shall* perish, and shall *not* have everlasting life, *i.e.*, shall perish everlastingly.[483] But whatever Christ meant by these words, the Creed means too, neither more nor less. Taken by themselves, they seem to point to the destruction of the wicked; or perhaps only to their failure to obtain the joys of heaven, without actually ceasing to exist.

[483] John 3. 16.

But however this may be, one thing is plain; that, according to the Creed, those who have been taught the truth about God, (*i.e.*, the Catholic Faith), must both *lead a good life*, (fighting against sin, etc.), and also *hold fast*, or *keep this faith*, if they wish to be saved. And St. Paul evidently regarded these as the two essentials; for at the close of his life, he rejoiced because he had *fought the good fight*, and *kept the faith*.[484]

[484] 2 Tim. 4. 7.

**(2.) Their truthfulness.**

Having thus shown what the warning clauses actually mean, we have next to consider whether they are true. Now, it is plain from the nature of the case that we can know nothing on such a subject, except what is revealed by God.

Is then, this doctrine stated or implied in the New Testament? Certainly it is, since belief in Christ is everywhere laid down as *necessary* to salvation. He is not one Saviour among many, nor is Christianity one means among many of getting to heaven. But Christianity is always represented as the *only* means, and Christ as the *only* Saviour.

We have already alluded to one text on this subject, that about the *perishing*; and we will now quote five others, each from a different writer, thus showing that the doctrine was not peculiar to any one Apostle or Evangelist. We are told then, that while he that believeth and is baptized shall be saved, he that disbelieveth shall be condemned; that unless men believe in Christ they shall die in their sins; that His is the only Name under heaven wherein men can be saved; that public confession of Him as Lord, together with belief in His Resurrection, leads to salvation; and that His Blood alone can redeem us from our sins.[485]

[485] Mark 16. 16; John 8. 24; Acts 4. 12; Rom. 10. 9; 1 Pet. 1. 19.

And the early Christians acted in entire accordance with this. When, for instance, the gaoler at Philippi asked St. Paul, *What must I do to be saved?* the answer was, *Believe on the Lord Jesus, and thou shalt be saved.*[486] Repentance, baptism, and amendment of life, would of course follow in due time; but first of all, before all other things, it was necessary that he should *believe in Christ*. This was the great essential.

[486] Acts 16. 31.

Now it is obvious that the belief in Christ, which is thus everywhere insisted on, must mean believing the truth about Christ, and not a false belief. If, then, the statements in the Creed represent the truth about Christ, as we have shown they do, then belief in these is necessary to salvation. And the Bible, like the Creed, expressly says that the great and fundamental truth about Christ, which we must both believe and *confess*, is His Incarnation, that He *is come in the flesh*.[487] And this involves His relationship to God the Father, and the doctrine of the Trinity. Thus the warning clauses as to the importance of a true belief, especially in regard to these two great doctrines, seem fully justified.

[487] 1 John 4. 2-3.

Three further remarks may be made before leaving this subject. The first is that the Creed is addressed to *Christians* only. This is clear from its opening sentence, *Quicunque vult salvus esse*, which means literally, 'Whoever *wishes* to be saved'; and this takes for granted that the persons addressed have heard of salvation. And, as we have shown, the following words, that they must *hold fast* or *keep* the Faith, also imply that they have been already taught it. The Creed cannot therefore be held to refer to any but Christians, no matter how general the language may be.

Secondly, among Christians the Creed is meant chiefly for *theologians*. This is plain from its technical language, which is so worded as to prevent a recurrence of several old errors. And it seems only fair to assume that children and unlearned persons belonging to a Church holding these doctrines would be considered as believing them. But though a child's belief,[488] which is merely trust and love, may be sufficient *for a child*, something more may reasonably be expected from well-instructed Christians. And this is that they should believe these doctrines *rightly* (v. 29), though this is a most unfortunate translation of the Latin word *fideliter*, as it seems to connect it with the *right* faith (*fides recta*) of the following verse. It would be better rendered by *faithfully*, as it is in v. 24, or *heartily*. Thus a *heartfelt belief* in the doctrines of the Trinity and the Incarnation—a belief which leads at once to *worship*, for 'the Catholic Faith is that we *worship* one God':—is what the Creed says is so essential.

[488] Matt. 18. 6.

Lastly, all these statements, like so many passages in the Bible,[489] are only *general rules*; to which there are often some exceptions. And in the present case, we may feel sure (from other passages)[490] that God will make exceptions, wherever unbelief or misbelief has not been due to a person's own fault. Our conclusion, then, as to the *warning clauses* is this; that if the other statements of the Creed are *true* (as we have shown they are), these clauses do not present any great difficulty.

[489] *E.g.*, 1 Cor. 6. 12.

[490] *E.g.*, 1 Tim. 1. 13.

### (3.) The objection as to dogmatism.

An important objection has still to be considered. It is that the Athanasian Creed *dogmatises* too much. Granting, it is said, that all its doctrines are contained in the New Testament, yet why not be content with the *simpler* statements in the Apostles' and Nicene Creeds? These were *sufficient* for the Church for several centuries, so why not leave other matters open for discussion, instead of treating them as *closed questions*? We will consider these points in turn.

And first as to *dogmatism*; by which is meant the exact statement of any truth. Now on all other subjects which influence our conduct, such as diseases or science, it is admitted to be of great importance that we should know the truth, and act accordingly. Why, then, should it be thought that in Religion alone this is immaterial, and that a false Creed is as good as the true one, if a man honestly believes it?

Moreover, a certain amount of dogmatism in matters of Religion seems essential. No one can intelligently serve or pray to a God of Whose Nature he has formed no idea, and the moment he begins to form such an idea he is involved in difficulties. Take for example what some will consider a very simple prayer, *May God forgive my sins for Christ's sake*. Who, we may ask, is God; who is Christ; what is the relation between them; why should One be asked to forgive for the sake of the Other; and what would happen if the sins were not forgiven? Such difficulties cannot be avoided; and if the statements in the Athanasian Creed are their true explanation, the more clearly this is stated the better.

In the next place, it is very doubtful whether the earlier Creeds are *simpler* and more easy to believe than the Athanasian. To a thoughtful reader it may well seem otherwise. For example, referring to the Trinity, the Apostles' Creed teaches us to believe in God the Father, in His Son Jesus Christ, and in the Holy Ghost, but it does not attempt to answer the simplest questions concerning Them. Are They, for instance, all three Persons? if so, are They all three Divine? and if so, are They three Gods? And the Nicene Creed is even more puzzling, for it first says that there is one God the Father, and soon afterwards that the Son is also God. So in regard to the Holy Spirit, He is called the Lord, yet it has been already stated that there is only one Lord Jesus Christ. How can all this be reconciled? And much the same applies to the future state of the wicked. The two earlier Creeds speak of the life everlasting (for the good), but what is to become of the bad? These and many other questions are suggested by the earlier Creeds, and answered by the Athanasian. And to many it seems easier to believe the Creed which answers difficulties, than those which merely suggest them.

And it was for this very purpose of answering difficulties, not making them, that the Athanasian Creed was composed. Its object was not to assert any new doctrines, or to suggest that those previously received were not *sufficient*, but merely to explain them, and to prevent them from being misunderstood. All the doctrines, as we have seen, are contained in the New Testament, and they were in consequence always believed by Christians. But it was not till after much controversy that men learnt to express this belief with clearness and precision.

Lastly, as to these doctrines being *closed questions*. They are closed questions in much the same way as the fact that the earth goes round the sun, and not the sun round the earth, is a closed question in astronomy. That is to say, they have been thoroughly discussed, and (to those who believe the New Testament) the evidence in their favour is overwhelming. Of course anyone may go over the proofs again for himself, and if he wants to have an intelligent belief he should do so; but as a rule of conduct the subject cannot be re-opened.

And it should be noticed that the Church, in thus treating certain questions as closed for its members, is only acting as other societies would do. Would a society of engineers, for instance, allow one of its members to construct an iron bridge on the supposition that the expansion of iron by heat was an open question; which he might, or might not, think worth allowing for? Or would a society of doctors allow one of its members to attend patients if he asserted that whether scarlet fever was infectious or not was an open question; which each patient might decide for himself? In short, well-ascertained truth, or what is believed to be such, in every department of knowledge is looked upon as a closed question; and it must remain so, unless some important fresh evidence is produced. But with regard to the Creeds, no fresh evidence can be produced, unless God were to give a fresh Revelation; so, from the nature of the case, they are closed questions in an even stricter sense than ascertained truths on other subjects.

This concludes a brief examination of the doctrines of the Three Creeds, and, as we have seen, they are all either contained in, or logically deducible from, the New Testament.

# CHAPTER XXV.
## THAT THE TRUTH OF THE CHRISTIAN RELIGION IS EXTREMELY PROBABLE.

(*A.*) THE EVIDENCES OF CHRISTIANITY.

One remaining objection, why are there so many difficulties, and no more obvious proof? considered in detail.

(*B.*) SUMMARY AND CONCLUSION.

We have now examined all the more important arguments for and against the Truth of Christianity. Many of them, as we have seen, involve a good deal of study, and we have often been obliged to consider a few examples only of various classes of facts; but it is hoped that no important argument on either side has been entirely overlooked. One remaining objection has still to be considered.

**(A.) THE EVIDENCES OF CHRISTIANITY.**

Does not, it is urged, this very fact of itself form a difficulty? Can an ordinary man be expected to ponder over arguments, objections, and counter-arguments by the dozen, even supposing the balance of probability to be in favour of the Religion? Surely, if Christianity were true, and God wished men to believe it, there would not be so many difficulties. He would have provided an easier way of proving it than this; or, at all events, if this elaborate argument were examined, the inference in its favour would be simply overwhelming. This is a difficulty felt perhaps by some who have read the present *Essay*; fortunately it can be answered satisfactorily.

And first, as to there being so many difficulties. Several of these are simply due to the evidence in favour of Christianity being so strong. If, for instance, we had only one Gospel instead of four, the difficulties caused by the discrepancies between them would disappear, but the argument in favour of Christianity would not be strengthened in consequence. Still putting aside these, it must be admitted that there are many difficulties connected with the Religion.

But what is the cause of this? It is the very magnitude of the Christian Religion which opens the way for so many attacks. A religion which claims to be the only true one in the world; to have been founded by God Himself; to have been prepared for by prophecies and introduced by miracles; to be the centre of the world's history, all previous history leading up to it, and all subsequent history being influenced by it; to be suitable for all ages and countries; to hold the key to all mental and moral problems; to be man's guide and comfort in this life, and his only hope for the next;—such a religion *must* be assailable at a great many points. But provided all these assaults can be repelled, provided this long *frontier-line*, so to speak, can be properly defended, it does not show the weakness of the religion; on the contrary, it shows its enormous strength. A religion which made less claims would, no doubt, have less difficulties; but it would be less likely to be the true one. If God became Incarnate, no claims can be too vast for the Religion He founded. And to many, this unspeakable grandeur of Christianity, so far from being a difficulty, constitutes one of its greatest charms.

Next, as to there being no *easier* means of proof. It is a simple matter of fact that the vast majority of men, both educated and uneducated, who believe in Christianity, have not arrived at this belief by a long line of reasoning, such as we have examined. They assert that there is an easier way. They say that God has given them a faculty of *Faith*, which, though it may be hard to explain, just as man's free will is hard to explain, yet gives them the most certain conviction of the truth of Christianity. And starting with this inward conviction, they say it is confirmed by their daily experience, just as a man's belief in his free will is confirmed by his daily experience. Of course, this appeal to faith is no argument to those who do not possess it. On the other hand, to those who do possess it, no arguments can really weaken or strengthen it. It is a thing by itself, and absolutely convincing.

It may be pointed out, however, that if man is a partly spiritual as well as a partly material being, which we have already admitted; then the existence of some spiritual sense, or faculty, by which to perceive spiritual truths, just as the body has material senses by which to perceive material objects, cannot be thought incredible. And this is what faith claims to be; it is a means to spiritual discernment, and may be compared to eyesight. It does not enable us to believe what we might otherwise think to be untrue; but it enables us to know for certain, what we might otherwise think to be only probable (*e.g.,* the existence of God). In the same way a blind man might, by feeling, think it probable that there were a certain number of pictures in a room, but if he could *see*, he would know for certain. And, just as a man, who had always been blind, ought not to reject the testimony of those who see, so a man who has no faith ought not to reject the testimony of those who have. And the existence of such a faculty will account for the very different views taken of Christianity by men of apparently equal intelligence and candour.

Still, it may be asked, why should some persons be given this faculty of faith, while others are not? The subject is no doubt a difficult one. But very possibly the faculty is *latent* in every one, only it needs (like other faculties) to be exercised and developed. And the man himself may be responsible for whether he takes suitable means (prayer, etc.) for doing this. However, we need not pursue this subject, since, as said above, no arguments can prove, or disprove Christianity to those who believe by faith.

But now comes the most important part of the objection. Granting, it is said, that the subject is a difficult one, and demands a long investigation, yet when we do go through the arguments on both sides the conclusion is not irresistible. In short, why are not the evidences in favour of Christianity *stronger*? Of course they might be so, but we have no reason for thinking that they would be. In our ordinary daily life we have never absolute certainty to guide us, but only various degrees of probability. And even, in Natural Religion, the reasons for believing in a Personal God and the freedom and responsibility of man, though to most people quite convincing, are certainly not irresistible; since, as a matter of fact, some men resist them.

And if God intends us to act on such evidence in common life, and also with regard to the great truths of Natural Religion, why should He not do the same with regard to Christianity? He seems, if we may use the word, to *respect* man's momentous attribute of free will even in matters of Religion; therefore in His sight a right belief, like right conduct, may be of no value unless it is more or less voluntary. It is to be a virtue, rather than a necessity. And this fully accounts for the evidences of Christianity not being overwhelming. They are amply sufficient to justify anyone in believing it; but they are not, and were probably never meant to be, sufficient to compel him to do so.

If, however,—and this is a matter of practical importance—they are strong enough to show that the Religion is *probably* true, a man who admits this is obviously bound to accept it. He cannot adopt a neutral attitude, because the evidence is not conclusive; since, as just said, in every other subject we have only probability, not certainty, to guide us; and why should religion alone be different? Then, if he accepts it, he is obviously bound to try and live accordingly, no matter what the sacrifice may be; for Christianity, if it is worth anything, is worth everything. Such tremendous truths cannot be half acted on if believed, any more than they can be half believed; it must be a case of all for all. And then, if he tries to live accordingly, he may find (as Christians in all ages have found) that for himself the probability becomes a certainty.

Lastly, it may be pointed out that though perhaps the evidences of Christianity are not so strong as we should expect, they are precisely of such a *kind* as we should expect; for they exhibit each of the three great attributes of God. His Omnipotence is shown in the miracles, His Omniscience in the prophecies, and His perfect Goodness in the Character of Christ; so that, judged by its evidences, Christianity is a Religion which might very reasonably have come from the God Who is All-Powerful, All-Wise, and All-Good.

## (*B.*) Summary and Conclusion.

It now only remains to give a summary of the previous chapters, and then point out the final choice of difficulties.

In Chapter XIII. we considered the *credibility* of the Christian Religion, and decided that some of its leading doctrines, especially those of the Incarnation and the Atonement, seemed very improbable. All that can be said on the other side is practically this, that we have no adequate means of judging; and that when we apply similar reasoning to subjects about which we do know, such as the freedom of man or the existence of evil, it generally leads us wrong. But still the fact remains that the Religion appears, at first sight, very improbable.

In Chapter XIV. we considered the *external testimony* to the *Four Gospels*, and decided that this was very strongly in their favour. At the close of the second century they held the same position among Christians as they do at present; during the middle of that century Justin shows that they were publicly read, together with the Old Testament Prophets; while the few earlier writers whose works have come down to us also seem to have known them.

In Chapter XV. we considered their *internal evidence*, and found that it strongly supported the above conclusion; so combining the two, we have an almost overwhelming argument in favour of their genuineness.

In Chapter XVI. we considered an additional argument of great importance, derived from the *Acts of the Apostles*. There are strong reasons for dating this book about A.D. 60; and if so it proves a still earlier date for the first three Gospels.

In Chapter XVII. we considered the *Resurrection of Christ*, and the accounts we have of it in the Four Gospels. And we decided that these Narratives, in spite of some obvious discrepancies and omissions had every appearance of being thoroughly trustworthy. Indeed their complete agreement in important points, their mutual explanations, and their signs of early date are all strongly in their favour.

In Chapter XVIII. we considered the testimony of the First Witnesses, and examined in detail their veracity, knowledge, investigation, and reasoning; and each seemed to be supported by irresistible evidence. Therefore the opposite theories, which are based on denying these points, and are called respectively the *Falsehood*, the *Legend*, the *Vision*, and the *Swoon* Theory, are quite untenable. So we must either accept the Resurrection of Christ; or deny it, in spite of all the evidence, and solely because of the miraculous nature of the event.

In Chapter XIX. we considered the other New Testament *Miracles*, and came to the conclusion that they also occurred. Indeed their marks of truthfulness, and their publicity together with the fact that they were never disputed at the time, make the evidence in their favour extremely strong.

In Chapter XX. we considered the argument from *Prophecy*; and discussed in detail Isaiah's Prophecy of the Lord's Servant, and the Psalm of the Crucifixion, and then glanced at several others. And we pointed out how completely these prophecies were fulfilled in Christ, and how utterly hopeless it was to find any other fulfilment of them. So here again the choice lies between either accepting these prophecies, or disputing them simply because they are prophecies, and imply superhuman knowledge. In other words, we must either admit the marvel of a Divine Revelation, or else we must face the *mental* difficulty of believing that all these coincidences were due to chance, the improbability of which can scarcely be calculated.

In Chapter XXI. we considered the *Character of Christ*; and the admitted excellence of His moral teaching seems quite inconsistent with deliberate falsehood on His part. Yet He kept asserting His superhuman and Divine Nature, and was finally put to death in consequence. So here once more we have a similar choice before us. We must either accept the Divinity of Christ, with all the wonders it involves; or else we must face the *moral* difficulty of believing that the best moral teaching the world has ever had, was given by One, whose own life was full of falsehood and presumption.

In Chapter XXII. we considered the *History of Christianity*, and found that its marvellous progress at first, in spite of its immense difficulties, and without the use of any force, could only be accounted for by its truth. So here for the last time we have the same alternatives to choose from. We must either admit the supernatural origin and spread of Christianity; or else we must face the *historical* difficulty of believing that its first preachers were able to convince men without evidence, conquer them without force, and found the greatest religion the world has ever seen on claims which at the time everyone must have known to be untrue.

In Chapter XXIII. we considered the *other evidence* on the subject, and briefly examined various arguments for and against Christianity, such as its connection with prayer; its adaptation to human nature, and its relation to other religions; but all of comparative unimportance.

Lastly, in Chapter XXIV. we decided that the *Three Creeds* were deducible from the New Testament; so the religion which has all this evidence in its favour is the *Christian Religion*, as we have used the term.

From the above summary it will be seen that the arguments against Christianity are all what may be called *antecedent* (or *a priori*) ones. The Religion itself, its doctrines, its claims, its miraculous origin, all seem most improbable. Thus the objections to Christianity all lie on the surface. They are obvious and palpable to everyone.

On the other hand, the arguments in its favour have often to be sought for; but when found they are seen to be stronger and stronger the more they are examined. There are four main arguments. These are of a widely different character, and each appeals most strongly to a certain class of minds, so each is often said to be the chief argument for Christianity, but they are probably of equal value. They may be conveniently called the argument from *Miracles*, including of course the Resurrection of Christ; from *Prophecy*; from *Christ's Character*; and from *History*. And it should be noticed in passing, that they mutually support one another. Miracles, for instance, are less difficult to believe when it is seen that they were to establish a religion which has for centuries exercised a greater influence on mankind than anything else; and prophecies become stronger when it is seen that the Life foretold was one that had such supreme and far-reaching effects.

Now, it is important to remember that the actual facts on which these arguments rest are in each case absolutely *unique*. Once, and only once in the history of the world, have men appeared who asserted that they were actual witnesses of miracles, and who faced all forms of suffering and death solely in consequence of this. Again, once, and only once in the history of the world, has a long series of prophecies, uttered many centuries apart, united in a single Person, in whom they one and all find a complete fulfilment. Yet again, once, and only once in the history of the world, has a Man appeared of faultless moral character, who asserted that He was also God, and who boldly claimed all that this tremendous assertion involved, and submitted to the consequences. While, lastly, once, and only once in the history of the world, has a Religion, most improbable in itself, and without using any force, succeeded in conquering nation after nation.

These, then, are the four chief arguments on the subject, and in every case we have the same choice before us. We must either face the antecedent (or *a priori*) difficulties in accepting Christianity, or the mental, moral and historical difficulties in rejecting it. There is no neutral ground, no possibility of avoiding both sets of difficulties. But the difficulties on the one side concern what we do *not* know—God's purpose in creating man—and may be due to our ignorance only. The difficulties on the other side concern what we *do* know. They are practical, they are derived from experience. We do know that men will not lay down their lives for what they believe to be false, and that the first preachers of Christianity must have known whether it was false or not. We do know that prophecies uttered at random through centuries would not all unite in a single Person. We do know that even moderately good men do not make extravagant claims. And we do know that no natural causes can account for such a religion as Christianity obtaining such a triumph as it did.

The choice, then, seems to lie between what we may call *unknown* difficulties and *known* ones. The unknown difficulty of believing that the Eternal God could so love man as to humble Himself even to death to win man's love; and the known difficulty of believing that evidence so vast and so various, so cumulative and so apparently irresistible, could all unite in making a monstrous falsehood appear to be a momentous truth. Between these two sets of difficulties we have to make our choice. But to those who agree with the previous chapters, the choice cannot be doubtful; for however hard it is to believe Christianity, it is, as we have shown, harder still to disbelieve it. This, then, is our final conclusion, that the truth of the Christian religion is *extremely probable*, because, to put it shortly, though the difficulties of accepting Christianity are great, the difficulties of rejecting it are far greater.

Milton Keynes UK
Ingram Content Group UK Ltd.
UKHW030903151124
451262UK00006B/1069

9 789362 511850